PROBLEMS AND PROCESS

Problems and Process

INTERNATIONAL LAW AND
HOW WE USE IT

ROSALYN HIGGINS

CLARENDON PRESS · OXFORD

OXFORD

UNIVERSITY PRESS

Great Clarendon Street, Oxford OX2 6DP

Oxford University Press is a department of the University of Oxford.
It furthers the University's objective of excellence in research, scholarship,
and education by publishing worldwide in

Oxford New York

Athens Auckland Bangkok Bogotá Buenos Aires Calcutta
Cape Town Chennai Dar es Salaam Delhi Florence Hong Kong Istanbul
Karachi Kuala Lumpur Madrid Melbourne Mexico City Mumbai
Nairobi Paris Sao Paulo Singapore Taipei Tokyo Toronto Warsaw
with associated companies in Berlin Ibadan

Oxford is registered trade mark of Oxford University Press
in the UK and in certain other countries

British Library Cataloguing in Publication Data

Data available

Library of Congress Cataloging-in-Publication Data

Higgins, Rosalyn.
Problems and process: international law and how we use it!
Rosalyn Higgins.
p. cm.
Includes index.
1. International law. I. Title.
JX3091.H54 1993
341—dc20   93–35770

ISBN 0–19–825767–8
ISBN 0–19–876410–3 (pbk)

Printed and bound in Great Britain
on acid-free paper by
Biddles Ltd, *www.biddles.co.uk*

PREFACE

To every international lawyer, an invitation from the Curatorium of the Hague Academy to deliver the General Course in International Law is the greatest possible honour. The last Briton to give the General Course was James Fawcett in 1971. I express my appreciation for the invitation to offer my views on international law in fifteen lectures—and the firm indication from the Curatorium that what was sought was a personal statement.

But it is hard to describe the magnitude of the task that this honour bestows; or the difficulties that it presents. Can there really be anything new or interesting still to say, or is not all wisdom and scholarship already gathered in the Collected General Courses? The problem was accentuated by the fact that in recent years there had been some exceptionally admired General Courses: I may particularly mention those of Professor Michel Virally, Professor Oscar Schachter, and Professor Lou Henkin.

There were further problems. Would not a *tour d'horizon* of the corpus of international law in fifteen lectures necessarily result in dealing with any given subject in a shallow way? After all, on any topic that one might choose for a single lecture, there would exist a vast literature in a variety of languages, and often a very substantial jurisprudence as well. How could one conceivably begin to do justice to any one of these topics?

For several months these seemed insoluble, and indeed overwhelming, problems. But then a beam of light was shown to me by Judge Sir Robert Jennings QC, President of the International Court. He offered the wise advice that one should never lose sight of the fact that one was not writing the definitive treatise on the entirety of international law, but rather lecturing to students about the ideas underlying international law.

From that moment the task seemed marginally less daunting. Of course, it would still be necessary to immerse oneself in as much as possible of the vast literature on each topic. But my job would not be to summarize or synthesize all that had ever been said on a given theme, but rather to offer my own perspectives and ideas. The learned writings, the state practice, the judicial and arbitral decisions would assist in helping me decide what seemed the key issues on which I wished to comment.

That decision, together with the insistence with which it had been put to me that the General Course is intended as a vehicle for one's personal views and philosophy, led rapidly to another decision. My course would not follow the traditional chapter headings of the textbooks; nor would it endeavour to deal with every matter that should properly be covered in a textbook, or in a university course. Our tasks were different.

But, if the lectures were not to follow the textbook headings, what should their theme be? A colleague suggested to me that I might focus on international law and the settlement of disputes. But international law in the settlement of disputes is only part of the story. International law, properly understood, is about avoiding disputes, or containing them, as much as about settling them. And indeed, the perception that international law is primarily about dispute settlement entails certain philosophical assumptions that should usefully be explored.

This General Course is neither a treatise nor a textbook. It is a series of lectures in which I endeavour to do two main things. First, I try to show that there is an essential and unavoidable choice to be made between the perception of international law as a system of neutral rules, and international law as a system of decision-making directed towards the attainment of certain declared values. Secondly, instead of recounting all the well-agreed principles of international law, I have deliberately written about many of the difficult and unanswered issues in international law today. And I have tried to show how the acceptance of international law as process leads to certain preferred solutions so far as these great unresolved problems are concerned.

I have had two further subsidiary objectives. One is to show that the process we call international law is not just about dispute resolution. I have also been very keen to show the students how things fit together. The traditional structuring of textbooks makes it hard to see how concepts apply in unexpected circumstances and locations. But this discovery—how one legal concept bears on another apparently unrelated matter—is one of the great excitements of international law. I wanted to show the students how the jigsaw fits together, how one matter bears on another, how there is always a new interrelationship to be discovered.

These are the objectives of this General Course. In my endeavours to realize them I owe a debt of gratitude to many people. First, to Professor Daniel Bardonnet, the Secretary General of the Curatorium, for his endless guidance, support, and encouragement, for his practical suggestions and personal friendship. Secondly, several students of mine at the University of London have enthusiastically helped with bibliographical research, harvesting the literature, assembling the evidences of practice, and chasing recalcitrant footnotes. My warm thanks go to Deborah Strachan, Greg Maggio, Charles Gottlieb, and Chanaka Wickremasinghe. My very great thanks go to Danesh Sarooshi, who engaged in this and assisted greatly on work on the typescript at the editing stage. Thirdly, the publication of these lectures affords me the opportunity of publicly recording my great appreciation to my secretary, Susan Hunt. Her unflappable assistance, in the face of chaotic piles of books and papers, illegible instructions, lengthy overnight faxes, wandering footnotes, and impossible deadlines, has been invaluable. Finally, my husband Terence has, as always, not only tolerated what others would surely have found intolerable, he has given every moral and practical support.

R. H.

London
January 1993

CONTENTS

ABBREVIATIONS

ACABQ	Advisory Committee on Administrative and Budgetary Questions
AJIL	*American Journal of International Law*
AOI	Arab Organization for Industrialization
BFSP	British Foreign and State Papers
BYIL	*British Year Book of International Law*
Canadian YBIL	*Canadian Year Book of International Law*
CAT	Committee Against Torture
CEDAW	Convention on the Elimination of All Forms of Discrimination against Women
CERD	Convention on the Elimination of Racial Discrimination
CPC	Committee on Programme and Co-ordination
CSCE	Conference on Security and Co-operation in Europe
EC	European Community
EEZ	exclusive economic zone
EJIL	*European Journal of International Law*
GAOR	General Assembly Official Records
German YBIL	*German Year Book of International Law*
HRLJ	*Human Rights Law Journal*
HRQ	*Human Rights Quarterly*
HRJ	*Human Rights Journal*
IBRD	International Bank for Reconstruction and Development
ICAO	International Civil Aviation Organization
ICCPR	International Covenant on Civil and Political Rights
ICJ	International Court of Justice
ICLQ	*International and Comparative Law Quarterly*
IFC	International Finance Corporation
ILC	International Law Commission
ILM	*International Legal Materials*
ILO	International Labour Organization
ILR	International Law Reports
IMCO	Intergovernmental Maritime Consultative Organization
IMF	International Monetary Fund
IMO	International Maritime Organization
Iran–USCTR	Iran–US Claims Tribunal Reports

ITC	International Tin Council
LNOJ	League of Nations Official Journal
LNTS	League of Nations Treaty Series
NYIL	Netherlands Yearbook of International Law
OAU	Organization of African Unity
ONUC	Opération des Nations Unies au Congo
Parl. Deb.	Parliamentary Debates
PCIJ	Permanent Court of International Justice
PLO	Palestinian Liberation Organization
Proc. ASIL	*Proceedings of the American Society of International Law*
RGDIP	*Revue général de droit internationale privé*
RIAA	*Reports of International Arbitral Awards*
UDI	Unilateral Declaration of Independence
UNCIO	United Nations Conference on International Organization
UNCLOS	United Nations Convention on the Law of the Sea
UNEF	United Nations Emergency Force
UNEP	United Nations Environment Programme
UNESCO	United Nations Educational, Scientific, and Cultural Organization
UNFICYP	United Nations Peace-Keeping Force in Cyprus
UNIFIL	United Nations Interim Force in the Lebanon
UNOGIL	United Nations Observer Group in the Lebanon
UNOSOM	United Nations Operations in Somalia
UNPROFOR	United Nations Peace-keeping Forces
UNTS	United Nations Treaty Series
UPU	Universal Postal Union
WHO	World Health Organization

TABLE OF CASES

FRANCE

GERMANY

INTERNATIONAL COURT OF JUSTICE

INTERNATIONAL CASES

BELGIUM

ITALY

ISRAEL

PERMANENT COURT OF INTERNATIONAL JUSTICE

SOUTH AFRICA

UNITED KINGDOM

UNITED STATES

TABLE OF NATIONAL LEGISLATION

TABLE OF INTERNATIONAL CONVENTIONS

THE NATURE AND FUNCTION OF
INTERNATIONAL LAW

INTERNATIONAL law is not rules. It is a normative system. All organized groups and structures require a system of normative conduct—that is to say, conduct which is regarded by each actor, and by the group as a whole, as being obligatory, and for which violation carries a price. Normative systems make possible that degree of order if society is to maximize the common good—and, indeed, even to avoid chaos in the web of bilateral and multilateral relationships that that society embraces. Without law at the domestic level, cars cannot safely travel on the roads, purchases cannot be made, personal safety cannot be secured. Without international law, safe aviation could not be agreed, resources could not be allocated, people could not safely choose to dwell in foreign lands. Two points are immediately apparent. The first is that this is humdrum stuff. The role of law is to provide an operational system for securing values that we all desire—security, freedom, the provision of sufficient material goods. It is not, as is commonly supposed, only about resolving disputes. If a legal system works well, then disputes are in large part *avoided*. The identification of required norms of behaviour, and techniques to secure routine compliance with them, play an important part. An efficacious legal system can also *contain* competing interests, allowing those who hold them not to insist upon immediate and unqualified vindication. Of course, sometimes dispute-resolution will be needed; or even norms to limit the parameters of conduct when normal friendly relations have broken down and dispute resolution failed. But these last elements are only a small part of the overall picture.

The second point is that, in these essentials, international law is no different from domestic law. It is not, as some suppose, an arcane and obscure body of rules whose origin and purpose are shrouded in mystery. But, if the social purpose of international law and domestic law is broadly similar, there are important differences arising from the fact that domestic law operates in a vertical legal order, and international law in a horizontal legal order. Consent and sovereignty are constraining factors against which the prescribing, invoking, and applying of international law norms must operate.

In this book I will endeavour to show international law as a normative system, harnessed to the achievement of common values—values that speak to us all, whether we are rich or poor, black or white, of any religion or none, or come from countries that are industrialized or developing.

What is International Law

When we ask 'What is international law?', we are in fact asking several questions. We are asking: What is its nature? Is it a body of rules? To whom does it apply? Who 'regulates' the application of international law? Why should anyone comply with it? Where is international law to be found? I shall now try to answer each of these component elements in the global question: What is international law? Some will be addressed in this chapter. Some will be reserved for the second. Chapter 1 addresses what we can broadly describe as the nature and function of international law; Chapter 2 is concerned with how we recognize it and where we find it. But it is essential to understand that these are essentially intertwined.[1]

There is a widely held perception of international law as 'rules'—rules that are meant to be impartially applied but are frequently ignored. It is further suggested that these rules are ignored because of the absence of effective centralized sanctions—and, in turn, that all of this evidences that international law is not 'real law' at all.

The view that international law is a body of rules that fails to restrain states falls short on several counts. In the first place, it assumes that law is indeed 'rules'. But the specialized social processes to which the word 'law' refers include many things beside rules. Rules play a part in law, but not the only part. I remain committed to the analysis of international law as process rather than rules and to the view I expressed many years ago, when I said:

When . . . decisions are made by authorized persons or organs, in appropriate forums, within the framework of certain established practices and norms, then what occurs is *legal* decision-making. In other words, international law is a continuing process of authoritative decisions. This view rejects the notion of law merely as the impartial application of rules. International law is the entire decision-making process, and not just the reference to the trend of past decisions which are termed 'rules'. There inevitably flows from this definition a concern, especially where the trend of past decision is not overwhelmingly clear, with policy alternatives for the future.[2]

---

[1] My views on these matters remain those elaborated in more detail in R. Higgins, 'Integrations of Authority and Control: Trends in the Literature of International Law and Relations', in B. Weston and M. Reisman (eds.), *Towards World Order and Human Dignity* (1976).

[2] R. Higgins, 'Policy Considerations and the International Judicial Process' (1968) 17 *ICLQ* 58 at 58–9.

Thus 'rules' are just accumulated past decisions. And, if international law was just 'rules', then international law would indeed be unable to contribute to, and cope with, a changing political world. To rely merely on accumulated past decisions (rules) when the context in which they were articulated has changed—and indeed when their content is often unclear—is to ensure that international law will not be able to contribute to today's problems and, further, that it will be disobeyed for that reason.

The rejection of the perception of law as 'rules' entails a necessary consequence. It means that those who have to make decisions on the basis of international law—judges, but also legal advisers and others—are not really simply 'finding the rule' and then applying it. That is because the determination of what *is* the relevant rule is part of the decision-makers' function; and because the accumulated trend of past decisions should never be applied oblivious of context. Although this reality has been regarded as anathema by many traditionalists, it was well understood by Sir Hersch Lauterpacht. He rejected the notion that the judicial function meant finding the appropriate 'rule' in an impartial manner. The judge, he argued, does not 'find rules' but he 'makes choices'—and choices 'not between claims which are fully justified and claims which have no foundation at all but between claims which have varying degrees of legal merit'.[3]

The reasons why some insist that international law is 'rules', and that all international lawyers have to do is to identify them and apply them, are not hard to find. They are an unconscious reflection of two beliefs, deeply held by many international lawyers. The first reason is that, if international law is regarded as more than rules, and the role of the authorized decision-maker as other than the automatic applier of such rules, international law becomes confused with other phenomena, such as power or social or humanitarian factors. The second reason is that it is felt by many that only by insisting on international law as rules to be impartially applied will it be possible to avoid the manifestation of international legal argument for political ends.

I want to deal with each of these reasons in turn, and tell you why I do not agree with them. To seek to contrast law with power (in which task the perception of law as 'rules' plays an essential task) is fundamentally flawed. It assumes that law is concerned only with the concept of authority and not with power, or control. International law *is* indeed concerned with authority—and 'authority' not just in the sense of binding decisions, but in the broader sense of jurisdictional competence, and more. Myres McDougal has explained:

---

[3] H. Lauterpacht, *The Development of International Law by the International Court* (1958), 399.

By authority is meant expectations of appropriateness in regard to the phases of effective decision processes. These expectations specifically relate to personnel appropriately endowed with decision-making power; the objectives they should pursue; the physical, temporal and institutional features of the situations in which lawful decisions are made; the values which may be used to sustain decision, and so forth . . .[4]

So far, so good. But it is *not* the case, as is frequently supposed, that international law is concerned with authority *alone*, and that 'power' stands somehow counterpoised to authority, and is nothing to do with law, and is indeed inimical to it. This view—which banishes power to the outer darkness (that is to say, to the province of international relations)—assumes that authority can exist in the total absence of supporting control, or power. But this is a fantasy. The authority which characterizes law exists not in a vacuum, but exactly where it intersects with power. Law, far from being authority battling against power,[5] is the interlocking of authority with power. Authority cannot exist in the total absence of control. Of course, there will be particular circumstances when power overrides authority. On such occasions we will not have decision-making that we can term lawful. But that is *not* to say that law is about authority *only*, and not about power too; or that power is definitionally to be regarded as hostile to law. It is an integral element of it.

What then of the other argument—that a perception of international law as other than neutral rules inevitably leads to bias and partiality? A classical statement of this view was made by Judges Fitzmaurice and Spender in the *South West Africa Cases* in 1962, when they wrote:

We are not unmindful of, nor are we insensible to, the various considerations of a non-judicial character, social, humanitarian and other . . . but these are matters for the political rather than for the legal arena. They cannot be allowed to deflect us from our duty of reaching a conclusion strictly on the basis of what we believe to be the correct legal view.[6]

This formulation reflects certain assumptions: that 'the correct legal view' is to be discerned by applying 'rules'—the accumulated trend of past decisions, regardless of context or circumstance—and that 'the correct legal view' has nothing to do with applying past decisions to current contexts by reference to objectives (values) that the law is designed to promote.

---

[4] M. McDougal, H. Lasswell, and M. Reisman, 'The World Constitutive Process of Authoritative Decision' (1966) 19 *Journal of Legal Education* 253 at 256.

[5] For expression of this view, see G. Schwarzenberger, 'The Misery and Grandeur of International Law', Inaugural Lecture 1963; see also M. Bos, *A Methodology of International Law* (1984), esp. ch. XI.

[6] *South West Africa Cases*, ICJ Reports (1962) 466 (joint diss. op.).

The classical view, so brilliantly articulated by Fitzmaurice but shared by very many others, is that international law can best perform its service to the community exactly by distancing itself from social policy. As the International Court of Justice put it in 1966: 'Law exists, it is said, to serve a social need; but precisely for that reason it can do so only through and within the limits of its own discipline. Otherwise, it is not a legal service that would be rendered.'[7] Of course, the International Court of Justice thought it self-evident as to where the law *does* draw 'the limits of its own discipline'. But what is self-evident to one is merely question-begging to another.[8]

Reference to 'the correct legal view' or 'rules' can never avoid the element of choice (though it can seek to disguise it), nor can it provide guidance to the preferable decision. In making this choice one must inevitably have consideration for the humanitarian, moral, and social purposes of the law. As I have written elsewhere:

Policy considerations, although they differ from 'rules', are an integral part of that decision making process which we call international law; the assessment of so-called extralegal considerations is *part of the legal process*, just as is reference to the accumulation of past decisions and current norms. A refusal to acknowledge political and social factors cannot keep law 'neutral', for even such a refusal is not without political and social consequence. There is no avoiding the essential relationship between law and politics.[9]

Because I believe there is no avoiding the essential relationship between law and policy, I also believe that it is desirable that the policy factors are dealt with systematically and openly. Dealing with them systematically[10] means that all factors are properly considered and weighed, instead of the decision-maker unconsciously narrowing or selecting what he will take into account in order to reach a decision that he has instinctively predetermined is desirable. Dealing with policy factors openly means that the decision-maker himself is subjected to the discipline of facing them squarely (instead of achieving unconsciously desired policy objectives by making a particular choice, which is then given the label of 'the correct legal rule'). It also means that the choices made are open to public scrutiny and discussion.

All this being said, there is still a problem we have to address. If international law is not the mere application of neutral rules in an impartial

---

[7] *South West Africa Cases*, ICJ Reports (1966) 6 at para. 49.
[8] See C. W. Jenks, *Law in the World Community* (1967), 54.
[9] Higgins, 'Integrations of Authority and Control', 85.
[10] Much of the work of M. McDougal and his associates has been directed towards elaborating a systematic method of inquiry for decision-makers. See, among many others, 'Some Basic Theoretical Concerns about International Law: A Policy Oriented Framework of Enquiry' (1960) 4 *Journal of Conflict Resolution* 337.

fashion, but requires choices to be made between alternative norms that could, in context, each be applicable, then do we really have something other than a justification of the end by the means? This is the serious question, made the more so by the events of the early 1980s. During the administration of President Reagan, the United States engaged in various acts of foreign policy which were designed not only to secure national goals but to secure certain objectives perceived as being in the interests of international order and justice. In particular, there occurred various military interventions designed to remove totalitarian rulers and to allow a democratic freedom of choice to the peoples of the countries concerned. We may cite military action in Nicaragua in 1983, in Grenada in 1983, and in Panama in 1989. There has also been military action to punish perceived terrorism: here we may cite the US bombing of Libya in 1986. Each of these actions occasioned significant debate, among Americans and friends of the United States as much as among others.[11] There were widely differing views as to the lawfulness of these various actions under international law. The Legal Adviser to the Department of State and the scholars who supported the military interventions very much emphasized the social purposes of international law in their analysis of what was and was not permitted under the United Nations Charter and under customary international law.[12]

My intention is not to enter the fray on the substance of these matters (though I shall have some things to say that bear upon them). Rather, I ask this question: if one shares the belief in the preferability of democracy over tyranny, and if one is committed to the policy-science approach to international law, whereby trends of past decisions are to be interpreted with policy objectives in mind, does it necessarily follow that one would have viewed all these actions as lawful? I think not.

In the first place, I do not believe that the policy-science approach requires one to find every means possible if the end is desirable. Trends of past decisions still have an important role to play in the choices to be made, notwithstanding the importance of both context and desired outcome.

---

[11] See, inter alia, F. Boyle et al., 'International Lawlessness in Grenada' (1984) 78 AJIL 172; T. Farer, 'Panama: Beyond the Charter Paradigm' (1990) 87 AJIL 503; C. Greenwood, 'International Law and the US Air Operation against Libya, (1987) 89 West Virginia Law Review 933; L. Henkin, 'The Invasion of Panama under International Law: A Gross Violation' (1991) 29 Columbia Journal of Transnational Law 293; V. Nanda, 'The Validity of US Intervention in Panama under International Law' (1990) 84 AJIL 494; J. Norton-Moore, 'Grenada and the International Double Standard' (1984) 78 AJIL 145; E. Schumacher, 'The US and Libya' (1986) 65 Foreign Affairs 329; P. Thornberry, 'International Law and its Discontents: The US Raid on Libya' (1986) 8 Liverpool Law Review 53.
[12] See the statement by the US Ambassador Walters to the UN Security Council (15 Apr. 1986), repr. in the Department of State Bulletin (June 1986), 19. See also 'Protection of Nationals', US Digest, ch. 4, para. 1, repr. in (1984) 78 AJIL 200, and A. d'Amato, 'The Invasion of Panama was a Lawful Response to Tyranny' (1990) 84 AJIL 516.

Where there is ambiguity or uncertainty, the policy-directed choice can properly be made. Some will say that, in a decentralized legal order, to allow one party to interpret the law to achieve desirable outcomes merely will allow another, less scrupulous party to claim to do the same. I am not greatly impressed with that argument. There is no escaping the duty that each and every one of us has to test the validity of legal claims. We will each know which are intellectually supportable and which are not, and it is a chimera to suppose that, if only international law is perceived as the application of neutral rules, it will then be invoked only in an unbiased manner. But it is in the common interest that some prohibitions should be absolute (for example, the prohibitions against some kinds of weaponry); and it is in the common interest that other kinds of limitation on conduct should be regarded as compelling, even if, on any single occasion, that prevents the achievement of an outcome otherwise to be regarded as desirable.

That being said, it is still quite wide of the mark to suggest, as some do, that, in the absence of third-party determination, the policy-science approach means simply whatever the policy-maker wants.[13] It really carries matters no further for critics to say that this approach 'can lead to international law being used by states as a device for *post facto* justifying decisions without really taking international law into account'.[14] This simply begs the question of what international law is. Such a comment merely presupposes that there is a 'real' international law that all men of good faith can recognize—that is, rules that can be neutrally applied, regardless of circumstance and context. And that is where the debate began.

Of course the debate on legal theory is not only about whether international law is 'rules' or 'process'.[15] But this is a critical aspect. Emphasis on rules is associated with, but not limited to, legal positivists—that is to say, those who conceive of law as commands emanating from a sovereign. Austin, the founding father of legal positivism, put it thus: 'Every positive law, or every law simply and strictly so-called, is set by a sovereign individual or a sovereign body of individuals, to a person or

---

[13] See W. Friedmann, 'Law and Politics in the Vietnamese War: A Comment' (1967) 61 *AJIL* 776 at 783.

[14] G. J. H. Van Hoof, *Rethinking the Sources of International Law* (1983), 43.

[15] There have been many important schools of thought, to which only brief reference can here be made. They include, among others, the naturalists, legal realism, inductivism, functionalism, structural positivism, and systems analysis. There is an impressive literature by and on the members of these schools of thought. Two interesting surveys of the ideas of many of these schools (from totally different viewpoints) are offered by Van Hoof, *Rethinking the Sources of International Law*, 13–84; and M. McDougal and M. Reisman, 'Theories about International Law: Prologue to a Configurative Jurisprudence' (1967) 8 *Virginia Journal of International Law* 188–299.

persons in a state of subjection to its authority.'[16] Kelsen, seeking to give meaning to positivism in a horizontal, decentralized international legal order, where command and sovereignty are notably lacking, proposed the existence of a *grundnorm*—the highest fundamental norm from which all others derived their binding force.[17]

Some leading scholars have sought to reconcile the 'rule' and 'process' approaches.[18] Yet others, while showing an interest in these matters, have sought to avoid taking positions, insisting that they will merely address the substantive problems of international law on a pragmatic level.[19] My view is that, superficially attractive though 'reconciliation' or 'synthesis' or 'middle views' may seem (as writers frequently want to claim to offer these attractive middle ways[20]), they avoid or blur the essential questions rather than provide an answer to them. And pragmatism itself entails certain assumptions about legal philosophy, no matter how much it seeks to cut clear of the argument.

So I should state clearly that these lectures are predicated on the view that a choice has to be made. The choice is for a perception of international law as a process. As we will see, this entails harder work in identifying sources and applying norms, as nothing is mechanistic and context is always important. But law as process does *not* entail a rejection of that core predictability that is essential if law is to perform its functions in society.[21]

To an extent, all of these debates are now well rehearsed. While profoundly important, they are not new. A recent important phenomenon has been writing on international law that is characterized as critical legal

[16] J. Austin, *Lectures on Jurisprudence or the Philosophy of Positive Law* (5th edn., 1954), i. 34.
[17] H. Kelsen, *General Theory of Law and State*, trans. A. Wedberg (1949), 113.
[18] M. Koskenniemi, *From Apology to Utopia* (1989), 159, categorizes the General Courses given by Schachter and Virally as 'appealing to a combination of the "rule" and "process" aspects of the law'. See *Recueil des cours* (1982, V; 1983, V).
[19] The writings of Jennings are characterized by a lively interest in theory coupled with a resolutely pragmatic approach on any given issue. See *Recueil des cours* (1967), 320. See also M. Sørensen, *Recueil des cours* (1960, III), 11; and citations in Koskenniemi, *From Apology to Utopia*, 159 n. 73.
[20] If Schachter and Virally are to be regarded as reconciliationist (a characterization of these writers that is in my view an oversimplification and not entirely apt), then one may refer to the writings of C. W. Jenks, *The Common Law of Mankind* (1955), for exhortation of the merits of 'synthesis' of diverse views and to Van Hoof, *Rethinking the Sources of International Law*, for an exposition of the 'middle path of structural positivism'. In a striking passage Van Hoof writes: 'The die-hard Positivist is like a photographer who once makes a picture with a defective camera which does not even register the most relevant aspects of reality. In addition he refuses to update his picture at regular intervals. The Policy-Oriented jurist, on the other hand, tries to make a continuing three-dimensional movie of society. The former was said to be likely to come up with fictitious answers. The latter cannot provide that minimum of certainty and stability which is required for the law to be able to perform its ordering and regulating function.' (p. 44)
[21] But see A. d'Amato, *The Concept of Custom in International Law* (1971); and H. Thirlway, *International Customary Law and Codification* (1972), 51.

studies. It has more in common with policy science than either the policy scientists or the critical realists might wish to acknowledge. For both schools, the legal theory is applicable to law in general and not just to international law (even if we, as international lawyers, are interested in its application to our branch of law). Both take as the starting-point that law is deeply rooted in social theory. Both locate legal process in social context and make the place of values quite explicit. Both reject law as rules and exceptions. But the critical-studies scholar will see law as contradictions[22] or as essentially indeterminate at its core[23] rather than as complementary or competing norms between which choices have to be made in particular circumstances. The critical-studies scholar believes that these contradictions are either historically contingent or inherent in the human experience. This view leads to the pessimistic conclusion that what international law can do is to point out the problems but not assist in the achievement of goals.

But one can accept the characterization of the origins of the place of contradictions in the legal system without concluding that there is no prospect of rationally choosing, for the common good, between these contradictions. Koskenniemi, for example, seems to preclude the possibility of making such choices on two key grounds. First, issues of contextual justice require 'venturing into fields such as politics, social and economic casuistry which were formally delimited beyond the point at which legal argument was supposed to stop in order to remain "legal" '.[24] But this is to rejoin the ultra-classicist position of Fitzmaurice. Of course law cannot *alone* achieve justice. The making of legal choices will not even contribute to justice if it purports totally to ignore political and social contexts. To remain 'legal' is not to ignore everything that is not 'rules'. To remain 'legal' is to ensure that decisions are made by those authorized to do so, with important guiding reliance on past decisions, and with available choices being made on the basis of community interests and for the promotion of common values. Secondly, Koskenniemi contends that liberalism is inherently flawed in that its guiding premiss—that the only basis of constraint is to prevent harm to others—presupposes in fact that some rights should prevail over others. One sees the intellectual point, but choice-making does not have to be structured on such an extreme application of liberalism—i.e. the imposition of no values at all save the avoidance of harm. To propose—as, for example, the policy-science

---

[22] See D. Kennedy, 'The Structure of Blackstone's Commentaries' (1979) 18 *Buffalo Law Review* 205; D. Kennedy, 'Theses about International Law Discourse' (1980) 23 *German YBIL* 353; and G. Binder, *Treaty Conflict and Political Contradiction: The Dialectic of Duplicity* (1990).

[23] See Koskenniemi, *From Apology to Utopia*.

[24] M. Koskenniemi, 'The Politics of International Law' (1990) 1 *EJIL* 4 at 32.

approach would do—guiding principles for choice does of course predicate
that certain views or assumptions as to what is desirable should prevail over
others. But I have no problem about this persuasive character of legal
jurisprudence. It is the necessary stuff of our very existence in community
with others. Everyone is entitled to participate in the identification and
articulation as to what they perceive the values to be promoted. Many
factors, including the responsive chords struck in those to whom the
argument is made, will determine whether particular suggestions prevail.

There are certain related matters that we must discuss. The first is that,
the further one moves away from positivism and rules, the less important
becomes the distinction between *lex lata* and *lex ferenda*—the law as it is
and the law as it might be. If law as rules requires the application of
outdated and inappropriate norms, then law as process encourages
interpretation and choice that is more compatible with values we seek to
promote and objectives we seek to achieve. But it is only to a rule-based
lawyer that this is to be classified as 'law as it ought to be', standing in
contrast to 'law as it is'. To the law as process, this is in large measure a
false dichotomy, a cleavage that we can ourselves banish from existence.

Closely related to this is the question of *lacunae*. There might well exist
topics on which there are no specific rules of international law: the liability
of states for the debts of international organizations of which they are
members, for example; or the question of whether a procedural delict that
entails no substantive harm requires the payment of compensation. The
rule-based lawyer can say only that international law has nothing to say on
the matter. But to the person who views international law as process, there
are still the tools for authoritative decision-making on the problem (by the
use of analogy, by reference to context, by analysis of the alternative
consequences) notwithstanding the absence of a precise rule which must be
applied.

A further consequence of analysing international law as a system, a
process, rather than rules or commands, is that we will be interested in a
variety of phenomena—claims and counterclaims, state practice, decisions
by a variety of authorized decision-makers. All of this makes up the fabric
of international law. In trying to identify what is international law, our
focus will not only be on the International Court of Justice. We will not be
embracing the view of those who have written that international law is to
be understood as what an impartial court would say if seized of the issue.[25]
That view rests on the perception of international law as the truly neutral
application of rules. This book, taking as its starting-point the perception
of international law as an authoritative system of decision-making available
in a decentralized system to all authorized decision-makers, will not be

---

[25] Thirlway, *International Customary Law and Codification*, 52.

centred on the International Court of Justice, hugely important though its role is.

I began with the question: *What is international law?* But the answer to this first question cannot be concluded without also asking whether it is really a universal system, or whether different views of its nature and content are not held in the socialist and in developing countries. For pre-perestroika marxists, international law was part of the superstructure of law, that would—along with the state—wither when the classless society was achieved. It was an attribute of the foreign policy of states,[26] an expression of the will of the ruling class. Where the will of the ruling classes of the socialist and capitalist systems coincided, international law could exist. It existed side by side with socialist international law, which was said to exist between the various socialist countries. Although this perception of the nature of international law was fundamentally different from that held in the West, there was none the less an operational agreement on the existence of international law as a system, and on substantial parts of its content. A major difference was over third-party determination of disputes; the Marxist approach to international law found it inappropriate for international courts to resolve disputes by determining the content of the law. And, although treaty obligations were undertaken, there was until recently resistance to international monitoring of compliance with these obligations. From the socialist perspective, international law was not universal—but not because it was imposed by the West. It was not universal because of its nature—the co-ordination of the wills of socialist and capitalist states.

In the last three years the emphasis has been less on international law as the co-ordination of clashing wills, than on international law as the articulation of a universal interest. That universal interest is exemplified by the common threat to human survival. The central idea of new political thinking within the former Soviet Union is now said to be the priority of universal human values;[27] and international law is seen as the vehicle for achieving these.

The developing countries have not had the Marxist historical tradition of preoccupation with legal theory. They have rather noted that much of the substance of customary international law was formulated before they

[26] See V. Vereshchetin and R. Mullerson, 'International Law in an Interdependent World' (1990) 28 *Columbia Journal of Transnational Law* 291. For a very original and radical analysis which challenges our state-centred perception of the international system (and thus of international law), see P. Allott, *Eunomia* (1990).

[27] See Vereshchetin and Mullerson, 'International Law'. They cite as universal values matters that a policy scientist would describe rather as desired outcomes: 'Diminishing the threat of world war, nuclear catastrophe . . . protection of the environment . . .' etc. (p. 292). They also state that 'Class interests in the international arena, as a rule, are expressed as national interests' (p. 293).

themselves had become independent, and that their contribution to the articulation of these norms was therefore limited.[28] This did not lead them to insist either that these norms were definitionally inimical to their interests or that they were not bound by them on achieving independence. International law as a whole has been readily accepted by the Third World as of universal application. However, two phenomena have undoubtedly been present. The first has been that individual norms have been challenged as being inequitable and as perpetuating the interests of the economically advantaged countries. Efforts have been made, often successful, to develop and change these norms to reflect contemporary realities and aspirations. All this has been done as part of the law-developing process—itself part of international law—which is the subject of Chapter 2. The second qualification to the general acceptance of international law has been that newly independent countries are no longer regarded as succeeding to every international law obligation (including treaties) incumbent upon the parent state.[29]

What is striking is that there has been no suggestion by emergent countries that they are not bound upon independence by international law as a whole, even if its formation owed much to Western European history;[30] nor indeed that the doctrine of state succession would be inapplicable in its entirety. More generally, this debate has been engaged on the substance and content of international law—but its universality has not been challenged. Indeed, the detailed provisions of international law have been accepted and relied on—and rightly so, for international law is the property of no one grouping but is rather a system that is relevant to us all.

To Whom does International Law Apply?

We can safely say that international law applies to states in their relationship with each other. But that response is far from complete. I will say only that international law today applies to international organizations also. It also applies in some circumstances directly to individuals (for example, in their responsibility for their conduct in war, or in their rights

---

[28] But it is an error to suppose that the main themes of international law reflect only Western ideas and contributions: see C. Alexandrowicz, *An Introduction to the History of the Law of Nations in the East Indies* (1967).

[29] For an affirmation of an emergent state's succession to treaties made for it by the parent state, see *United States Nationals in Morocco Case*, ICJ Reports (1952) 176 at 193–4. For an excellent detailed but succinct survey of the complex issue of the 'clean slate' and state succession, see *Oppenheim's International Law* 9th edn., ed. R. Jennings and A. Watts (1992), i. pt. 1, pp. 227–34.

[30] For a strongly Western perspective of the solely European contribution to international law, and its mere acceptance by the East, see B. Verzijl, 'Western European Influence on the Foundation of International Law' (1955) 1/4 *International Relations* 137–146.

regarding fundamental freedoms); and in some circumstances indirectly (as when they are required, through the intervention of necessary state legislation, to comply with UN trade sanctions against a particular country). I shall return to this issue in Chapter 3.

What is the Basis of Obligation of International Law?

To an Austinian positivist, the concept of law is that of a sovereign command made effective by the application of sanction. Because sanction plays so little a role in the international legal system, international law is not properly to be called law at all. Even to the non-positivists, there are some difficult questions that must be answered. All are agreed that a system cannot be described as 'law' unless there exists a sense of obligation that its norms are binding, and that states are required to comply with them in their behaviour. The issue arises at two levels. First, there is the question as to why any normative system should be regarded, in its generality, as binding (I say 'in its generality', because there will always be debate about the legal status of any given norm at any moment of time. That is something to which we will return later.) Secondly, there is the question as to why states should comply with the norms of international law. The two questions are often dealt with interchangeably, as if they are the same question. But they are not, although they are closely related. The Austinian imperative—that there must exist an effective sanction—is relevant to the second question, but not to the first. Let us take them each in turn.

What is it that makes states regard international law as 'binding' and thus capable of being a true system of law? This question has generated an enormous literature[31] and the answers are far from easy. For some writers the answer lies in origins other than in international law itself. They suggest that it is in the natural order of things that certain matters should be regulated in a compulsory manner. An obligatory foundation to the basic precepts of justice is to be found in natural law. Natural law itself originally had certain religious connotations,[32] but over the years has come to be a

---

[31] e.g. J. L. Brierly, *The Basis of Obligation in International Law* (1958); H. Lauterpacht, 'The Grotian Tradition in International Law' (1946) 23 *BYIL* 1; P. Corbett, 'The Consent of States and the Sources of International Law' (1925) 6 *BYIL* 20; G. Tunkin, 'Coexistence and International Law', *Recueil des cours* (1958), 5 at 32 ff.; H. Kelsen, *Principles of International Law* (2nd rev. edn., 1966), 563 ff.; Jenks, *The Common Law of Mankind*, ch. 1; M. Kaplan and N. Katzenbach, *The Political Foundations of International Law* (1961), 55–80 and 340–55.

[32] See J. Bodin, *Six Livres de la Republique* (1593); J. Finnis, *Natural Law and Natural Rights* (1980); E. Midgley, *The Natural Law Tradition and the Theory of International Relations* (1975); S. Pufendorf, *De jure naturae et gentium libri octo*, trans. C. and W. Oldfather (1934).

relatively secularized notion.[33] It has been suggested in the recent writing of Koskenniemi[34] that 'natural' obligations of justice became not those of divine law but essentially what is necessary for subsistence and self-preservation. Others have focused on consent as the key to the binding nature of international law. Norms are binding because states consent that they should be. This view is based closely on the sovereignty of states, which in turn emphasizes their freedom to act unilaterally save to the extent they agreed to be constrained. For socialist scholars, the problem of the basis of obligation and of the sources of international law is one and the same thing. International law is made by the concordance of the wills of states; and that is enough for it to follow that this brings 'mandatory legal rules' into existence. Notwithstanding the very important changes that took place in the early 1990s in Soviet policy, this apparently remains the current orthodoxy.[35] Western scholars have traditionally distinguished the basis of obligation from the question of the sources of international law—while acknowledging their close interrelationship. But they too have widely accepted consent as the basis of obligation. Socialist scholars have had the advantage of this logic: that, if consent is the basis of obligation, treaties are the prime source of international law, and custom, being less clearly based on consent, is to be regarded with suspicion. Western lawyers who—at least until their numerical majority in international decision-making was lost to the Third World—were comfortable with custom as the source of law have to explain why it is binding. Again, there has been some confusion as to whether the question is 'why is custom *as a genre* deemed binding?'; or 'why should norm X, which derives from customary law, bind state Y, who has not consented to it?'.

Although this problem is most sharply perceived in relation to custom-derived norms, it exists (as Fitzmaurice rightly showed) even in respect of treaties. Why, he asked, should we deem even the *expression of consent*, *pacta sunt servanda*, as binding? The only answer, he felt, was an infinitely

---

[33] See Locke, *Two Treatises*, Second Treatise, ch. III, s. 16, 125; Pufendorf, *De Jure Naturae*, bk. II, ch. 1, 5.8, 152–3; Hume, *A Treatise*, bk. III, s. II, 547.

[34] Koskenniemi, *From Apology to Utopia*, 70.

[35] See G. Tunkin, in G. Tunkin (ed.), *International Law*, trans. X. Pikarski (1990), chs. 1, 3, at pp. 20 and 39. Tunkin states that 'Law is the sum total of rules which are considered binding on the subjects of a given system of law' (p. 20). He continues that 'before explaining why rules of law are deemed binding' it is necessary to trace the origin of law as a specific social phenomenon. But he never does explain why rules are deemed binding, merely explaining that rules come into existence with the consent of states. Although the new post-perestroika political thinking emphasizes that international law must be based on universal values (rather than the co-ordinated wills of states representing different values), there is nothing to indicate a retraction from the central role of consent. See Vereshchetin and Mullerson, 'International Law in an Interdependent World', 291.

regressive concept of the consent of states, anterior to the international law system itself.[36]

In so far as consent has been regarded as central to obligation, there has been a tendency to mitigate its rigours through a variety of techniques. This 'forward consent' can be given to an obligation to resolve disputes through judicial means: this is done through the Optional Clause. And acquiescence and unilateral acts each have a role to play as evidence of presumed or deemed intent to be bound, even when consent has not been clearly given.[37]

Koskenniemi elaborates the consent-based theory thus: since international law is, according to modern doctrine, based on the consent of states, it is open to the criticism that international law is whatever states choose to regard as law, so that the law cannot be an effective external constraint on their behaviour.[38] In so far as it is responded that states *do* accept these obligations, and do *not* insist that consent also allows them to change their minds, or deny consent already given, then (says Koskenniemi) international law is open to the criticism that it is *apologist*, merely providing a semblance of justification and legitimation for what states choose to do. If states simply *want* to obey, the basis of obligation is apologist; if it is claimed norms exist which states are not prepared to obey, then the basis of obligation is utopian. He thus carries the Fitzmaurice thesis further. Fitzmaurice says the basis of obligation must lie in something anterior to international law itself. Koskenniemi says that, if states consent, then it is not law at all, but just an agreement by them that their behaviour will be regarded as normative.

Both Fitzmaurice and Koskenniemi rely on derivational logic to construct these seemingly awesome problems. But international law is not the vindication of authority over power (which is the supposition at the heart of Koskeniemmi's 'apologist' argument). It is decision-making by authorized decision-makers, when authority and power coincide. It is the initial faulty perspective of law as the vindication of authority over power that leads Koskenniemi to suppose that, if power is in harmony with

---

[36] G. G. Fitzmaurice, 'The Foundations of the Authority of International Law and the Problem of Enforcement' (1956) 19 *Modern Law Review* 1.

[37] Koskenniemi argues that the International Court has allocated this role to silence even where it is quite clear there was never any intention to be bound—e.g. in the *Anglo-Norwegian Fisheries Case* (see *From Apology to Utopia*, 255–8). For an interesting analysis of the mitigation of the consent constraint in practice, see E. Lauterpacht, *Aspects of the Administration of International Justice* (1991), ch. III, pp. 23–58.

[38] This summary is taken from the summary conveniently provided by V. Lowe in his review of Koskenniemi in *Cambridge Law Journal* 3 (1989), 527–9. For an interesting review article on Koskenniemi, and on V. Krotochvil, *Rules, Norms and Decisions: On the Conditions of Practical and Legal Reasoning in International Relations and Domestic Affairs* (1989), see I. Scobbie, 'Towards the Elimination of International Law: Some Radical Scepticism about Sceptical Radicalism' (1991) 61 *BYIL* 339.

authority (through consent, in his model), then what one has cannot be law.

In any event, we have in international law a system in which norms emerge either through express consent, or because there is no opposition— or because it is thought that, sovereignty notwithstanding, opposition would not succeed—to obligations being imposed in the absence of such specific consent. We will return to these matters in Chapter 2, which deals with sources. As for the basis of obligation,[39] reciprocity is a central element. As notions of natural justice were replaced by consent, so consent has gradually been replaced by consensus. States have undoubtedly come to regard themselves as bound by norms to which they have not given their express consent, either because they were not party to the law-making agency or because they did not wish to approve the specific proposals. If consensus, often tacit and sometimes unenthusiastic, is the basis of international law, then that consensus comes about because states perceive a reciprocal advantage in cautioning self-restraint.[40] It rarely is in the national interest to violate international law, even though there might be short-term advantages in doing so.[41] For law as a process of decision-making this is enough. The search for some other basis of obligation is unnecessary; and the terming of this basis as 'apologist' does not change a normative system of decision-making into something other than law.

What, then, of sanctions? In contrast to the question of the basis of legal obligation, there is little controversy among contemporary international lawyers about the place of sanctions in identifying what we mean by international law. There are very few today who believe that international law cannot exist in the absence of effective sanctions, or that sanctions predicate the existence of particular norms of international law.[42] While, as we have shown, there is a wide range of views on the basis of obligation—natural law, consent, principles anterior to the legal system itself, consensus, reciprocity—it is interesting that they all exclude imposed obligation by the enforcement of sanctions.

[39] The classic starting-point remains Brierly, *The Basis of Obligation in International Law*. See also McDougal and Reisman, 'Theories about International Law', 188–94; and myriad others.

[40] This brings one back to the utilitarian variation of natural justice identified by Koskenniemi (*From Apology to Utopia*, 74).

[41] Henkin's analysis of the way in which the international system is geared to law compliance remains outstanding (L. Henkin, *How Nations Behave*, 2nd edn., 1979).

[42] G. Schwarzenberger is sometimes regarded as having donned the mantle of Austin and Kelsen in this regard. But his argument does not centre on sanctions as such. Rather, he contends that, if particular rules of international law are constantly breached, we cannot continue to call them law. But he does not argue that all rules *will* be breached in the absence of sanctions; or that without sanctions international law does not exist. See *The Misery and Grandeur of International Law* (1963); *A Manual of International Law* (5th edn., 1967); *The Inductive Approach to International Law* (1962).

2

SOURCES OF INTERNATIONAL LAW:
PROVENANCE AND PROBLEMS

CHAPTER I dealt with what international law is, and the purposes that it serves. It also tried to explain why states believe that it is binding on them; and why, even in the absence of physical compulsion, it is usually obeyed.

This chapter also is concerned with what international law is—but in a different sense of the term. Where do we find the substance of international law? What constitutes international law? What is the difference between a political proposal and a binding rule? Whereas what we dealt with in Chapter I might conveniently be termed the *identity* of international law, what we are concerned with in this chapter is the *identification* of international law. This latter topic is commonly termed 'the sources of international law'. It is really all about the provenance of norms.

As international lawyers, we have perhaps ceased to notice how very strange it is that we spend so much time talking about the provenance of the norms that bind the participants in the international legal system. In domestic legal systems the sources of legal obligation are treated in a much more matter-of-fact way: legislation primary or secondary, and, in the common law, judicial decisions, are the sources. And that is the end of it. Of course, the opacity of particular legislation can be noted, the content of particular judicial decisions criticized—but that is an entirely different matter. But we have become so preoccupied with jurisprudential debate about the sources of international law that we have, I think, lost sight of the fact that it is an admission of an uncertainty at the heart of the international legal system. I do not mean that there are uncertainties about what particular norms provide (which there may be), but about how we identify norms. And until the answers to the question of identification, of provenance of norms, are more settled, then we do not have the tools for rendering more certain the content of particular norms.

The question of sources is thus of critical importance; and the jurisprudential and philosophical debates that continue to range have much more than an academic significance. It is right and proper to find them absorbing, and to participate in the intellectual exchanges. But we should not ignore that the need for them is a damaging acknowledgement of inadequacies in a legal system.

It is well known that the starting-point for any discussion of sources is

Article 38 (1) of the Statute of the International Court of Justice. That provides:

The Court, whose function is to decide in accordance with international law such disputes as are submitted to it, shall apply:
  (a) international conventions, whether general or particular, establishing rules expressly recognized by the contesting states;
  (b) international custom as evidence of a general practice accepted as law;
  (c) the general principles of law recognized by civilized nations;
  (d subject to the provisions of Article 59, judicial decisions and the teachings of the most highly qualified publicists of the various nations, as subsidiary means for the dermination of rules of law.

It is interesting that the route to the identification of sources is via an identification of what rules the International Court of Justice will apply in resolving legal disputes. That has led some writers to contend that international law is defined as that which the Court would apply in a given case.[1] I find this too narrow: international law has to be identified by reference to what the actors (most often states), often without benefit of pronouncement by the International Court of Justice, believe normative in their relations with each other.

In this chapter I do not intend simply to run through the headings of certain treaties, general principles, judicial decisions, and learned writings. There is excellent treatment of each of these topics in many leading textbooks. Instead, I want to focus on a few key *problems*—problems which are both interesting and operationally important.

Custom

I want first to address the question of custom, and in particular the continuing controversy on practice, custom, and *opinio juris*.

Article 38 of the Statute contains the injunction that the Court should apply 'international custom, as evidence of a general practice accepted as law'. This formulation, the unsatisfactory nature of which has been much commented upon,[2] speaks of custom as evidence of a practice. Yet it is generally accepted that it is custom that is the source to be applied, and that it is practice which evidences custom. But practice by itself is not evidence of the existence of a custom—the norm must be 'accepted as law'. Thus Article 38 could more correctly have been phrased to read 'international custom as *evidenced by* a general practice accepted as law'.

---

[1] H. Thirlway, *International Customary Law and Codification* (1972).
[2] e.g. P. Van Hoof, *Rethinking the Sources of International Law* (1983), 87.

In fact, this is the way the clause is interpreted in practice. But, there are still many problems about the relationship between practice and *opinio juris* (the belief that a norm is accepted as law).

One of the special characteristics of international law is that violations of law can lead to the formation of new law. Of course, this characteristic is more troublesome for those who regard law as rules, and less troublesome for those who regard law as process. But whether one believes that international law consists of rules that have been derived from consent or natural law; or whether one believes international law is a process of decision-making, with appropriate reliance on past trends of decision-making in the light of current context and desired outcomes, there still remains the question of how the 'rules' or the 'trend of decision' change through time. And, in so far as these rules or trends of decisions are based on custom, then there is the related question of what legal significance is to be given to practice that is inconsistent with the perceived rules or trends of decision.

Some rule-based international lawyers are apt to see rules as immutable. Repeated violations of these rules are to them a reflection of the reality that at the end of the day international law is dependent upon power: and, if there is a divergence between the two, it is power politics that will prevail. This was the view of Georg Schwarzenberger and, of course, is a view widely held by non-lawyers, and by students of international relations. From this perspective, the reality is that there continue in existence certain rules which regrettably are widely disobeyed, and it is the task of the international lawyer to point to the existence of these rules and to take every opportunity to urge compliance with them—even if the battle against power politics takes very many years. For those who regard international law as a process, however, the situation presents itself rather differently. That which we describe *as law* is the confluence of authority and control. Where there is substantial non-compliance, over a period of time, the norms concerned begin to lose their normative character. What has been lost is the community expectation that claimed requirements of behaviour reflect legal obligation.

But even for those who view international law as process, there are some difficult questions. What exactly causes a norm to lose its quality as law? Conceptually, this question is, of course, the same as that to be put regarding the formation of custom. To ask what is evidence of practice required for the loss of obligatory quality of a norm is the mirror of the evidence of practice required for the formation of the norm in the first place. As we have seen, for the formation of custom, practice and *opinio juris* are required.

If a customary rule loses its normative quality when it is widely ignored, over a significant period of time, does this not lead to a relativist view of the substantive content of international law, with disturbing implications?[3] Let us take a spectrum of possibilities. In the *South West Africa Cases* South Africa argued that there was not in reality any norm of non-discrimination, as—regardless of the way states voted on resolutions on this issue—the great majority of states routinely discriminated against persons of colour. This argument really arose in the context of whether a norm of non-discrimination had ever developed and come into existence.[4] A second example: all states agree that international law prohibits genocide (and that this total prohibition is today rooted in customary international law and not just in treaty obligations). So what if some states from time to time engage in genocide? Here we may safely answer that genocide, while it sometimes occurs and while its very nature makes *all* norm compliance shocking, is certainly not the majority practice. The customary law that prohibits genocide remains intact, notwithstanding appalling examples of non-compliance. Let us look at a third, more difficult example. No one doubts that there exists a norm prohibiting torture. No state denies the existence of such a norm; and, indeed, it is widely recognized as a customary rule of international law by national courts.[5] But it is equally clear from, for example, the reports of Amnesty International, that *the great majority* of states systematically engage in torture.[6] If one takes the view that non-compliance is relevant to the retention of normative quality, are we to conclude that there is not really any prohibition of torture under customary international law? The International Court of Justice touched on this issue in a rather general way in *Nicaragua* v. *United States*, when determining the law on intervention and permitted use of force. It said:

If a state acts in a way prima facie incompatible with a recognized rule, but defends its conduct by appealing to exceptions or justifications contained within the rule itself, then whether or not the State's conduct is in fact justifiable on that basis, the significance of that attribute is to confirm rather than to weaken the rule.[7]

For lawyers who do not approach matters from the perspective of the battle between 'legal rules' and 'power politics', this last type of example presents very real difficulties. The answer seems to have been found by some in embracing, if not a hierarchical normativity, then a weighted normativity. Thus, for example, Oscar Schachter has explained that 'The rules against aggression and on self-defence are not just another set of

---

[3] For an interesting and wide-ranging discussion, see A. Cassese and J. Weiler (eds.), *Change and Stability in International Law Making* (1988).

[4] *South West Africa Cases* (Second Phase), ICJ Reports (1966).

[5] See e.g. *Filartiga* v. *Pena-Irala* 630 F. 2d 878 (2d Cir. 1980).

[6] Amnesty reports that, out of a UN membership of 179 in 1990, some 104 states engaged in acts of torture against their citizens.

[7] *Military and Paramilitary Activities in and against Nicaragua*, ICJ Reports (1986) 14 at 98.

international rules. They have a "higher normativity", a recognised claim to compliance that is different from the body of international law rules.'[8] I am not sure from where one gets this notion of 'higher normativity', still less the suggestion that the requirements of practice do not operate in the normal way. Essentially, the argument seems to be that, if these are not treated as 'rules of higher normativity' than ordinary rules, then they cannot be treated differently from ordinary rules so far as the evidence of practice is concerned; and, if they cannot be treated differently, then disaster will ensue. To assert an immutable core or norms which remain constant regardless of the attitudes of states is at once to insist upon one's own personal values (rather than internationally shared values) and to rely essentially on natural law in doing so. This is a perfectly possible position, but it is not one I take.

Schachter speaks of the rules against aggression, also of the rules on self-defence, as well as on genocide, prisoners of war, torture, and large-scale racial discrimination, as falling within this 'special category', and says that is why states and tribunals do not question the continued force of those rules because of 'inconsistent or insufficient practice'. He refers to cases of genocide and to the killing of prisoners by their captors as not leading to the conclusion that the proscriptions no longer exist.

My approach is somewhat different. To say, as for example McDougal and Feliciano have said, that the prescriptions against aggression and on self-defence are 'necessary rules of coexistence' and 'principles of minimum world order'[9] is not to render these (together with those orders which I have just listed) as a species of *grundnorm* in respect of which the normal requirements of practice do not apply. Nor is the matter disposed of by noting that the prescriptions relating to aggression, use of force, protection of prisoners of war, and genocide are widely regarded as *jus cogens*.[10] A norm that is *jus cogens* cannot be limited or derogated from by agreement between states in their relations with each other. State A and State B cannot agree that, *inter se*, they will allow prisoners of war that they hold to be freely killed. I believe that to be exactly because the *community as a whole* regards these norms as of critical importance, such that particular states cannot 'contract out' of them. But that is not to say

---

[8] O. Schachter, 'Entangled Treaty and Custom', in Y. Dinstein (ed.), *International Law at a Time of Perplexity: Essays in Honour of Shabtai Rosenne* (1989) 717 at 734.

[9] M. McDougal and F. Feliciano, *Law and Minimum World Public Order* (1961).

[10] See, *inter alia*, E. Jimenez de Arechaga, *Recueil des cours* (1978, I) 9 at 64–7; I. Sinclair, *The Vienna Convention on the Law of Treaties* (2nd edn., 1984), 203–26; F. Munch, in R. Bernhardt, W. Geck, G. Jaenicke, and H. Steinberger (eds.), *Volkerrecht als Rechtsordnung Internationale Gerichtsbarkeit Menschen rechte: Festschrift für Hermann Mosler* (1983), 617–28; L. Hannikainen, *Peremptory Norms (ius cogens) in International Law: Historical Developments, Criteria, Present Status* (1988); F. A. Mann, *Further Studies in International Law* (1990), 84–102.

that these prescriptions would somehow retain their normative quality if the world community *as a whole* did not regard them as such. The status of norms that we hold dear is to be protected by our efforts to invoke and apply them, in turn ensuring that they do not totally lose the support of the great majority of states. But they cannot be artificially protected through classifying them as rules with a 'higher normativity' which will continue to exist even if we fail to make states see the value of giving such prescriptions a normative quality.

The answer, in my view, lies elsewhere. First, we must not lose sight of the fact that it is the practice of the vast majority of states that is critical, both in the formation of new norms and in their development and change and possible death. Thus, even if genocide and the killing of prisoners of war regrettably sometimes occur, if this is not the usual practice of most states, the status of the normative prohibitions is not changed. No special attribution of a 'higher normative status' is needed. More difficult is the question of torture, because we are told, by reputable bodies in a position to know, that the majority of states in the world do engage in this repugnant practice. It is at this point that a further factor comes into play.

New norms require both practice and *opinio juris* before they can be said to represent customary international law. And so it is with the gradual death of existing norms and their replacement by others. The reason that the prohibition on torture continues to be a requirement of customary international law, even though widely abused, is not because it has a higher normative status that allows us to ignore the abuse, but because *opinio juris* as to its normative status continues to exist. No state, not even a state that tortures, believes that the international law prohibition is undesirable and that it is not bound by the prohibition. A new norm cannot emerge without both practice and *opinio juris*; and an existing norm does not die without the great majority of states engaging in both a contrary practice and withdrawing their *opinio juris*.

Resolutions of International Organizations

In 1963 I wrote the following about the role of the United Nations in law-making:

The United Nations is a very appropriate body to look to for indications of developments in international law, for international custom is to be deduced from the practice of States, which includes their international dealings as manifested by their diplomatic actions and public pronouncements. With the development of international organizations, the votes and views of States have come to have legal significance as evidence of customary law . . . Collective acts of States, repeated by and acquiesced in by sufficient numbers with sufficient frequency, eventually attain the status of law. The existence of the United Nations—and especially its accelerated trend towards universality of membership since 1955—now provides a very clear, very concentrated focal point for state practice. Here, then, is the reason for looking to United Nations practice in a search for the direction of the development of international law.[11]

Looking back at this from a distance of some thirty years, two points are striking. The first is how modest and indeed cautious those views are today, though in 1963 they were regarded as somewhat radical. There is nothing in this approach that suggests a belief in 'instant custom', or that the distinction between decisions and recommendations is to be ignored.

Matters are put in much the same way by Judge Tanaka in his dissenting opinion in the *South West Africa Cases* in 1966. Judge Tanaka indicated that the requirements of custom—practice, repetition, *opinio juris*—may occur at an accelerated pace in the world of an international organization. But he did not suggest that the mere existence of a resolution obviated the need for these requirements:

A State, instead of pronouncing its view to a few States directly concerned, has the opportunity, through the medium of the organization, to declare its position to all members of the organization and to know immediately their reaction on the same matter. In former days, practice, repetition and *opinio juris sive necessitatis*, which are the ingredients of customary international law might be combined together in a very long and slow process extending over centuries. In the contemporary age of highly developed techniques of communication and information, the formation of a custom through the medium of international organizations is greatly facilitated and accelerated . . .[12]

He returned to the theme of accelerated practice (on which Judge Sir Robert Jennings has also written[13]) in his dissent in the *Continental Shelf Cases*. He said that the speed of present communications had 'minimised the importance of the time factor and has made possible the acceleration of the formation of customary international law. What required a hundred years in former days now may require less than 10 years.'[14]

The second point is this: the views I expressed in 1963 were directed to the place of UN practice in the development of international law. There was in the theoretical analysis virtually no reference to *resolutions* as such. Resolutions are but one manifestation of state practice. But in recent years there has been an obsessive interest with *resolutions* as an isolated phenomenon. Intellectually, this is hard to understand or justify. We can

[11] R. Higgins, *The Development of International Law through the Political Organs of the United Nations* (1963), 2.
[12] Dissenting opinion of Judge Tanaka, ICJ Reports (1966) 248 at 291.
[13] See R. Jennings, 'Recent Developments in the International Law Commission: Its Relation to the Sources of International Law' (1964) 13 *ICLQ* 385, and R. Jennings, 'Treaties as Legislation', in G. Wilner (ed.), *Jus et Societas: Essays in Tribute to Wolfgang Friedmann* (1979) 159 at 166.   [14] ICJ Reports (1969) 3 at 177.

only suppose that it is easier—that is, that it requires less effort, less rigour, less by way of meticulous analysis—to comment on the legal effect of a resolution than to look at a collective practice on a certain issue in all its complex manifestations. The political bodies of international organizations engage in debate; in the public exchange of views and positions taken; in expressing reservations upon views being taken by others; in preparing drafts intended for treaties, or declarations, or binding resolutions, or codes; and in decision-making that may or may not imply a legal view upon a particular issue. Some of these activities may result in resolutions of one sort or another. But the current fashion is often to examine the resolution to the exclusion of all else. We are examining only a part of the picture.

Binding quality of resolutions

One important element in the phenomenon of the examination of resolutions is the question of their binding quality. For certain commentators, that is enough: a negative answer indicates the irrelevance of resolutions in the law-making process.

It is, of course, beyond all doubt that the drafters of the Charter deliberately declined to give the General Assembly legislative authority. In other than budgetary matters, the resolutions of the General Assembly are recommendatory and not directly binding: see the wording of Articles 10, 11, 12, 13, and 14.

The binding or recommendatory quality of resolutions is closely related to the concept of state consent. But, as was remarked by Sir Kenneth Bailey in 1967: 'To say that a resolution is recommendation only is undoubtedly to assert that governments are under no legal obligations to comply with it. Does this relegate General Assembly resolutions wholly to the sphere of moral or legal precepts, with no relevance to law?'[15]

But the passing of binding decisions is not the only way in which law development occurs. Legal consequences can also flow from acts which are not, in the formal sense, 'binding'. And, further, law is developed by a variety of non-legislative acts which do not seek to secure, in any direct sense, 'compliance' from Assembly members; we refer here to the 'law-declaring' activities of the Assembly.[16]

It is exactly this appreciation of the distinction between the development of law and the binding or non-binding nature of a resolution that was at the heart of the finding of the International Court of Justice in the *Namibia Advisory Opinion*.[17] The Court was faced with both General Assembly and Security Council resolutions that purported to terminate South

[15] K. Bailey, 'Making International Law in the UN' (1967) *Proc. ASIL* 235.
[16] R. Higgins, 'The United Nations and Lawmaking' (1970) *Proc. ASIL* 37 at 42.
[17] *Legal Consequences for States of the Continued Presence of South Africa in Namibia (South West Africa)*, ICJ Reports (1971) 50.

Africa's mandate over South-West Africa. It found the Security Council resolution binding, even though it could not be clearly identified as a traditional 'Chapter 7' resolution; and it found that the General Assembly resolutions, while manifestly not binding, were not without legal effect, given the existence of a right to terminate and the Assembly's constitutional role in monitoring the mandate. As the Court pertinently put it: 'It would not be correct to assume that, because the General Assembly is in principle vested with recommendatory powers, it is debarred from adopting, in specific cases within the framework of its competence, resolutions which make determinations or have operative design.'[18]

In some international organizations even the term 'recommendation' in its context sometimes signals more than one would expect from a literal reliance on that word. Thus 'recommendation' may still in context entail a duty of compliance or an obligation to act: see Article 14 (3) of the European Coal and Steel Community or Article 19 (b) of the International Labour Organization.[19]

Further, other recommendations—those to establish subsidiary bodies, for example—entail financial consequences which are legally incumbent upon all members, whether they voted for them or not. The ICJ Advisory Opinion on the *Expenses Case* established that lawfully established subsidiary bodies—that is to say, bodies established with the objects and purposes of the UN Charter and given tasks not specifically prohibited thereunder—generate financial and legal obligations for UN members.

There is a further matter that must be mentioned, on the borderline of what might be called the internal and external competence of a UN organ. The *travaux* have always made clear that 'in the course of the operations from day to day of the various organs of the organisation it is inevitable that each organ will interpret such parts of the Charter as are applicable to its particular function'.[20] The repeated practice of the organ, in interpreting the treaty, may establish a practice that, if the treaty deals with matters of general international law, can ultimately harden into custom. Although organ practice may not be good evidence of the intention of the original state parties, it is of probative value as customary law.[21] Here the United Nations is a participant in the international legal process.

Declaratory resolutions

We turn to those activities where the international organization is

---

[18] ICJ Reports (1971) 50.

[19] C. Joyner, 'UN General Assembly Resolutions: Rethinking the Contemporary Dynamics of Norm-Creation' (1981) 11 *California Western International Law Journal* 445 at 452.   [20] Report Committee IV/2, UNCIO, 1945, ix. 70.

[21] R. Higgins, 'The Development of International Law by the Political Organs of the United Nations' (1965) *Proc. ASIL* 118–19.

unambiguously facing outwards—that is, concerned with general international law rather than its own procedural powers or even the direct interpretation of its own constituent instrument. Prominent among such activities is the passing of resolutions that purport to be declaratory of contemporary international law. Can we reject their legal relevance *simply* on the ground that they are recommendatory, or incapable of directly binding the membership at large? What status is therefore to be accorded to them?

There are a great range of opinions. Looking along a spectrum, we can perhaps see at one end those who are deeply sceptical, in the generalized fashion, about the relevance of General Assembly resolutions—such writers as Judge Sir Gerald Fitzmaurice, Judge Stephen Schwebel, and Sir Francis Vallat, Professors David Johnson and Gaetano Arangio-Ruiz.[22] The Englishmen in this group all arrive at their position primarily by an emphasis in their writings, or judicial decisions, on the recommendatory nature of Assembly resolutions and their inability to bind. The difficulties with that approach have already been indicated. Judge Schwebel and Professor Arangio-Ruiz arrive at their position through a different route. They fully accept that resolutions can contribute to the formation of customary international law, but express deep scepticism as to whether this really happens.

Professor Arangio-Ruiz says that General Assembly resolutions do not in fact contribute to the evolution of custom because states 'don't mean it'. 'That is to say, states often don't meaningfully support what a resolution says and they almost always do not mean that the resolution is law.'[23] Judge Schwebel then adds a piercingly important point. Agreeing that states 'don't mean it', he says: 'This may be as true or truer in the case of the unanimously adopted resolutions as in the case of majority-adopted resolutions. It may be truer still of resolutions adopted by "consensus".'[24] Thus the size of the majority has nothing to do with the intentions of the states voting for it.

Somewhere towards the middle of the spectrum there are other international lawyers who downplay the significance of Assembly resolutions as non-binding, but accept that it would be wholly exceptional for any

---

[22] G. Arangio-Ruiz, 'The Normative Role of the General Assembly of the United Nations and the Development of Principles of Friendly Relations', *Recueil des cours* (1972 III), 431; S. Schwebel, 'The Effect of Resolutions of the UN General Assembly on Customary International Law' (1979) *Proc. ASIL* 301; F. Vallat, 'The General Assembly and the Security Council of the United Nations' (1952) 39 *BYIL* 96; G. Fitzmaurice, 'The Future of Public International Law and of the International Legal System in the Circumstances of Today', in *Institut de Droit International, Livre du Centenaire* (1973) 270–4; D. Johnson, 'The Effect of Resolutions of the General Assembly of the UN' (1955–6) 32 *BYIL* 97.

[23] Arangio-Ruiz, 'The Normative Role'.

[24] Schwebel, 'The Effect of Resolutions', 302.

single resolution to have normative results. They argue rather than the decentralized method of international law-making can cause the metamorphosis of 'General Assembly recommendations from non-binding resolutions to inchoate normative principles'.[25] Certain resolutions may be a first step[26] in the process of law creation; and, looked at as a whole, they may in certain circumstances (depending on subject-matter, size and nature of majorities, *opinio juris*) be evidence of developing trends of customary law.[27]

At what could be termed the radical end of the spectrum are those who invest Assembly resolutions with considerably greater legal significance. In this context can be mentioned Richard Falk, who has written of the 'quasi-legislative' competence of the General Assembly,[28] and Jorge Castaneda, who has argued that, through its repeated efforts to declare principles of international law, the General Assembly has secured powers beyond the recommendatory powers listed in the UN Charter.[29]

Underlying these positions are many complicated and interesting issues, one or two of which may be mentioned briefly. When we look at resolutions as a first step in the formation of custom, or as part of the evidence of the existence of general practice, is it enough that we look at the resolutions alone?

Judge Schwebel has insisted that, because *opinio juris* remains a critical element, one must look to see if states 'mean' what they have voted for—and looking at their practice outside the United Nations is one way we can ascertain this. The arbitral award of Professor Dupuy in the *Texaco Case*[30] is interesting in this context, as well as in many others. It will be recalled that (unlike Judge Lagergren, when faced with similar issues in the *BP* v. *Libya Case*[31]) Dupuy closely examined the series of resolutions that are collectively regarded as the New International Economic Order resolutions, to see whether the traditional requirements for compensation had changed. He found that General Assembly Resolution 1803 represented current international law, for it had been passed with the support of the industrialized capital exporting states as well as the capital importing states; however, the same consensus was never really apparent in the voting on the Charter for Economic Rights and Duties and the Declaration

[25] Joyner, 'UN Resolutions and International Law', 464.
[26] M. Lachs, 'The Threshold in Law Making', in Bernhardt *et al.*, *Volkerrecht als Rechtsordnung*, 497.
[27] I believe that among this group would be Lachs, Schachter, Joyner, Julius Stone, and myself, as well, of course, as many others.
[28] R. Falk, 'On the Quasi-Legislative Competence of the General Assembly' (1966) 60 *AJIL* 782.
[29] J. Castaneda, *Legal Effects of United Nations Resolutions* (1970).
[30] *Texaco Overseas Petroleum Co.* v. *Libyan Arab Republic*, 53 *ILR* 389.
[31] *BP* v. *Libyan Arab Republic*, ibid. 297.

on the New International Economic Order. In other words, Dupuy was engaged in trying to ascertain whether a resolution expressed a consensus on what was the existing customary rule. But one must take care not to use General Assembly resolutions as a short cut to ascertaining international practice in its entirety on a matter—practice in the larger world arena is still the relevant canvas, although UN resolutions are a part of the picture. Resolutions cannot be a *substitute* for ascertaining custom; this task will continue to require that other evidences of state practice be examined alongside those collective acts evidenced in General Assembly resolutions.[32]

So far we have spoken of Assembly resolutions. Yet we must not lose sight of Security Council resolutions in our examination of the process of creating norms in the international system. Professor Tunkin, in his 1956 study on the fundamental principles of contemporary international law,[33] indicated that decisions of the UN Security Council are not strictly speaking sources of international law. They have an *ad hoc* effect and may create binding obligations, but they are not sources of general applicability. This brings us back to our earlier discussion. I think that this view is largely right—though sometimes the substance of the Security Council work, and the fact that it is legal work repeated year in and year out, makes it engage in the processes of customary development as well as the mere imposing of obligation.

Conclusion

As with much of international law, there is no easy answer to the question: What is the role of resolutions of international organizations in the process of creating norms in the international system? To answer the question we need to look at the subject-matter of the resolutions in question, at whether they are binding or recommendatory, at the majorities supporting their adoption, at repeated practice in relation to them, at evidence of *opinio juris*. When we shake the kaleidoscope and the pattern falls in certain ways, they undoubtedly play a significant role in creating norms.

The Overlap between Treaty and Custom

Provisions formulated in a treaty can in certain circumstances be binding even on states which are not parties to the treaty. This can occur if the provisions articulate what is already customary international law. This may

---

[32] See the interesting article on the point by G. Kerwin, 'The Role of the United Nations General Assembly Resolutions in Determining Principles of International Law in United States Courts' (1983) *Duke Law Journal* 879 esp. at 885–6.

[33] G. Tunkin, *Osnovy sovremennogo mezhdunarodnogo prava* (1956).

often be true of elements in a treaty—for example, much of what is in the Vienna Convention on Diplomatic Relations of 1969 was a codification of pre-existing customary law. But some elements of that Convention represent new law, and those elements are undertaken only by the parties to the Convention. And, if a treaty has certain procedural or dispute settlement provisions built into it, a non-party will not be bound by those provisions, even if it is bound by certain substantive norms contained in the treaty, because they are already customary law. Thus, while not being bound by all the particular provisions of the Genocide Convention, no non-ratifying state could claim to be free to commit genocide because it was not a party to that legal instrument. The prohibition against genocide clearly pre-existed the Convention as a prohibition of customary international law.

A much more difficult possibility may occur—namely, that provisions in a treaty are new at the time they are formulated (and not just a repetition of existing customary international law); but that customary international law then develops in such a way as itself to embrace those new norms. This of course was the possibility addressed by the International Court of Justice in the *North Sea Continental Shelf Cases*. The Netherlands and Denmark claimed that the equidistance rule of Article 6 of the 1958 Continental Shelf Convention was binding upon the Federal Republic of Germany (a non-party) as a matter of customary law. The argument was that the equidistance rule of delimitation

is, or must now be regarded as involving, a rule that is part of the *corpus* of general international law; and, like other rules of general or customary international law, is binding on the Federal Republic automatically and independently of any specific assent, direct or indirect, given by the latter.[34]

Part of the proposition was based on an argument that the equidistance principle had a 'juristic inevitability' in continental-shelf delimitation. That argument does not concern me here. But the other part of the Dutch and Danish claim was that the work of international legal bodies, state practice, and indeed the influence of the Geneva Convention itself had 'cumulatively evidenced or been creative of the *opinio juris sive necessitatis* requisite for the formation of new rules of customary international law'.[35]

After a detailed analysis of the Court reached the conclusion that Article 6 of the Geneva Convention 'did not embody or crystallize any pre-existing or emerging rule of customary international law',[36] but then moved to see if such a rule had since come into being, 'partly because of its own impact, partly on the basis of subsequent state practice—and that this rule, being now a rule of customary international law [is] binding on all states . . .'.[37]

---

[34] *North Sea Continental Self Cases*, ICJ Reports (1969) 3 at para. 37.
[35] Ibid.   [36] Ibid., para. 69.   [37] Ibid., para. 70.

The Court noted that this would involve treating Article 6 of the 1958 Convention as a norm-creating provision which has constituted the foundation of or has generated a rule which, while only conventional or contractual in its origin, has since passed into the general *corpus* of international law, and is now accepted as such by the *opinio juris*, so as to have become binding even for countries which have never, and do not, become parties to the Convention.[38] The Court characterized the process as one that is 'perfectly possible', but the result was 'not lightly to be regarded as having been attained'.[39]

In identifying what would be needed for the result to be attained, the Court said that the norm had first to be of a fundamentally norm-creating character. While these words might have been seen as an allusion to the distinction drawn by some jurists between law and obligation, the Court's mind seemed turned in another direction. It was unlikely, said the Court, that a provision that expressly allowed of derogation, qualification, or reservation would have a norm-creating potential.

In an interesting passage, the Court thought that, 'even without the passage of any considerable period of time', a very widespread participation in the Convention might suffice, 'provided it included that of states whose interests were specially affected'. This aspect—'substantial participation by those whose interest are affected'—was later to be echoed by Professor J. Dupuy in the *Texaco* v. *Libya* arbitration, and to which we have referred above. Looking at the legal status to be accorded to a series of General Assembly resolutions on permanent sovereignty over natural resources he gave critical weight to whether they had the support of the capital-exporting as well as the capital-importing states.

Further, where non-parties applied the equidistance principle, said the Court, 'the basis of their action can only be problematical and must remain entirely speculative'. The Court found there was 'not a "shred of evidence" that they believed themselves to be applying a mandatory rule of international law'.[40] This leads us right back to the problem of evidence for the establishment of custom, and in particular evidence as to *opinio juris*. And there is a related question: is the evidence of *opinio juris* the same when the norm tells one *what to do* (e.g. draw an equidistant line) as when it proscribes certain actions (e.g. do not commit genocide)? Applying the same tests that it enunciated in the *Continental Shelf Cases* to the question of genocide, would the Court have determined that there were relatively

[38] *North Sea Continental Shelf Case*, ICJ Reports (1969) para. 70.
[39] Judge Lachs thought it 'too exacting to require proof that every state applies a general rule out of a sense of obligation' (ibid. 231).
[40] Ibid., para. 76.

few ratifying parties to the Genocide Convention, that they did not include most of the potential butchers, and that the basis of the practice of most states in not committing genocide has to remain 'entirely speculative'?

The character of the alleged emerging norm seems important in the analysis. We may take two further examples to explore the matter further. The first is the concept of the exclusive economic zone (EEZ). This doctrine was formulated early during the negotiations for a revised UN Convention on the Law of the Sea. It found general favour and in its refined form appears as Articles 55–70 of the 1982 Convention text. That Convention has not, of course, entered into effect, so the question we now put is even more striking than the one the Court had to address in the *North Sea Continental Shelf Cases*: can a provision, appearing for the first time in a treaty that has not entered into effect, rapidly come to represent customary international law even for those who have not ratified the unexecuted treaty? There seems to be a widespread support for the view that it can. But again, we should note that the provision is different in kind from those of the Genocide Convention and from Article 6 of the 1958 Continental Shelf Convention. It concerns neither proscribed behaviour nor mandatory techniques. The EEZ provisions are rather jurisdictional entitlements allowed to states in certain maritime areas.

The provisions were widely supported for inclusion in the Convention text, even by those who later refused, on other grounds, to become ratifying parties. And a substantial number of states, with diverse maritime interests potentially affected by the provisions, have since enacted legislation based, overtly or covertly, on the EEZ provisions.[41] The 'basis of their action', to use the Court's words, must here too be 'entirely speculative': but they seem to feel they are entitled so to act—and, indeed, the lack of protest at these evidences of state practice has been affirmed by the Court as evidencing a general consensus as to a new norm which entitles the establishment of EEZs.[42]

A further interesting example is that of abandonment of petroleum rigs and installations after the life of the petroleum field is exhausted. What is to be done about removing these structures? In particular, does international law have a role in balancing the interests of the shelf state in keeping abandonment costs low with the interests of navigation, or fishing, or the environment? Article 5 (5) of the Geneva Convention of 1958 on the

---

[41] See e.g. the Decree of the Presidium of the Supreme Soviet of the USSR on the Economic Zone of the USSR in the publication by the UN Office for Ocean Affairs and the Law of the Sea, No. 4 *Law of the Sea Bulletin* (Feb. 1985) at p. 31 and Act No. 15/1984 of 12 Nov. 1984 on the Territorial Sea and Exclusive Economic Zone of the Republic of Equatorial Guinea, No. 6 *Law of the Sea Bulletin* (Oct. 1985) at p. 19.
[42] See *Continental Shelf (Libya v. Malta) Case*, ICJ Reports (1985) 13 at 33.

Continental Shelf simply provides: 'Any installations which are abandoned or disused must be removed entirely.' The issue here is not so much whether Article 5 (5), any more than Article 6, came to represent a mandatory norm of customary international law. There was virtually no international practice in field abandonment between 1958 and 1982, so the problem of *opinio juris* in relation to practice simply does not arise. Rather, the issue is whether the provisions of the 1982 Convention prevail, although that Convention is not in force, the relevant provisions are ambiguous, and they contain a reference on to a further institution. Article 60 (3) provides that abandoned installations or structures *shall be removed* to ensure safety of navigation, taking into account any generally accepted international standards established in this regard by *the competent international organization*. Notification is to be given of any installations or structures *not entirely removed*.

In the event, the International Maritime Organization (IMO) has asserted its right to be treated as 'the competent international organization', and it has adopted Guidelines and Standards for the Removal of Offshore Installations and Structures. A mandatory requirement in the 1958 Convention, which was probably binding only on parties thereto, has been replaced by a softer clause in another treaty which is not in effect, which makes reference to standards to be adopted by another body. A substantial percentage of states who have offshore petroleum deposits are members of the IMO; but the IMO's resolutions are not binding. The evidence seems to be that states in their national legislature and action thereunder are making serious efforts to comply with the IMO's Standards and Guidelines. Of course, it is easier for states to comply with these Standards and Guidelines, as they alter the 1958 treaty rule from full removal to partial removal. Even those states which are parties to the 1958 Convention, but are not ratifying parties to the 1982 unexecuted Treaty, seem to feel entitled to rely both on Article 60 of the 1982 Convention and on the non-binding resolution of the IMO.

What conclusions do we draw from all of this? We can only say that the sources of international law are not compartmentalized, but do indeed overlap. And it will always be harder to show an emerging mandatory requirement that is obligatory for states than to show an emerging relaxation of a mandatory requirement, upon which states are entitled to rely.

Sources of Law and Legal Obligations

Article 38 of the Statute speaks of general or special conventions as a source of law. Thus bilateral or multilateral conventions each have a place in the sources of international law.

It has been suggested by Fitzmaurice that treaties are not a source of law *stricto sensu*, but only a source of obligation between the parties.[43] Judge Sir Robert Jennings has spoken of this as an insight whose truth, upon reflection, is apparent.[44] Fitzmaurice's point is general, because he suggested that a treaty either contained already accepted norms, which themselves were thus the source of the law, or contained new provisions, which were an exchange of obligations between the treaty parties. But his observation is particularly striking in relation to bilateral treaties, where the rehearsal of existing norms is often relatively muted, and the exchange of new bilateral obligations of behaviour is often particularly marked.

Is this distinction correct, and if so, is it meaningful? It is largely a definitional matter. If existing norms are repeated in a treaty, an obligation would exist in respect of those norms, even were they not contained in that treaty. This is exactly the point illustrated by the International Court of Justice—in somewhat controversial circumstances, to be sure[45]—when it applied customary norms relating to the use of force even when it decided that its jurisdictional competence did not extend to the application of the provisions of Article 2 (4) and Article 51 of the UN Charter. But of course multilateral treaties rarely simply repeat existing norms. Sometimes broad norms are filled out as to detail; sometimes existing norms will in a treaty be placed side by side with new norms. (The Vienna Convention on Diplomatic Relations provides a useful example. Much of it was declaratory of existing international law. A few provisions—such as the simple prohibition on a right to search diplomatic bags, which replaced the entitlement of a state to return a bag unopened if a state was not willing to submit it to search—were new.)

In so far as a treaty contains provisions not reflective of prior customary international law, it is true, as Fitzmaurice has said, that it provides for an exchange of obligations between the parties. But does it mean to say that this is therefore not a source of law? It can only mean that Fitzmaurice viewed law as something in respect of which an 'obligation' existed—that is, that 'law' and 'obligation' were two different phenomena. If State A and State B agree upon cultural exchanges, there would be an *obligation* existing between them, but no *law* of cultural exchange.

What it seems to boil down to is that, in the Fitzmaurice view, if obligations are binding only upon parties who agree to them, and no others (because they are new, albeit contained in a treaty), they are not law. The

[43] G. Fitzmaurice, *Symbolae Verzijl* (1958), 153 ff.

[44] Jennings, 'Recent Developments in the International law Commission', 388. But cf. Thirlway, *International Customary Law and Codification*, 26–7, who finds the distinction unhelpful.

[45] For criticism, see M. Mendelson, 'The Nicaragua Case and Customary International Law' (1989) 26 *Coexistence* 85.

argument has now become one of definition. It is of course possible to choose to define law as norms of univeral application. There is an echo of this view in the position taken by Professor Tunkin in 1956[46] when he wrote that decisions of the UN Security Council are not strictly speaking sources of international law. They have an *ad hoc* effect and may create binding obligations but are not of general application beyond the moment and effect to which they are directed. But it is equally possible to take a different definitional position, and to define law not as norms of general application, but as the conjoining of authority and law in a particular target. On that view law *embraces* obligation, and a Security Council resolution or a treaty commitment is still law for the addressee or ratifying party, and no less so because it is not obligatory on the world at large.

Looked at from this starting-point, custom is obligation involuntarily undertaken—that is, not based on the consent of any given state. No state has a veto over the emergence of a customary norm, which attains its status as such through repeated practice accomplished by *opinio juris*. Occasional views have been expressed to the contrary.[47]

But this is really a different phenomenon—that of *non-opposability*. Where does non-opposability fit into our study of sources? A treaty is non-opposable to third parties, unless they accept its terms or unless it is a treaty whose terms a third party inherits by virtue of the law of state succession of treaties. States can also contribute to the formation of customary international law by unilateral practice. Striking examples of that phenomenon have been the Truman Proclamation, and other such unilateral acts, being the first claims of rights over the continental shelf; and the Norwegian claims to draw straight baselines on heavily indented coastlines. The Court found that the unilateral practice in the latter case *was* opposable to the United Kingdom, because of its failure of consistent protest. But we should not draw from that the conclusion that, if it had protested, it would not have been bound by an emerging customary rule of law. The role of protest is to slow the formation of the new legal rule, or to prevent a unilateral act from being opposable. But, if a rule of general application *does* emerge (perhaps because the phenomenon is a more general one, widely practised), then an initially protesting state will not remain exempt from the application of the new customary rule.

We may summarize the discussion on *sources* and *obligations* as follows. General international law creates and contains norms which are always obligatory. Treaties, in so far as they repeat the existing norms, create neither the norms nor the obligation. Law-making treaties that seek to develop new norms are both the source of the creation of the norm (though

---

[46] Tunkin, *Osnovy sovremennogo mezhdunarodnoga prava*, 13.
[47] See Judge Sørensen, in *Anglo-Norwegian Fisheries Case*, ICJ Reports (1969) 3 at 247–8.

of course one can say the treaty is the vehicle for the *consent* that created the norm) and the mechanism for making it obligatory upon the ratifying parties. If treaties are concerned with norm-creation or elaboration *and* obligation, then there are other ways by which *obligations simpliciter* are undertaken. Thus treaties can be made opposable to a third party, by specific acceptance of their contents or, in certain categories of treaties, by state succession to such a treaty when it has been concluded by a state to which another state succeeds. Again, unilateral acts may be the source of an obligation undertaken but not of the norm which thereby becomes opposable.

Unilateral acts will be binding on the state making them only if they evidence an intention to be bound. That is a question of appreciation, on the basis of all the facts and the context. The distinction that has been drawn is between an intention to create a binding obligation, and the expression of a mere political intention. The celebrated case of *Eastern Greenland*[48] (regarding the so-called Ihlen declaration) and the *Nuclear Tests Case*[49] (regarding the French statement of an ending of atmospheric testing) are leading examples where it has been held that the unilateral acts concerned—each very different from the other—were held to amount to the undertaking of a binding obligation. In *Nuclear Tests* a statement made by one party, but not formally communicated to the other, was held binding as the conduct indicated therein. By contrast, in *Nicaragua* v. *United States* (Merits),[50] a formal communication that had been committed to the Organization of American States was held *not* to be a formal undertaking, but rather to be a political pledge. One can say only that an appreciation of all the circumstances will have to be made in every case. The law can signal the criteria, but the difficult problem of application of the criteria remains and cannot be short-circuited.

Sometimes it is suggested that there has been a unilateral assumption of obligations not by statements made, but by virtue of a state's conduct— that is to say, an implicit assumption of obligation. The International Court of Justice has made clear, in the *North Sea Continental Shelf Case*[51] and elsewhere[52] that the unilateral assumption of obligations by conduct is not 'lightly to be presumed' and a 'very consistent course of conduct' is necessary.

Nor is it to be lightly presumed that unilateral acts amount to a waiver of prior claimed rights: *Norwegian Loans Case.*[53]

To be binding, a unilateral act will require to be a representation of fact

[48] (1933) PCIJ, Ser. A/B, no. 53, pp. 52 ff.   [49] ICJ Reports (1974) 457.
[50] ICJ Reports (1986) 14 at 132.   [51] ICJ Reports (1969) 3 at 25.
[52] *Legal Status of Eastern Greenland* (1933) PCIJ, Ser. A/B, no. 53, p. 22 at 45–6; and (per Spender) *Case Concerning the Temple of Preah Vihear*, ICJ Reports (1962) 6 at 139. See also Lagergren in *Rann of Kutch Arbitration* 50 ILR 2.   [53] ICJ Reports (1957) 9 at 26.

or promised conduct, notified to the other party (or at least known by it: *Nuclear Test Case*).[54] A failure to direct the obligation to a specific party will make the assumption of an obligation less likely (*Burkina Faso* v. *Mali* Case).[55] The intention to be bound by such representation remains essential. The unilateral act may be in oral or written form.

Detrimental reliance upon the representation or promise by the addressee of the unilateral representation or promise is frequently referred to in the writings on unilateral acts. But, properly analysed, detrimental reliance seems more relevant to *estoppel* than to the *binding nature of the unilateral act*. A unilateral act is either binding or not, depending upon all the circumstances and whether it was intended to create a legal obligation between the parties. Estoppel operates as a procedural rule, whereby the party making the representation is precluded from denying to a party that has relied to its detriment thereon that it is bound thereby. It would seem that estoppel through detrimental reliance can operate to prevent such denial even when the unilateral act would not of itself have been regarded as binding.

The case law seems tolerably clear that detrimental reliance is distinct from the assumption of legal obligation. See, for example, the *Eastern Greenland Case*, where there was no detrimental reliance by Denmark.[56] Yet the Court held that Norway's unilateral declaration did 'constitute an engagement obliging Norway to refrain from occupying any part of Greenland'. In the *Nuclear Tests Case*, far from there being reliance by Australia and New Zealand, these countries insisted that the French statements were inconclusive. The Court rested rather on its own view that a legal obligation had been created.

Less clear is whether detrimental reliance really is required for estoppels to operate. Although the literature generally assumes this to be a requirement, the case law is more ambiguous. In the *Preah Vihear* case it is difficult to discern detrimental reliance by Cambodia. Two of the dissenting judges (Judges Wellington Koo and Spender) thought that estoppel was applied without evidence of such reliance. Judge Fitzmaurice thought that detrimental reliance was not necessary to estoppel. And in his important separate opinion, Judge Alfaro insisted that estoppel requires detrimental reliance.

But in the *North Sea Continental Shelf Cases*[57] the majority (including Judge Fitzmaurice) indicated that estoppel required detrimental reliance.

---

[54] ICJ Reports (1974) 253.

[55] ICJ Reports (1986) 554.

[56] PCIJ, Ser. A/B, no. 53 at 37 ff. Cf. T. Franck, 'Word Made Law: The Decision of the ICJ in the Nuclear Test Cases' (1975) 69 *AJIL* 612 at 617, who classifies consequential Danish action as 'reliance'.

[57] ICJ Reports (1969) 3 at 30.

Conclusion

Thirlway, in his stimulating book *International Customary Law and Codification*, takes the view that at the end of the day international law is what the International Court of Justice would declare it to be. He cautions against a loose approach to the question of sources. But the reality is that the Court itself often seems to approach the question of sources with a certain looseness. In many judgments and opinions resolutions are referred to without any clear indication as to what legal purpose their invocation serves: are those resolutions mere historical events, or evidence of practice, or carrying some normative weight? One could cite many examples (and the arbitral award in the case of *The Rainbow Warrior* is also replete with such examples). But the *Nicaragua* v. *United States* (Merits) case is a clear illustration of the Court using Assembly resolutions as *opinio juris*, without going further. It was important for the Court in that case, because of jurisdictional difficulties it faced in dealing with the UN Charter as a treaty-based applicable law, to find a parallel customary international law. And it found it in the practice under the Treaty that it was beyond its jurisdictional competence to rely on. Referring to 'certain General Assembly resolutions and in particular Resolution 2625 (XXV)' (the 'Friendly Relations Resolution'), the Court said that the effect of consent to the text of such resolutions must be understood 'as an acceptance of the validity of the rule or set of rules declared by the resolution by themselves'.[58] The Court relied also on Resolution 3314 (XXIX) on the Definition of Aggression.[59]

In the same case the Court—in defining the customary international law on the use of force—invoked the Helsinki Final Act and the Inter-American Treaty of Reciprocal Assistance. In the *North Sea Continental Shelf Case*, as we have seen, the Court warned against too ready assumption that treaties evidence customary international law, although in appropriate circumstances that might be the case. No explanation is given in the *Nicaragua Case* as to why *these* treaties met the test.

I am led to the following conclusion. Where the status of a treaty or a resolution at the heart of the very issue under consideration by the Court is

---

[58] *Military and Paramilitary Activities in and against Nicaragua*, ICJ Reports (1986) 14 at 100.

[59] Ibid. at 103–4. The Court prefaced this passage with the words 'with all due caution': but Professor Mendelson suggests that such 'due caution' has not been exercised. To show *opinio juris* an examination would be needed, he says, 'by a careful analysis of the language used in the Declaration and, probably, of its drafting history, including the explanatory statements made by governments. But all of this is conspicuously absent from the judgment of the Court' (Mendelson, 'The Nicaragua Case and Customary International Law' (1989) 26 *Coexistence* 85 at 93).

invoked, a rather rigorous analysis of its status will ensue. But where resolutions or treaties are invoked somewhat incidentally as evidence of law, a much looser approach will suffice. If international law is what the International Court of Justice is likely to say it will be (in Thirlway's definition), then—all the intellectual arguments notwithstanding—the Court, as much as the rest of us, is caught in the psychological moment: resolutions and treaties apparently *do* matter.

3

PARTICIPANTS IN THE INTERNATIONAL
LEGAL SYSTEM

I N this chapter we address the questions: What is the reach of international law? To whom does it apply? And, given its decentralized, horizontal nature, who are the participants in the international legal system? It is possible, as I have sought to explain, to view international law as a body of neutral rules or, as I prefer, as a flow of authoritative decision-making, with all that that implies. The classic view has been that international law applies only to states. But, as we will see, there is a growing perception that it is relevant to international actors other than states. But on one thing everyone can agree. International law is, for the time being, still *primarily* of application to states. States are, at this moment of history, still at the heart of the international legal system.

States

International law stipulates the criteria by reference to which an entity is to be termed 'a state'; it stipulates the rights and obligations of states; and it is the body of law which will most usually govern the relations of states with each other.

In a rapidly changing world, the definition of 'a state' has remained virtually unchanged and continues to be well described by the traditional provisions of the Montevideo Convention on the Rights and Duties of States: 'The state as a person of international law should possess the following qualifications: (*a*) a permanent population; (*b*) a defined territory; (*c*) government; and (*d*) capacity to enter into relations with the other states.'[1] No further serious attempts at definition have been essayed. But it should not be thought that, because the formal definition of statehood has remained unchanged, the concept of statehood is rigid and immutable. Its component elements have always been interpreted and applied flexibly, depending on the circumstances and the context in which the claim of statehood is made. For example, one has to be a state to be admitted to the United Nations.[2] Further, states may appear before specific organs of the United Nations,[3] bring matters affecting peace and

---

[1] 26 Dec. 1933, Art. 1, 49 Stat. 3097, TS No. 881.
[2] Art. 4 UN Charter.   [3] Art. 32.

security to the notice of the United Nations,[4] and be a party to the Statute of the International Court of Justice.[5] Initial membership of the United Nations was, for some of the entities claiming this right, undoubtedly part of a wider political package. The position of India and the Philippines was anomalous at the time of their admission, and that of Byelorussia and the Ukraine has remained so until after the dissolution of the Soviet Union, when the form and reality of statehood coincided for the first time. Previously, it had been quite unclear as to what it was that purportedly made them independent states, when the rest of the Soviet republics were not. But in assessing the statehood of applicants for subsequent membership, the criteria have been more seriously applied. The application of the requirement of defined territory has allowed states with unresolved border disputes to be admitted to the United Nations (for example, Israel); while claims by an existing UN member to reversionary title over all of a newly decolonized territory, which claimed independence, occasioned greater delays in admission. Generally, the claims of reversionary title were not accepted. This was true, for example, of the claims of Morocco over Mauritania in 1960 and of Iraq over Kuwait in 1962.[6] The International Court of Justice effectively rejected the claims of both Mauritania and Morocco over Western Sahara many years ago. It is to be hoped that its long-proclaimed entitlement to independence will soon become effective. The requirement of stable and effective government was always problematic for countries newly independent from colonial rule. We have only to mention Rwanda, Burundi, and Congo (Zaire) to recall that statehood, for purposes of UN admission, was attributed even when the new governments clearly lacked effective control. The invocation of the right to self-determination prevailed over the political realities; and no interest was seen as being served in refusing to allow precarious new entities to become part of the international community of states.[7] What is absolutely clear is that a loss of 'stable and effective government' does not remove the attribute of statehood, once acknowledged. Often the loss of stable and effective government is associated with intervention by other powers. Sometimes the result is simply uncertainty and chaos and an absence of objectively effective control by any government. The situation in Cambodia affords an unhappy example. Sometimes the result is that effective control has passed from central government elsewhere, either dispersed within the body politic (as in Lebanon) or abroad (as in the case of Yemen in the 1960s). In none of these cases has the international community suggested that these countries have ceased to be 'states'.

In the Balkans the appreciation of the loss of statehood by the former

---

[4] Art. 35 (2).   [5] Art. 93 (2).
[6] On all these matters, see R. Higgins, *The Development of International Law through the Political Organs of the United Nations* (1963), 13–25.   [7] Ibid., 23.

Yugoslavia has been irresistible. But the ambivalence of the international community about the new realities has been evident. On the one hand, Slovenia, Croatia, and Bosnia-Herzogovina were admitted as new member states to the United Nations in 1992. It would seem inexorably to follow that federal Yugoslavia no longer existed. And General Assembly Resolution 47/1 (1992) suspended 'Socialist Federal Yugoslavia' (Serbia-Montenegro) from participation in the General Assembly. But Serbia-Montenegro was also *not* recognized as being the legal successor to federal Yugoslavia; and was invited under the same resolution to apply *de novo* for UN membership. And for the time being 'Yugoslavia' (which surely no longer exists) remains a member of the United Nations, able to participate in everything save the Security Council. The situation can only be described as legally confused.

The number of states has only lessened where there has been an agreed merger of the legal personality of two states, whether on the basis of applications of the legal regime of one state to another (as in the unification of the two Germanys in 1990) or on a different basis (as with the foundation of the United Arab Republic from Egypt and Syria in 1958).[8] We may conclude that, once in the club, the rules by which admission was tested—and that always with a degree of flexibility—become less important.

No state is totally without dependence on some other state. A degree of interdependence is in the nature of things. But it is important that, when an entity makes its claim to be a state for a comprehensive purpose such as joining the United Nations, it is not simply an emanation of another state, lacking an essential core of independence. Thus the Indian army that had assisted in the birth of Bangladesh, after civil war in Pakistan, was required to leave Bangladesh before that country was admitted to the United Nations.

Very small nations, such as Andorra, San Marino, and Monaco, whose foreign-affairs power has been in the hands of others, have not sought to become members of the United Nations (in part also for reasons of size and resources). In 1920 Liechtenstein had been denied admission to the League of Nations on grounds that, although a sovereign state, it had freely chosen to give away some of its sovereignty and was thus not in a position to carry out all the international obligations imposed by the Covenant.[9] However, in 1990 Liechtenstein successfully secured admission to the United Nations. What had changed?

We have mentioned that invitations under Article 32 and Article 35 (2) of the Charter (to appear before the Security Council) may also be extended to states who are not members of the United Nations. Practice

---

[8] See generally J. Crawford, *The Creation of States in International Law* (1979).
[9] LNOJ 1st Ass. (1920) 667. See also Higgins, *The Development of International Law*, 34 n. 30.

shows that 'statehood' for this limited purpose is viewed more flexibly than 'statehood' for the more comprehensive claim of UN membership. Entities whose status was sufficiently controversial or insecure, and who would not have secured admission to the United Nations, have been invited under these provisions to participate in the work of the United Nations. Once again, there has been no policy interest in a narrow interpretation of the term 'state' for purposes of this limited claim to participate in the resolution of an international problem. This same flexibility has been shown in respect of claims to become a party to the Statute of the International Court of Justice—the Statute being, by virtue of Article 93 of the UN Charter, open to 'a state which is not a member of the United Nations'.[10]

Strikingly, pragmatism has also been the key to admission to the UN Specialized Agencies. Not all Agencies' constitutions use the term 'state'; and this is not the place for a detailed examination of the very complex practice. We may merely note that, notwithstanding the fact that the legal basis for admission has often been the subject of very detailed scrutiny with the Agencies, countries have been admitted to UNESCO, ICAO, the WHO, the UPU, and the ILO when they would have been unable to secure admission to the United Nations itself. No facile conclusions may be drawn and the practice admits of several different analyses. My purpose here is merely to say that, while the concept of what constitutes a state has a certain undeniable core, the application of the component elements will also depend upon the purpose for which the entity concerned is claiming to be a state, and the circumstances in which that claim is made.

If it is states who are leading actors, they find their physical manifestation in governments. Treaties are formally concluded between states; but we all know that sometimes treaties will be signed by 'The State of X' and sometimes by 'The Government of the State of X'. The legal question of recognition arises in respect of each of them. Recognition is the formal acknowledgement by the state that another exists. From the perspective of the recognized state, such acknowledgment is obviously welcome. There is a doctrinal dispute as to whether recognition by a significant number of states is in fact a further *requisite* for statehood (effectively forming an additional category to those stipulated in the Montevideo Convention).[11]

[10] San Marino and Liechtenstein (before it became a member of the UN) were parties to the Court's Statute.
[11] H. Lauterpacht, *Recognition in International Law* (1947), 52–8 (recognition is 'constitutive', i.e. a necessary element for statehood; but is compulsory when the elements objectively exist). Cf. Crawford, *The Creation of States*, 17–20; R. Jennings, 121 *Recueil des cours* (1967), 350; J. Verzijl, *International Law* (1969), ii. 587; T. Chen, *The International Law of Recognition with Special Reference to Great Britain and United States* (1951), 18 n. 41; J. Verhoeven, *La Reconnaissance internationale dans la pratique contemporaine: Les Relations publiques internationales* (1975), 714–15.

Whatever position one takes on that, it is the case that no entity has had access to generalized arenas—for example, to UN membership, to participation in multilateral conferences—without being recognized by substantial numbers of existing states.

International law has provided criteria for the existence of statehood (which other states then recognize, believing it to be politically important and perhaps also significant as a constitutive element in the statehood of the country concerned). But international law has said nothing about governments—which have also been the subject-matter of recognition—or whether all that is required under international law for a government to be recognized is that it is in effective control of the state concerned. And it is for each state to appreciate in good faith whether an entity claiming to be the government of another state is indeed in effective control of the territory. But certain issues of law and policy still arise. May one state properly add additional criteria, refusing to recognize a government whose politics are not its own? Or is the test not just effective control, but *only* effective control? In the 1950s the United States took one view, the United Kingdom another. The United States refused to extend recognition to the communist government of China, regarding its access to power as having been achieved through the unlawful use of force. The United Kingdom early recognized the Government of Mao Tse Tung on the basis of its manifest exercise of effective control over mainland China. To the political sophisticate in the 1960s the latter view seemed much more attractive. After all, it was the representatives of the government who would be allowed to speak for a state in the United Nations. Did not a refusal to recognize the communist government of China—and in turn, a refusal to support the representation of China by that government in the United Nations—effectively deny 600 million people any place in the family of nations?

Today the answers seem less clear. In the 1950s and 1960s the important policy consideration, for those who took the view that 'effective control' was the exclusive requirement for the recognition of a government, was that the United Nations should be an organization of universal membership, seeing to bring good to all the peoples of the world through access to their governments—regardless of the nature of those governments. It is a fact that 85 per cent of governments represented at the United Nations are dictatorships of one sort or another.

But since the mid-1960s the idea has come to take hold that people are entitled to a more direct participation in decisions over their own lives. Mere membership of their countries in the United Nations has been a totally insufficient guarantee of such participation. Instead, there has developed the concept of internal self-determination (which will be examined in detail in a later chapter).

There is a growing tendency in the United Nations to ensure not only that the remnants of colonialism are transferred to independence, but that the newly independent countries are governed by representative governments. This policy (somewhat selective in its application, but a discernable trend none the less) is being achieved by two main means. First, by calls for non-recognition of claims to independence by manifestly unrepresentative governments: the calls for non-recognition of Ian Smith's government in Rhodesia[12] upon its unilateral declaration of independence from the United Kingdom; and for the non-recognition of the Bantustans' purported independence from South Africa,[13] are cases in point. Secondly, the United Nations has in recent years been engaging in much technical assistance to ensure that power is transferred to the elected representatives of the people, offering a real choice.

Taking all this into account, does it really do today to say that each state is free to recognize any other government on the exclusive grounds that that government is in effective control of the territory concerned? Every ratifying party of the International Covenants on Human Rights acknowledges the right of peoples to self-determination. That commitment will, as we approach the twenty-first century, require the international community to harness every means at its disposal to encourage democracy and free choice. The making of recognition conditional upon not only effective control, but the representative quality of a government, is one such means. A graphic illustration of the new tendency is afforded by events in the early 1990s in the former Soviet Union and Yugoslavia. Other states have made recognition of the new entities emerging from those former states dependent not only upon representative government, but upon the expression of willingness by the new states to accept commitments under international human-rights treaties.[14]

The pressure for self-determination, and the growing importance of representative government, has seemingly led to another phenomenon—namely, a willingness to recognize the independence of entities which have shown commitment to representative government (and where they have broken away from former totalitarian rule), even when there is no government really yet in effective control. The recognition by the EC states of Croatia[15] would seem to fall into that category. The recognition was constitutive not only in the legal sense, but in the political sense that it

---

[12] SC Res. 277 (1970).

[13] GA Res. 2775E (XXVI) 1971; GA Res. 3411D (XXX) 1975.

[14] See *Declaration of the EC on Yugoslavia and on Guidelines of Recognition of New States* (1992) 31 *ILM*, 1485; and see also the Legal Opinions of the Yugoslav Arbitration Commission established under the International Conference on Yugoslavia (ibid. 1494).

[15] Germany recognized Croatia on 19 Dec. 1991. The remaining eleven members of the EC recognized Croatia on 15 January 1992.

was an essential element in securing the later 'statehood' that was recognized before it became an effective reality.

What purpose, from the point of view of the recognizing state, does recognition serve? A state may, of course, share our view that recognition may be a useful tool for securing certain social ends. Beyond that, the requirements of international intercourse make it hard to avoid some public statement when a new state comes upon the scene: the birth of Bangladesh, or the unification of Germany, could hardly go unacknowledged. Nor could the tumultuous events affecting the Baltic states, the Soviet republics, and the countries comprising the former Yugoslavia. Further, states will have to vote for or against the admission of state-applicants to the United Nations, or its Specialized Agencies. It may well be necessary to take a position on certain legal issues; and, indeed, the voting may give rise to implied recognition.[16]

But recognition of governments is another thing. Some states, such as the United Kingdom,[17] have found it possible to avoid formal recognition of governments, simply choosing whether or not to open trade or cultural contacts or to seek diplomatic relations. But what we must also remember is that in many countries recognition—or at least a formal indication by the authorities as to how they regard an entity terming itself the government of a foreign country—serves certain domestic purposes, too. In many countries an unrecognized state or government will not be able to sue in the courts of the forum;[18] nor will private persons be able to claim title through decrees or legislative acts of an unrecognized government;[19] nor will an unrecognized government be able to claim those privileges and immunities from jurisdiction afforded by international law.[20] The extent to which recognition is determinative for these domestic purposes is a matter

[16] For State A to be a member of the same organization as State B implies no recognition (unless it is an organization of very limited membership). But for State A to vote for the admission of State B, to an organization the members of which must be states, implies recognition of State B as a state.

[17] In 1980 the United Kingdom announced it would no longer formally recognize new governments (although formal recognition of new states would continue): *Hansard*, Parl. Deb. (Commons), vol. 983, cols. 277–9 (Written Answers, 25 Apr. 1980)). For comment, see C. Warbrick, 'The New British Policy on Recognition of Governments' (1981) 30 *ICLQ* 568.

[18] See, *inter alia*, *City of Berne* v. *Bank of England* (1804) 9 Ves. Jun. 347; cf. *Gur Corporation* v. *Trust Bank of Africa Limited* [1986] 3 AER 449; *Russian Socialist Republic* v. *Cibrario* (1923) 235 NY 255; cf. *Diggs* v. *Dent* (1975) 14 *ILM* 795; *Société Despa et Fils* v. *USSR* (1931–2) 6 *Annual Digest of Public International Law Cases*, Case No. 28. For an excellent general survey of the question of recognition in international law in its entirety, see *Oppenheim's International Law*, 9th edn., ed. R. Jennings and A. Watts (1992), vol. i, pt. 1, pp. 126–203.

[19] See, in the United Kingdom, *Luther* v. *Sagor* [1921] 3 KB 532; *Carl Zeiss Stiftung* v. *Rayner and Keeler* [1967] AC 853.

[20] *Arantzazu Mendi* [1939] AC 256; cf., in the United States, *Wulfsohn* v. *Russian Socialist Republic* (1923) 234 NY 372, 138 NE 24; and s. 1116 (c) (ii) Protection of Diplomats Act 1971 (1972) 11 *ILM* 1405.

for each country. In the United States, with its formal separation of powers, the courts have traditionally deferred to the executive in matters touching on foreign relations.[21] In the United Kingdom the Foreign and Commonwealth Office provides a certificate on the recognition of a state, or a letter in reply to the court's request for information—but the legal consequences are left for the court to draw. The courts show a tendency to draw conclusions that they regard as in accordance with social or commercial realities.[22] But in areas of current political importance—such as during the life of the rebellion in Rhodesia, or with reference to the UN call for non-recognition of Iraq's claim to govern Kuwait—courts are likely to be sensitive to speaking with the same voice as the executive. Recognition is the legal tool by which this is achieved.

International Organizations

International organizations may be participants in the international legal system in a variety of senses. They will often be established by international treaty and their governing law—that is to say, the law that determines their status and functions and responsibilities—is international law.[23] They may be endowed by their constituent instruments with international personality—they are legal persons distinct from the states who established them and agreed to their constituent instruments. In the words of Fischer Williams, the entity is the bearer of rights and obligations. The classic indicia are (1) an ability to contract, (2) an ability to sue and be sued, (3) an ability to own property, and (4) a *volonté distincte*—in other words, a capacity to take decisions which bind the membership, perhaps even when not all of the members have favoured the decision concerned.

It can thus be seen that certain types of intergovernmental institutions can be set up, through which states choose to conduct their affairs, but they will not have these attributes of independent legal personality. Of course, this does not mean that they are not actors on the international plane, or that international law does not govern their status and attributes, or that they are governed by any single national law. It means only that such an institution is, at the end of the day, indistinguishable from the states that created it. But other international organizations, which have these indicia

---

[21] But see *Third Restatement of the Law: The Foreign Relations Law of the United States* (1987), 7–15, esp. p. 9 on the separation of powers.

[22] See *Carl Zeiss Stiftung* [1967] AC 853; and the views of Lord Denning as expressed in *Hesperides Hotels Ltd.* v. *Aegean Turkish Holidays Ltd.* [1979] AC 508.

[23] Very exceptionally, an international organization set up by international treaty will be placed under the governing law of a single state: see the Bank for International Settlements, whose governing law is Swiss.

of international legal personality, are truly international actors in their own right.

Sometimes a treaty establishing an international organization will state in terms whether it has international legal personality. On other occasions it may be necessary to deduce personality from powers that are given in the constituent treaty, and from the functions that the organization has been given. Thus, in the famous Advisory Opinion in *Reparation for Injuries*,[24] the International Court of Justice was asked whether the United Nations could bring a legal suit to recover damages for the death of its employee, Count Folke Bernadotte. It could only do so if it had legal personality, on which the UN Charter is silent. The International Court noted:

the Organization was intended to exercise and enjoy, and is in fact exercising and enjoying functions and rights which can only be explained on the basis of the possession of a large measure of international personality and the capacity to operate upon an international plane . . . it could not carry out the intentions of its founders if it was devoid of international personality.[25]

Some further points may be made on international organizations as participants in the international legal system. The first is that, if an organization does not have personality, its member states will be liable for its defaults and wrongful acts. But the converse is not necessarily true. The fact that an organization has legal personality means that it is liable for its own defaults. But whether the member states have a concurrent or a secondary liability (that is to say, a liability to creditors or those harmed, if the organization fails to pay) depends upon the particular constituent instrument. This is a controversial area, but, in my view, in the absence of any such provisions, there is no liability upon member states; and nor is there any provision of general international law that makes states liable.[26]

There are those who take the view that the international legal personality of an organization is opposable only to those who have 'recognised' the organization, in the sense of being a member of the organization or engaging in some transaction with it, or granting privileges to it.[27] But this is to ignore the objective legal reality of international

---

[24] Reparation for Injuries Suffered in the Service of the United Nations, ICJ Reports (1949 174.   [25] Ibid. 179.

[26] These issues have been at the heart of the massive litigation following the collapse of the International Tin Council in 1985. See *Maclaine Watson and Co. Ltd.* v. *International Tin Council* [1988] 3 WLR 1169; *In re International Tin Council* [1988] 3 WLR 1159; *J. H. Rayner Ltd* v. *Department of Trade and Industry* [1989] 3 WLR 969. The matter is under examination by the Institut de Droit International and has also been addressed in the international arbitration concerning *Westland Helicopters* v. *Arab Organization for Industrialization*— though note that in this case the Arab Organization for Industrialization was, as the first Arbitral Tribunal put it, 'in effect indistinguishable from the states' (80 ILR 596 at 622).

[27] G. Schwarzenberger, *A Manual of International Law*, (3rd edn., 1957), i. 128–30; R. Bindschedler, 'Die Anerkennung im Volkerrecht' (1961–2) 9 *Archiv des Volkerrechts* 387–8; I. Seidl-Hohenveldern, 'Die Volkerrechtliche Haftung fur Handlungen internationales

personality. If the attributes are there, personality exists. It is not a matter of recognition. It is a matter of objective reality.[28]

Closely related is the difficult question of the legal status in domestic law of a body having personality in international law. Does the fact that an international organization has, under its constituent instrument, expressly or by implication, powers to sue or be sued, to enter into contracts, to bear responsibilities, mean that it is to be recognized as a legal person in domestic law? The answer to that question lies in the laws of the various jurisdictions. Some domestic courts will take the provisions of the international instrument as a guide to what status the local forum should accord the organization. Others will require the source of the personality to be accorded the organization to be found in domestic law. This is especially likely to be the case if the jurisdiction concerned does not automatically 'receive' treaties as part of domestic law, but requires them to be incorporated into domestic law before local effect will be given to them. Thus the courts of the United Kingdom found that the International Tin Council (ITC) had legal personality—not because it was clearly provided for in the International Tin Agreement, but because that provision was made part of English law by a statutory instrument.[29] Thus, said the House of Lords in a striking and disturbing phrase, the statutory instrument 'created' the ITC in English law. It necessarily followed that, when another international organization, the Arab Monetary Fund— clearly and objectively existing in any real-world sense—was not accorded personality by any provision of English law, it was held by the House of Lords to be a non-existent international organization, legally speaking.[30]

Individuals

International law has traditionally been defined by reference to those to whom it is said to apply. The classic definition of it as law binding on states has been expanded to include also international organizations. As for the place of individuals in this scheme of things, rational debate has been constrained first by the notion that the appropriate framework of enquiry is

Organisationen im Verhaltnis zu Nichtmitgliedstaaten' (1961) 11 *Osterreichische Zeitschrift fur offentliches Recht* 497–506; I. Seidl-Hohenveldern, 'Recentsbeziehungen zwischen Internationalen Organisationen und den einselnenstaaten' (1953–4) 4 *Archiv des Volkerrechts* 33; H. Mosler, 'Reflexions sur la personnalité juridique en droit international public', *Mélanges offerts à Henri Rolin* (1964); W. Wengler, *Actes officiels du Congres international d'études sur la Communauté Européene du Charbon et de l'Acier* (1958), iii. 10–13, 318–19.

[28] See *ITC v. Amalgamet Inc.* 80 ILR 31.

[29] *J. H. Rayner Ltd.* v. *Department of Trade and Industry* [1989] 3 WLR 969. For comment and criticism, see R. Jennings, 'An International Lawyer Takes Stock' (1990) 39 *ICLQ* 513.

[30] See *Arab Monetary Fund* v. *Hashim* (No. 3) [1991] 2 WLR 729.

that of the concept of 'subjects and objects of international law'; and, secondly, by a conservative belief that what presently is, necessarily always has to remain so.

Let me begin my argument at the beginning. Plutarch and later Francisco de Vitoria in 1532 both wrote in terms that effectively acknowledged that non-state entities had internationally recognized legal rights. De Vitoria, of course, was speaking of the Indian Kingdoms of America. A century later Grotius, in his *De jure belli ac pacis* of 1625, was refining the idea. Verzijl has suggested that the first scholar to use the technical term 'subject of international law' (in fact to describe the status of a state) was Liebnitz in the preface to his *Codex juris gentium diplomaticus*, of 1693.

The designating of states as 'subjects' within the international legal system in turn led to an embracing, especially by the leading jurists of the positivist school of international law, of the position that under a legal system there exist only 'objects' and 'subjects'. This starting-point has received a widespread and uncritical acceptance and has necessarily dictated the framework of any examination. We have all been held captive by a doctrine that stipulates that all international law is to be divided into 'subjects'—that is, those elements bearing, without the need for municipal intervention, rights and responsibilities; and 'objects'—that is, the rest. Certain authors have contended vigorously that only states are the subjects of international law.[31] And to the positivist there is no permissive rule of international law that allows individuals to be bearers of rights and duties.[32] They must, therefore, be *objects*: that is to say, they are like 'boundaries' or 'rivers' or 'territory' or any of the other chapter headings found in the traditional textbooks.

I believe every step of this argument to be wrong. I have already argued that international law is not to be understood as a set of 'rules'. First of all, international law is not only 'rules'; moreover, its norms are not fixed indefinitely and are thus wholly responsive to the needs of the system. Further, the positivist definition assumes that some specific rule is required 'permitting' the individual to be a 'subject' of international law. Finally, the whole notion of 'subjects' and 'objects' has no credible reality, and, in my view, no functional purpose. We have erected an intellectual prison of our own choosing and then declared it to be an unalterable constraint.

There are others who reject the positivist view that the individual is a mere object under international law, and suggest that the individual can be

---

[31] D. Anzilotti, *Cours de droit international* (1929), 134; Gihl, *Folkratt under Fred* (1956); M. Siotto-Pintor, *Recueil des cours* (1932, III), 356.

[32] Schwarzenberger, *Manual*; *International Law as Applied by International Courts and Tribunals* (3rd edn., 1957), i. 140–55.

a subject having, in certain limited cases, rights and duties.[33] But this view, too, is based upon the assumption that the correct starting-point is an examination of whether individuals can or cannot be 'subjects' of international law.

But I believe that there is room for another view: that it is not particularly helpful, either intellectually or operationally, to rely on the subject–object dichotomy that runs through so much of the writings. It is more helpful, and closer to perceived reality, to return to the view of international law as a particular decision-making process. Within that process (which is a dynamic and not a static one) there are a variety of participants, making claims across state lines, with the object of maximizing various values. Determinations will be made on those claims by various authoritative decision-makers—Foreign Office Legal Advisers, arbitral tribunals, courts.

Now, in this model, there are no 'subjects' and 'objects', but only *participants*. Individuals *are* participants, along with states, international organizations (such as the United Nations, or the International Monetary Fund (IMF) or the ILO), multinational corporations, and indeed private non-governmental groups. Elsewhere I have put it this way:

In the way our world is organized, it is States which are mostly interested in, for example, sea space, or boundaries, or treaties; it is thus States which advance claims and counter-claims about these. Individuals' interests lie in other directions: in protection from the physical excesses of others, in their personal treatment abroad, in the protection abroad of their property interests, in fairness and predictability in their international business transactions and in securing some external support for the establishment of a tolerable balance between their rights and duties within their national state. Thus, the topics of minimum standard of treatment of aliens, requirements as to the conduct of hostilities and human rights, are not simply exceptions conceded by historical chance within a system of rules that operates as between states. Rather, they are simply part and parcel of the fabric of international law, representing the claims that are naturally made by individual participants in contradistinction to state-participants.[34]

Among the few writers who rejected the subject–object dichotomy was the late Professor D. P. O'Connell, who as early as 1965 had realized that the debate over the position of the individual in international law 'goes to the heart of legal philosophy'. He continued:

Does it suffice to admit that the individual's good is the ultimate end of the law but refuse the individual any capacity in the realisation of that good? Is the good in fact attained through treating the individual as an instrumentality of law and not as an

---

[33] e.g. C. Norgaard, *The Position of the Individual in International Law* (1962).
[34] R. Higgins, 'Conceptual Thinking about the Individual in International Law' (1978) 4 *British Journal of International Studies* 1 at 5.

actor? Philosophy and practice demonstrate that the answer to all these questions must be in the negative . . .[35]

There are certain other matters concerning the individual in international law which must also be mentioned. Undoubtedly, whatever view one takes on the somewhat philosophical matters we have been discussing, individuals are extremely handicapped in international law from the procedural point of view. They have little access to international arenas; and are dependent upon the nationality-of-claims rule, whereby an individual must, generally speaking, pursue a claim at the international level by getting his government to take it up on his behalf. There is, of course, a close relationship between the notion of nationality of claims and the unavailability of most[36] international tribunals to the individual. Articles 35 and 65 of the Statute of the International Court allow only states and international organs to obtain, respectively, judgments and advisory opinions. Why can an individual not bring a claim before the Court in respect of a subject-matter of immediate legal interest to him—an expropriation issue, for example? The traditional view is that, if State A expropriates the property rights of Mr X, a foreigner, without compensation, it has violated no right of Mr X (because he *has* no rights under international law) but has caused damage to his national state, State B, through harm to one of its nationals. Accordingly, it is for State B to decide whether it wishes to bring a legal claim. (The same principle operates should State B decide to make a diplomatic protest, rather than commence litigation.)

Does harm to a state's national amount to harm to the state? And, even if the answer is 'yes', does that *also* mean that the individual has no rights under international law himself, either substantive or procedural? Some states take the view that physical harm to their citizens abroad is to be assimilated as harm to the state itself such that it triggers the right to self-defence for 'an armed attack upon the state'. That view is a controversial one. To claim that *all* damage to individuals, including material damage, is damage to the state is to press the legal fiction even further. If the harm were really harm to the state, there would surely be a requirement that *all* instances of such harm be reported to the state, so that that state would be in a position to decide whether to make diplomatic representations or pursue legal remedies. But the state does *not* decide how to protect itself on the basis of such necessary information. The reality is that individuals who have been harmed will seek their own remedies (often through negotiation, through action in the courts of the foreign state); but, if

[35] D. P. O'Connell, *International Law* (1965), i. 116.
[36] cf. the European Court. The Court acts, *inter alia*, as an administrative tribunal in respect of the acts or omissions of Community organs; and as a constitutional court, interpreting the Treaty at the request of national courts: See Art. 177, EEC Treaty.

unsuccessful, will *then* engage in protracted dialogue with their own government to urge it to take up the case on their behalf. We know that there are techniques available when a state truly *does* regard action taken against an individual or corporation as action harming the national state itself: that is exactly what so-called Blocking Statutes are about, which *require* the reporting to the national authorities of assertions of jurisdiction deemed excessive and damaging to the national interest.[37] But, generally speaking, no specific harm is done to the state itself through injury to the individual. Its natural general interest in seeing that its citizens should be unmolested and properly treated could be met by the individual being allowed to bring an international claim himself.

Not only does this seem right as a matter of analysis, but the individual has in fact been badly served by the nationality-of-claims rule. All too often his national government is not at all interested in pursuing his claim (or in rectifying the harm allegedly done to itself, to rephrase it in the classic formula). It has broader interests to concern itself with, and the instigation of litigation may not fit with these broader considerations.[38] The individual is thus left with no effective remedy: international law does not oblige his government to protect him, and his national law will almost certainly not allow any judicial review of a government's failure to act on his behalf.

The Permanent Court of International Justice noted in 1933: 'it is scarcely necessary to point out that the capacity to possess civil rights does not necessarily imply the capacity to exercise those rights oneself.'[39] What are the implications of this procedural inability suffered by individuals?

International law lays certain obligations upon states in how they treat aliens. Do aliens therefore have certain *rights* under international law to be treated according to an international minimum standard? Or does it not work that way? While states are under certain obligations *vis-à-vis* aliens, do aliens none the less have *no* international law rights *vis-à-vis* foreign states with which they have contact?

The answer is, of course, at once muddied by the ever-intrusive presence of the nationality-of-claims requirement. If a state mistreats an alien, an international suit will only lie against it at the hands of the national state of the alien concerned. Does this fact mean that the individual has no rights under international law against the foreign state? Or merely that it cannot make them good without the intervention of its national state? Are we speaking here of procedure or of substance? Is it indeed a distinction without a difference, in the sense that a right without a remedy is, contrary

---

[37] e.g. UK Protection of Foreign Trading Interests Act 1980.
[38] For a graphic example, see the *Barcelona Traction, Light and Power Company Case*, ICJ Reports (1970), 18.
[39] Ser. A/B, no. 61, p. 231.

to what was said by the Permanent Court of Justice,[40] virtually no legal right at all? Or is that something that international lawyers, operating in a decentralized system, are not allowed to think?

As international lawyers, all too familiar with the realities of power, we have long had a vested interest in rejecting the Austinian and Kelsenian precept of the dependence of international law upon the existence of an effective sanction. I realize, of course, that effective remedy and sanction are not wholly coterminous, and I simply make the point that we are not unaccustomed to separating our definition of a right from our appraisal of a remedy. We can look at the question in another way. Is the obligation under international law not to mistreat aliens an international law right in *the hands of the alien*? Is there some inevitable inner truth in the answer 'No, because international law duties are owed *between states* and not between states or private parties'? Do these words describe an immutable truth or are they just a linguistic shorthand for the legal fact that, as presently structured, international law does not permit individuals to sue directly on the international plane in respect of matters of international law? Is the statement that international law is about inter-state obligations only, the *consequence* of a procedural disability under which the individual labours, or is it the *cause* of that procedural disability?

My own view is that the individual does have certain rights owed *to him* under international law (and not just to his state). Sir Hersch Lauterpacht, in *International Law and Human Rights*, puts it thus:

The position of the individual as a subject of international law has often been obscured by the failure to observe the distinction between the recognition, in an international instrument of rights enuring to the benefit of the individual and the enforceability of these rights at his instance. The fact that the beneficiary of rights is not authorized to take independent steps in his own name to enforce them does not signify that he is not a subject of the law or that the rights in question are vested exclusively in the agency which possesses the capacity to enforce them. Thus in relation to the current view that the rights of the alien within foreign territory are the rights of his state and not his own, the correct way of stating the legal position is not that the state asserts its own exclusive right but that it enforces, in substance, the right of the individual who, as the law now stands, is incapable of asserting it in the international sphere.[41]

Lauterpacht spoke of rights enuring to the benefit of an individual under an *international instrument*. My suggestion is that the principle is equally applicable without the intervention of an international instrument, and

---

[40] A view embraced by Lord Denning in *Gouriet* v. *Union of Post Office Workers* [1977] 2 WLR 696. This point was not approved by the House of Lords, which reversed the Court of Appeal's decision favouring Mr Gouriet.

[41] H. Lauterpacht, *International Law* (1950), 27.

that individuals *can* be the beneficiaries of international law rights which fall upon states to perform as a matter of general international law.

What exactly do we mean when we ask if international law *applies* to individuals? Do we mean, are they obliged to follow its precepts? Or do we mean can they *invoke* it as the required standard of behaviour in other actors, such as states? These are difficult questions, and we will need to approach the underlying issues step by step.

The increasing importance of international arbitration is an area that we should perhaps be watching in this area. It is now commonplace for a foreign private corporation and a state who have entered into contractual relations to agree to international arbitration in the event of a dispute. (And, in principle, the private party could be an *individual*, though as such he will probably have less leverage than a foreign corporation and may well have to accept the local legal system rather than reference to international arbitration.) The applicable law clause may designate a national legal system, but more usually it will refer to 'general principles of law' or 'the law of country X and the relevant principles of general international law', or some such similar formula. At one bound, therefore, the private party has escaped the need to have his claim brought by his national government, and can invoke international law. Thus, if State X and Mr Y have a contract, State X's ability to vary the terms of that contract will be interpreted by reference to the relevant principles of international law; and compensation due to Mr Y will likewise be appraised by reference to international law. Thus, even if the purists wish to say that State X owes Mr Y no international law obligations about his property (owing them only to Mr Y's national state), the reality is that Mr Y *can* invoke such legal norms and it is as if international law obligations were owed by the state to the individual. Arbitral clauses which refer to international law as the applicable law effectively remove the alleged inability of individuals to be the bearer of rights under international law. This is being done by mutual consent, of course—but the point is that there is *no inherent reason* why the individual should not be able directly to invoke international law and to be the beneficiary of international law.

Developments in this area, as elsewhere in international law, occur as much through the force of circumstances as through any conscious intellectual processes. The arrangements for the litigation of issues arising out of the Iran revolution is an interesting case in point. The Agreements with Iran that resulted in the release of the US hostages included provision that a Claims Tribunal should be set up in The Hague. This Tribunal was

---

[42] Art. V, Declaration of the Government of the Democratic and Popular Republic of Algeria concerning the Settlement of Claims by the Government of the United States of America and the Government of the Islamic Republic of Iran (1981) 20 *ILM* 230.

given jurisdiction over claims of nationals of the United States against Iran and Iran against the United States concerning debts, contracts, expropriations, and other measures affecting property rights. The applicable law shall be 'such choice of law rules and principles of commercial and international law as the Tribunal determines to be applicable'.[42] Under this clause, private parties have claimed violation of a treaty (the 1954 Treaty of Amity) which was made between two states. They have invoked international law principles. And they have invoked the law on state responsibility (in the context of questions relating to the personal security of the plaintiffs). In none of these areas did the government of Iran, according to the precepts of classical international law, owe duties to the individuals or corporations concerned. The duties were owed to their nation states. We have here not only a waiver of the usual nationality-of-claims requirements, but also the bearing by private parties of substantive international law rights.

4

ALLOCATING COMPETENCE: JURISDICTION

IN Chapters 1–3 I discussed what international law is, and what function it serves; how we identify its substantive content; and to whom it applies. This was the introductory section of a book designed to show that, if we do not insist upon international law as the mechanistic application of rules, without regard to context, it is a system that can assist in the avoidance, containment, and resolution of disputes.

Chapters 4–15 show some of the ways in which international law helps to avoid conflicts. Of critical importance is the issue of *jurisdiction*, because that is all about allocating competence. There is no more important way to avoid conflict than by providing clear norms as to which state can exercise authority over whom, and in what circumstances. Without that allocation of competences, all is rancour and chaos.

Any textbook will tell you that there are the following bases of jurisdiction:

territorial jurisdiction, by which a state can make laws for, and apply them to, persons and events within its territory;
nationality jurisdiction;
protective jurisdiction;
passive personality jurisdiction;
universal jurisdiction;
effects jurisdiction, claims for which are more controversial.

I do not plan to go through each of these in turn. The topic is extensively covered elsewhere, including in the two outstanding sets of lectures given in the Hague Academy in 1964 and 1984 by the late Dr Francis Mann.

Rather, as in the earlier chapters, I have chosen to focus on what is not yet clear, what is controversial, what is uncertain—in short, the key problems within this topic. Accordingly, I will have some things to say on universal jurisdiction, on passive personality jurisdiction, on abduction and the exercise of jurisdiction, and on extraterritorial jurisdiction.

Universal Jurisdiction

International law permits the exercise of jurisdiction in respect of certain offences against the international community. That is to say, the nature of the act entitles a state to exercise its jurisdiction to apply its laws, even if the act has occurred outside its territory, even if it has been perpetrated by a non-national, and even if nationals have not been harmed by the acts.

Often cited in this context is a celebrated dictum of the International Court of Justice in the *Barcelona Traction Case*. Contrasting the obligations that one state may owe another with the obligations owed to the international community as a whole, the Court said of the latter: 'By their very nature [they] . . . are the concern of all States. In view of the importance of the rights involved, all States can be held to have a legal interest in their protection, they are obligations *erga omnes*.'[1] The Court continued by citing examples in contemporary international law: aggression, genocide, and the basic rights of the human person, including protection from slavery and racial discrimination.

This dictum of the Court is often incorrectly used as authority for more than it can sustain. It is spoken of as if it provides guidance for the contemporary application of the principle of universality of jurisdiction—as if the Court was affirming universal jurisdiction in respect of each of these offences. Of course, the Court was doing nothing of the kind. Its dictum was made in the context not of the assertion of jurisdiction but of an examination of the law relating to diplomatic protection. Usually, it is necessary for a state, before bringing an international claim, to show that the defendant state has broken an obligation towards the claimant state in respect of its nationals. Only the party to whom the international obligation is due can bring a claim in respect of its breach.[2] The Court was suggesting that, in respect of these offences, the restrictive requirements of the nationality-of-claims principle would not apply.

Further, the nationality-of-claims rule concerns diplomatic representation in civil claims. This is true of the stated exception to the rule, where obligations are owed *erga omnes*.[3] The universality principle, by contrast, is concerned with the application of criminal jurisdiction.

[1] *Case Concerning the Barcelona Traction, Light and Power Company Limited* (2nd Phase), ICJ Reports (1970) 3 at para. 33.
[2] See *Reparation for Injuries Suffered in the Service of the United Nations*, Advisory Opinion, ICJ Reports (1949) 174 at 181–2.
[3] The Court's dictum has yet to be tested and seems to this writer to be couched in overly broad terms. Is it really the case that State A could bring a claim before the International Court of Justice on behalf of Mr X, a non-national, on the grounds that he has been racially discriminated against by State B? Would the answer differ if the claim was being brought under a treaty or by reference to an alleged right of protection which 'entered into the body of general international law'? (see *Barcelona Traction Case*, Judgment, para. 34). The whole matter is baffling, as it is uncertain where such rights of protection have entered into general international law; and in the alternative basis referred to by the Court—instruments of a universal or quasi-universal character—the possibilities of state action on behalf of non-nationals are very limited indeed. See e.g. Art. 24, European Convention on Human Rights, and cases brought thereunder, which are technically not 'on behalf of' a non-national, but for breach of treaty in the form of violation of the human rights of national or non-national. See

To some international lawyers, the universality principle is an exception to the basic principle that a state does not have any rights of criminal jurisdiction in respect of acts done abroad by aliens.[4] This approach is part of the wider issue referred to in Chapter 1—namely, whether one views international law as a set of rules, with exceptions, or as complementary norms, the selection of which must be made in the context of all the facts and circumstances. The universality principle is, in my view, a well-established norm, which stands alongside other norms of jurisdiction and is not to be seen as an exception from any one of them.

In any event, it may readily be said that the offences which are agreed to be subject to the universality principle are very limited in number. The requirement is that these are acts which are commonly treated as criminal[5] in the local jurisdiction of most states, and which they perceive also as an attack upon *international* order. As has rightly been said, 'By its very nature this principle can apply only in a limited number of cases . . . It is founded upon the accused's attack upon the international order as a whole.'[6] The right to exercise jurisdiction under the universality principle can stem either from a treaty of universal or quasi-universal scope, or from acceptance under general international law. The latter provides the basis for the most commonly[7] accepted example of an offence allowing of universal jurisdiction: piracy.[8] Slavery, too, is generally regarded as being subject to universal jurisdiction.[9] The Nuremberg Tribunal took jurisdiction over war crimes—that is to say, major violations of the customary or conventional laws relating to the conduct of hostilities, as exemplified in

e.g. Application 9940/82, *France, Norway, Denmark, Sweden and Netherlands* v. *Turkey* 26 *Yearbook of the European Convention on Human Rights* (1983), Part II, 1; Application 4448/70, *Denmark, Norway, Sweden and Netherlands* v. *Greece* 12 *Yearbook of the European Convention on Human Rights* (1969), 12.

[4] See F. A. Mann, 'The Doctrine of Jurisdiction in International Law', *Recueil des cours* (1964, I), 1. Mann writes of universality as an exception to the principle that 'the legislating state has no rights in respect of acts done abroad by aliens'; but the universality principle concerns jurisdiction to *apply*, not to legislate (p. 93).

[5] The Third *Restatement of the Law: Foreign Relations Law of the United States*, correctly states that although universal jurisdiction is commonly exercised in the form of criminal law, 'international law does not preclude the application of non-criminal law on this basis, for example, by providing a remedy in tort or restitution for victims . . .' (s. 404, comment *b*).

[6] Mann, 'Doctrine', 95.

[7] The Second *Restatement of the Law: Foreign Relations Law of the United States*, cited only piracy as an offence subject to universal jurisdiction (see s. 34).

[8] See M. McDougal and W. J. Burke, *The Public Order of the Oceans* (1962), 805–23. See also Art. 19, Geneva Convention on the High Seas 1948, 450 UNTS 82.

[9] See claim to this effect in M. McDougal, H. Lasswell, and L. C. Chen, *Human Rights and World Public Order* (1980), 354. The instruments to which they refer (ch. 7 and accompanying notes, pp. 132–283) indicate a general condemnation of slavery. But relatively few of them contain any further element that would underpin a general norm of universal jurisdiction.

the 1907 Hague Conventions.[10] Today, major violations of the 1949 Geneva Conventions would be included in the small list of offences allowing universal jurisdiction.[11]

A classic example is the assertion of jurisdiction by the courts of Israel in the case of *Eichmann*. Here jurisdiction was exercised over the principal executioner of Hitler's 'final solution' in respect of acts carried out elsewhere than on the territory of the state of Israel, against persons who were not Israeli citizens (indeed, the state of Israel did not exist at the time). While objections were raised by other states to the manner by which Eichmann was brought to Israel, no protest was made as to Israel's right to assert a universal jurisdiction over the offences.[12] In the case of *Demjanyuk*, a US court accepted the competence of Israel to try a person charged with murder and related offences in concentration camps in Eastern Europe. The court observed, 'international law provides that certain offences may be punished by any state because the offenders are common enemies of all mankind and all nations have an equal interest in their apprehension and punishment'.[13]

While, from the perspective of international law, there is clear universal jurisdiction to try and punish war crimes, there is some uncertainty as to whether anything further is required in domestic law for this possibility to be acted upon. It is not simply a matter of how any given national law 'receives' general international law.[14] It may be the case that, even if the domestic law of a country acknowledges the international law universality principle that allows it jurisdiction over an offence, as a practical matter it will be necessary for the offence to be defined in domestic legislation.

This point is well illustrated by a controversy which occurred in the United Kingdom. *The British Manual of Military Law* states in clear terms:

War crimes are crimes *ex jure gentium* and are thus triable by the courts of all States . . . British military courts have jurisdiction outside the United Kingdom over war

---

[10] Art. 6, Charter of the International Military Tribunal, established jurisdiction for crimes against peace, war crimes, and crimes against humanity.

[11] See R. Baxter, 'The Municipal and International Law Basis of Jurisdiction over War Crimes' (1951) 28 *BYIL* 382; M. McDougal and F. Feliciano, *Law and Minimum World Public Order: The Legal Regulation of International Force* (1961), 706–21. Parties to the Conventions are under a duty to search for, prosecute, and punish persons committing grave breaches thereunder, regardless of their nationality.

[12] See *Attorney General of Israel* v. *Eichmann* 36 ILR 277. In fact, the District Court of Jerusalem based its jurisdiction also on the protective principle: see 36 ILR 5, para. 30.

[13] In matter of *Demjanyuk*, 603 F. Supp. 1468 (ND Ohio) aff'd 776 F. 2d 571 (6th Cir. 1985), cert. denied 457 US 1016, 106 S. Ct. 1198, 89 L. Ed. 2d. 312 (1986). The US court was addressing the issue in the context of a request for extradition.

[14] Although states vary greatly in how they 'receive' treaty law, virtually everywhere general international law is simply treated as part of the law of the land, without any specific act of incorporation being required.

crimes committed . . . by . . . persons of any nationality . . . It is not necessary that
the victim of the war crime should be a British subject.'[15]

This is to be contrasted with the statement of the Home Secretary in 1988,
when faced with the question of what action could or should be taken (if
any) in respect of seventeen alleged war criminals said to be living in
Britain. He said:

The British courts have jurisdiction over British citizens who have committed
manslaughter or murder abroad, but do not have jurisdiction over people who may
now be British citizens, or who may now live here and have done so for some time,
if the allegations relate to events before they became British citizens or before they
came to live here.[16]

It was assumed that no action could be taken, without amending the law of
the United Kingdom, 'to prosecute for war crimes persons who are now
British citizens or resident in the United Kingdom'.[17] The thinking seemed
to be that there is no jurisdiction over non-nationals for murder committed
abroad; that war crimes are murder; that therefore there is no jurisdiction
in respect of war crimes committed by non-nationals; and that special
legislative jurisdiction would need to be taken in respect of alleged
perpetrators who were now British citizens or resident in the United
Kingdom.

The Inquiry that was ordered largely put things right in its Report,
however, when it explained that legislation 'would merely empower British
courts to utilise a jurisdiction already available to them under international
law'.[18]

The Report recommended that 'British courts be given jurisdiction over
murder and manslaughter committed as war crimes (violations of the law
and customs of war) in Germany or German occupied territory during the
period of the Second World War by persons who are now British citizens or
resident in the United Kingdom'.[19] Several points may be noted. First, the
assumption still seems to be that jurisdiction could not be taken if the
offenders were not currently citizens or long-time residents. The United
Kingdom appeared to take the view that, notwithstanding the universality
principle in respect of war crimes, it would not be able to assert jurisdiction
over a war criminal who was not now a citizen or resident, but who came to
the United Kingdom on a vacation. That may reflect a policy decision but it
is not a correct reading of the universality principle, which requires no such
links to found jurisdiction. In the context of Iraq's invasion of Kuwait in
August 1990, the United Kingdom urged that in due course President

---

[15] *Manual of Military Law*, III (1956), para. 637.
[16] Hansard, Official Report, 8 Feb. 1988, col. 32.
[17] Report of War Crimes Enquiry, 16 June 1989, para. 1.6.
[18] Ibid., paras. 6.35–6.44.   [19] Ibid., paras. 9.22–9.30, and 10.3.

Saddam Hussein should be brought to trial for war crimes. The legislation to give effect to the universality principle is clearly also too narrow to deal with anything other than Second World War crimes. It would not, for example, allow trials for war crimes committed in the Gulf. Secondly, the recommendation of the Report excluded war crimes other than murder or manslaughter;[20] and also crimes against humanity. This last was excluded, not because of doubt about the availability of universal jurisdiction, but because of anxieties about retrospection. The Report found that 'In 1939 there was no internationally accepted definition of crimes against humanity.'[21]

The British government secured with great difficulty passage of legislation to act upon the proposals of the Report. Although the proposed legislation secured a substantial majority in the House of Commons, it was twice defeated in the House of Lords.[22]

Beyond this, there is controversy as to what other offences allow universal jurisdiction. It is often simply loosely asserted that universal jurisdiction exists over a variety of other matters. Article 6 of the Charter of the Nuremberg Tribunal provided for jurisdiction not only over war crimes but also over crimes against peace and crimes against humanity. The former entailed the planning of an aggressive war; the latter has correctly been described as 'war crimes writ large'[23]—extermination, murder, deportation, etc., committed against any civilian population before or during the war. The principles of the Nuremberg Charter and Judgment were unanimously adopted by the UN General Assembly in 1946.[24]

Thus we may say that universal jurisdiction today exists over war crimes, crimes against peace, and crimes against humanity, committed immediately before, or during, war. The Nuremberg Tribunal did not, however, provide for a universal jurisdiction over crimes against humanity which

---

[20] Many of the war crimes alleged related to offences other than murder or manslaughter—e.g. the taking of foreign hostages, the maltreatment of Kuwaitis. See Hansard, 6 Sept. 1990, col. 174; and *Financial Times*, 16 Apr. 1991, p. 4, for proposal of EC countries to UN Secretary-General. Referring to 'grave breaches' specified in the four 1949 Geneva Conventions, the Report notes 'it can be said that in many ways the concept of grave breaches of the Geneva Conventions has largely replaced the concept of war crimes in international law, and in the domestic law of many countries' (para. 5.32). In the context of the 'ethnic cleansing' carried out by Serbian authorities in the former Yugoslavia, there have been calls for prosecution of a number of Serbian officials who are alleged to be responsible. See e.g. the statement by the US Secretary of State Lawrence Eagleburger, as reported in *Newsweek*, 11 Jan. 1993, p. 30. See also G. Gilbert, 'Punishing the Perpetrators' (1992) 142 *New Law Journal* 1237–8.   [21] para. 5.43.

[22] See Hansard, House of Lords, 4 Dec. 1989, col. 604; 4 June 1990, col. 1080; 5 June 1990, col. 1177. There is comparable legislation in many other countries, some asserting a more general jurisdiction than others.

[23] I. Brownlie, *Principles of Public International Law* (4th edn., 1990), 560.

[24] GA Res. 95/1, 1945.

occurred during times of peace.[25] The Genocide Convention, which addresses the offence in this form, provides for both territorial jurisdiction and a *potential* universal jurisdiction. In Article I the parties confirm that genocide is 'a crime under international law which they undertake to prevent and punish'. Article VI provides for persons charged with genocide to be tried in the state where the acts were committed, or 'by such international penal tribunal as may have jurisdiction with respect to those Contracting Parties which shall have accepted its jurisdiction'. Of course, no such international penal tribunal yet exists; and the provisions of Article VI fall short of universal jurisdiction in the sense of an entitlement of any *national* court to assert competence over the offence.

A detailed analysis of the international law of jurisdiction is to be found in the Third *Restatement of the Law: The Foreign Relations Law of the United States*. It deals with these matters in a somewhat loose way, simply asserting: 'That genocide and war crimes are subject to universal jurisdiction was accepted after the Second World War.' It contends that 'universal jurisdiction to punish genocide is widely accepted as a principle of customary international law', but the only authority that it gives is that genocide is a violation of customary international law. But the fact that an act is a violation of international law does not of itself give rise to universal jurisdiction. Later, and more pertinently, the Commentary notes that genocide is characterized as an 'international crime' in the International Law Commission (ILC) Draft Articles on State Responsibility.[26] The Draft Articles do not purport to deal with jurisdiction, but the Restatement Commentary adds: 'An international crime is presumably subject to universal jurisdiction.'[27] This would seem to be correct, in so far as only two purposes are really served by attributing the notion of 'crime' to certain breaches of international law. The first is to attach a generalized sense of opprobrium to the offence in question. The second is to suggest that universal jurisdiction would be tolerated.

However, Article 19 of the ILC Draft Articles also classifies as crimes under international law: apartheid; a serious breach of the right of self-determination; and a serious breach of the duty to prohibit massive pollution. It is hard to see how these give rise to universal jurisdiction.[28] It

---

[25] See Brownlie, *Principles of International Law*, 563. For a recent examination of genocide more generally, see M. Shaw, 'Genocide and International Law', in Y. Dinstein (ed.), *International Law at a Time of Perplexity: Essays in Honour of Shabtai Rosenne* (1989), 797–821.

[26] Art. 19, Report of ILC, GAOR 33rd sess., suppl. 10, p. 193.

[27] Third Restatement, s. 404, p. 257.

[28] But the International Convention on the Suppression and Punishment of the Crime of Apartheid, GA Res. 3068 (XXVIII) 1973, does contain in Art. 4 (*b*) provisions for universal jurisdiction and an undertaking to adopt the necessary judicial and administrative measures.

is simply too big a leap to say that a listing in Article 19 is a basis for universal jurisdiction.

The Third Restatement stipulates the existence of universal jurisdiction over certain offences which we have already mentioned (piracy, slave trade, genocide, and war crimes) and mentions also 'attacks on or hijacking of aircraft', and 'perhaps certain acts of terrorism'. These latter are now listed in the suggested list of 'international crimes' in Article 19 of the ILC Draft Articles on State Responsibility. Is it correct that there is universal jurisdiction in respect of them?

The first point to be made is that, so far as the hijacking of aircraft is concerned, the jurisdictional basis permitted by international law is largely to be discovered by the examination of relevant treaties. Let us briefly review some of the leading instruments.

The provisions of the Tokyo Convention on Offences and Certain Other Acts Committed On Board Aircraft, 1963,[29] are complex. They provide for jurisdiction on a variety of bases—the registration of the aircraft, the place where the aircraft arrives, the nationality of personnel harmed, obligations under any treaty—but none of these amounts to universal jurisdiction.

The Montreal and Hague Conventions are early examples of what has recently become an important treaty basis of jurisdiction—the *aut dedire aut punire* principle. The Montreal Convention[30] and the Hague Convention[31] envisage jurisdiction being taken when the offence is committed on board an aircraft registered in that state, and when the aircraft on board which the offence is committed lands in its territory with the alleged offender still on board.[32] Again, nothing excludes criminal jurisdiction exercised in accordance with national law. Importantly, contracting states are required to make the offences punishable by severe penalties,[33] and to take such measures as are necessary to establish jurisdiction over the offence and the offender.[34] In a now classic formula, it is then provided in Article 7 that:

The Contracting State in the territory of which the alleged offender is found shall, if it does not extradite him, be obliged, without exception whatsoever and whether or not the offence was committed in its territory, to submit the case to its competent authorities for the purpose of prosecution.

In so far as this provides for the jurisdiction of *all parties to the Convention* (now standing at over 140), it is perhaps understandable that it

---

[29] 704 UNTS 219.

[30] Montreal Convention for the Suppression of Unlawful Acts against the Safety of Civil Aviation, 23 Sept. 1971, UNTS 974 (1975), 177.

[31] Hague Convention for the Suppression of Unlawful Seizure of Aircraft, 16 Dec. 1970, UNTS 860 (1973), 105; (1973) 10 *ILM* 133.

[32] Art. 4.   [33] Art. 2.   [34] Art. 4 (1), 4 (2).

is spoken of as universal jurisdiction. But it is still *not* really universal jurisdiction *stricto sensu*, because in any given case only a small number of contracting states would be able to exercise jurisdiction on the basis of Articles 2, 4, and 7. All that is 'universal' is the requirement that all states parties do whatever is necessary to be able to exercise jurisdiction *should the relatively limited bases* of jurisdiction arise in the circumstances. Contrary to the views sometimes expressed elsewhere,[35] this is not treaty-based universal jurisdiction (and so the question of such a treaty basis 'passing into' general international law does not arise). The Third Restatement offers no convincing authority that there exists treaty-based universal jurisdiction in respect of hijacking, still less any general principle of international law.

Other treaties referred to by the Third Restatement as showing a universal jurisdiction do not in fact do so. The 1973 Convention on Prevention and Punishment of Crimes against Internationally Protected Persons including diplomatic agents provides for territorial jurisdiction, flag jurisdiction, and nationality jurisdiction.[36] The same jurisdiction (extended to stateless persons who are habitually resident) is present in the International Convention against the Taking of Hostages.[37] In the 1980 Convention on Physical Protection of Nuclear Material[38] jurisdiction is based on territoriality, flag, or nationality of the offender. The jurisdictional basis of the UN Convention against Torture and Other Cruel and Inhuman or Degrading Treatment or Punishment[39] is a little wider, the nationality of the victim providing a further ground. The 1961 Single Convention on Narcotic Drugs,[40] as amended by the 1972 Protocol,[41] provides that the parties will make the prohibited acts offences under their penal law, and either prosecute when offenders are found upon their territory, or extradite them to the state where the offence was committed. Although these treaties seek to provide wide alternative bases of jurisdiction, they are not examples of universal jurisdiction. Universal jurisdiction, properly called, allows *any* state to assert jurisdiction over an offence.

Nor is the situation different in respect of terrorism, though that too is claimed in the Restatement, and also in the 1990 Report of the Council of Europe European Committee on Crime Problems[42] as allowing of

---

[35] See e.g. the Report of the European Committee on Crime Problems, *Extraterritorial Criminal Jurisdiction* (Strasburg, 1990), which too broadly asserts '[some] conventions clearly envisage or require the taking of universal jurisdiction: treaties on counterfeiting, piracy, hijacking and actions envisaging the safety of civil aviation afford examples' (p. 15).

[36] 1035 UNTS 167.   [37] GA Res. 146 (XXXIV), UKTS 81 (1983), Cmnd 9100.
[38] (1979) 18 *ILM* 1419.   [39] GA Res. 46 (XXXIX), Misc. 12 (1985), Cmnd 9593.
[40] 520 UNTS 151.   [41] (1972) 11 *ILM* 804.
[42] Report of the European Committee on Crime Problems, *Extraterritorial Criminal Jurisdiction*, 15 n. 35.

universal jurisdiction. This latter Report asserts, again too loosely, that 'conventions envisaging the taking of universal jurisdiction are those relating to the combat against terrorism, the prevention of torture, the protection of diplomatic staff, the physical protection of nuclear material and the taking of hostages'.

But none of them, properly analysed, provides for universal jurisdiction. They provide for various bases of jurisdiction coupled with the *aut dedire aut punire* principle—that is, that a state party to the treaty undertakes to try an offender found on its territory, or to extradite him for trial.

Of all of these, it is the European Convention on the Suppression of Terrorism that comes nearest to truly universal jurisdiction. It lists offences to be deemed terrorist offences, stipulates that none of them shall be regarded as a 'political offence' for the purpose of refusing extradition, and provides again that each contracting state shall take such measures as may be necessary to establish jurisdiction 'where the suspected offender is present in its territory and it does not extradite him'. Thus no connection with the offence beyond being a Convention party is required.[43]

Passive Personality

The so-called passive-personality principle is a claim to jurisdiction over events occurring outside one's territory when these harm nationals who are also outside one's territory. Thus, the basis of jurisdiction is protection of one's nationals, without anything more. It can be contrasted with the so-called effects or impact jurisdiction, where the harm resulting from extraterritorial acts is to one's nationals (or economy) within one's territory. The SS *Lotus*[44] is traditionally cited as authority for this principle, but it should be looked at with great caution. In that case a collision occurred on the high seas between a Turkish vessel and a French vessel, occasioning the loss of life of Turkish crew. When the *Lotus* put into Constantinople, the master was put under arrest and charged and convicted of manslaughter. France protested at Turkey's assertion of jurisdiction, and the issue went to the Permanent Court of International Justice. The Court found in favour of Turkey, though the grounds of its decision are not wholly clear. The effect on the Turkish vessel was assimilated to an effect on Turkish territory. But neither ships nor embassies are 'national territory', and this artificial approach merely obscures the jurisdictional issues.

It must be noted that passive personality has not been adopted as the jurisdictional basis for vessel collision in the Brussels Convention 1952,[45]

[43] (1977) ETS 90. [44] (1927) PCIJ Ser. A, no. 10.

[45] International Convention on Certain Rules Concerning Civil Jurisdiction in Matters of Collision, 439 UNTS 217.

the Geneva Convention on the High Seas of 1958,[46] or the UNCLOS Convention of 1982.[47] These treaties have preferred, in relation to comparable facts, simple flag jurisdiction.

Further, in the *Lotus Case* the Court was faced with a collision on the high seas. Its broad dictum, to the effect that jurisdiction can be asserted by a state unless a prohibitory rule prevents this,[48] cannot be regarded as authority for passive-personality jurisdiction within the territory of *another* (as if, for example, a motor accident had occurred in France between French and Turkish cars, with Turkey claiming criminal jurisdiction over the French driver).

These caveats having been duly noted, we must also admit that since the 1990s there has been a revived interest in invoking the passive-personality principle. This has occurred against the background of the explosion of international terrorism. Here the problem has not been a clash of contending jurisdictions, but rather the fact that those who clearly do have jurisdiction have been reluctant to exercise it—either for reasons of political sympathy with the terrorist, or because it is feared that to exercise jurisdiction will invite further acts of terrorism. Accordingly, other states with a direct legal interest in the events and a strong political belief in the need to combat terrorism have sought to identify a possible basis for asserting jurisdiction themselves. The United States and France provide interesting examples.

The matter is fairly summarized in the Third Restatement of the Foreign Relations Law of the United States,[49] where it is said that victim nationality as a basis for jurisdiction

has not been generally accepted for ordinary torts or crimes,[50] but it is increasingly accepted as applied to terrorist and other organised attacks on a state's nationals by reason of their nationality, or to assassination of a state's diplomatic representatives or other officials.

Little international authority is given for this,[51] but undoubtedly the United States has in recent years robustly asserted such a right.

The position of the United States appears to have been that, if a national

---

[46] 450 UNTS 82.   [47] A/CONF./62/121, 1982.
[48] (1927) PCIJ Ser. A, no. 10, at p. 19.   [49] (1987), i. 240.
[50] For a famous US example of strong opposition to the passive-personality principle, see the *Cutting* case (1887), For. Rel. 751 (1888), repr. 2 JM Moore, *International Law Digest* (1906), 232–40. Here the US Secretary of State rejected as contrary to international law the suggestion that a person may be tried in a country other than that where the offence was committed, simply because its objects happen to be a national of the country of the forum (ibid. 228–42).

[51] The Reporter's Note (p. 243 n. 3) does refer to Art. 5 (1) (*c*), Convention against Torture, and other Cruel, Inhuman or Degrading Treatment or Punishment, which authorizes a state party to exercise jurisdiction 'when the victim is a national of that state if that state considers it appropriate'.

is harmed abroad, that is a matter for the jurisdiction of the country concerned—but may also fall within the jurisdiction of the country of nationality to the extent that there exists a provision in the legislation of that country prohibiting such harm to citizens abroad.[52]

Relevant legislation on hostage-taking was designed for that purpose.[53] It stipulates that, if the conduct in question occurred outside the United States, then US courts will not have jurisdiction under the Act, unless the offender or the hostage is a US citizen or if the offender is found in the United States.[54] The passive-personality principle was clearly relied upon in the case of the *Achille Lauro*, where a US citizen aboard an Italian vessel in the Mediterranean was killed by terrorists.[55] The US Terrorist Prosecution Act of 1985 likewise provides in pertinent part for 'the prosecution and punishment of persons who, in furtherance of terrorist activities or *because of the nationality of the victims, commit violent attacks upon Americans outside the United States . . .'.*[56] This too seeks to establish a passive-personality basis of jurisdiction. However, it would seem that the assertion of jurisdiction is still intended to be limited to offences that would commonly be described as 'terrorist' offences. There appears to be no intention to assert jurisdiction (notwithstanding the broad wording of the Act) where, for example, Americans abroad are the victims of bar-room violence or robberies.

In 1986 Congress enacted the Omnibus Diplomatic Security and Antiterrorism Act.[57] Chapter 113A of this Act, entitled 'Extraterritorial Jurisdiction over Terrorist Acts Abroad against US Nationals' provides in

---

[52] See Statement of National Security Adviser Robert McFarlane ((1985) 24 *ILM* 1509 at 1522). Mr McFarlane was speaking in the context of the apprehension of terrorists (through interception of a flight over high seas) who had hijacked the Italian vessel *Achille Lauro* in the Mediterranean; held US citizens, among others, hostage; and killed a US citizen. The terrorists were turned over in the first instance to the Italian authorities; later their extradition was sought under the US–Italy extradition treaty of 1984.

[53] The legislation referred to is Public Law 98–473–Oct.12.1984, esp. Ch. XX, Part A: 'Act for the Prevention and Punishment of the Crime of Hostage Taking'. For text, see (1985) 24 *ILM* 1551.

[54] The wording of the Hostage Taking Act is unclear as to whether these are cumulative or alternative requirements. Other clauses are linked by the word 'or'; these two provisions (ss. 1203 (*b*) 1 (A) and (B)) are not.

[55] Though the indictment refers also to 'piracy under the law of nations' and the relevant US legislation in respect thereof, as alternative bases of jurisdiction. See (1985) 24 *ILM* 1556–7.

[56] 99th Cong., 1st sess., 132 Cong. Rec. 1382–8. This Act is now incorporated into the 1986 Omnibus Diplomatic Security and Antiterrorism Act, 100 Stat. 896 (1986); USC s. 2331 (1986).

[57] Ibid. For commentary, see C. Blakesley, 'Jurisdictional Issues and Conflicts of Jurisdiction', in C. Bassiouni (ed.), *Legal Responses to International Terrorism, US Procedural Aspects* (1988), 131–81. Blakesley criticizes generally the attempts to extend the reach of US jurisdiction; and specifically the US Restatement as contrary to international legal principles. (ibid. n. 26).

§2331 (*a*) that there shall be jurisdiction over 'whoever kills a national of the United States, when such national is outside the United States . . . if the killing is a murder, manslaughter, and involuntary manslaughter'. The apparent breadth of this passive-personality jurisdiction is circumscribed by §2331 (*e*), which stipulates that a prosecution in the United States shall take place only when 'such offense was intended to coerce, intimidate or retaliate against a government or a civilian population'.

Thus the passive-personality principle is invoked by the United States, but only in relation to terrorist-type offences.[58] In so far as the *Lotus* is thought to be authority for this basis of jurisdiction (which is doubtful), it of course contains nothing that limits the principle to this category of subject-matter. The confinement of a passive-personality claim to terrorist-type cases points to a constellation of facts which touches on a state's sovereignty and the security of its citizens in relation thereto. It has been pointed out that this 'triggers the protective principle. Thus, there is no need to call upon the more controversial and less accepted passive personality theory.'[59]

In France too[60] traditional hostility to the passive-personality principle has been overtaken by legislation based on this principle. Once again, it has been explained by those responsible for such legislation that its invocation is intended to be restricted to cases involving national security. Article 689 of the Code of Criminal Procedure in 1975 made it possible for France to assert jurisdiction over extraterritorial offences committed against its nationals.[61] In response to those opposing this law,[62] it was explained that French jurisdiction is subsidiary to that of the country in which the offence occurs, and would in any event not be invoked, save where national security was involved.[63] As in the United States, this assertion of jurisdiction followed a series of events of a terrorist nature

---

[58] There is a long line of earlier US cases which state in terms that the fact that a victim abroad happens to be a US citizen does *not* give US courts of jurisdiction to try the offence. See 2 Hackworth, *Digest of International Law* (1942), 179.

[59] Blakesley, 'Jurisdictional Issues', 144. In the case of *United States* v. *Yunis*, 681 F. Supp. 909, 914–15 (DDC 1988), the Court relied on both the universality and the passive personality principle, so far as international law was concerned, to assert jurisdiction over a foreigner who hijacked a foreign aircraft, in foreign airspace—when US citizens happened to be on that aircraft. The aircraft flight did not terminate in the United States. For comments, see A. Lowenfeld, 'U.S. Law Enforcement Abroad: The Constitution and International Law' (1989) 83 *AJIL* 880; and Abramovsky, 'Extraterritorial Jurisdiction: the United States' Unwarranted Attempt to Alter International Law in *United States* v. *Yunis*' (1990) 15 *Yale Journal of World Public Order* 121.

[60] This aspect is very well explained in Blakesley, 'Jurisdictional Issues', 172–7. France had, of course, strongly objected to the Turkish assertion of jurisdiction in the *Lotus*.

[61] Law of 11 July 1975, No. 75–624, 1 *Dalloz* 1975.

[62] Notably, J. P. Cot. See Blakesley, 'Jurisdictional Issues', 175 nn. 158, 159, for references.

[63] Ibid. n. 159.

against French nationals that those with territorial jurisdiction were unwilling to prosecute.

Legislation in those countries invoking this jurisdiction is not limited to terrorist offences; but in reality its application is. Diplomatic protest is hard to discern. Usually the problem is not conflicting concurrent jurisdiction, but rather that a state with alternative jurisdiction does not wish to assert it. We should also note that several recent conventions, such as the 1979 International Convention against the Taking of Hostages, do include passive personality as one of the jurisdictional possibilities. It is to this that we now turn.

Protests are not usually over the assertion of such (limited) passive-personality jurisdiction *as such*, but over something else—the forcible bringing of the alleged offender into the territory of the state of the victim, so that protection on this basis can then effectively take place.

Abduction as the Precursor for Jurisdiction

Abduction cannot be a *basis* for jurisdiction. But it can sometimes be the means by which a person is brought within the territory, to stand trial for an offence over which jurisdiction is asserted on some other basis. Often, that asserted jurisdictional basis will be either universality or passive personality. Thus, in the *Eichmann* case the accused was abducted from Argentina to stand trial in Israel for crimes against humanity committed in Eastern Europe; in the *Yunis Case* the accused, a Lebanese, was lured on to a yacht in international waters and then arrested and brought to the United States, to stand trial for hijacking and destroying a Royal Jordanian plane in Beirut.[64] Three US passengers who had been aboard the plane survived the ordeal. But no violation of the territorial sovereignty of another state was involved. And in the *Achille Lauro Case*, terrorists were interrupted during a flight over high seas and were turned over to the Italian authorities (the *Achille Lauro* was an Italian vessel). Their extradition was later sought under the USA–Italy extradition treaty of 1984, for trial for the murder of a US citizen.

The relevance of abduction in the asserting of jurisdiction has remained largely a matter for determination by the domestic court concerned. Here one may draw an analogy with evidence that is improperly obtained. Some courts exclude the use of such evidence. Others do not, cautioning only as to its weight in all the circumstances. Similarly, some courts have refused to take jurisdiction over offenders brought before them by abduction. Many, such as the Israel Supreme Court in the *Eichmann Case*, have

---

[64] *United States* v. *Yunis* 924 F. 2d 1086 (DC Cir. 1991).

insisted that *how* a person is brought before them is not a matter for them. They are concerned only with the fact of his presence and the need to establish a separate basis of jurisdiction.

Does international law itself have anything to say on the impact of abduction on the issue of jurisdiction? Is the manner of bringing a defendant before a court relevant to the jurisdiction of the court over him? There are, I believe, various relevant points of law and policy, each of which needs clearly to be understood in answering this question.

Because abducted persons are brought for trial in diverse national jurisdictions, the problem is often dealt with largely as a matter of the diverse domestic laws. But in such cases, which definitionally involve elements occurring beyond the borders of the forum state, it is also understood that principles of international law are also relevant. The first question, therefore, is whether the effective assertion of jurisdiction is dependent upon a violation of international law. The answer to this question is not as simple as it seems. From the perspective of an individual, his forcible detention and removal (whether or not from one jurisdiction to another, whether or not to stand trial) violate his human rights, in that everyone is entitled to security of the person and only to be restrained in accordance with due process. This is provided for in all the leading instruments on human rights.[65] Although the precise due-process requirements may be treaty-based, the principle would seem to be of general application and to be a norm of customary international law. Like all human rights, it is a right which villains and criminals, as well as the innocent, are entitled to invoke.

From the perspective of the other state concerned, the answer to whether a violation of international law has occurred depends upon the particular circumstances. If the defendant has been abducted from foreign territory, a violation of that state's sovereignty has occurred. It is contrary to international law, too, for the officers of one state to enforce, without permission, their criminal law within the territory of another. In many of the leading cases, abduction has indeed occurred from another state's territory.[66] Sometimes, however, the abduction will carefully have been arranged in or over international waters, precisely to avoid violating the territorial sovereignty of another state.[67] The issue then becomes whether an injurious act against an individual is—as traditional international law would have it—harm done to his national state. Whatever may be the general answer to that question (and I believe it should be in the

---

[65] Art. 5, European Convention on Human Rights; Art. 9, International Covenant on Civil and Political Rights; Art. 7, Inter-American Convention on Human Rights.

[66] The *Eichmann Case* is perhaps the most celebrated. See also *USA* v. *Alvarez-Machain*, Judgment of the Supreme Court of 15 June 1992, repr. in (1992) 31 *ILM* 901.

[67] e.g. *United States* v. *Yunis* 924 F. 2d 1086 (DC Cir. 1991).

negative),[68] an action that violates a person's human rights is not to be regarded as harm done to his national state. The whole purpose of human rights is to distinguish the individual from his state, not to make them coterminous.[69]

Assuming that international law has been violated by an abduction in a given case, should this disbar a court from acting upon otherwise existent jurisdiction? This has been the subject of keen controversy, with different writers and courts taking different views. The US Supreme Court has in a series of cases declined to set aside jurisdiction on the grounds of the prior kidnapping of the defendant. It has held that, where no treaty is invoked, a court may properly exercise jurisdiction even though the defendant's presence is procured by means of a forcible abduction.[70] It has further held that a defendant may not be prosecuted in violation of the terms of an extradition treaty.[71] In the *Alvarez-Machain Case* in 1992 the US Supreme Court acknowledged that an abduction might violate general international law—but that would not be grounds for setting aside jurisdiction. Only if a *treaty* is violated would jurisdiction have to be set aside. And, held the Supreme Court, it is not to be presumed, by reference to general principles of international law, that the existence of an extradition treaty necessarily implies that abductions are to be prohibited between the parties.[72] The argument that abductions are so clearly prohibited in international law that there was no reason to include a prohibition against abduction in the Treaty itself found no favour with the Court. It is hard to disagree with those dissenting Justices who found it 'shocking that a party to an extradition treaty might believe that it has secretly reserved the right to make seizures of citizens in another's territory'.[73]

But it must be noted that the Supreme Court was discussing whether the abduction violated the treaty, not the underlying issue of whether jurisdiction should be exercised if the abduction violated international law generally or a specific treaty. It had already answered the former in the affirmative (*Ker*) and the latter in the negative (*Rauscher*). The distinction in consequence between violations of general international law and treaty law seems hard to follow. But the underlying question remains an important one. Many leading writers have vigorously contended that

---

[68] The legal fiction that harm to an individual is harm to his state is a consequence of the procedural incapacity of individuals to bring claims before international tribunals, and their need to rely on the diplomatic protection of their states. The fiction has no inherent merit.

[69] Where states can bring claims against another state for violations of human rights, this is not tied to claims on behalf of one's own nationals (see e.g. Art. 24, European Convention on Human Rights).

[70] *Ker* v. *Illinois* (1886) 119 US 436.

[71] *US* v. *Rauscher* (1886) 119 US 407.

[72] *US* v. *Alvarez-Machain* (1992) 31 *ILM* 901.

[73] Ibid. 914.

jurisdiction should not be asserted in these circumstances.[74] Thus Francis Mann has argued[75] that a kidnapping is an international wrong, and the application of the principle *ex injuria juris non oritur* means that an otherwise existing basis for jurisdiction should therefore not be exercised. If one looks behind the rule to the policy underpinnings, the answer is perhaps less clear. The *ex injuria* rule was to ensure that those who act unlawfully in international law should not be able, in their relations with third parties, to consolidate their illegality *at the expense of those wronged*.

In the *Eichmann* type of case the assertion of jurisdiction over Eichmann did not exacerbate or perpetuate the undoubted violation of Argentina's sovereignty. There was no consolidation of a gain at the expense of the wronged party. The exercise of jurisdiction over Eichmann entailed, for example, no affirmation of title over Argentinian territory.

At the same time, it cannot be denied that there are important policy factors that support the view that international illegality is to be discouraged, and that to permit jurisdiction is to encourage the illegality. As the South African Supreme Court put it, in setting aside jurisdiction over a defendant kidnapped from Swaziland by the security services, 'Society is the ultimate loser when, in order to convict the guilty, it uses methods that lead to decreased respect for the law.'[76]

There are also important policy considerations that support the bringing to trial of those who engage in universally condemned offences, such as war crimes, or hostage-taking. Those policy ends could arguably be better served by the decoupling of the illegal method of seizing the accused, and the exercise of an otherwise existing jurisdiction over him. International law should be able to furnish its own remedies for the violation represented by the abduction—though in a decentralized legal order the remedy may have to lie in a diplomatic or economic response, and not necessarily in an international judicial finding of wrongdoing.

In order to prevent abuse by states who simply seek to enforce their police powers overseas, this proposed 'decoupling' should apply to the assertion of universal jurisdiction only over that limited category of offences regarded as international crimes—war crimes, crimes against

---

[74] See the important series of articles by A. Lowenfeld on this issue: 'US Law Enforcement Abroad: The Constitution and International Law' (1989) 83 *AJIL* 880; 'US Law Enforcement Abroad: The Constitution and International Law, Continued' (1990) 84 *AJIL* 444; 'Kidnapping by Government Order: A Follow-Up' (1990) 84 *AJIL* 712; 'Still more on Kidnapping' (1991) 85 *AJIL* 655.

[75] In F. A. Mann, 'Reflections on the Prosecution of Persons Abducted in Breach of International Law', Y. Dinstein (ed.), *International Law at a Time of Perplexity*, (1989) 407.

[76] *State* v. *Ebrahim*, South Africa Supreme Court, Appellate Division, 16 Feb. 1991, repr. in (1992) 31 *ILM* 888 at 898.

humanity, and arguably slavery. Abduction to secure the presence of persons to be tried for other offences should, however, cause jurisdiction to be set aside.

Extraterritorial Jurisdiction

Logically, all exercises of jurisdiction that are not based on the territoriality principle are exercises of extraterritorial jurisdiction. The nationality principle, by which states in certain circumstances make their criminal law applicable to nationals abroad, is an extraterritorial form of jurisdiction. International law in principle tolerates this basis of jurisdiction, so long as its exercise is not excessive and so long as there is no attempt to enforce it within the territory of another state. To take a simple example, should an Islamic country wish its citizens to remain subject to the prohibition on alcohol while abroad (even though they may lawfully drink under the laws of the country they are visiting), it is at liberty to draw up its legislation in these terms and, if it wishes, bring deviant citizens to trial upon their return home. But it would not be acceptable for the authorities of that country to endeavour to enforce its laws upon its own citizens within the territory of that other jurisdiction where they are residing. The greatest problem in regard to nationality jurisdiction has arisen over identifying who *is* a national abroad, particularly in the corporate area. For the United States, particularly, subsidiaries of US companies abroad, even if locally incorporated in that foreign country, really remain 'US companies'—and thus subject to those US laws drawn up in terms to apply even to nationals overseas. The host country, however, where these subsidiaries are incorporated, regards them as of local nationality and subject only to local law. Sometimes these differences of perception about nationality have caused great problems. Thus in 1979 the United States, in response to the seizure of US diplomatic and consular staff in Tehran, froze all Iranian assets under its jurisdiction.[77] This it interpreted as applying not only to assets within the United States, but also to dollar-denominated accounts held by US banks and their subsidiaries abroad. In 1981 and 1982 the United States, in response to the imposition of martial law in Poland, introduced measures to prohibit supplies of material for the construction of the projected gas pipeline from Siberia to Europe. This prohibition applied to US companies and their subsidiaries, even if abroad, and even to material made abroad.[78] In the former case doubts were expressed as to the legality of the United States' insistence on the reach of its freezing

---

[77] 44 Fed. Reg. 65, 956, 1979, consolidated in 1980, 3 CFR, 535, 1980.
[78] For the US measures, see (1982) 21 *ILM* 855, 864, 1098, 1115.

law.[79] And the measures affecting the Siberian pipeline contracts occasioned official protests from the European Community.[80]

In these cases the problem was twofold—whether nationality jurisdiction could properly be asserted while the national was still 'abroad'; and the anterior issue of how one determines the nationality to which the extraterritorial law is said to apply. What is the 'nationality' of a dollar account abroad, or a local subsidiary of a US company?

The protective principle, by which a state may exercise jurisdiction over a limited range of measures directed outside its territory at its security, is another relatively unproblematic example of an extraterritorial exercise of jurisdiction.

The passive-personality principle, of which I have already spoken, because it exercises jurisdiction on the basis of harm to a national while abroad, is also an extraterritorial jurisdiction.

But, all that being said, 'extraterritorial jurisdiction' has come to have a discrete meaning of its own, over and above nationality, protective, and passive-personality jurisdiction. It has come to mean a much more controversial claim—namely, to be able to exercise jurisdiction over persons abroad (even non-nationals) for acts occurring abroad, which were intended to have, and did indeed have, significant harmful effects within the territory asserting jurisdiction. This formulation, first articulated by the US Supreme Court in the *Alcoa Case* in 1945, has become known as 'the effects doctrine'.[81] It has had particular importance in the fields of criminal and antitrust law and it has been very controversial.

One position, most strongly insisted upon by the United Kingdom, has been that such an exercise of jurisdiction is simply unlawful under international law. Viewing territoriality as 'the primary rule', all other bases of jurisdiction are, in the eyes of the United Kingdom, to be regarded as *exceptions to the rule*, and as such to require justification under international law. While such justification may be found for nationality and protective-principle jurisdiction, and even for universal jurisdiction in relation to a limited range of offences, it cannot in the view of the United Kingdom be found in the effects doctrine. No rule of law *permits* it, and it is contended that it would lead to unacceptable interferences in the freedom of others to conduct their economic affairs as they choose. Why should not, the United Kingdom asks, Company A and Company B be free to engage in restrictive trading practices, for example, to fix prices, if *their* law allows it? Why should the courts of State C have jurisdiction over them

---

[79] For a detailed analysis of the issues, see R. Edwards, 'Extraterritorial Application of the US Iranian Assets Control Regulations' (1981) 75 *AJIL* 870.

[80] See (1982) 21 *ILM* 891–904.

[81] *United States* v. *Aluminium Co. of America*, 148 F. 2d 416 (1945).

because their conduct has a significant adverse effect on prices within State C?

Many Commonwealth jurisdictions have supported this view, joining the fight against what they see as an overreaching of US jurisdiction beyond its shores. The position of the EC countries is not quite so clear. They have certainly joined with the United Kingdom—as has the European Community itself—in formally protesting against certain US extraterritorial jurisdiction. But the requirements of Article 85 of the EC Treaty have themselves arguably involved the exercise of an extraterritorial jurisdiction by the Community. Article 85 prohibits agreements which may restrict or distort competition within the common market. The European Court has over the years interpreted the geographical reach of that jurisdiction as not being limited to practices of corporations incorporated in, or themselves having their headquarters in, EC territory.[82] Is it correct, then, that the EC is in favour of the effects doctrine, save when it is applied by the United States against EC interests, when it then joins the United Kingdom in protest?

Until recently there was room for some uncertainty. The leading EC cases had been based on the concept of 'economic unity' rather than extraterritoriality as such. They acknowledged that entities within the European Community might not behave autonomously, but would follow the directives of the parent company—and, if that parent company was outside the European Comunity, then the concept of 'economic unity' would allow jurisdiction over that parent company too, if there was action violating Article 85. The United Kingdom, which initially opposed the concept of economic unity, came in due course to accept that jurisdiction could be exercised on this basis if the subsidiary did indeed engage in conduct *within* the Community. It was even prepared to say, in the *Wood Pulp* cases before the EC Court,[83] that it would be acceptable—because it was not really an exercise of *extra*territorial jurisdiction—for jurisdiction to be asserted over corporations that, through the act of agents (i.e. not even subsidiaries) within the Community, harmed competition. But the Court in that case, affirming the exercise of jurisdiction over overseas foreign firms selling through agents within the European Community, spoke in broader terms, and indeed asserted EC jurisdiction over not only these foreign corporations but also a cartel that had itself never sold through agents or otherwise within the Community. The effects doctrine has now been accepted in all but name.

The controversy has been especially keen where a state exercising effects jurisdiction has categorized economic behaviour, lawful in the country

---

[82] *Dyestuffs Case* [1972] ECR 619; *Béguelin Case* [1971] ECR 949.

[83] *Ahlstrom and Others* v. *Commission of European Communities (Wood Pulp)* [1988] ECR 5193.

where it was done, not only as unlawful but as criminal. Many states have responded by introducing 'blocking legislation'—that is to say, statutory provisions which prohibit the furnishing of information or evidence to another state for criminal proceedings instituted by it in respect of restrictive trade practices.[84] Many non-US commentators have acclaimed these statutes,[85] but I regret them. The UK statute goes in my view far beyond what is reasonable, resisting even the right of the United States to categorize prohibited conduct as criminal, and to award multiple damages in consequence when committed by foreign incorporated entities having offices there and operating within the United States—that is to say, not merely operating *externally* or having a harmful effect within the United States.[86]

There is evidence, however, that each side now wishes to contain the dispute. Some countries with blocking legislation have not acted on it; and the United Kingdom has given a broader interpretation to what constitutes conduct *within* a territory. A broad interpretation of territoriality overlaps in part with what has been defined by others as *extra*territorial. For their part, the US courts have suggested that, before extraterritorial jurisdiction be exercised, a balancing should be made of the entitlement of the United States with the foreign interests involved. The elements to be weighed, as identified in the leading cases,[87] included: degrees of conflict with foreign law or policy; relative importance of the alleged violation of conduct in each country (i.e. if it was prohibited and/or criminal); availability of a remedy abroad and the tendency of litigation there; existence of intent to harm US commerce and its foreseeability; the possible effect upon foreign relations of the exercise of extraterritorial jurisdiction; and whether the matter is covered by a treaty.

The problem for the moment seems to lie dormant, in the face of a clear desire by both sides to avoid further disputes on the matter if at all possible.

Two final points. First, it is arguable that special considerations obtain in respect of extraterritorial jurisdiction over conduct that is *generally* regarded as criminal. While countries may take different views as to

---

[84] e.g. Protection of Trading Interests Act 1980 (UK); Foreign Proceedings (Prohibition of Certain Evidence) Act 1976 (Australia); Limitation of Danish Shipowners' Freedom to Give Information to Authorities of Foreign Countries 1967 (Denmark); Law Prohibiting a Shipowner in Certain Cases to Produce Documents 1968 (Finland)..

[85] e.g. V. Lowe, 'Blocking Extraterritorial Jurisdiction: The British Protection of Trading Interests Act, 1980' (1981) 75 *AJIL* 257; S. April, 'Blocking Statutes as a Response to the Extraterritorial Application of Law', in C. Olmstead (ed.), *Extraterritorial Application of Laws and Responses Thereto* (1984), 223.

[86] See the broad wording of s. 6 (1) of the 1978 Act.

[87] Notably, *Timberlane Lumber Co.* v. *Bank of America*, 549 F. 2d 597 (1976), and *Mannington Mills* v. *Congoleum Corp* 595 F. 2d 1287 (1979). For a useful collection of materials on the controversy, see V. Lowe, *Extraterritorial Jurisdiction* (1983).

whether restrictive trade practices are lawful, unlawful, or criminal, *all* are agreed that, for example, murder and extortion and drug-running are criminal. In an interesting Report on Extraterritorial Criminal Jurisdiction, the Legal Affairs Committee of the Council of Europe has suggested that in these circumstances extraterritorial jurisdiction ought to be regarded as a justified exception. Basing itself on a principle of 'international solidarity between states in the fight against crime', the Committee states: 'Public international law does not impose any limitations on the freedom of states to establish forms of extraterritorial criminal jurisdiction where they are based on international solidarity between states in the fight against crime.' The *exercise* of that jurisdiction should be based upon whether the international solidarity would be helped or harmed.[88]

In the great debate on extraterritorial jurisdiction those who believe it lawful (the United States and, from time to time, the European Community) have invoked the *Lotus Case* as authority for the proposition that, unless conduct is *prohibited* by international law, it is permitted. Although I am not unsympathetic to the exercise of extraterritorial jurisdiction over certain conduct, I do feel that one cannot read too much into a mere dictum of the Permanent Court. This is, for me, another example of the futility of deciding law by reference to an unclear dictum of a court made long years ago in the face of utterly different factual circumstances. We have better ways of determining contemporary international law.

Applying a more flexible approach to decision-making, I believe that the key to the issue lies in the protection of common values rather than the invocation of state sovereignty for its own sake. The fight against restrictive practices, which harm the consumer and keep prices high, in my view deserves international solidarity, along with the fight against common criminality. The exercise of extraterritorial jurisdiction to that end seems to me as acceptable as its exercise in the other non-territorial bases of jurisdiction.

[88] European Committee on Crime Problems, Council of Europe, *Extraterritorial Criminal Jurisdiction* (1990), 27.

5

EXCEPTIONS TO JURISDICTIONAL COMPETENCE: IMMUNITIES FROM SUIT AND ENFORCEMENT

IN Chapter 4 we saw the way in which international law provides norms for the allocation of competences among states: the doctrine of jurisdiction. The most basic ground for the exercise of jurisdiction is that of territoriality. It is natural that, within a territory, a state expects its laws to apply. And that law will apply, in principle, to all within the territory—nationals and foreigners, residents and visitors. When you go to another country, you put yourself within its laws and legal system. Any English person visiting The Hague expects to have to drive on the right-hand side of the road. And an English resident in The Hague expects to be taxed on his income under Dutch law. Some elements of self-restraint do enter the picture, where common sense prevails. If our Englishman visits for one day only, he must still drive on the right. But he would *not* expect a one-day visit to result in being made subject to the Dutch tax system. But, in general terms, territorial jurisdiction applies.

There are really two major categories of jurisdiction: some writers describe them as jurisdiction to legislate and jurisdiction to enforce. I think the better division is between jurisdiction to *prescribe* and jurisdiction to *apply*.

Within its own territory a state would expect both to prescribe law *and* to apply it. In this chapter we consider whether there are exceptions to the authorization to *apply* law *within one's own* territory. The topic of 'state immunity' concerns the exception to the territorial application of law.

There have, in classical international law, been two beneficiaries of an exception to the normal application of law on the basis of territoriality: foreign states and foreign diplomats. To these two beneficiaries must now be added a third recipient of some benefits of immunity—international organizations. Each of these requires some attention.

STATE IMMUNITY

Under classical international law, states, including governments thereof, were granted immunity from the territorial jurisdiction of other states. Various reasons of policy have been suggested, all interrelated. First, a reason may be found in the doctrine of sovereign equality: *pari parem non habet imperium*. No state could be expected to submit to the laws of another. Secondly, it has been said that it would offend the dignity of a state to submit to the jurisdiction of another. In *Parlement Belge*, Brett LJ spoke of the duty of 'every sovereign state to respect the independence and dignity of every other sovereign state'.[1]

The doctrine of absolute immunity of states from the jurisdiction of other states prevailed until the very end of the last century.[2] As states began to engage in functions not wholly reserved to the state, this doctrine of absolute immunity began to be questioned. It began to be asked why, if two identical contracts were made, one with a private person and another with his government, the former could be sued on his contract and the latter could not. The problems became more acute with the widespread contracting for trade by socialist governments—and, indeed, by non-socialist governments too. Absolute immunity increasingly seemed an inappropriate phenomenon in the face of the requirements of the contemporary commercial world and of notions of stability, fairness, and equity in the market place.[3]

Absolute immunity had been based on status. It was enough for a potential defendant to show that it was a state, or a government, and that it was being impleaded directly or indirectly (through claims relating to property over which it claimed title),[4] for it to be accorded immunity. But from the 1950s onwards an increasing number of states began to move towards the restrictive or qualified doctrine of immunity, following the early example of Italy and Belgium, which had adopted restrictive immunity since the turn of the century. Many states were now engaging in trade, and it was increasingly felt unsatisfactory that, if they broke their contracts, they were protected by an absolute immunity from the exercise of local jurisdiction. The Federal Republic of Germany and the United States[5] in turn indicated that they would no longer emphasize the *status* of the defendant, but rather the activity or transaction in which it had been engaging. Under the restrictive doctrine of immunity, a distinction was to be made between *acta jure imperii*—acts in public authority in respect of which there would still be immunity—and *acta jure gestionis*—commercial or private acts in respect of which no immunity now lies. *Status* remained important only to put a defendant within the category of persons who

---

[1] (1880) 5 PD 197 at 214–15.

[2] For a good historic survey, see S. Sucharitkul, *State Immunities and Trading Activities* (1959), 3–23.

[3] R. Higgins, 'Certain Aspects of the Law of State Immunity' (1982) 29 *NILR* 265.

[4] The classic case on indirect impleading is *Juan Ysmael and Co. Inc.* v. *Indonesian Government* [1954] 3 WLR 531.

[5] See S. Sucharitkul, 'Immunities of Foreign States before National Authorities', *Recueil des cours* (1976, I), ch. III.

potentially could claim immunity; but his actual entitlement so to claim would now depend upon the activity or transactions in question. The 1970s and 1980s saw the adoption by several common-law countries, including the United States and the United Kingdom, of statutes based essentially on this distinction, and directed to tidying up the various anomalies that inevitably arise when law develops through the cases.[6]

There are very many detailed and fascinating questions to be asked about state immunity. International law requires that a state limit the exercising of its jurisdiction in respect of a foreign state or government. The debate is about the extent and scope of that requirement limitation. As with any other normative requirement of international law, it is necessary to look at treaties, state practice as evidence of custom, judicial decisions, and leading writings. These are the source materials on the international law of state immunity. But, so far as treaties are concerned, for the moment there is no treaty of universal application. The formulation of articles by the International Law Commission (ILC) has been completed and is directed towards providing the text for such a treaty.[7] After great debates over the years within the ILC, the Draft Articles do affirm the restrictive approach, rather than the absolute approach to state immunity. Interestingly, this is dealt with in terms of implied consent[8]—that is, in entering into such a contract the foreign state is considered to have consented to the exercise of jurisdiction.

There exists in the European Convention on State Immunity of 1972 an example of an influential regional treaty. This treaty is largely directed towards reciprocal enforcement of judgments, but is firmly based on the

---

[6] e.g. Foreign Sovereign Immunity Act 1976 (USA); State Immunity Act 1978 (UK); State Immunity Act 1981 (Canada); Foreign State Immunities Act 1981 (South Africa); Australian Foreign States Immunities Act 1985.

[7] The topic 'Jurisdiction Immunities of States and their Property' was taken up by the ILC at its 30th session in 1978. The ILC received a preliminary and seven further reports from its Special Rapporteur, Mr Sucharitkul: see *Yearbook of ILC* (1979), ii. pt. 1, p. 227, A/CN. 4/323; (1980), ii. pt. 1, p. 199, A/CN.4/331 and Add. 1; (1981), ii. pt. 1, p. 12, A/CN.4/340 and Add. 1; (1982), ii. pt. 1, p. 199, A/CN.4/357; (1983), ii. pt. 1, p. 25, A/CN.4/363 and Add. 1; (1984), ii. pt. 1, p. 1, A/CN.4/376 and Adds. 1 and 2; (1985) ii. pt. 1, p. 21, A/CN. 4/388; (1986), ii. pt. 1, p. 8, A/CN.4/396. At its thirty-ninth session the ILC appointed Mr Ogiso Special Rapporteur. At the next session he provided a preliminary report: (1988), ii. pt. 1, p. 96, A/CN.4/415 and Corr. 1 and 2. Two further reports followed: (1989), ii. pt. 1, p. 59, A/CN.4/422 and Corr. 1 and Add. 1; and a preliminary segment in 1990 for purposes of conducting the second reading of the Draft Articles. In 1991 the ILC adopted a set of Draft Articles, which were then submitted to the General Assembly with a recommendation that it convene a conference to conclude an international convention on the subject. See Report of the ILC on the work of its 43rd sess., GAOR 46th sess., suppl. 10 (A/46/10), p. 9.

[8] For an interesting suggestion that the same function is performed by waiver at the municipal level as originating consent at the international level, see R. Jennings, 'The Place of the Jurisdictional Immunity of States in International and Municipal Law' (1987) 108 *Vortrage, Reden und Berichte aus dem Europe-Institut* 3–22 at 4.

restrictive principle of immunity.[9] Council of Europe states are parties to the Convention.[10]

As for state practice, it cannot be said to be uniform. Most of the industrialized world has moved to limiting immunity, making it unavailable for commercial acts or transactions. These jurisdictions now classify the activity, and not the status, of the dependent—and it is for the courts to determine the nature of that activity. But this generalization has not been true of the Soviet Union or industrialized Eastern Europe, which while under Marxism insisted upon absolute immunity. There is some evidence of rethinking in this new era, but any such revising process is only just beginning. Latin America remains solidly opposed to restrictive immunity; and so does much of the new Commonwealth.[11]

Judicial decisions are of course a source of international law. Singularly, in respect of the topic of state immunity it is almost entirely to national decisions that we must look. It is before domestic courts that, definitionally, issues of immunity from local jurisdiction arise. And they arise not in cases concerning two sovereign states (which would usually come before an international tribunal) but in cases concerning a private individual and a foreign state. These domestic courts recognize that they must, in any given case, provide answers in accordance with international law. Sometimes, where there is statute law or a civil code on the matter, they must follow that legislative enactment. But that legislation, in turn, will be based on what the local legislature has understood to be required and permitted by international law. The topic of state immunity is endlessly fascinating, both substantively and because of this intriguing interplay between international law and domestic law.

There has been a prodigious amount of well-informed writing on all aspects of the topic of immunity.[12] And, in addition to the proposals of the ILC, the matter has received the detailed attention of the Institut de Droit International, under the guidance of its rapporteur, Professor Ian Brownlie.[13]

[9] (1972) 11 *ILM* 470.

[10] The United Kingdom gave its desire to ratify this Convention as one of the reasons for the promulgation of its State Immunity Act 1978, which confirmed and accelerated the common-law retreat in the 1970s from the doctrine of absolute immunity.

[11] An excellent survey of practice can be deduced from the early reports of the Special Rapporteur to the ILC (see n. 7) and from the series of Research Papers prepared by the Australian Law Reform Commission 1983, under the direction of Professor Crawford.

[12] Including Sucharitkul, *State Immunities* and 'Immunities of Foreign States'; C. Schreuer, *State Immunity: Some Recent Developments* (1988); G. Badr, *State Immunity, an Analytical and Prognostic View* (1984); J. Dellapenna, *Suing Foreign Governments and their Corporations* (1988).

[13] *Annuaire Yearbook* (Cairo, 1987), i; and resolution adopted in 1991, *Annuaire Yearbook* (Basle, 1991), vol. ii. p. 389; I. Sinclair, 'The Law of Sovereign Immunity: Recent Developments', *Recueil des cours* (1980, II), 130; and very many others. See also R. Higgins,

Surveying these sources of international law, we may say that international law today does not require the courts of one state to afford absolute immunity from jurisdiction to a foreign state or government. But a state or government will be entitled to invoke a limited immunity, in the courts of another, for its *acta jure imperii*.

That being said, there are prodigious difficulties left and very many technical problems still unresolved. I cannot hope in this chapter to do more than refer to some of the most interesting problems that still remain.

The key problem undoubtedly is *how* one distinguishes an *actus jure imperii* from an *actus jure gestionis*. Even if we accept the distinction between *acta jure imperii* and *acta jure gestionis*, it is not always self-evident into which category any specific transaction falls. A contract for sale and purchase is generally regarded as a commercial transaction, an *actus jure gestionis*. What about a contract to purchase missiles? Is that to be regarded as an exercise of sovereign authority? If contracts are to be regarded as *acta jure gestionis*, would that be true of a contract for the employment of a diplomat?

Is everything done within an embassy to be regarded as *acta jure imperii*? Or should there be no immunity regarding matters, including non-diplomatic employment, that are of a mundane, everyday character? In *Sengupta* v. *Republic of India*[14] an English court found that all matters concerning an embassy were *acta jure imperii* and immune from the local jurisdiction. But in another English case, *Alcom* v. *Republic of Columbia*,[15] the Court of Appeal took the view that an embassy bank account was designated for commercial purposes, as it would necessarily be used to make purchases and to pay bills. The House of Lords reversed this decision, finding that it was not for a local court to require to know the nature of each and every expenditure made under an embassy bank account.[16] The important point is that, while the rejection of absolute immunity removes the preoccupation with the status alone of the defendant state, it cannot provide a mechanistic answer: the court will always have to appraise whether the transaction in question was commercial or in sovereign authority, and sometimes that will not be easy.

It used to be thought that assistance was to be derived in this task by seeing the *purpose* for which a contract was being entered into. Thus, in

'Recent Developments in the Law of Sovereign Immunity in the United Kingdom' (1977) 71 *AJIL* 424; R. Higgins, 'Execution of State Property: United Kingdom Practice', in (1979) 10 *Netherlands Yearbook of International Law* 35; and R. Higgins, 'La Pratique britannique en matière d'immunité d'execution', in *L'Immunité d'execution de l'état étranger* (1990).

[14] 64 ILR 352.   [15] (1984) AC 580.
[16] The case was in the context of an attempt to execute prior judgment. The 1978 State Immunity Act provides in s. 13 (4) that process may be issued in respect of property which is in use or intended for use for commercial purposes.

the example of a contract to purchase missiles, the answer to the question 'is this *gestionis* or *imperii*?' would be given by noting that the object of the contract was undoubtedly a high state matter—a matter of sovereign authority. But there has come to be a general rejection of reliance on 'purpose' as being incompatible with the requirement to focus on the *nature* of the transaction. Thus the purpose of a contract was said by Lord Denning in the *Trendtex Case*[17] to be irrelevant to its designation as attracting absolute or qualified immunity. And in the famous *Empire of Iran Case*[18] the German Constitutional Court stated: 'As a means of determining the distinction between *actus jure imperii* and *jure gestionis* one should rather refer to the nature of the state transaction or the resulting legal relationships, and not to the motive or purpose of the state activity.'[19]

The US Foreign Sovereign Immunities Act of 1976 expressly provides that the character of an activity shall be determined by its nature, rather than by reference to its purpose.[20] By contrast, the UK Act is silent on the point. But in case law subsequent to the entry into force of the Act in 1978 the English courts have affirmed that it is the nature of the transaction and not its purpose that is relevant for characterizing a transaction as *imperii* or *gestionis*.[21]

Given the continuing difficulty, in marginal cases, of making this characterization, and given further the inappropriateness of 'purpose' as an aid, is there another aid or test? There is undoubtedly a recent tendency to turn towards the test of whether an act is one that may be performed by anyone, or only by a sovereign. This test, already signalled in the *Empire of Iran Case*, has been applied elsewhere, including the *1° Congreso del Partido*. For some it goes further than assisting in identifying an act as *imperii* or *gestionis*, it is seen as *replacing* a test in itself unsatisfactory. Thus Sir Gerald Fitzmaurice criticized the *imperii/gestionis* distinction, saying 'a sovereign state does not cease to be a sovereign state because it performs acts which a private citizen might perform';[22] and Sir Hersch Lauterpacht wrote that, 'in engaging in economic activities ostensibly removed from the normal field of its political and administrative activities, the state nevertheless acts as a public person for the general purposes of

---

[17] *Trendtex Trading Corp.* v. *Central Bank of Nigeria* [1977] 1 QB 529.

[18] *Claims against the Empire of Iran* (1963), BVerfGE 16; 45 ILR 57.

[19] This was cited with approval by Goff J. in first instance in the famous case of *1° Congreso del Partido* [1978] 1 QB 500.

[20] s. 1603 (*d*).

[21] See e.g. *Trendtex Trading Corp.* v. *Central Bank of Nigeria* [1977] 1 QB 529, per Lord Denning MR at 558 and Shaw LJ at 579; and *1° Congreso del Partido* [1981] 3 WLR 328 per Lord Wilberforce at 262–3.

[22] G. Fitzmaurice, 'State Immunity from Proceedings in Foreign Courts' (1933) 14 *BYIL* 101 at 121.

the community as a whole'.[23] The solution, suggests Sir Robert Jennings, is
to see if an act is one done in the exercise of sovereign activity, which
excludes the doing of something which an ordinary private person might
also do.[24]

I think the test a useful one too; but, at the end of the day, its application
on the facts will still remain a matter for appreciation by the courts. The *1°
Congreso Case* seems tellingly to make the point. In that case contracts of
affreignment had been agreed by the government of Cuba and a private
firm of importers in Chile. The goods were sent on Cuban government
ships to Chile. The government of President Allende of Chile was
overthrown by a military *coup* and the masters of the vessels concerned
were ordered by the government of Cuba not to discharge their cargo at
Valparaiso port in Chile. Thus there was, on the one hand, an undoubtedly
commercial contract and, on the other, an order, taken for highly political
reasons, to breach the contract. But Goff J. at first instance, and Lord
Wilberforce in the House of Lords, held that the test was whether the
relevant act could be done only by a private person. Goff J. said that an
actus jure imperii would be an act which 'is of its own character a
governmental act, as opposed to an act which any private citizen can
perform'.[25] He found that immunity lay for the acts of ordering the vessel
not to discharge its cargo. Lord Wilberforce relied eventually on the same
test, but said that, in denying the cargo to its purchasers, the Republic of
Cuba, 'had not exercised and had no need to exercise, sovereign powers. It
acted, as any owner of the ship would act, through Mambisa, the managing
operations. It invoked no governmental authority.'[26] He found that no
immunity *actus jure imperii* could therefore be claimed. Thus the
application of the same test to the same facts by different courts still does
not necessarily lead to the same outcome. On Lord Wilberforce's view of
things, virtually nothing would be left protected by immunity *acta jure
imperii*—perhaps the declaring of war, the conclusion of a treaty, and the
nationalization of property.[27]

The fine line between purpose and private law activity has recently been
illustrated in the United Kingdom in *Kuwait Airways Corporation* v. *Iraqi*

---

[23] H. Lauterpacht, 'The Problem of Jurisdictional Immunities of Foreign States' (1951) 28
BYIL 220 at 224.

[24] Jennings, 'The Place of the Jurisdictional Immunity of States', 8.

[25] [1978] QB 500 at 528.   [26] [1983] AC 244 at 268.

[27] The articles of the ILC adopted on first reading included one which stipulated that the
'present articles shall not prejudice any question that may arise in regard to extra territorial
effects of measures of nationalization'. This bizarre provision clearly has no place within a
scheme relating to immunities, and the question of immunity—from the jurisdiction of foreign
courts—in relation to nationalized resources seems sufficiently covered by the application of
the principle of *actus jure imperii*. This misconceived provision did not survive into the articles
finally adopted.

Airways Company and Another.[28] In this case the judge found that the passing by Iraqi government officials of Kuwait Airways aircraft to Iraqi Airways Company, after the invasion of Kuwait, was not an *actus jure imperii*. This was not because the motive was commercial (which it was), but because the facts of the case showed the circumstances called for its categorization as *gestionis*.

Of course, even after entering the market place, a government may need to act as a government and not as a trader. But why should it have immunity from suit on the trading transaction? Let it pay if its action has caused damage—all said and done, there is no specific performance in international law, and the government will still be perfectly free to take whatever action it feels it needs to for the public good. But it cannot expect an innocent private party to bear the costs of that liberty. In the distribution of benefits and burdens in the international legal system, there is no reason why private traders should pay for the freedom of states to pursue their political and foreign-policy objectives.

There are many other unresolved problems, which can here be only mentioned. Should an agreement to arbitrate be regarded as a waiver of any claim to immunity in any action that arises in a domestic court in connection with that arbitration? Should the general rules on immunity apply to torts as well as to contracts? Should contracts of employment be included in the general rules? Should state enterprises be treated as states for purposes of immunity?[29] In the countries which apply a restrictive immunity, the answer to all these questions has been fairly clearly in the affirmative. But these matters have all been put in doubt in the ILC— either by the rapporteur's draft or by the comments of members which show their dissatisfaction with an article as drafted. The finally adopted draft articles pull back towards answers preferred by those favouring qualified immunity.

There are other issues which have never been the subject of clear agreement, even within those states which practise restricted immunity. Some countries provide for immunity for central banks, while others do not. A major topic, that can here only receive brief mention, is the distinction between immunity from suit and immunity from execution. They are closely related but distinct concepts. If a state is immune from suit—that is, from legal action against it—then definitionally no question of execution of a judgment against it arises. But, if it is *not* immune from suit, and a judgment is given against it, then does it follow that the judgment may be executed against its property? The extent to which an

[28] *Financial Times Law Reports*, 17 July 1992. This case has now been reversed on appeal. The text of the judgment is pending.

[29] See particularly the strange proposal in Article 11 bis of the Third Report of the Special Rapporteur of the ILC, A/CN.4/431, 11 Apr. 1990.

absence of immunity from execution is to be regarded as simply consequential upon an absence of immunity from suit seems to be largely a matter for national determination. In some countries—and the Netherlands would be one of them—the two phases are closely integrated. In other countries, such as the United Kingdom and the United States, there are distinct legal requirements for each phase. Some allow execution of judgments on the property of states and simply follow the same immunity criteria as applied to jurisdiction—that is, the property must be 'commercial' property rather than 'public' property. Thus, even though a judgment may be secured against a state, it remains hard to get execution of that judgment against the foreign state's property. Section 13 (5) of the UK Act allows the Ambassador of a foreign state to certify that property is in use, or destined for use, for public purposes, and this acts as rendering it immune from execution.[30] In all of these matters it is clear that these are no obligatory requirements of international law. If the work of the ILC results in a treaty, some of these matters will become clarified by international treaty for the parties. In the formulation of norms that are still in the making, the object should be to identify and sustain the interest of the international community as a whole, and to fashion our legal prescriptions accordingly.

DIPLOMATIC IMMUNITY

Permanent diplomatic missions are only one of a variety of institutional means through which states can conduct diplomacy with each other. These include visits by heads of government (or other leading officials), special missions, and official representation at *ad hoc* or regular conferences. Permanent diplomatic missions may be established at the headquarters of many international organizations: the law relating to their status is at an early stage of development. The privileges and immunities of member representatives to international organizations was codified in the Vienna Convention on the Representation of States in their Nations with International Organizations of a Universal Character of 1975;[31] but the Convention has not been sufficiently ratified to enter into force. By contrast, diplomatic law, which applies to the permanent missions that states have established within each others' territories since the fifteenth century, is well developed. Until the end of the 1950s the sources of diplomatic law were largely customary international law, although various bilateral treaties also existed on the topic. Some limited attempts at codifying certain aspects of diplomatic relations had occurred in 1815

---

[30] UK State Immunity Act 1978, s. 13 (5).
[31] A/CONF. 67/16, reported in (1975) 69 *AJIL* 730.

(Congress of Vienna) and in the 1920s under the League of Nations. But not until the 1961 Vienna Convention on Diplomatic Relations was the topic generally codified. This treaty—which includes, but is not limited to, the question of privileges and immunities—in large measure confirmed existing customary international law, and the great majority of states are parties to it.

Diplomatic immunity, like state immunity, is an exception to the general international law provided for territorial jurisdiction. Its purpose is to allow diplomats to carry out their functions within the framework of necessary security and confidentiality. They are not usually exempt from the local jurisdiction to prescribe laws (though certain tax laws are sometimes not only not *applied* to diplomats or to diplomatic premises, but are not prescribed for them in the first place). Generally, diplomats are required to comply with local law, but will be immune from the local jurisdiction to apply and enforce such laws.

The person of the diplomatic agent is inviolable. He is to be treated with respect, protected against attack, and may not be detained or arrested.[32] The diplomatic agent is immune from the criminal jurisdiction of the recessing state.[33] The premises of the mission are inviolable;[34] and the archives and documents of the mission are inviolable whether they are on or off the premises.[35] Communications for diplomatic purposes are to be protected,[36] and the diplomatic bag is not to be opened or detained.[37]

Although significant elements in the substance of the law on state immunity are uncertain, the substantive content of the law of diplomatic immunity is fairly clear. There are some remaining uncertainties that we may mention. Given the varying national practices on marriage and different understandings of the concept of 'family', this scope of Article 37 of the Vienna Convention is open to some debate. That provides immunities from 'the members of the family of a diplomatic agent forming part of his household'. Receiving states interpret this variously. The United Kingdom, for example, interprets the expression to include 'the spouse and minor children', with 'minor' being construed in accordance with UK law as meaning a child under 18.[38] There has been some uncertainty as to whether the prohibition on opening or detaining the diplomatic bag would include X-ray (which it almost certainly would) or external search for explosives or drugs by 'sniffer dogs'.

The principle of inviolability of the archives of a diplomatic mission is well established and free from controversy. The classic case, in which the principle in general international law is clearly established, is *Rose* v.

[32] Art. 29, Vienna Convention on Diplomatic Relations of 18 Apr. 1961.
[33] Art.31. [34] Art. 22. [35] Art. 24.
[36] Art. 27. [37] Art. 27 (3).
[38] For details, see E. Denza, *Diplomatic Law* (1976), 225.

King.[39] But its scope and application has recently required some attention, particularly in the light of Article 24 of the 1961 Vienna Convention on Diplomatic Relations. This provides that the 'archives and documents of the mission shall be inviolable at any time and wherever they may be'. A textual reading might be thought to indicate that 'archives' and 'documents' are two separate things—albeit that the intention was to provide inviolability for both.[40] The Vienna Convention on Consular Relations of 1963 avoids giving this impression by *defining* consular archives as 'all the papers, documents, correspondence, books, films, tapes and registers of the consular post, together with the ciphers and codes, the land indexes and any of the articles of furniture intended for their protection and safekeeping'. This point arose for consideration in the litigation following the collapse of the ITC, under the Headquarters Agreement[41] made with the United Kingdom, guaranteed that its archives should have the same privileges and immunities as are accorded to the archives of a diplomatic mission under Article 24 of the Vienna Convention. It was argued by the creditors of the ITC (which had ceased trading in tin and was unable to meet the debts it owed to brokers and bankers) that the organization had inviolability only for its archives but not for its documents more generally. In the Court of Appeal one judge[42] held that the 'archives' referred only to those records of the ITC that it was intended to retain as a formal record. Thus, in his view, working papers of the Secretariat or other incidental documentation were not 'archives' within the meaning of Article 5 of the Headquarters Agreement. This view was not upheld by the House of Lords, which was prepared to give the term 'archives' the broader meaning, in the sense of the definition in the Consular Convention (notwithstanding the different terminology in Article 24 of the Convention on Diplomatic Relations).[43]

Article 24 stipulates that the archives and documents shall be inviolable at any time and 'wherever they may be'. It is clear that this last phrase is meant to cover circumstances where a building other than embassy premises is used for storage of the archives; and also the circumstance in which an archived document has been, for example, taken there by a member of the Secretariat staff for overnight work—or even inadvertently left by him on the train or in a restaurant. What would happen if the Secretariat member, or a diplomat, took an overseas trip, and mislaid the document while abroad? The English High Court was disturbed by the idea that 'wherever located' could, on the face of it, mean even in Australia or

---

[39] [1947] 3 DLR 617. See also the English case of *Fayed* v. *Al Tajir* [1987] 3 WLR 102.
[40] See para. 2 of the ILC commentary on Draft Article 22: *Yearbook of ILC* (1958), ii. 96.
[41] 9 Feb. 1972, Cmnd. 4938.
[42] *Shearson Lehman Brothers Inc.* v. *Maclaine Watson & Co. Ltd. (No. 2)* [1988] 1 AER 116 per Mustill LJ at 122.   [43] Ibid.

Japan. It is true that an English court is not likely to be in a position to enforce the inviolability of a document from the authorities in another country where that particular document happens to be located. But it is entirely another thing to say that, because a document happens to be outside the jurisdiction, an English court is thereby entitled to treat it, in matters that do fall within its own competence, as non-archival and thus without benefit of such inviolability as it is in a position to bestow.

But it is the underlying policy issue of diplomatic immunity that has attracted most attention: if these immunities or inviolability are given to allow the performance of the diplomatic function, should they continue to be available if the diplomatic function is manifestly being abused? To take some examples that have occurred in the United Kingdom that have excited public opinion: should a diplomat who has committed indecent assault upon a child escape prosecution by virtue of his immunity from criminal jurisdiction? Shall the local law remain helpless to assist a landlord to recover his property from diplomatic tenants who refuse to move out when their lease expires? And, if a policewoman is shot from the window of an embassy, can it be right both that the embassy should not be entered by the local police and that no arrests should be made from the crime?

While the disquiet is understandable, the answer has to be that immunity *should* continue to be available in these circumstances. In the first place, one cannot *assume* criminal guilt in advance of a trial, to argue that there should therefore be no immunity from trial. Secondly, it would be very easy for a receiving country to insist that a foreign diplomat was abusing his position and that in those circumstances was not entitled to rely upon immunities. It can readily be seen that unscrupulous governments could use such a line of argument to harass foreign diplomats and bring pressure to bear on them. Even if, in particular cases, a diplomat has behaved in a thoroughly reprehensible manner, it is important for the larger good to maintain the integrity of the Vienna Convention.

This does not mean that the receiving state is powerless in the face of diplomatic abuse. The receiving state has the right to notify the sending state, without even having to give explanation let alone prove an allegation, that a member of the diplomatic staff is *persona non grata*.[44] The receiving state may also limit the size of the mission.[45] In an extreme case it can always decide to suspend or terminate diplomatic relations. Except in the case of espionage—and not always then—states have often been reluctant to invoke these powers.[46] It is not in the community interest

---

[44] Art. 9.   [45] Art. 11.

[46] This was very much the finding of the Foreign Affairs Committee of the House of Commons in its 1984–5 session: see further its report from this session, *The Abuse of Diplomatic Immunities and Privileges*. It urged a firmer policy towards application of the Vienna Convention and made specific recommendations to that end. These were accepted by

that states should fail to avail themselves firmly of available remedies against abuse, but should instead seek to undercut the immunities, which are needed to protect the bona-fide work of diplomats and would become unavailable as an effective protection if immunities could be withdrawn by the receiving state upon its unilateral determination of an action as 'abusive'.

INTERNATIONAL ORGANIZATIONS

International Organizations, though not 'accredited to' a particular country, are none the less located in a particular country. They require certain privileges and immunities from the jurisdiction of that state, and from all its member states should there be the potential of its acts or staff or property coming under their jurisdiction also. These immunities are those that are necessary for the fulfilment of the purposes of the organization.

So far as the United Nations is concerned, the need for such protection was envisaged in Article 103 of the Charter. Inviolability of its premises and archives, diplomatic immunity of its most senior officials, and immunity of senior officials from jurisdiction and execution on a functional basis, are provided for in the Convention on Privileges and Immunities of the United Nations.[47] The United Nations was immune 'from every form of legal process'. There is a Convention in very similar terms for the Specialized Agencies.[48] Furthermore, these multilateral provisions are often supplemented by a bilateral headquarters agreement between the organization and the host state. The position is broadly similar in respect of those international organizations which are not specialized agencies of the United Nations, save that there exists no general convention on their privileges and immunities. (The ILC is examining relations between international organizations and host states and a treaty may eventually emerge.) The need for immunities is usually referred to in the constituent instrument and the details filed in a Headquarters Agreement. Often a state will need to make such treaties, including a headquarters agreement to which it is party, effective in domestic law by enacting appropriate domestic legislation.

Are these immunities dependent on provision for them in specific governing instruments or are they enjoyed by international organizations as a matter of customary international law? The Third Restatement takes

---

the UK Government. See R. Higgins, 'The Abuse of Diplomatic Privileges and Immunities: Recent United Kingdom Experience' (1985) 79 *AJIL* 641; R. Higgins, 'UK Foreign Affairs Committee Report on the Abuse of Diplomatic Privileges and Immunities: Government Response and Report' (1986) 80 *AJIL* 135.

[47] 1 UNTS 15.   [48] 33 UNTS 261.

the view that international organizations are so entitled, as a matter of customary law, to 'such privileges and immunities as are necessary for the fulfilment of the purposes of the organization, including immunity from legal process and from financial controls, taxes and duties'.[49] The Reporters' Notes in support of this in fact all relate to universal international organizations.

Do organizations of limited membership, albeit with separate legal personality, receive immunities from the jurisdictions of the host state as a matter of customary international law? The English High Court thinks not. The judge said, in one of the main cases arising out of the ITC debate:

international organizations such as the ITC have never so far as I know been recognized at common law as entitled to sovereign status. They are accordingly entitled to no sovereign or diplomatic immunity in this country save where such immunity is granted by legislative instrument, and then only to the extent of such grant.[50]

This statement was invoked with approval in subsequent litigation, by counsel for creditors and by Bench alike. But in reality there is no suggestion that the ITC—or any international organization—is entitled to *sovereign* or *diplomatic* immunity. The issue is really quite different: it is whether international law requires that a different type of international person, an international organization, be accorded functional immunities. The basis for an affirmative answer—which I believe to be correct—lies in good faith (that is, provision of what is necessary for an organization to perform its functions) and not in deference to sovereignty or to its representation through diplomacy. And I can see no difference in principle between an organization of universal membership and one of limited membership. The issue is not, *so far as the membership is concerned*, one of 'recognition' of the personality of the organization. It is simply that members—and *a fortiori* the headquarters state—may not at one and the same time establish an organization and fail to provide it with those immunities that ensure its role as distinct from that of the host state.[51] This point—a combination of good faith and functionalism—runs like a thread throughout the International Court of Justice's Advisory Opinion in the *Mazilu Case*, and finds explicit articulation in the separate opinion of Judge Shahabuddeen.[52]

[49] Third *Restatement of the Law: The Foreign Relations Law of the United States* (1987) i. s. 467 (1).

[50] Bingham J., as he then was, in *Standard Chartered Bank* v. *International Tin Council* [1987] 1 WLR 641 at 647–8. This dictum emerged from the concession by Counsel that under common law the ITC enjoyed no sovereign or diplomatic immunity.

[51] This point is also made by P. Reuter, *Le Droit au secret et les institutions internationales* (1956) 53 AFDI 60.

[52] *Applicability of Article VI, s. 22 of the Convention on the Privileges and Immunities of the United Nations*, ICJ Reports 1989.

Regrettably, the Fifth Report of the Special Rapporteur on Relations between States and International Organizations is not clear on this point. It cites certain treaties that provide for inviolability of archives,[53] but also concludes that 'doctrine and state practice' fully supports the principle of the inviolability of archives.[54] It deduces this rule from customary law relating to diplomatic missions, simply asserting that 'the principle is equally valid in the case of international organizations'.[55] The matter is still treated by assimilation to diplomatic missions.

It is important to determine whether the immunities of an international organization are customary, and not based solely on the treaty setting it up, in the following circumstances. First, there may exist no relevant headquarters agreement.[56] Secondly, it may be necessary to know whether the terms of a headquarters agreement are exhaustive of the immunities that may be claimed, or whether, if its text is deficient, other immunities may be claimed by reference to customary international law. Thirdly, in some jurisdictions the courts will not give effect to the terms of a treaty unless that treaty has been incorporated in domestic law. If no such law has been enacted, or if its terms do not fully match those of the treaty,[57] the question may arise as to whether there is none the less an obligation incumbent upon the local courts by virtue of the requirements of customary international law.

Do states other than the host state have to give immunities to an international organization? In the *Amalgamet Case*[58] a New York court held that no such obligation existed in the absence of a treaty commitment by the United States.

What does seem clearly established is that, in respect of a wide range of international organizations, domestic courts regard customary international law as prohibiting the assertion of jurisdiction over employment claims.[59] Further, it is not always necessary for an international organiza-

---

[53] A/CN.4/432, p. 4, 11 May 1990: Agreement between the Government of Chile and the Economic Commission for Latin America, Art. 1 (1) (9), UN Leg. Ser. St/LEG/SER.B/10, p. 218.   [54] para. 48.   [55] para. 46.
[56] For many years no headquarters agreement existed between the Intergovernmental Maritime Consultative Organization (IMCO) and the United Kingdom. See R. Higgins, *The Development of International Law through the Political Organs of the United Nations* (1963), 248 n. 37.
[57] cf. e.g. Art. 8 of the ITC Headquarters Agreement with Art. 6 of the relevant Order in Council of 1972.
[58] *International Tin Council* v. *Amalgamet Inc.* (1988) 524 NYS 2d 971.
[59] *Shamsee* v. *Shamsee* 102 5 Ct. 389, 70 L. 2d 207 (1981); *Weidner* v. *International Telecommunications Satellite Org* 392 A. 2d 508 (DC App. L578); *Int. Institute of Agriculture and Profile*, Court of Cassation, Italy 1931; See also *Law Suits Against International Organizations: Cases in National Courts Involving Staff and Employment* (World Bank Legal Dept., 1982).

tion to have full immunity from suit and enforcement for it to fulfil its purposes. That will depend upon the organization. Many organizations in the banking field permit suits by bondholders and related creditors (though usually the property and assets of the bank will remain immune from attachment before final execution).[60]

Does the *imperii/gestionis* distinction apply to international organizations? This question only arises, of course, if one accepts that the immunities of an international organization are not necessarily determined *only* by legislative provisions. This seems an unsettled matter, though in some cases this distinction has been referred to, and immunity has not been allowed when an organization has entered into a contract with a private person.[61] But how can an organization act 'in sovereign authority'? To suggest that this distinction has any relevance to organizations is to assimilate them to states, which is not correct. Their basis of immunity is different. The relevant test under general international law is whether an immunity from jurisdiction to prescribe is necessary for the fulfilment of the organization's purposes. That question cannot be answered by reference to whether it was, in respect of the matter under litigation, acting 'in sovereign authority' or 'as a private person'.

The international tin litigation has highlighted another problem related to what documents constitute archives that receive protection of inviolability. International organizations prepare papers for meetings which are then sent to state members for their study and consideration, prior to the deliberation of the organization. In my view these papers are received by the states members not as 'third parties'—in which case the papers would cease to be the papers 'of the organization', and have no inviolability by reference to Article 24 of the Vienna Convention. Rather, working documents are received by the states parties in their capacity as organs of the international organization. They retain their status as documents of the international organization, and the benefit of the protection of Article 24. Any other conclusion leads to the untenable result that as soon as the Secretariat (one organ of an international organization) shares with members (who constitute another organ) confidential documents, those documents cease to have any protection from disclosure by the host state. On this thesis the papers of an international organization can only be protected if the organization is never in a position to use them for its work, because they remain only within one organ, the Secretariat.

None the less, this is the position taken by the House of Lords, which has

---

[60] e.g. Art. VII, s. 3, IBRD, 2 UNTS 134 at 80; Art. 50 of the Asian Development Bank 571 UNTS 123; Articles of Agreement by the IFC, 264 UNTS 117. The ITC had no immunity from suit in respect of trading agreements made on the metal exchange.
[61] e.g. *Branno* v. *Ministry of War* 22 ILR 756.

held that documents issued by the ITC cease to be the documents 'of' the
ITC once they are sent to member states.[62]

The protection to be given to the archives of international organizations
has been considered by the ILC. Unfortunately, the Fifth Report of the
Special Rapporteur on Relations between States and International
Organizations[63] does not address the range of problems that have actually
arisen. The text merely refers to Article 24 of the Vienna Convention and
insists that international organizations are subject of international law and
thus enjoy inviolability of their archives. There is no deeper discussion on
what constitutes the archives of an international organization.

Conclusion

1. The immunities from suit that a state needs in order to be able to fulfil
   its governmental functions are really very limited indeed.
2. There is a case for allowing greater possibilities of execution of
   judgments against defaulting states than exist in many countries at the
   moment.
3. The diplomatic immunities represented in the 1961 Convention do
   represent the minimum of what is required for diplomats to be able to
   pursue their functions without harassment or interference from the
   receiving state. If they abuse them, they should be required to leave—
   but the immunity should not be narrowed, for they protect those who
   act in a proper, law-complying way.
4. More attention should be paid to the immunities of international
   organizations, and local courts should be encouraged to appreciate that
   their required immunities are based on functional needs of their own,
   not on any artificial assimilation to states and diplomatic missions.
   Immunities serve an important purpose, but the appropriate limits to
   them can only be drawn by a full understanding of the social purposes
   which this exception to territorially based jurisdiction serves.

---

[62] This conclusion was reached by reliance on the fact that, in the English legislation that
gave effect to the Headquarters Agreement, separate provision was made for the inviolability
of documents of the states members of the ITC. *Shearson Lehman Bros. Inc.* v. *Maclaine
Waterson & Co. Ltd.* [1988] 1 WLR 16, HL. The author should properly mention that she was
counsel for the ITC in this case.
[63] (Second part of the Topic), A/CN.4/432, 11 May 1990.

6

RESPONDING TO INDIVIDUAL NEEDS:
HUMAN RIGHTS

As we have seen, international law is a system that provides normative indications for states in their relations with each other. We have also seen that the main participants in this system, naturally, are sovereign states, though there is no reason of principle to exclude individuals from its reach. But if the classic content of international law is directed to stabilizing and facilitating interstate relations, how are we to guarantee that the needs of the individuals who comprise those states are not ignored? The amelioration of interstate relations is largely directed to other ends—ends that are important, and may not be inimical to the needs of the citizen, but are essentially different. The problem is not only that the norms underpinning interstate relations are rarely addressed in any direct sense to the needs of individuals, but that it is to his own government that the individual will look for his most basic needs. At the same time, it is from his own government that an individual often most needs protection.

It is clear that classical international law has relatively little to offer in this regard. States may, it is true, enter into treaties with each other about the protection of the ethnic, national, or religious groups of one party who are resident in the territory of the other. Indeed, it can be provided that an international tribunal will resolve any dispute about the application of such treaties. This was essentially the system adopted by the Inter-War Minority treaties, and useful protections were undoubtedly provided.[1] But it clearly does not go far enough. The individual is left with no direct access to a forum, no legal right that he can call his own, no redress against his own state.

The special body of international law characterized as human-rights law is strikingly different from the rest of international law, in that it stipulates that obligations are owed directly to individuals (and not to the national government of an individual); and it provides, increasingly, for individuals to have access to tribunals and fora for the effective guarantee of those obligations. Once it is recognized that obligations are owed to individuals

---

[1] See J. Fouques-Duparc, *La Protection des minorités de race, de langue et de religion* (1922); P. de Azcarate, *The League of Nations and National Minorities* (1945). For texts of the minority treaties, see H. Temperley, *A History of the Peace Conference of Paris* v. (1969) 432 ff. See also *Oppenheim's International Law*, 9th edn., ed. R. Jennings and A. Watts (1992), vol. i., pts. 2–4, pp. 973–5.

(because they have rights), then there is no reason of logic why the obligation should be owed only to foreign individuals, and not to nationals. It becomes unsustainable to regard the treatment of one's own nationals as matters falling essentially within domestic jurisdiction, and thus unreviewable by the international community.

Why should obligations be owed directly to individuals? The answer can only be because they have rights, human rights. What then do we mean by human rights? What distinguishes, for example, the right that an individual may have in respect of a contract with his government that his government may have broken, from his right not to be tortured? They are surely both *legal* rights. We can put the answer this way. Human rights are rights held simply by virtue of being a human person. They are part and parcel of the integrity and dignity of the human being. They are thus rights that cannot be given or withdrawn at will by any domestic legal system. And, although they may most effectively be implemented by the domestic legal system,[2] that system is not the source of the right. International human-rights law is the source of the obligation, albeit that the obligation is reflected in the content of the domestic law. It further follows that the right will be the same in all the various jurisdictions; other legal rights, even though present in most legal systems, will depend for their substance and formulation upon the domestic legal system. To return to our example: the right to have redress for breach of contract is present in virtually every legal system. But the extent to which governments have freedom to abrogate contracts, or to be immune from legal process for such breach, will depend upon the proper law of the contract. But the prohibition placed upon a government from the use of torture is not dependent at all, as a matter of law, upon its own legal system: the obligation is one of international law.

It is sometimes suggested that there can be no fully universal concept of human rights, for it is necessary to take into account the diverse cultures and political systems of the world.[3] In my view this is a point advanced mostly by states, and by liberal scholars anxious not to impose the Western view of things on others. It is rarely advanced by the oppressed, who are only too anxious to benefit from perceived universal standards. The non-universal, relativist view of human rights is in fact a very state-centred view and loses sight of the fact that human rights are *human* rights and not dependent on the fact that states, or groupings of states, may behave

---

[2] This is exactly why the exhaustion of local-remedies rule is present in every international human-rights instrument. See also A. Drzemszewski, 'The Domestic Application of the European Human Rights Convention' (1980) 30 *ICLQ* 118.

[3] On this see, *inter alia*, I. Nguema, 'Human Rights Perspective in Africa' (1990) 11 *HRLJ* 261; D. Donoho, 'Relativism Versus Universalism in Human Rights: The Search for Meaningful Standards' (1991) 27 *Stanford Law Journal* 345; H. Gros Espiel, 'The Evolving Concept of Human Rights: Western, Socialist and Third World Approaches', in B. Ramcharan (ed.), *Human Rights Thirty Years after the Universal Declaration* (1979), 41 ff.

differently from each other so far as their politics, economic policy, and culture are concerned. I believe, profoundly, in the universality of the human spirit. Individuals everywhere want the same essential things: to have sufficient food and shelter; to be able to speak freely; to practise their own religion or to abstain from religious belief; to feel that their person is not threatened by the state; to know that they will not be tortured, or detained without charge, and that, if charged, they will have a fair trial. I believe there is nothing in these aspirations that is dependent upon culture, or religion, or stage of development. They are as keenly felt by the African tribesman as by the European city-dweller, by the inhabitant of a Latin American shanty-town as by the resident of a Manhattan apartment.

The debate about political and cultural relativism in human rights has taken many forms over the years. It is worth recalling how the situation was viewed in Eastern Europe in the early 1990s. In the early post-war years it was insisted that the treatment of one's own nationals was a purely domestic matter, on which neither other states nor the organs of the United Nations could properly pronounce. From the mid-1960s, the Soviet Union and other Eastern European states began to become party to a variety of international instruments on human rights. They now accepted that they had, as an exercise in state sovereignty, agreed to international law obligations about provision of these rights. But the position was taken that the manner of implementation of rights was still a matter for national discretion. In the Helsinki Final Act system the old socialist states took the view that *monitoring* by other states, or by human-rights groups, was interference in domestic matters. While there was an international obligation to provide the right, that did not provide others with an entitlement to interfere by monitoring compliance. So far as the system under the International Covenant on Civil and Political Rights was concerned, a slightly different point was made. The Covenant itself provided for an international monitoring mechanism, through the Committee on Human Rights. That was fully accepted by the socialist countries—indeed, it should be said that their record on providing the required reports in timely fashion, and sending well-qualified represent-atives to co-operate in the examination of such reports, was generally exemplary. But the argument was made that it was to be expected that the *manner* of implementation would vary according to the particular political system.[4] Thus all the constitutions that allowed freedom of speech, but contingent upon it being directed at the promotion of the socialist system

---

[4] B. Graefrath, 'The Application of International Human Rights Standards to States with Different Economic, Social and Cultural Systems', in *The United Nations after Forty Years: Human Rights* (1986). Cf. C. Tomuschat, 'Human Rights in a Worldwide Framework: Some Current Issues' (1985) *Zeitschrift für auslandisches offentliches Recht und Volkerrecht* 547; and R. Higgins, 'Human Rights: Some Questions of Integrity' (1989) 52 *Modern Law Review* 1.

of government, were to be regarded as permitted diversity of implementation reflecting a multicultural and politically differentiated world.

With the changes that have occurred in Eastern Europe in the early 1990s, those arguments are no longer heard. While states may indeed implement rights in different ways (by legislation, through the constitution, through the common law), the *content* of what is to be implemented depends on the international standard and will not vary.[5]

The areas in which the topic of diversity now most frequently arises are twofold: religion and internal self-determination. Two particular issues arise in relation to religion, as is evidenced by a reading of the Reports of the Human Rights Committee on its examination of State Reports.[6] Certain Islamic countries (but not all) believe that adherence to Islam requires the offence of Apostasy (renunciation of the faith) to be punishable by death. Again, some, but not all, Islamic countries interpret Islamic law as requiring punishment by particularly severe means for a range of offences that would not attract punishment at all, or only lighter punishment, elsewhere.

How is cultural and religious diversity to be respected if universal human-rights standards are set? The answer, in my view, cannot lie in the suggestion that the standards adopted are not in principle of universal application. The International Covenants, in particular, benefited in their formulation, which took place over a long period of years, from the participation of states from all parts of the world, representing all the different political and religious systems. The texts were adopted with general approval; and states of all the varying political and religious systems have had a free choice as to whether to become a party to the Covenants. If particular elements in the Covenant were really to be regarded as incompatible with a profound religious tenet or political point of departure, then the correct course of action was to enter a reservation as to those elements. It is striking that this has in fact not been done— reservations rarely go to these rather important points of religious and political philosophy. If it is not done, then in my view sensitivity to political and cultural diversity does not require that a state be regarded as exempted from what it has undertaken.

There are philosophical problems of a different order about which we must speak, also. A human right is a right held *vis-à-vis* the state, by virtue of being a human being. But what *are* those rights? The answer to that

---

[5] See R. Mullerson, *Human Rights: Ideas, Norms, Reality* (1991) (in Russian), ch. 2, pp. 13, 26; R. Mullerson, 'Human Rights and the Individual as a Subject of International Law' (1990) 1 *European Journal of International Law* 33.
[6] cf. the examination of the reports of Tunisia (CCPR/C/SR/990–2, 15–16 July 1990) and Jordan (CCPR/C/SR/1077–9, 17 and 18 July 1991) with the examination of the report of Iran (CCPR/C/SR/193, 29 Nov. 1992).

question depends, once again, on the approach you take to the nature and sources of international law. Some will answer that the *source* of human-rights obligations is to be found in the various international instruments; and that whatever rights they contain and designate as human rights *are* thereby human rights, at least for the ratifying parties. They may in time become reflected in customary international law, and thus become human rights more generally. Others will say that the international instruments are just the vehicle for expressing the obligation and providing the detail about the way in which the human right is to be guaranteed. It is an interaction of demands by various actors, and state practice in relation thereto, that leads to the generation of norms and the expectation of compliance in relation to them. Many further questions have been debated. Are human rights, properly so called, limited to the field of civil and political rights? That was for many years the traditional Western view, though that position appears now to be softening. A variety of reasons in support of this view has been offered. Rights suppose a correlative obligation on the part of the state. All states, no matter what their political system, or what their level of economic development, are in a position to comply with civil and political rights. Abstention from torture, toleration of free speech, liberty of religion, are essentially a matter of good faith on the part of the state. In contrast, claims that are said to be economic and social rights—claims to education, to paid holidays, to food and housing—are often simply not within the ability of the state to provide. This is particularly true of the poorer states. Again, this is to define a right by reference to the ability of the party upon whom the obligation lies—the state—to provide it immediately. If that cannot be done, then there is no right. This does of course echo a well-known aphorism of law generally that, without a remedy, there may not be a right. But when we analyse this, the analogy is less than exact. The aphorism reminds us, that without a remedy, a right may be but an empty shell. That is clearly correct (though in the decentralized system of international law it has been evidenced that 'remedies' may take a myriad of forms). But that is not to say that therefore the disappointed claimant must be taken to have had nothing that could be identified as a right from the outset. This approach again looks at things from the perspective of the state, rather than from that of the individual. Problems about delivery leave his right a right none the less. There will, of course, need to be careful analysis about what exactly a state is obliged to do in relation to economic and social rights, and in what manner: and to that I will return.

It is also sometimes said that economic and social rights cannot be rights at all, because 'rights' implies something in respect of which legal claims can be brought, and economic and social rights are not justiciable. What would it mean, it is said, for a citizen of a poor African country to go to a court in his country to say that the government has violated his right to education, or health care? The correlation of rights with justiciability is an understandable attitude from the domestic-law point of view. But, of course, international lawyers are very familiar with the phenomenon that, for a variety of reasons (sometimes jurisdictional, sometimes more substantive), it is not possible to bring claims in vindication of rights held in international law. The absence of the possibility of recourse to third-party judicial procedures is certainly not the test of whether the right exists or not. To the international lawyer, the existence of the right is tested by reference to the sources of international law.

It is further suggested that economic, social and cultural rights are not real rights for two more reasons: they are imprecise as to content, and, in any event, because these demands are mostly incapable of immediate delivery, it must be recognized that they are mere aspirations. Here imprecision of content of the right in the hands of the beneficiary is in reality being confused with uncertainty as to the scope of the obligation incumbent upon the state. From the perspective of the holder of the right, the entitlement to free primary education is as clear as the entitlement to be free from torture. The *real* difference is that in large part the state's duties in respect of civil and political rights are covered in terms of abstention from prohibited conduct, whereas the provisions of economic and social rights usually require specific action by the state. A state will fulfil its obligation to provide freedom of speech if it does nothing to interfere with the exercise of that right; but the right to food requires action by the state.[7] It must immediately be said that a right is just as much a right if its implementation requires positive steps rather than negative abstinence. Moreover, the concept of positive duties is increasingly becoming part and parcel of the normative requirements of civil and political rights. The European Court of Human Rights has, in respect of several rights, indicated that their fulfilment places positive duties upon states.[8] An obvious example is the entitlement, implicit in the right to fair trial, of access to the courts. A mere failure to bolt the doors to the courtroom will not guarantee access without discrimination to the courts. The provision of information about legal services, the holding of courts in accessible locations and perhaps also, in certain circumstances, the provision of legal aid, may all be needed.

The Committee on Human Rights, operating under the International

---

[7] A. Eide, *Report on the Right to Adequate Food as a Human Right*, UN Doc. E/CN.4/Sub.2/1987/23.

[8] For cases where the European Court of Human Rights has interpreted an article of the European Convention as requiring a state party to take positive action see: *Airey* v. *Ireland*, Ser. A, no. 32, 9 Oct. 1979 at para. 25; *Marckx* v. *Belgium*, Ser. A, no. 31, 13 June 1979 at para. 31; and *Johnston* v. *Ireland*, Ser. A, no. 112, 18 Dec. 1986 at para. 74.

Covenant on Civil and Political Rights, has indicated that, in order effectively to guarantee rights (even those cast in non-interventionist terms), it is frequently necessary for states to take positive measures. For example, the protection of privacy, guaranteed by Article 17 of the Covenant, requires states not to interfere with mail and communications beyond the limits permitted by that clause. But that is not enough. The Committee has made clear that, in order to make this right effective in the complicated world in which we live, it will be necessary for states to have legislative and other measures identifying the limits of permitted inter-ferences with privacy, safeguards that require their exercise to be authorized by a judge, procedures for review against abuse. The whole field of violation of privacy through the inadequate control of data information equally requires positive measures. States are requested by the Committee on Human Rights to provide information on the positive measures they are undertaking.[9] Even the prohibition against torture and inhuman and degrading treatment often requires positive measures: prison guards and police need to be educated; programmes are required to ensure that they are familiar with the international-law prohibitions and with the International Minimum Rules for the Treatment of Prisoners; and, where there is a problem, vigorous prosecution and appropriate punishment of those found guilty are necessary.[10] All this is part and parcel of guaranteeing a right that is covered as a 'freedom *from*' maltreatment.

That being said, it must be conceded that problems remain so far as the economic and social rights are concerned. The entitlement to, for example, free primary education or two weeks' paid holiday is clear enough. But other rights—such as freedom from hunger and the right to adequate food—are indeed less precise as to their content. And there does indeed remain the underlying problem that, even if it is known exactly what has to be provided, many states are simply not in a position to deliver the right at the present time.

The Committee acting under the International Covenant on Economic, Social, and Cultural Rights has shown the way forward on these issues. Its starting-point has been that these are present rights and not long-term aspirations. States are under an immediate obligation to do what they can to provide these rights. They are required to identify a programme for the progressive achievement of those rights, in some considerable detail. As the obligation is a present one, they must prepare a realistic programme and show the Committee, in regular period examinations, how they are complying with the timetable they themselves have set. As for the content

---

[9] See General Comment 6 (16) (Art. 6) adopted 27 July 1982; and General Comment 16 (32) adopted 28 Mar. 1988.

[10] See General Comment 20 (44) (Art. 7); and General Comment 21 (44) (Art. 10), both adopted 7 Apr. 1992. See generally also Arts. 2 (2) and 3 of the ICCPR.

of the right, the Committee is able to lend assistance in formulation where necessary. The identification of minimum nutritional requirements, for example, can be called in from various expert sources. The Committee has used an expert study on the right to food initially prepared for the Subcommission on Human Rights both to elaborate the substance of the work and to explore the variety of mechanisms for achieving it.[11] States are expected to participate in erecting building blocks, or stepping stones, to put into place the obligation to provide the right. The task of the Committee is to assist in the formulation of these building blocks and to monitor that they are being complied with. Its approach is at once imaginative and realistic, a further example of the creativity that goes into the formulation of international law norms.[12]

If we accept that human rights comprise individuals' economic and social rights as well as their civil and political rights, what are we to make of collective rights; and, even more, of so-called 'third-generation' rights?[13] There seems no reason of principle why an entitlement held by a group cannot be termed a human right. The right of self-determination, on which I shall have more to say in Chapter 7, is just such a right. It is a right of peoples, rather than a right held by Mr X or Mrs Y. Why should that make it less a right? The answer can only be because 'peoples' do not readily fall into the category of plaintiffs, cannot readily bring legal actions. But we have already seen that justiciability is not the yardstick by which the status of a provision as a human right is to be judged. It is to be judged by reference to the authoritative nature of the sources that purport to identify it, by community expectation that an obligation exists.

On these grounds, and not because I am opposed in principle to such rights being acknowledged as *real* rights, it seems to me that not all so-called collective or third-generation rights *are* in fact rights. The 'right of peoples to peace' seems to me so indeterminate as not properly to be termed a human right. The 'peoples' who are holders of the right of self-determination are identifiable (and this will be elaborated in the next

[11] Eide, *Report on the Right to Food*; E/C.12/1989/SR.20, pp. 2–9.

[12] P. Alston and G. Quinn, 'The Nature and Scope of States Parties' Obligations under the International Covenant on Economic, Social and Cultural Rights' (1987) 9 *HRQ* 157–93; P. Alston, 'The Second Session of the UN Committee on Economic, Social and Cultural Rights' (1988) 82 *AJIL* 603; P. Alston, 'The Committee on Economic, Social and Cultural Rights', in P. Alston (ed.), *The United Nations and Human Rights: A Critical Appraisal* (1992), 473 ff.

[13] See P. Alston, 'Conjuring Up New Human Rights: A Proposal for Quality Control' (1984) 78 *AJIL* 607; S. Marks, 'Emerging Human Rights: A New Generation for the 1980s?' (1981) 33 *Rutgers Law Review* 435; V. Nanda, 'Development as an Emerging Human Right under International Law' (1984–5) 13 *Denver Journal of International Law and Policy* 161; D. Shelton, 'Human Rights, Environmental Rights and the Right to the Environment' (1991) 28 *Stanford Journal of International Law* 103; I. Hodkova, 'Is there a Right to a Healthy Environment in the International Legal Order?' (1991) 7 *Connecticut Journal of International Law* 65.

chapter). The 'peoples' who are entitled to peace are surely, each and every one of us, individuals. Upon whom does an obligation lie? Particular states? All states? Who owes duties to whom? And what are the duties owed? It is difficult enough, in a world where different views are taken about the economic role of government and the place of the market, to formulate normative building blocks about the provision of food, or housing. There seems as yet no body of expert opinion that can define, in a manner that will be regarded as authoritative, what steps must be taken to guarantee peace. Of course, there is a widespread consensus that certain weapons are prohibited, that certain types of weapon-testing is unlawful, that arms sales should be controlled, and that a measure of disarmament is desirable. But beyond that there remain profound differences as to what further measures would best guarantee peace.

The existence of a treaty may not be the only test as to whether a right exists. Rights may, of course, exist in customary international law. But a treaty will be an important indication, and the claim that a right exists in customary international law will need to be established by reference to the normal criteria of that source, including state practice, which may be expected to be evidenced in resolutions and declarations of international bodies. That is notably lacking in, for example, the so-called right to peace. So far as the right to development is concerned, it has been much supported by leading writers and there does exist a UN General Assembly Resolution on the subject,[14] and it has been frequently invoked by various international bodies. But it is notably absent from the International Covenant on Economic, Social, and Cultural Rights. In my view, formidable problems remain about classifying it as a human right. The right-holders are presumably the peoples of developing territories. But what the right *entails* is for the moment very unclear. Indeed, much of the literature that proclaims the existence of the right ignores this question entirely, concentrating instead upon the legitimacy of collective or fourth-generation rights (a necessary but insufficient issue). Is the right to development simply what we have when all the rights enumerated in the Economic, Social, and Cultural Covenant are fulfilled? In other words, is it a shorthand term for the compendia of the right to food, to shelter, to education, to health? Or is it the *prerequisite* to the achievement of any one of these rights?[15] And, if so, what exactly is the duty incumbent upon states—and, indeed, upon *which* states? Does the right to development mean that certain poorer countries are entitled, as a legal right, to increase their industrial base by x per cent per annum? Or that they are to be

---

[14] GA Res. 41/128, 1986.
[15] See A. Eide, 'Developmentalism and Human Rights—Toward a Merger? Some Provisional Reflections', in L. Rehof and C. Gulman (eds.), *Human Rights in Domestic Law and Development, Assistance Policies of the Nordic Countries* (1989), 69 ff.

protected against the terms of trade? Or that price supports are to be provided for their commodities? All of this is uncertain. Does it perhaps mean that they have a legal entitlement to receive foreign aid? Or investment? If so, does this mean that states must not leave aid and investment to the private sector, but must make these provisions themselves? And to what is the aid and investment to be directed? What activity may be said to support economic development? Is this a matter on which international institutions such as the World Bank may properly pronounce, or is it a matter of sovereign choice for the receiving state? One has only to put such questions to see that there is no consensus on what is required and no expectation that any specific obligations to provide exist.

If we think of human rights in the classical sense as an obligation running between a person, or persons, and the state which has jurisdiction over them, then the so-called right to development undeniably goes beyond that pattern. It is really a purported right of one state to receive benefits from others—and indeed, from international institutions—for the good of its citizens. A final problem, so far as a right to development is concerned, is that it is unclear whether it is compatible with emerging environmental norms. There is frequently an environmental price to pay for development. It is no longer clear that states have *carte blanche* in these matters, regardless of the consequences for others—and indeed for their own citizens in the longer term. These citizens begin to invoke the right to a safe environment—a claim whose status as a human right is also uncertain at this stage, and in an early phase of evolution. Development and environmental needs often pull in opposite directions.[16]

I have tried to show where I draw the line between what are human rights and what are not. It is more than an academic matter, because the articulation of claims as human rights is part of the process of according priority to decision-making processes. The question is often asked as to whether there is a finite list of rights, or whether it can be expanded indefinitely.[17] The answer to *that* question depends upon one's perception of what constitutes a human right. For some, it is a core set of civil and political rights. For some, it is all civil and political rights, but not economic, social, and cultural rights. For others, economic and social

[16] See B. Conable, 'Development and the Environment: A Global Balance' (1990) 5 *American University Journal of International Law and Policy* 235; R. Houseman and D. Zaelke, 'Trade, Environment and Sustainable Development: A Primer' (1992) 15 *Hastings International and Comparative Law Review* 535; R. Munro and J. Lammers, *Environmental Protection and Sustainable Development: Legal Principles and Recommendations* (1987); P. Alston, E. Lutz, S. McCaffrey, I. Shihata, and D. Wirth, 'Environment, Economic Development and Human Rights: A Triangular Relationship? A Panel', *Proc. ASIL* (1988), 40.
[17] This issue is addressed in an impressively analytical manner in R. Bilder, 'Rethinking International Human Rights: Some Basic Questions' (1969) 2 *HRJ* 557.

rights could be included on a 'basic-needs' basis—thus the right to food and shelter would be regarded as rights, but other matters as aspirations. Where does our sense of something being a 'right', an 'entitlement', come from?[18] Beyond the 'basic-needs' approach to human rights, it is hard to pinpoint an objective basis. The philosophy of the social contract, whereby the state protects the liberty and security of the person, and his property, in return for loyalty, provides one answer—but also a very short list of civil and political rights. I myself prefer the position that human rights are demands of a particularly high intensity made by individuals *vis-à-vis* their governments.[19] Thus it is that we now have an unprecedented ratification rate for a treaty on the rights of the child, whereas a decade ago there would have been serious doubt that there was any such human right. In principle, therefore, the list could be infinite. In practice, the continued expansion of the list of rights presents problems. If states accede to this expansion for reasons of political convenience, rather than conviction, then the coinage will undoubtedly become debased, and the major operational importance of designating a right a human right—that opprobrium attaches to ignoring it—will be lost.

There are functional problems, too, associated with an expanding list of rights—and, indeed, with the instruments detailing in more precise terms how existing rights can better be protected. But this requires one first to identify the main methods by which attempts are today made to protect human rights.

The prime task is necessarily the identification and articulation of the right. Customary international law has undoubtedly had a role to play in this, with the interplay between the standard-setting UN Declaration on Human Rights, and its acceptance in many national constitutions and before many courts, providing an important example. But the greatest push in the formulation of human rights has undoubtedly been through the treaty process. The International Covenants, one on Civil and Political Rights, one on Economic, Social, and Cultural Rights, provide instruments that deal with the comprehensive range of rights on a universal basis. The instruments cover all the major rights, and are open to all the states of the world. The Covenant on Civil and Political Rights, for example, has 150 state parties, from the various corners of the world. An alternative—or often complementary—method is for the provision for the protection of the comprehensive range of rights, but on a regional basis. The idea is that

[18] There is a vast literature on this philosophic question. See particularly O. von Gierke, *Natural Law and the Theory of Society, 1550–1800*, 2 vols. (1934); J. Finnis, *Natural Law and Natural Rights* (1980); R. Dworkin, *Taking Rights Seriously* (rev. edn., 1978). See also generally the footnotes accompanying the text of pp. 1–38 of C. Palley, *The United Kingdom and Human Rights* (1991).

[19] M. McDougal, H. Lasswell, and L. C. Chen, *Human Rights and World Public Order* (1980), 80 ff.

the rights may be formulated on a basis that will command confidence in the region, and that in turn will allow rather effective enforcement measures. Thus the European Convention on Human Rights generally contains fewer rights than those found in the Covenant on Civil and Political Rights. Those that exist in both are often formulated in comparable terms (with some notable exceptions). And the machinery for the enforcement of those rights is undoubtedly somewhat stronger in the European model than in a global version. However, generalizations cannot readily be made about the relative qualities of regional and universal instruments. The rights contained in the International Covenants on Human Rights are similar but often not identical to those in the European Convention and the Inter-American Convention. The institutional machinery has certain similarities to each and also some notable differences. The African Charter has strikingly different formulations of the rights, with much broader powers of limitation being permitted to governments, greater emphasis on collective rights, the introduction of the concept of individuals' duties to the state and family, and relatively weak institutional measures directed at compliance.[20]

The universal and regional instruments on the broad range of rights have over the years been supplemented by universal instruments directed towards the elaboration of single rights. Thus international conventions now exist on Genocide, on Racial Discrimination, on the Rights of Women, on Torture, and on the Rights of the Child. A new Protocol to the Covenant on Civil and Political Rights, which provides for the abolition of the death penalty, entered into force in 1991.

Here then we have the norms identified and articulated. Their invocation (and invocation is part of the process of implementation and not, as some think, separate from it and irrelevant to the 'more serious task' of implementation) takes place in a variety of fora. Some of these bodies have their own special human-rights mandate; some do not. In the latter category we should refer to the Security Council. None the less, in performing its own peace and security tasks it sometimes places reliance on human-rights issues. In dealing with peace and security matters it may be that human-rights concerns are also present—or, indeed, are exactly the element that is occasioning the threat to international peace. The Security Council may then pass resolutions that pronounce upon such human-rights matters. Resolutions on the provision of arms to South Africa, the Namibia question, the treatment of Palestinians in the occupied territories, and the situation of the Kurds and Shi'is in the Gulf all provide examples.

While human-rights questions arise incidentally in some organs of the

[20] See M. Hamalengwa, C. Flinterman, and E. Dankwa, *The International Law of Human Rights in Africa* (1988), 1–77; E. Bello (1981) 30 *ICLQ* 628; S. Neff (1984) 33 *ICLQ* 331; E. Kodjo (1990) 11 *HRLJ* 271.

United Nations, other bodies are specifically mandated to deal with human-rights questions. The UN Commission on Human Rights is such a body.[21] It is undeniably political, in that those who serve on it are representatives of their states, and the debate—both as to what should go on to the agenda and as to the substance—is often contentious. But, together with the Subcommittee on Non-Discrimination and Minorities (whose members are individual experts and which is able to work in a slightly less politically charged atmosphere), it has enshrined some important methods and procedures. We may particularly mention the 1503 procedure, whereby complaints may be made against states that are claimed to have a gross pattern of violation of a particular right. The procedure is cumbersome, with certain political protections for states built in, but it may be seen as part of the technique for the mobilization of shame. The great efforts that states make to prevent findings against them under the 1503 procedure seems to indicate that they do care about it.

The Commission has also made important contributions to fact-finding—itself an important technique for the protection of human rights—through the establishment of special rapporteurs. Sometimes these are so-called 'country rapporteurs' (those who have reported on Chile and Afghanistan may be cited as examples) and sometimes they are thematic (for example, the Special Rapporteur on Summary Executions). The Rapporteurs will seek the cooperation of the countries they need to visit. Sometimes good working relationships can be established, and the confidence of the state that its position will be fairly reported will be a contributing factor to an amelioration of the human-rights position. This was true of the Chilean attitude to the Special Rapporteur. But, even when co-operation is denied, as it was by Afghanistan, careful work can be done to provide impartial factual information.

Fact-finding in human rights can take many forms. The European Commission on Human Rights has certain modest powers of fact-finding in the context of individual cases brought before it.[22] It can ask to visit prisons, to meet detainees, to talk to witnesses. The Inter-American Commission on Human Rights[23] has strikingly broad fact-finding powers, being able to make on-site investigations in the member states both in response to an invitation and of its own volition. It issues extremely detailed reports on its findings. Fact-finding in the form of on-site visits is an important element in the prevention of torture. The European

[21] See H. Tolley, *The UN Commission on Human Rights* (1987); T. Van Boven, 'The UN and Human Rights', in A. Cassese (ed.), *UN Law/Human Rights: Two Topics in International Law* (1979).
[22] Art. 28, European Convention on Human Rights.
[23] Arts. 41 and 48 (1), Inter-American Convention on Human Rights. Also R. Norris, 'Observations *in loco*: Practice and Procedure of the Inter-American Commission' (1980) 15 *Texas ILJ* 46.

Convention on Torture contains provisions for such fact-finding by its Committee and, under the Chairmanship of Professor Cassese, has begun to produce important and immensely detailed information.[24] And, of course, non-governmental organizations have an especially important role in fact-finding. Sometimes such bodies will be invited by the country concerned to examine prisons and detention centres, or to attend trials. On other occasions they will have to rely for information, following careful procedures to ensure its reliability, on victims or other persons within the country concerned.[25]

The regional systems each have their own institutional machinery. In the European system the Commission and Court are largely dedicated to human-rights litigation, whether in the form of applications by individuals against states, or inter-state disputes. The Inter-American system combines judicial and quasi-judicial functions in the Court and Commission with other fact-finding functions performed by the Commission. The International Covenant on Civil and Political Rights broke new ground in the universal treaty system by providing for efficacious monitoring machinery in the form of the Committee on Human Rights.[26] Other more single-topic treaties (such as the Committee on the Elimination of Racial Discrimination (CERD), the Committee against Torture (CAT), and the Committee on the Elimination of All Forms of Discrimination against Women (CEDAW)) have also been provided with monitoring committees. They have to a considerable extent followed the practices of the Human Rights Committee under the Covenant, and it has been found that monitoring is best achieved through a combination of state-reporting and the bringing of applications by individual claimants. The state-reporting system is compulsory. The right of the Committee to sit in a quasi-judicial capacity and hear cases is optional. If a state accepts the special procedures in the treaty in question, procedure may be set in motion for such applications ('communications') in the future.

The Human Rights Committee under the Covenant now has considerable experience both of state reporting and of hearing cases. States are required to submit a report within one year of the Covenant entering into effect for them, and then to submit further reports on a five-year cycle. The Committee has the right to call for further reports outside the regular cycle. State parties attend an examination of their reports by the

---

[24] Art. 10 (1), European Convention for the Prevention of Torture and Inhuman or Degrading Treatment or Punishment. For an interesting report consequential upon fact finding in Austria, see CPT/Inf(91)10, 3 Oct. 1991.

[25] B. Ramcharan (ed.), *International Law and Fact Finding in the Field of Human Rights* (1982).

[26] R. Higgins, 'Encouraging Human Rights', *LSE Quarterly* (1986), 249; T. Opsahl, 'Instruments of Implementation of Human Rights' (1989) 10 *HRLJ* 13.

Committee in open session. This examination, in which the Committee endeavours to have a 'constructive dialogue' with the state concerned, rather than a confrontational and hostile cross-examination, is proving a useful means of monitoring compliance and encouraging progress. The states are provided with Guidelines as to what their reports must cover, and in what form. Committee members (following somewhat different procedures for each of the different rounds of examination—i.e. for the initial, second, and third periodic reports) will probe as to what is said in the reports, what is missing, and what is known from other sources of information. At the end of the examination the Committee members will offer their comments on how they find the state of human rights in the country concerned. The Committee then provides its own Observations.

The Committee now also has a considerable jurisprudence under its case law, since the 1980s having provided an exponential growth in the use of the communications procedure. In this way efforts are made to assist individuals whose rights have been violated and to assist governments in specifying certain legal obligations under the Covenant. If the pattern of compliance with the decisions of the European Court is strikingly good, the picture is more mixed so far as the case law under the Covenant is concerned. The European Convention has its own treaty procedures for ensuring compliance. Because states parties have not, under the Covenant, undertaken in terms to give effect to the views of the Committee, there are not comparable procedures. But the Committee has recently introduced certain procedures in order better to 'follow up' on compliance with its case law.[27]

The very success of these procedures has led to its own problems. The parties to the European Convention on Human Rights find that large amounts of time have to be given over to the preparation of cases before the Commission and Court. And the spread of the state-reporting system to so many UN human-rights treaty bodies has undoubtedly led to problems for states parties. It is difficult enough for wealthy developed states to put in all their reports to all the various bodies that now require them. It is an extraordinarily onerous task for smaller and developing countries, who often lack the resources of manpower to perform those tasks. Work is under way within the UN system to facilitate this burden. Part of the work is in the form of advisory services—for example, the provision of technical assistance in the form of regional seminars on the preparation of reports. An important and creative study of the problems arising from the requirements of the treaty bodies has been prepared by

---

[27] For details, see Report of the Human Rights Committee, 1991, A/46/40 (1991), GAOR 46th sess., 173.

Professor Philip Alston.[28] Efforts are now being made to provide as much uniformity as possible between the demands of the various bodies, so that preparation can be standardized; and to assist in the task through computerization.

The proliferation of treaty bodies has financial implications for the states, as well as consequences in terms of the need to produce reports. It also raises the worrisome spectre of divergent jurisprudence from the various treaty bodies dealing with a common right. It is perhaps arguable that there is little scope for further separate treaty bodies, and that, if it is desired to elaborate rights enumerated in the Civil and Political Covenant in more detail, this should be done by additional protocols to the Covenant, enabling the committee to perform the dual monitoring functions of state-reporting and case law. Such a solution would have its own implications for the nature and status of the Committee.

It is up to every one of us to participate in the fight for human rights. The international human-rights bodies cannot fight the battle alone. And states must do more than be watchful for human rights within their own territories; at the end of the day, their commitment to the promotion of human rights will be judged as much by their willingness to provide the resources to allow the impartial treaty-monitoring bodies to do their work effectively. States must also be willing to address the institutional problems within the human-rights treaty system, at both the regional and the global level. The World Conference for human rights, held in Vienna in June 1993, could have provided a vehicle for getting to grips with these institutional problems. But the states showed no interest in doing so.

[28] *Effective Implementation of International Instruments on Human Rights*, Including Reporting Obligations, A/44/668 (1989).

7

SELF-DETERMINATION

CHAPTER 6 was concerned with the international system for human rights. This chapter addresses one particular human right—that of self-determination. Why, of all the rights, should self-determination merit a separate chapter? There are, after all, other rights of the most profound importance—freedom from torture, for example. The reason that self-determination is the subject of a separate chapter is because it is difficult, extraordinarily intertwined with other norms of international law, controversial, topical, and well illustrates the complexities of the law-creating process.

There is a general assumption that self-determination is to do with independence. It is also widely assumed that the UN Charter provides for self-determination in such terms. In fact, there is no such provision in the UN Charter. Our contemporary understanding of the concept of self-determination has been generated by the interplay of a variety of historical factors. But, contrary to popular mythology, it does not find its origins in the UN Charter. Other law-making mechanisms have been at work.

When the Charter of the United Nations was drawn up, there were fifty-one original members, all independent, with the exception of India (which was very shortly to become independent) and Ukraine and Byelorussia. These last, somewhat anomalously and as the result of a political bargain, were treated as independent UN members while still republics of the Soviet Union. In 1946 the focus was on the rights and obligations of the sovereign member states. It was not yet fashionable to think about the rights of those not yet independent. There were, certainly, recognized duties that colonial powers had towards the peoples they governed. But at that time that did not clearly include any duty to grant independence. The common assumption that the UN Charter underwrites self-determination in the current sense of the term is in fact a retrospective rewriting of history.

The First Phase: Self-Determination and Independence from Colonial Rule

The Charter contains rather few references to self-determination. The first reference appears in Article 1 (2), which provides that one of the purposes of the United Nations is 'to develop friendly relations among nations based on respect for the principle of equal rights and self-determination of peoples'. That phrase—'equal rights and self-determination of peoples'—is the formula that appears elsewhere. Thus Article 55, on Economic and Social Co-operation, instructs the United Nations to promote higher standards of living, solutions to health and cultural problems, and universal respect for human rights—all in order to create conditions necessary for peaceful and friendly relations among nations 'based on equal rights and self-determination'. In both Article 1 (2) and Article 55, the context seems to be the rights of the peoples of one state to be protected from interference by other states or governments. We cannot ignore the coupling of 'self-determination' with 'equal rights'—and it was equal rights of *states* that was being provided for, not of individuals.[1] The concept of self-determination did not then, originally, seem to refer to a right of dependent peoples to be independent, or, indeed, even to vote.

The incorrectness of popular assumptions about what the UN Charter provides on self-determination is further strikingly illustrated by turning to those parts that deal with dependent territories. Here, it might be assumed, would be found the references to the duty to provide self-determination on the basis of independence. But in fact Chapters XI and XII do not use the phrase 'self-determination'. Chapter XI, which is concerned with non-self-governing territories, refers in Article 73 (*b*) to the duty of the governing state to 'develop self government, to take due account of the political aspirations of the peoples, and to assist them in the progressive development of their free political institutions, according to the particular circumstances of each territory and its peoples and the varying stages of advancement'. While laudable, this falls quite short of what today is generally thought of as self-determination. Chapter XII, which covers the trusteeship system, comes a little nearer to what one would today expect to find in its governing provisions. Article 76 provides that the basic objective of Trusteeship shall be '(*b*) to promote . . . their progressive development towards self government *or* independence as may be appropriate to the particular circumstances of each territory and its peoples and the freely expressed wishes of the peoples concerned'. But there is still no use of the term 'self-determination', and independence was not assumed as the only proper outcome.

It can now be seen that self-determination is *not* provided for by the text of the UN Charter—at least not in the sense that it is generally used. But international law does not develop from written words alone. On other

---

[1] The *travaux préparatoires* of the Charter confirm this understanding of the phrase: see VI UNCIO 300. For a thorough analysis of the diplomatic history of the references to self-determination in the Charter, see A. Cassese, *Self-Determination of Peoples: A Legal Reappraisal* (1993), 34–42.

matters, too, contemporary norms seem to deviate from the written text of the Charter. That necessarily presents us with the problem: Which is the *real* international law? The first point to be made is that not every deviation from the written word is the same. Some develop and elaborate rather limited statements of principle; other deviations appear actually to contradict clear written prescriptions. In the case of self-determination, the term originally had a rather limited and state-based meaning. But there was nothing in the Charter that actually *prohibited* the emergence of a norm that required states not only not to interfere with each other but also to provide to dependent peoples the right to determine their own destiny. But, as will be seen in a later chapter, on the use of force, the deviation between the Charter text and contemporary practice is of a different nature: the written text seems to prohibit the current practice, giving rise to the question of whether the practice is to be seem as an exception to the Charter norm or an amendment of it. We will return to these aspects of law development later.

For the moment it suffices to note that, notwithstanding the cautious way in which self-determination is referred to in the Charter, there began in the 1950s to be a moral stand taken on the issue by the General Assembly. And, with the increase in Afro-Asian membership in the 1960s, self-determination became increasingly invoked as a right of dependent peoples. At first, several of the colonial powers resisted the idea that there was a legal right of self-determination. It was, in their view, merely a political aspiration. But gradually their resistance to the idea of a legal right became more muted. They accepted broader interpretations of their duties under 73 (*e*), especially in terms of the provision of information to the United Nations on political progress. The development of the concept of self-determination was historically bound up with decolonization—with the growing agreement that it was obligatory to bring forward dependent peoples to independence if they so chose, even though Article 73 had spoken only of self-government.[2]

While self-determination began to be accepted as a legal right in the context of decolonization,[3] it was never restricted to a choice for

---

[2] See R. Higgins, *The Development of International Law through the Political Organs of the United Nations* (1963), 90–106.

[3] For differing early views on the status of self-determination as a legal norm, see R. Jennings, *The Acquisition of Territory in International Law* (1963), 78; R. Emerson, 'Self-Determination' (1971) 65 *AJIL* 464–5; M. Pomerance, *Self-Determination in Law and Practice* (1982), 70–1; cf. Higgins, *The Development of International Law* 101–6; G. Scelle, 'Quelques reflexions sur le droit des peuples à disposer d'eux-mêmes', in *Mélanges Spiropoulos* (1957), 385–91. By 1971 the International Court was clear that the development of international law meant that the principle of self-determination was applicable to all non self-governing territories (*Legal Consequences for States of the Continued Presence of South Africa in Namibia notwithstanding Security Council Resolution 276* (1970), Advisory Opinion, ICJ Reports (1971) 16 at 31).

independence. A choice by the peoples of a territory to join with another state,[4] or to remain in a constitutional relationship with the former colonial power,[5] was equally acceptable. Usually, of course, the choice has been for independence. Very often the United Nations has played a role in that exercise in choice, by itself organizing a referendum or plebiscite, or by monitoring such exercises.[6]

The Second Phase: Self-Determination and Human Rights

The next phase in legal development was the building of a bridge from self-determination as a legal obligation in the process of decolonizing, to self-determination as a human right. Two resolutions of the General Assembly, passed within twenty-four hours of each other, spoke about the right of peoples to self-determination: General Assembly Resolution 1514 (XV) and General Assembly Resolution 1541 (XV). In Resolution 1514—the Declaration on Granting Independence to Colonial Countries and Peoples, the reference to the term 'peoples' is conditioned by many allusions to colonialism. And it provided, in operative paragraph 2, that all peoples subject to colonial rule have the right to 'freely determine their political status and freely pursue their economic, social and cultural development'. Resolution 1541 (XV) made clear that this exercise in self-determination could result in various outcomes, and stipulated the processes required to ensure that informed, free, and voluntary choices were being made. But, within six years of the passing of these key resolutions on decolonization, the right of peoples to self-determination was to appear as a free-standing precept, beyond the confines of normative practices on decolonization.

In 1966 the texts of the Covenant on Civil and Political Rights and of the Covenant on Economic, Social, and Cultural Rights were concluded. Common Article 1 of each of these provides: '1. All peoples have the right of self-determination. By virtue of that right they freely determine their political status and freely pursue their economic, social and cultural development.' From this time onwards we see repeated reference to self-determination in human-rights terms. The Helsinki Final Act interestingly builds on the old UN Charter language, while at the same time making it clear that self-determination is a right of *peoples*. It speaks of 'the principle

---

[4] e.g. the integration of the Northern Cameroons into Nigeria, and the Southern Cameroons into Cameroon.

[5] e.g. Gibraltar *vis-à-vis* the United Kingdom; Puerto Rico *vis-à-vis* the United States.

[6] See e.g. GA Res. 944 (X), 15 Dec. 1955, and the ensuing plebiscite in British Togolands in May 1956; GA Res. 1350 (XIII), and the ensuing plebiscite in Northern Cameroons and in Southern Cameroons in Nov. 1956 and Feb. 1961; GA Res. 1580 (IV) and the ensuing referendum in Rwanda of Sept. 1961; and very many others.

of equal rights and self-determination of peoples' by virtue of which 'all peoples always have the right, in full freedom, to determine, when and as they wish, their internal and external political status, without external interference, and to pursue as they wish their political, economic, social and cultural development'.[7] The African Charter on Human and Peoples' Rights also provides that all peoples shall have the right to self-determination.[8]

If self-determination has developed from its modest beginnings in the UN Charter to a legal entitlement of decolonization and to a free-standing human right, there are still very many questions to be answered. As will become apparent, the questions are very interlinked and the answer to any one is apt to depend on the answer you give to any other. But for analytical purposes some effort to separate the various questions is necessary.

Self-determination beyond colonialism

If self-determination has come to be accepted as a legal right, is its application limited to decolonization? In the *Namibia* Advisory Opinion the Court had affirmed that 'the subsequent development of international law in regard to non-self-governing territories, as enshrined in the Charter of the United Nations, made the principles of self-determination applicable to all of them'.[9] In the *Western Sahara* Advisory Opinion[10] the Court again affirmed the linkage between self-determination and the right of peoples under colonial rule, when it spoke of 'the principle of self-determination as a right of peoples, and its application for the purpose of bringing all colonial situations to a speedy end'. More recent reference to the principle, but still in the context of decolonization, is to be found in the *Burkina Faso* v. *Mali Case*[11] and in the arbitral award in the *Guinea-Bissau* v. *Senegal Case*.[12]

It came further to be accepted that the right of self-determination was applicable not only to peoples under colonial rule, but also to peoples subject to foreign or alien domination. This was spelled out in the UN Declaration on Friendly Relations of 1970, which has been widely invoked on this point, although the Declaration is contained in an Assembly resolution rather than a binding instrument, and although the two Covenants do not mention this circumstance. The Declaration speaks of self-determination being available in situations of colonialism, and the 'subjection of peoples to alien subjugation, domination and exploitation'. Those supporting this clause clearly had two very different circumstances in mind. The first concerned South Africa—an independent state, but one perceived by many as subject to 'alien domination', and foreign support for

---

[7] (1975) 14 *ILM* 1292.

[8] Art. 20 (1982) 21 *ILM* 59.

[9] ICJ Reports (1971) 16 at para. 52.

[10] ICJ Reports (1975) 12 at para. 162.

[11] ICJ Reports (1986) 554 at paras. 25–6.

[12] (1990) *RGDIP* 240; and 83 ILR 1.

that minority domination. The second was a very different matter—the status of occupied territories upon the termination or suspension of military hostilities. It was felt that the position of peoples in such territories was to be protected not just by humanitarian law, but by insistence upon their right to self-determination.[13] In any event, there have been many UN resolutions referring to the right of self-determination in circumstances of alien occupation. These include resolutions on Afghanistan and Arab-occupied territories.[14]

The wording of the UN Declaration on Friendly Relations[15] seems at first sight to support the view that self-determination is limited to a specific moment of decolonization. It provides, *inter alia*, that a colonial or non-self-governing territory continues its separate existence 'until the people of the colony or Non-Self-Governing Territory have exercised their right of self-determination in accordance with the Charter . . .'.

For a considerable period of time there was substantial resistance to the suggestion that self-determination might have any application outside the colonial context. That resistance was shared by the Eastern European states and the new territories. Under the old Eastern Europe there was obviously little desire to concede that peoples had an entitlement to determine their own political and economic destiny. The phenomenon was appropriate for decolonization only. And many of the new states regarded self-determination as a matter between them and their former colonial masters, but not as between them and their own population. Indeed, this much was declared in terms by India when ratifying the International Covenant on Civil and Political Rights[16] and has recently been repeated by India during the course of the examination of its Third Periodic Report by the Committee on Human Rights.[17] Part of the fear of Third World states was that post-colonial self-determination would necessarily result in the fragmentation of the new nation states, with ethnic groups in one country seeking to secede or to join with the same ethnic groups in another country. But the idea has been consistently fostered by the Committee on Human Rights, acting under the Covenant on Civil and Political Rights, that self-determination is of continuing applicability; and the idea has undoubtedly taken a general hold.[18] The Committee on Human Rights,

---

[13] For a good survey of the different positions taken on this clause during the drafting of the Declaration on Friendly Relations, see Cassese, *Self-Determination of Peoples,* 72–6.

[14] See GA Res. 2535 (XXIVB) 1970 and 2672-C, 1970; GA Res. 3236 (XXIX) 1974 (Palestine); GA Res. 2144 (XXV) 1987 (Afghanistan).

[15] GA Res. 2625 (XXV) 1970, Principle (e).

[16] France, the Netherlands, and the FRG all entered objections to this reservation.

[17] See Second Periodic Report of India, CCPR/C/37/Add. 13, and examination thereon, CCPR/C/SR/1039–42, 26–7 Mar. 1991.

[18] The ILC supported this view in its 1988 Report to the General Assembly, albeit relying on the revisionist view of what the Charter requires. It stated there: 'The principle of self-

when examining the report of a state party to the Covenant, asks not only about any dependent territories that such a state party may be responsible for (external self-determination) but also about the opportunities that its own population has to determine its own political and economic system (internal self-determination). Virtually no states refuse to respond to probing comments and questions on internal self-determination, and the Committee is not told that no such right exists. Rather, it is accepted that the right exists, and the debate most frequently is about the forms that it can take.

The reference in the African Charter on Human and Peoples' Rights to Self-Determination is in terms that does not tie it to colonialism. Article 20 stipulates:

1. All peoples shall have the right to existence. They shall have the unquestionable and inalienable right to self-determination. They shall freely determine their political status and shall pursue their economic and social development according to the policy they have freely chosen.
2. Colonial or oppressed peoples shall have the right to free themselves from the bonds of domination by resorting to any means recognised by the international community.
3. All peoples shall have the right to the assistance of the States Parties to the present Charter in their liberation struggle against foreign domination, be it political, economic or cultural.

While paragraph 3 is directed to colonialism, or foreign domination, paragraphs 1 and 2 are couched in broader terms. We have also noticed that the wording of the Helsinki Final Act provisions clearly presuppose the continuing and ongoing relevance of the principle of self-determination.[19]

This reality is a far cry from the position of certain writers who assume that self-determination is only about independence; that independence is achieved by the end of colonialism; and that further independence can only be achieved through secession. Because they believe—correctly, in my opinion—that there is no legal right of secession where there is representative government—they conclude that there is no self-determination permitted in these circumstances. Much of this debate has centred around General Assembly Resolution 2625 (XXV). After several paragraphs authorizing self-determination, the penultimate paragraph on self-determination provides:

determination, proclaimed in the Charter as a universal principle, had been applied mainly in eradicating colonialism, but there were other cases in which it had been and could and should be used. By not tying it exclusively to colonial contexts, it would be applied much more widely. In that connection, all members of the Commission believed that the principle of self-determination was of universal application' (*Yearbook of ILC* (1988), ii. pt. 2, p. 64).

[19] A point made by G. Arango-Ruiz, 'Human Rights and Non-Intervention in the Helsinki Final Act', *Recueil des cours* (1977, IV), 195 at 224–31.

Nothing in the foregoing paragraphs shall be construed as authorising or encouraging any action which would dismember or impair, totally or in part, the territorial integrity or political unity of sovereign or independent states conducting themselves in compliance with the principle of [self-determination] and thus possessed of a government representing the whole people belonging to the territory without distinction as to race, creed or colour.

Some writers have taken the view that self-determination applies only to those peoples living under racist regimes and contends that the wording of the resolution forbids self-determination where there is a non-racist representative government.[20]

But of course it assumes that self-determination means only independence—and that, in turn, independence in a post-colonial situation can only mean secession for some, violating the territorial unity of the whole. The starting-point is not, in my view, the correct one. It is certainly not the approach taken by the Committee on Human Rights—whose practice on this matter, and the concurrence of states as evidenced in the dialogues upon the examination of state reports, bears examination.

It has been clear from the outset that self-determination was not tied only to independence. The peoples of an independent territory have always had the right to choose the form of their political and economic future. While independence has been the most frequently chosen path, other possibilities have always existed and have sometimes been chosen. General Assembly Resolution 1541 (XV) spoke long ago of self-determination being exercised 'through independence, free association, integration with an independent state, or emergence into any other political status freely determined by a people'. The peoples of dependent Cyprus contemplated *enosis* (integration) with Greece as a possible option, before eventually deciding upon independence as a separate sovereign state.[21] The peoples of Gibraltar have by referendum[22] decided to maintain their present constitutional arrangement with the United Kingdom. It has been an act of self-determination freely to decide to leave ultimate sovereign powers to Westminster, with certain other powers being devolved locally. And the people of Puerto Rico have, through successive elections in which candidates have stood on 'independence' or 'association' or '51st State of the Union' platforms, made their own choices.[23] For the

---

[20] See A. Cassese 'The Helsinki Declaration and Self-Determination', in T. Buergenthal and J. Hall (eds.), *Human Rights, International Law and the Helsinki Accord* (1977), 83 at 88–92. Also Pomerance, *Self-Determination in Law and Practice*, 39. See also the useful survey of some of these issues in P. Thornberry, 'Self Determination, Minorities, Human Rights: A Review of International Instruments' (1989) 38 *ICLQ* 867.

[21] See R. Higgins, *United Nations Peacekeeping* (1981) iv. 33–4.

[22] Held on 10 Sept. 1967.

[23] See M. Reisman, *Puerto Rico and the International Process, New Roles in Association* (1975); J. Crawford, *The Creation of States in International Law* (1979) 372.

present they wish to remain in associated status with the United States, being neither a fifty-first state nor an independent sovereign state. Although for a period of years there was some opposition expressed in the UN Committee on Decolonization to such non-independence choices,[24] it cannot be seriously argued that peoples are not entitled to make their choices. What is important is that a proper range of options is laid before a dependent people and that they are given the opportunity to express their choice.

That opportunity to express choice has not always been given. The International Court of Justice in the *Western Sahara Case* acknowledged that

in certain cases the General Assembly has dispensed with the requirement of consulting the inhabitants of a given territory. Those instances were based either on the consideration that a certain population did not constitute a 'people' entitled to self-determination or on the conviction that a consultation was totally unnecessary, in view of special circumstances.[25]

The indigenous peoples of West Irian were not directly consulted through a plebiscite about the decision to integrate with Indonesia upon the completion of the United Nations' interim administration at the end of Dutch rule.[26] And in Western Sahara itself the plebiscite that the Court envisaged still had not, at the time of publication, been held.[27] But in many cases the United Nations has, through its expertise in organizing plebiscites or monitoring elections being run by others, been able to contribute to the exercise of free choice that underlies self-determination. The elections in Namibia are a classic example, ensuring not only the transition to independence but the free selection of government from among the various political parties.[28]

Self-determination has never simply meant independence. It has meant the free choice of peoples. During the era of colonialism, that choice was focused on the possibility of independence or other post-colonial status. That is the aspect of colonialism that reflects the entitlement referred to in Article 1 of the International Covenant on Civil and Political Rights that all peoples may 'freely determine their political status'. But the entitlement

---

[24] Thus the General Assembly, in Res. 2353 (XXII) of 19 Dec. 1967, disapproved the holding of a referendum in Gibraltar.

[25] ICJ Reports (1975) 33, at para. 59.

[26] See GA Res. 1752 (XVII), 21 Sept. 1962; GA Res. 2504 (XXIV), 19 Nov. 1969. For criticism, see M. Pomerance (1974) 12 *Canadian YBIL* 38–66. Further, J. Crawford, *The Creation of States in International Law* (1979), 382 n. 132.

[27] See SC Res. 690, 29 Apr. 1991, approving a schedule for a referendum. For strong (and justified) criticism, see also T. Franck, 'The Stealing of the Sahara' (1976) 70 *AJIL* 694.

[28] See the report of the Secretary-General, *Enhancing International Effectiveness of the Principle of Periodic and Genuine Elections*, GA Doc. A/46/609, 19 Nov. 1991, pp. 6–7.

goes beyond that (and this is the part that is conveniently forgotten by those who limit self-determination to a historical moment of decolonization)—the entitlement is also to 'freely pursue their economic, social and cultural development'. And how can that be done if self-determination does not also provide for free choice not only as to *status* but also as to *government*? It was exactly this duality of requirements for determination that the UN plebiscite in Namibia supported—as did the internationally supervised elections held at the transition from colonial minority rule in Zimbabwe.

And the right remains an ongoing one. It is not only at the moment of independence from colonial rule that peoples are entitled freely to pursue their economic, social, and cultural development. It is a constant entitlement. And that in turn means that they are entitled to choose their government. The Human Rights Committee has consistently told states appearing before it for examination of their periodic reports that the right of self-determination requires that a free choice be afforded to the peoples, on a continuing basis, as to their system of government, in order that they can determine their economic, social, and cultural development. It has been made clear—and not just recently—that this is virtually impossible to achieve in a one-party state. Even in one-party systems that allow some form of participatory democracy, the system itself is predetermined: the range of political, economic, and social choices is thereby already narrowed. In the experiments now beginning in Africa with political pluralism, the Committee has suggested to one state that, while the new permission for four political parties is welcome, the limitation on the number of parties is still not compatible with self-determination.[29] Pluralism can take many forms; but self-determination requires the ongoing choice of the people as to their governance, and, in turn, their economic, social, and cultural development.

This brings us to a further question. Given that another article of the Covenant on Civil and Political Rights—Article 25—contains provisions on voting and participation in public life, can it really be said that self-determination in Article 1 is to be understood as about anything other than colonialism and the vestiges of racist rule? In other words, can the view of Article 1 that I have offered stand up in the face of the existence of Article 25? Article 25 provides that every citizen shall have the right to take part in the conduct of public affairs, to vote and to be elected at periodic elections on the basis of universal suffrage, and to have access to public service in his country.

There is undoubtedly a close relationship between Article 1 and Article

---

[29] See Second Periodic Report of Zaire, CCPR/C/57/Add. 1 and examination thereon, CCPR/C/SR 993-995, 17–19 July 1990.

25. But Article 25 is concerned with the *detail* of how free choice (necessarily implied in Article 1) is to be provided—by periodic elections, on the basis of universal suffrage. And it covers matters clearly beyond those touched on by Article 1, namely, the entitlement to participate without discrimination in the public life of one's country, whether as a politician or as a civil servant. While there is a close relationship between Article 25 (1) and Article 1, nothing in the former requires a narrow reading of the right of self-determination. The two articles are complementary.

Self-determination and minorities

In recent times, old states (often under one-party undemocratic rule) have begun to disintegrate. The component parts of the Soviet Union and Yugoslavia have claimed independence as separate states. Those constituting the majority within the new state borders were minorities within the old union or federal structure; and now they claim that as minorities they are entitled to self-determination. Is it right, as is commonly asserted by the various nationalist factions, that minorities are entitled to self-determination, and that self-determination entails secession?

The question 'who exactly is entitled to the right of self-determination' cannot be answered without first understanding the relationship between self-determination and national unity. The evolving norms on self-determination contained—undeniably and consistently—an anxious refrain whereby self-determination is to be harnessed to, and not the enemy of, territorial integrity. Both General Assembly Resolution 1514 (XV) on the Granting of Independence to Colonial Peoples and General Assembly Resolution 2625 (XXV), the Declaration of Principles on Friendly Relations—each of which emphazises self-determination—caution against anything being interpreted to violate territorial integrity. In Resolution 1514 it is provided that 'any attempt aimed at the partial or total disruption of the national unity and the territorial integrity of a country is incompatible with the purposes and principles of the Charter of the UN'. In Resolution 2625 (XXV), it is provided that: 'Nothing in the foregoing paragraphs shall be construed as authorising or encouraging any action which would dismember or impair, totally or in part, the territorial integrity or political unity of sovereign or independent states . . .' This is a standard formula, and is almost invariably to be found in instruments that affirm the right of self-determination, as if to set the limits to that right, or at least to provide a counterweight. It is that counterpoising that has led some writers to conclude that self-determination can therefore apply only at the moment of independence.

I have tried to show that self-determination can be exercised through many ways, including an open and pluralistic political process, and that this is entirely compatible with the clauses in relevant instruments that call for the protection of territorial integrity.

What limits does the requirement of territorial integrity place upon the exercise of contemporary self-determination? Does it indeed mean that the right is limited to the exercise of political rights by the people as a whole?

It was always understood by states emerging from colonialism that there would be problems associated with the fact that their boundaries had been settled by the colonial powers, on the basis of political interests that did not necessarily coincide with their own. In the case of the emerging African states the problem of inherited boundaries has been particularly acute, and tribes have often straddled the new frontiers yet have continued to feel themselves a unit. But the inherited boundaries have been accepted by the emerging new states, in full knowledge of what they were doing: the importance of the stability and finality of frontiers was viewed as the paramount consideration. In the early nineteenth century the new states of Latin America adopted, upon independence from Spain and from Portugal, the boundaries that had been the administrative divisions of their former rulers. The acceptance that these colonial boundaries were not to be challenged after independence became known as the principle of *uti possidetis*. It is a principle that has found a more general reflection, including in Africa and in Asia. General Assembly Resolutions 1514 (XV) and 1541 (XV), carefully balance the references to self-determination with the importance of national unity and territorial integrity. This necessarily entails the consequence that they intended that the colonial boundaries function as the boundaries of the emergent state. It is not surprising that the principle has been found as necessary to independent Africa as to Latin America, because the underlying policy purposes that it serves are the same. As a well-placed African commentator has aptly put it, when writing of African boundaries at independence: 'Revindication of lost territories is not always practicable, especially when they have crystallized into new political formulae as solidified as the ancestral unit itself.'[30]

In 1964, at the height of African decolonization, the Organization of African Unity (OAU) adopted a celebrated resolution in Cairo which affirmed that the status quo was to be preserved on African boundaries and that these would mark the international frontiers within Africa as states emerged to independence. By this acceptance of the inheritance of colonial boundaries, the members of the OAU effectively acknowledged the applicability of *uti possidetis* to their continent. The point is not so much that the OAU resolution was the basis of legal authority for the *uti possidetis* principle to Africa. Rather it is that the resolution reflected an

---

[30] A. Cukwurah, *The Settlement of Boundary Disputes in International Law* (1967), 164.

underlying norm—that of commitment to territorial integrity and international stability. This way of looking at things has been confirmed in *Guinea-Bissau* v. *Senegal Case*.[31] Judge Bedjaoui, in his dissenting opinion, held that there was but a single concept of *uti possidetis*, applicable everywhere. And Judge Lachs, the President of the Tribunal in the *Guinea–Guinea-Bissau Maritime Delimitation Case*[32] arbitration, has affirmed the applicability of the principle to Africa and pointed out that it was a principle entirely consistent with the principles contained in the 1978 Vienna Convention on State Succession in respect of Treaties[33]—and, we may say, with the general international law on treaty succession.

The applicability of the principle to Africa is beyond doubt. It formed the basis of the reference by the parties to the International Court of Justice in the *Mali-Burkina Faso* case. But it is clear that in any event the Chamber of the Court would have found the principle applicable.

The Chamber in that case clearly regarded the principle as one of general international law.

Although historically the principle had been 'nécessairement lié à la decolonisation qu'elle a produisée',[34] it was now part of general international law. 'Le droit international—et par conséquent le principe de *l'uti possidetis*—est applicable au nouvel État.'[35]

We now return to our point of departure. Is the principle of *uti possidetis* compatible with the concept of self-determination? In other words, is self-determination really thereby to be understood as being limited to an exercise of rights within the inherited frontier? The Chamber in the *Burkina Faso Case*, while aware that 'at first sight' there appeared to be an incompatibility between the two concepts, found that *uti possidetis* did not detract from self-determination. And, in a striking passage, Judge Ad Hoc Abi Saab explained that, without the stability of frontiers, the exercise of self-determination is in reality a mirage. Turmoil is not conducive to human rights.

We may now summarize this point as follows: the right of self-determination continues beyond the moment of decolonization, and allows choices as to political and economic systems within the existing boundaries of the state. Of course, it is very desirable that there should be opportunities for free access to each other by members of the same tribe, group, or people living on opposite sides of an international boundary. But that is to be achieved by neighbourly relations and open frontiers, not by demands for the redrawing of international boundaries. *Uti possidetis* does

---

[31] See n. 12.
[32] 77 ILR 636.
[33] (1978) 17 *ILM* 1488. This treaty has, to date, not yet entered into force.
[34] ICJ Reports (1986) 554 at para. 23.
[35] Ibid., para. 30.

not prevent states freely agreeing to redraw their frontiers. But self-determination does not require this of them.

Again, the desire for secession from a state by certain groups—whether to form their own independent state or to join with another group or unit elsewhere—will be at its most intense when their human rights are being suppressed. Just as the desire of individuals to exercise their right to leave their country is strongest when their rights have been violated, so the desire of ethnic groups to break away is most noticeable when they are oppressed.

Where does this leave us with the question we are addressing, namely, whether minorities have the right to self-determination? Put differently, who exactly is entitled to the right to self-determination? We have seen from the Covenant and other instruments that it is 'all peoples' who are entitled to the right. But what are we to understand by that? There are really two possibilities—that 'peoples' means the entire people of a state, or that 'peoples' means all persons comprising distinctive groupings on the basis of race, ethnicity, and perhaps religion.

The emphasis in all the relevant instruments, and in the state practice (by which I mean statements, declarations, positions taken) on the importance of territorial integrity, means that 'peoples' is to be understood in the sense of *all* the peoples of a given territory. Of course, all members of distinct minority groups are part of the peoples of the territory. In that sense they too, as individuals, are the holders of the right of self-determination. But minorities *as such* do not have a right of self-determination. That means, in effect, that they have no right to secession, to independence, or to join with comparable groups in other states.

It is today fashionable among political leaders to invoke the legal right of self-determination (and for that we must be thankful). And there is also a genuine concern with the rights of minorities. But to the international lawyer the rhetoric is confused. It seems that many governments have come all the way from an insistence in the 1950s that self-determination was not a legal right (the Western view); and from an insistence that it had no application beyond decolonization (the Third World view); to an assumption, by many European leaders at least, that self-determination is a right that authorizes minorities to break away. I have explained why I do not believe this to be the case.

What follows from this view? Does it mean, on the one hand, that minorities are to be left unprotected and, on the other, that frontiers are frozen for all times, with new states never again to be formed and recognized? The answer is 'no' in each case. Let us take them each in turn. Minorities are indeed to be protected, through the guarantee of human rights that every individual is entitled to (including non-discrimination), and, more particularly, through the provision of minority rights. These rights, already presaged in the inter-war minority treaties[36] and in judgments and opinions of the Permanent Court of International Justice,[37] find contemporary formulation in Article 27 of the International Covenant on Civil and Political Rights. This provides:

In those states in which ethnic, religious or linguistic minorities exist, persons belonging to such minorities shall not be denied the right, in community with other members of their group, to enjoy their own culture, to profess and practise their own religion, and to use their own language.

In an ideal world these rights will be part of the fabric of life in a state. From time to time, when particular problems arise, the national government may need to be reminded of its duties to minorities. And in certain particular situations—and that may be true of Iraq today—internal autonomy may provide the best guarantee for the realization of these rights. (Autonomy is not, of course, independence.) Attractive though secession may seem at times of stress—particularly when the national government is undemocratic and represents only itself—the reality is that secession may not cure all the problems. There may be an area in a state where a particular minority is regionally predominant. If it feels oppressed, it may wish to secede. But within this regional area there may be a minority of the predominant minority—perhaps persons belonging to the national majority, or to yet another ethnic minority. We may recognize this situation in some of the republics of the Soviet Union and in some of the seceding provinces of Yugoslavia. Virtually every minority has its own minority, and the fear of oppression gets pushed further down the pyramid. The lesson we must draw is that the right of self-determination is interlocked with the proper protection of minority rights—but that they are discrete rights, not to be confused with each other.

As to the second question, it is not the case that this view of self-determination means that new frontiers can never be recognized. Even if, contrary to contemporary political assumptions, self-determination is not an *authorization* of secession by minorities, there is nothing in international law that *prohibits* secession or the formation of new states. The principle of *uti possidetis* provides that states accept their inherited colonial boundaries. It places no obligation upon minority groups to stay a part of a unit that maltreats them or in which they feel unrepresented. If they do in fact establish an independent state, or join with an existing state, then that new reality is one which, when its permanence can be shown, will in due course be recognized by the international community. The territorial rearrangements in the old Mali Federation, and in the Indian subcontinent

---

[36] For listing, see F. Capotorti, Study on the Rights of Persons Belonging to Ethnic, Religious, and Linguistic Minorities, UN Doc. E/CN.4/Sub.2/1979/384/rev. 1.

[37] e.g. *Minority Schools in Albania* (1935) PCIJ, Ser. A/B, no. 64, p. 4.

with the birth of Bangladesh, are examples of new states emerging after initial decolonization. Where no principle of *ex injuria non oritur* applies, international law will recognize new realities. And where secession has in fact occurred, and a new state has emerged with its own government, not dependent on another, and functioning effectively over the territory concerned, then recognition will follow.

If the 'peoples' entitled to self-determination are the entire peoples of a state, then it becomes unnecessary to answer the difficult question of whether a *particular* minority group, for example, Nagas in India, or Basques in France, or Indians in Canada—are 'peoples' for purposes of self-determination under Article 1 of the Covenant. But, of course, the question will still remain as to whether every such group is a minority for purposes of Article 27 (the article that deals with minority rights). That is beyond the scope of this chapter, but those who have assumed that self-determination is a right in the hands of special groups, rather than the people as a whole, have been faced with the two-step problem: What constitutes a minority? And are all minorities 'peoples' for purposes of self-determination?

The Committee on Human Rights under the Covenant on Civil and Political Rights has not—some apparently believe—decided that certain groups are not 'peoples' for purposes of self-determination. Its view of self-determination as a right of *all* the peoples in a territory has in fact precluded the necessity of such a finding. But it has had to make certain findings *of a jurisdictional nature* on self-determination that we may usefully mention at this point. Under the Optional Protocol individuals may bring complaints against state parties to the Covenant accepting that procedure. The Optional Protocol provides that claims may be brought concerning 'violations of any of the rights set forth in the Covenant' (Preamble, Articles 1 and 2) and 'any provision of the Covenant' (Article 4). Self-determination is undoubtedly a right 'set forth in the Covenant'. At first sight there would seem to be no difficulty in the Committee dealing with claims ('communications') on self-determination. But the Optional Protocol also stipulates that communications may be brought by '*individuals . . .* who claim to be victims of violation of any of the rights set forth in the Covenant' (Article 1). The Rules of Procedure of the Human Rights Committee in turn emphasize that the communication is to be submitted by the individual concerned. There is no possibility for group or class actions under the Covenant procedures. The Committee has thus been faced with the dilemma. The right of self-determination is a right in the Covenant—albeit a right of a different kind from the rest, standing alone in Part I of the Covenant. But it is a right by peoples, not of any individual; and only individuals may bring communications. Dealing with a series of cases in which groups have claimed that they were indeed 'peoples' for purposes of Article 1 of the Covenant (the Mikmaq Indians and Lubicon Lake Band Indians of Canada, and the Samis of Sweden), the Committee has determined as follows:

While all peoples have the right of self determination and the right freely to determine their political status, pursue their economic, social and cultural development and dispose of their natural wealth and resources, as stipulated in Article 1 of the Covenant, the question whether the Lubicon Lake Band constitutes a 'people' is not an issue for the Committee to address under the Optional Protocol to the Covenant. The Optional Protocol provides a procedure under which individuals can claim that their individual rights have been violated. These rights are set out in Part III of the Covenant, articles 6–27, inclusive.[38]

Of course, individuals may join in bringing a claim in which they each have had an individual right infringed. And it should be understood also that minority rights are *individual* rights. Article 27 is couched in terms of the rights of the *individual* as a member of a minority.

One further issue on self-determination remains to be mentioned. It follows from the principle of territorial integrity. It is often the case that self-determination is part of the armoury of rhetoric in what is essentially a dispute about territorial title. Both the case of Gibraltar and that of the Falklands illustrate the point. Title to Gibraltar is disputed between the United Kingdom and Spain. Title to the Falklands–Malvinas is disputed between the United Kingdom and Argentina. From the perspective of the United Kingdom, self-determination has a pertinent role to play. These are dependent territories, whose peoples have been given the opportunity to decide if they would like to remain in the status quo or not. From the British point of view, it is important that the wishes of the peoples of the territories be heard and heeded. But from the point of view of the Argentinians and the Spanish, that is an irrelevance. If the territory concerned belongs to Argentina, or to Spain, then the inhabitants have no right of self-determination—any more than would Spanish or Argentinian nationals happening to live in the United Kingdom. Judge Hardy Dillard's famous dictum in the *Western Sahara Case* has been much quoted: 'It is for the people to determine the destiny of the territory and not the territory the destiny of the people.'[39]

Attractive an aphorism though it is, it still has to be said that the territorial issue *does* come first. Until it is determined where territorial sovereignty lies, it is impossible to see if the inhabitants have a right of self-determination. Thus in the *Western Sahara Case* it was necessary first to see if the territory did indeed belong to Mauritania or Morocco. If so, the

[38] *Lubicon Lake Band* v. *Canada* UNDOC A/42/40 (1984), para. 32.1; Communication No. 167/1984.
[39] ICJ Reports (1975) 12 at 122 (sep. op. Judge Dillard).

peoples of Western Sahara would have had no right of self-determination (other than the ongoing right that all citizens of those countries have to determine their own political status and economic development). As neither country had sovereignty over Western Sahara, that territory was indeed a colonial dependency of Spain, whose peoples were entitled to exercise self-determination and choose their own destiny. It necessarily follows from all that I have said that I do not share the view of those who see the current problems of Hong Kong as problems of self-determination. At least so far as the leased territories are concerned, it is clear that title lies with China and must revert there in 1997. The issue in my view is to secure the generality of human rights of all in Hong Kong after that time rather than to insist that they have been denied the right of self-determination.

Conclusion

Self-determination, having for years been denied as a legal right by vested interests in the West, Eastern Europe, and Third World alike, now faces a new danger: that of being all things to all men.

The role of the international lawyer remains constant—to eschew current fashion when it is intellectually unsound, and to provide the analysis that shows how, properly understood, this important principle of international law can serve common values.

8

NATURAL RESOURCES AND
INTERNATIONAL NORMS

To study the international law of natural resources is rapidly to discover that it is not a single, monolithic topic. Almost everything depends, if not on the specific resource, on the category of natural resource that one is studying. Not only the answers, but indeed the questions that it is necessary to ask, will depend upon that initial matter. Let me take the following three broad examples of natural resources to illustrate the point: the mineral resources of the deep sea-bed; water, including water as it is carried along by the great international rivers; and petroleum found on shore, or beneath a state's territorial waters, or on its continental shelf. The mineral resources of the deep sea-bed are located in an area beyond national jurisdiction. Who may exploit them? Indeed, how will it be determined who may exploit them? How is it to be done, and within what constraints? And what of water carried by international rivers? Under whose jurisdiction do these rivers and their precious resource fall? Is each section of the river to be treated as a resource under separate national sovereignty? Does international law place any restraints on state freedom over the uses of water and control of water? And where do any such normative constraints come from? Petroleum is most usually found in areas within the jurisdiction of a state. Sometimes it will be found in areas of full sovereign jurisdiction, and sometimes in areas of functional jurisdiction. Sometimes it is located in areas of shared jurisdiction. What difference does all of this make? Does the location of the resource determine all the issues, giving the territorial state full freedom to do exactly what it wants, when it wants, in relation to the resource? And where do we find the legal answers to these questions?

Let me consider, briefly, each of these three categories, to elaborate in a little more detail the very different issues that they have generated.

The Resources of the Deep Sea-Bed

From the earliest days of international law there was developed the idea of the freedom of the high seas.[1] That was first codified in the UN Convention on the High Seas of 1958. Whereas specific provisions in that

[1] Grotius, *Mare liberum* (1609). Cf. Gentilis, *Advocatio Hispanica* (1613), and Selden, *Mare clausum sive de dominio maris* (1618). Cf. further Bynkershoek, *De dominio maris*

treaty may not have been binding on non-parties, the basic status of the
high seas undoubtedly represented what was already customary international law. It had always been assumed that the freedom of the high seas
also entailed a freedom to remove the resources that were found in those
waters. Fishing on the high seas requires no one's permission, because no
one has title over the high seas. During the 1950s it was beginning to be
apparent that fish were not the only important resource of the high seas.
Beneath the waters, in the sea-bed itself, there were resources of a
different kind—mineral resources certainly, with manganese, cobalt, and
nickel in clear evidence. It was also likely that petroleum too lay within
certain parts of the deep sea-bed. Moreover, the time could not be far
distant when it would be possible to exploit these resources, for human
benefit and for commercial gain. The Government of Malta in 1967
introduced into the UN General Assembly an idea that was to have a
profound effect on the way international law developed in relation to these
newly perceived realities.[2] It was there suggested that the resources of the
deep sea-bed were 'common heritage of mankind', and that this notion of
common heritage over a resource was different from the perception of, for
example, fish in the waters of the high seas. In the latter case, fish were *res
nullius*—that is to say, belonging to no one, and therefore exploitable by
anyone who wished to, and was in a position to, exploit them. But a
resource that was termed a 'common heritage' apparently meant something different: it meant a resource that could, like the fish swimming
above it, in principle be exploited by anyone—but only with the permission
of the world community and upon such conditions as the institutions
representing that community would lay down. It is hard to see any reason
of logic why, in areas beyond national jurisdiction, resources in water (fish,
plankton, indeed the water itself) should be treated as *res nullius*; whereas
in those same areas resources located in the sea-bed, rather than in the
water above it, should be treated as falling under a different regime—one
in which the legal consequences of commonality and lack of state
jurisdiction would be treated differently. But of course it was not simply a
matter of logic. There were economic and political considerations at play.
The economic consideration was that the resources of the deep sea-bed
were likely to be of profoundly more commercial value than the fish that
swim above them. And we live in a world of finite and dwindling natural
resources. The political consideration at play was that the *res nullius*
approach to commonality meant that, while *anyone* could exploit these

(1702); and on the history of evolving acceptance of the freedom of the high seas, D.
O'Connell, *International Law* (1982), i. ch. 1.

    [2] See the adoption by the General Assembly of the Declaration of Principles on the Seabed
and Ocean Floor, GA Res. 2749 (XXV), 1970.

resources, in fact only a few did so. To allow any state to explore and exploit the mineral resources of the deep sea-bed was not as open as it seemed, because only a handful of states would have the material wealth and the technical know-how to be able to engage in this activity. What was in principle open to all would in reality become a resource in the hands of a few. Of course, it might be argued that that did not matter, that indeed it made good sense for those states with the financial and technical capability to do the physical exploring and exploiting; what *did* matter was that these resources should then be made available, through the market, to the community as a whole. Whether one agrees with this will depend upon one's political philosophy. In any event, it was a reply clearly unacceptable to the numerical majority of the General Assembly, who also took the view that prices would inevitably be set by those who did the physical exploring and exploiting, and that the resources would often be put on the market at a price beyond the reach of the poor countries, making common access to a resource beyond any single state's jurisdiction an illusion.

It was these underlying policy purposes that the notion of 'common heritage of mankind' served. And it was interesting to see how, in a short space of time, this notion was widely perceived as having a normative quality. Repeated invocation before various organs, repetition in the texts of various instruments, analysis by scholarly writing, all began to attribute the concept with the quality of an emerging norm. The General Assembly before long passed a resolution calling for a moratorium on the exploitation of the deep sea-bed pending the conclusion of international agreement as to how the legal regime of the common heritage of mankind would operate.[3] In fact, that agreement was being sought within the wider framework of the multilateral negotiation for a new, comprehensive, law of the sea treaty—the United Nations Convention on the Law of the Sea (UNCLOS). The proposals for UNCLOS contained various separate parts, on the territorial sea, on the continental shelf, on the new concept of the exclusive economic zone, on scientific matters—and on the deep sea-bed. But these were to be a 'package deal'. They were negotiated together, over a period of fifteen years, and they were to stand or fall in their entirety. No state could expect to be fully satisfied with every element in the vast treaty; but it was hoped that all would find their interests sufficiently represented in most of the treaty that they would be prepared to accept the parts they did not like. For a while it appeared that this might be the case. The advanced industrial states that had the potential capability to exploit the sea-bed expressed deep reservations about the legal basis of the concept of 'common heritage of mankind', but were prepared to discuss its implications and participate in its fashioning. But the Assembly-recommended moratorium was resisted as lacking in legal basis, and

[3] GA Res. 2574 (XXIV) 1969.

virtually all the states concerned took domestic legal powers to exploit the deep sea-bed when the moment might be ripe.[4] It is an interesting illustration of the gradual fashioning of practice, and perhaps *opinio juris*, that some of these measures made provision for the putting-on-one-side of sums for contribution, in due course, to an international institutional fund that might be required if the UNCLOS proposals for the deep sea-bed succeeded. These proposals essentially envisaged a UN licensing authority which would, upon payment of a fee, grant a licence to explore and exploit; that certain parts of the proposed licence areas were, moreover, to be set aside for future exploitation by a different international body, which would sit on behalf of those poorer states that did not have the financial or territorial base to explore and exploit themselves. Royalties would also be paid by successful licence holders to help this body.[5]

At the end of the day the advanced industrial states found this unacceptable. While for the most part rather satisfied with UNCLOS as a whole, the section on the deep sea-bed was, from their perspective, so unsatisfactory that they were prepared to refuse to accept the treaty as a whole. At the time of writing the 1982 UNCLOS has not yet entered into force—though the number of ratifying parties is making that a less distant prospect, with the consequence that some further efforts are currently being made by all the parties concerned to see whether the gap in approach cannot still be bridged. At the same time, in significant part for economic reasons, no exploitation of the resources of the deep sea-bed has yet been attempted. There is thus a 'legal stand-off'. For the moment, therefore, there remains a somewhat uncertain range of questions, and answers, about mineral resources on the deep sea-bed. Would it really be unlawful under general international law for a state unilaterally to attempt to exploit the mineral resources of the deep sea-bed? The question, and its answer, is really all about the sources of international law—about emerging custom (especially when state practice is 'on paper' only), about *opinio juris*, about what evidences are required. If one applied the test offered by Professor Dupuy in the *BP–Texaco Case*,[6] where the UN resolutions had to have the support of the major actors in the practice in question (the capital-investing countries, in that case), the case would not seem to be made for the 'common heritage of mankind' to be regarded as a compulsory norm. But the matter is not entirely analogous to *BP–Texaco*—the support of the great majority of UN members for the common-heritage approach was evidenced by the text of a negotiated treaty, and that text was approved by many of the industrialized governments—albeit at the end of the day they

---

[4] See legislation of FRG (1980) 19 *ILM* 1330; France (1982) 21 *ILM* 808; Japan (1983) 22 *ILM* 102; United Kingdom (1981) 20 *ILM* 1217; USA (1980) 19 *ILM* 1003.
[5] See Part XI of the 1982 Convention, UN Doc. A/CONF. 62/122; (1982) 21 *ILM* 1261.
[6] *BP* v. *Libyan Arab Republic* 53 ILR 297.

did not ratify. And their national legislation, and their hesitation in acting under it, shows some sensitivity to the 'common-heritage' approach. The issues are far from easy to resolve. What we can say is that the key issues that have surrounded the natural resources of the deep sea-bed have largely concerned questions of jurisdiction and law development.

Water as a Resource

It has been somewhat different with the question of international rivers. International rivers carry water—the most important of all resources, providing the basis for life and sustenance, as well as sources of energy— through the territories of two or more states. Does the upper riparian state have lawful control over the river in its entirety, in the sense that it has territorial sovereignty over the river where it rises, and may do with it what it wants at that point? Or—a small variation on this possibility—does each state have full sovereignty over the river as it is present within its national territory, able to do what it wishes with the resources within the confines of its jurisdiction? Of course, if that is so, the state where the river waters rise may choose to exercise its entitlements in such a way that all or part of the water flow to the other riperians is cut off, so that what *they* in turn may freely exercise control over is non-existent, or substantially diminished. Some early views of interested parties were heard in support of the principle of full territorial sovereignty being applicable to the various segments of international rivers. Attorney-General Harmon's views on US entitlement on the Rio Grande are the classic example.[7] It follows, of course, that, if international law allows a state *full* freedom of action over a river within its territory, then no damage can lie for any consequences that ensue to other lower riparians.

As before, when we try to identify the substance of the international law on natural resources, the pertinent questions and answers cannot be studied without a keen appreciation of the diversity of the sources that assist in legal development. In matters relating to the deep sea-bed, we look at state practice, the role of the United Nations, the status of unratified treaty texts, etc. The development of the law on the non-navigable uses (i.e. resource uses) of international rivers has a rather different provenance. There are two or three important cases and arbitrations,[8] to be sure—but they were all against the background of agreed treaties, or of agreed *compromis*, and so have to be relied on rather cautiously. And there is an extremely complex pattern of state behaviour,

---

[7] 21 *Opinions Attorney-General* (1895) 274 at 282–3.
[8] See *Lake Lanoux Arbitration* 24 ILR 101; *Diversion of the Waters of the River Meuse Case* (1937) PCIJ Ser. A/B, no. 70, p. 70; *Trail Smelter Arbitration* (1939) 33 AJIL 182–212.

as revealed in various watercourse disputes, claims articulated, and solutions agreed. These too often have to be read on their special facts. There are also a huge number of international treaties, bilateral and multilateral on specific rivers, directed mostly to navigational aspects. Unusually, to date, the law on water as a natural resource has been mostly developed through attempts at codification by private international law bodies, notably, the International Law Association and the Institut de Droit International, each of which has over the years had this topic on its agenda. The International Law Association represents a wide gathering of international lawyers, of varying seniority and nationalities. The Institut de Droit International is smaller, with an invitational membership of lawyers of considerable seniority, with a preponderance of Western membership. But it is what has emerged as common ground from the codification efforts of each of these bodies that interests us—not least because, as we shall see, those principles are invoked as normative both by decision-makers and by those who seek today to carry forward the process of codification.[9]

Certain key principles have emerged. A state does indeed have sovereignty over the water resource in its own territory—but within the limits of what is permitted by international law. The important thing, therefore, is to identify the relevant international-law constraints. International law requires that, in the exercise of sovereignty, regard must be had to the legitimate interests of other users of the water. Legitimate interests have come to be defined as an equitable share in the beneficial use of the resource. It has not been possible to define 'equitable' and 'beneficial' in isolation of each other. The defining clauses are compendious. But the starting-point, in my view, has to be to decide what is a beneficial use. Then one can proceed to the even more difficult question of an equitable share in that use. Through the evolution of the international instruments to which I have referred, there has emerged a series of criteria (not hierarchical, but all important) that have to be taken into account when deciding whether a use is beneficial. What is the purpose of the use? Is it to provide drinking water; or irrigation; or an energy source; or is it recreational? Is the particular use to be provided for in a wasteful, or conserving, way? Has there been past waste of this precious resource? It is important to know, too, whether there are alternative water resources elsewhere in the country, or whether it is solely or primarily dependent on the proposed use of the particular stretch of international river.[10]

[9] See particularly the Madrid Declaration of the Institut de Droit International: (1911) 24 *Annuaire Yearbook* 365; the Salzburg Resolution of the Institut de Droit International: (1961) 49 *Annuaire Yearbook* ii. 381; New York Resolution of the ILA: *Report of 48th Conference*, pp. viii–x; Helsinki Rules of the ILA, *Report of the 52nd Conference* (1966).
[10] See Art. 4, Helsinki Rules.

The answers to all these questions will have to be compared, in a given case, with the same questions asked of a competing user of the resource. There may be desirable, and important, uses in several riparians: there is no avoiding the need to weigh them against the background of the criteria indicated. This weighing process (which allows one to ascertain the equitable share in a beneficial use) involves other questions, too. Does a beneficial use already exist in one of the states, which the other state wants to displace in favour of a new use of its own? Has the state that has already been using the resource (part of which is now demanded by another) used it prudently? Can water resources be 'put aside'—that is, not allowed for current use by another, because there are plans pending for a new beneficial use programme that would be preferable to the current use of the other state?

The contribution of the International Law Association and the Institut has been to develop the notion of sovereignty limited by international law obligation; to conceptualize the obligation as the entitlement of all watercourse states to an equitable share in beneficial use; and to provide the criteria for deciding whether uses fall into these categories. Norms on priority of present use against future use have emerged less clearly through these unusual sources. The emerging entitlement to an equitable share in beneficial use has, almost incidentally, resolved other long-running problems. The first is as to whether a riparian who wishes to alter the natural flow of a watercourse requires the consent of the other riparians. Many Spanish-speaking states have long insisted that the answer is in the affirmative: prior permission is required, because, even if no adverse consequences result for the other riparians from the diversion of the waters, their flow has passed from nature to another state. But the Arbitral Tribunal in the *Lake Lanoux Case* thought otherwise.[11] Prior consent was not needed and it was not to be assumed that a state would intend to act in a way to cause harm to a co-riparian. With one early exception,[12] none of the ILA or Institut resolutions require prior permission for change to the flow of water, whether as to line of its flow or as to its quantum or content. The essential test will be whether those changes meet the test of beneficial use, and whether they leave the other riparians with an equitable share in respect of their own beneficial uses.

The second element that is resolved as a necessary result of the equitable share of a beneficial-use formula is the question of whether compensation is due for change. As there is no duty *not* to change the flow of water, or to change the use by an upper riparian, there can be no duty to compensate on the basis of damage for unlawful acts. But some changes may be permitted that do in fact cause a *measure* of harm. The evolving

---

[11] 24 ILR 101 at 140.   [12] The Madrid Declaration of 1911.

international legal standard is that, unless appreciable and significant harm is caused, no compensation will be due.

The approach to the development of the international law on water as a resource has taken a significantly different turn since it has been under consideration by the ILC. The first Special Rapporteur was Judge Schwebel, before his elevation to the Court. He based himself on the emerging norms, and sought to build on them in a variety of ways, including by the introduction of a concept of a *watercourse system*, in which the emphasis was not so much on state sovereignty but on riparian states as participants in a *shared* resource. Although there has been some stepping back from the terminology introduced by Judge Schwebel, the underlying idea has taken root.[13] After a brief period under the special rapporteurship of Judge Evenson,[14] before *his* elevation to the Court, the matter passed into the hands of Professor McCaffrey, who guided the ILC's work to the adoption of the first reading of the draft articles in 1991.[15] His work has led to an entirely new layer being added to the emergent substantive rules. This layer consists of what we may call the procedural law of co-operation. The ILC text now contains a plethora of international obligations—not of substance, but obligations relating to a duty to *inform* on the one hand and to *consult* on the other. It has, in other words, been regarded as insufficient to resolve conflicts to have provided a list of criteria for the unilateral application by claimant states. Conflict can better be *avoided* by talking and by information sharing. The ILC text requires, in rather specific detail, the sharing of all sorts of technical information and planning intentions among watercourse states. And although there is no requirement of prior consent, there *is* an obligation to consult—and further detailed provisions for third-party procedures if the consultations do not lead to agreement. This striking interweaving of developing substantive norms, and the avoidance of conflict in relation to them through the specification of very detailed procedures for co-operation, is a phenomenon that one begins to see repeated elsewhere.

Petroleum Deposits

International law as it bears on petroleum is yet again different. Although there may well be petroleum deposits beneath the deep sea-bed, it has so far proved neither necessary nor attractive to seek to recover these.

---

[13] *Yearbook of ILC* (1980), ii. pt. 1, p. 159.
[14] Report of the ILC on the work of its 41st session, A/44/10, GAOR 44th sess. (1991), paras. 621–36.
[15] Report of the ILC on the work of its 43rd session, A/46/10, GAOR 46th sess. (1991), p. 152.

Virtually all known commercial petroleum deposits are either on-shore or under territorial waters (and clearly within state territory), or in the continental shelf. As for the latter, it is a commonplace that the initially unilateral acts[16] by which states asserted jurisdiction for the purpose of resources exploitation over the continental shelf rather rapidly became a permissive rule of customary international law, that was in turn recognized in the 1958 Geneva Convention on the Continental Shelf.[17] The definition of the outer limits of the continental shelf (and thus of lawful exploitability) speedily became problematic. The 1958 formula had been for the shelf to be measured either by a designated depth of 200 metres or by exploitability; and the assumption was that these were virtually identical.[18] But rapidly evolving technology soon made it apparent that it was possible to exploit the resources at deeper levels. Until the 1982 UNCLOS enters into force, it must remain questionable as to whether the new definition[19] of the outer limits of the shelf (in which legal entitlement is no longer clearly tied to considerations of geography and geology about the nature of the shelf) represents customary international law. It would seem that these provisions are so widely accepted, and that there has been such an absence of protest at states acting on reliance on the new definitions, that they *do* represent current international law. The remaining controversies are not about the definition of the shelf, but about the proposals for delimiting adjacent or overlapping shelves—a different question from the subject of this lecture.

Do we conclude, then, that petroleum reserves beneath the continental shelf are exactly the same, from the legal perspective, as reserves beneath a desert in the interior of a state? That would be an oversimplification. There is clear sovereignty over all of one's land mass. No other state has an entitlement and it is a matter for the discretion of the state concerned as to whether it takes title itself over all mineral reserves, or allows them to be owned by the owners of the superjacent soil. But the Continental Shelf Conventions—whether of 1958 or of 1982—provide that the coastal state has sovereign jurisdiction for purposes of the exploration and exploitation of the resource. It is a *functional* sovereignty. The distinction has been one of great legal importance. In the first place, states have had to take care that any legislation they pass which purports to have application on the shelf (criminal legislation, civil legislation, and tax legislation) is limited to matters relating to the exploration and exploitation of shelf resources. The reach of criminal jurisdiction and civil liability has led to interesting case law in a variety of jurisdictions. So too has the question of shelf taxation. The issue of whether a state may tax a company that operates on its shelf

[16] Truman Proclamation of 1946; and comparable claims by various UK dependent territories, large numbers of South American states, and others. For texts, see *Laws and Regulations on the Regime of the High Seas* (UN publ.), i. (1951), 38 ff.
[17] Art. 2. [18] Art. 1. [19] Art. 76, 1982 Convention.

without having any office within its jurisdiction, and which is not itself engaged in exploring and exploiting, has occasioned particular difficulty in the North Sea. Service companies, with vessels providing food or entertainment on platforms, have resisted their liability to tax at the hands of the coastal state. Again, the local jurisdiction will have to interpret the tax legislation against the specific jurisdiction authorized under international law.[20]

There is an even more important consideration. If on-shore mineral resources have been vested in the state, it is clear that it owns them. But it has no right of ownership in the resources *in situ* in the continental shelf—it has only sovereignty for the purposes of exploring and exploiting. This means no-one else may explore and exploit without permission; that it may grant licences for that purpose; but it does not *itself* 'own' the petroleum. What then does a licensee of off-shore petroleum get? The old style on-shore concession often passed title *in situ* to the holder of the concession. But the holder of an off-shore licence cannot thereby get title to a resource over which the licensing government does not itself get title. It gets, instead, an entitlement to explore and exploit (which action would otherwise be illegal) and to reduce into possession. It is the actual reduction into possession which gives the licensee title. Thus it is, for example, that in the North Sea title passes not with the granting of the licence but at the well-head, when the recovered petroleum is reduced into possession.

Why does all of this matter? It matters at the most prosaic level because there are implications for lending institutions. Loans to the licensee cannot be secured against collateral in the form of resources owned by the licensee. Any government could always stop the intended reduction into possession through unilateral action. In the event, investors and other non-licence-holding partners have evolved a variety of financial techniques, whereby repayment for a loan, or the recouping of profit on an investment, are made by reference to the barrels of oil produced, or the cash they represent. Complicated questions, relevant for domestic law, as to whether these various arrangements represent an interest in the petroleum itself, have also arisen.[21]

But it is important too in the context of a government's ability to terminate, alter, or indirectly take the benefit of a licence. The exact entitlement of a licensee under international law in these circumstances is a hard enough question. The question is harder still when what is altered or taken is not the title to petroleum, but the entitlement to reduce the petroleum into possession.

[20] See T. Daintith and G. Willoughby, *Manual of United Kingdom Oil and Gas Law* (1984), 1–1107.   [21] Ibid. i. 430.

It is to this aspect of state intervention that I now turn. But let me first set the scene. Where international rivers are concerned, the participants are various states and the constraints on their sovereign behaviour is a matter of pure international law. The constraints do not flow from any prior contractual relationship between them. Things are very different when we think of petroleum. The usual situation is that the resource is located within the jurisdiction of one state; that a foreign company (often private, though sometimes a public-sector company of another state) secures permission to search for and get the petroleum; the details of this arrangement are contained in one or more instruments to which both sides are party. The problems that occur thus present themselves in a very different manner. From the perspective of the foreign investor, the problem is sometimes put thus: how can he be sure that, given the vast investments he will be required to make, he will be allowed to reap the benefits of his investment and work effort, and that the rewards will not be taken from him just as his fulfilment of the contract terms begins to bear fruit (that is to say, petroleum)? From the perspective of the host government, the problem can be put thus: how can any arrangement entered into with a foreign oil company in respect of what is, all said and done, one's own natural resource, remain flexible enough so that one is not locked into terms that over a long period turn out to bear little relationship to changing market conditions? Further, how can one ensure that, notwithstanding the contractual arrangements with the foreign investor, the proper sovereign concerns of a government are met—that is to say, concern for health, safety, and regulatory standards; for ensuring that the local population do not suffer shortages on the one hand, and secure proper economic benefits from their natural resource on the other?

It is my firm view that the proper task of the international lawyer is not to pronounce upon who is 'right' or 'wrong', as if the investors or the governments have a monopoly of legal virtue. Rather, we must use the opportunities provided by international law to see whether these difficulties can be avoided, contained, and if necessary resolved, in a manner that is acceptable to both parties and is in the common interest.

The necessary first question is whether international law has a role to play at all. Some have suggested that, if in an international contract for the exploitation of natural resources the proper law is the national law, that is essentially the end of the matter.[22] If any changes imposed by government—whether in the form of more onerous contract terms, or higher taxation, or even a nationalization of the property—are lawful under the national law, then that is all that matters, as that is the law governing the

---

[22] F. A. Mann, 'State Contracts and State Responsibility' (1960) 54 *AJIL* 572. See also C. F. Amerasinghe, 'State Breaches of Contracts with Aliens and International Law' (1964) 58 *AJIL* 881.

contractual relationships. Others take a different view, saying that the proper law of the contract will indeed determine the interpretation and application of the specific provisions; international law remains ever-present in any transnational relationship, bringing into play all the norms relating not only to the treatment of foreigners, denial of justice, and good faith, but also those relating to the taking of property.[23]

But it is rather like a juggler's trick. There are so many balls in the air at once that it is hard to see which one is actually critical at any particular moment. Are we sure it is *property* we are speaking about? In an old-style concession the investor secured title to the petroleum *in situ*. In off-shore petroleum, for reasons that I have explained, he does not. But it is now well accepted that contract rights are themselves a form of property.[24] Why does it matter? Why is it not enough for us to deal with the matter as one of contract law? The answer is that international law has rather a lot to say on property and relatively little on transnational contracts (save by analogy with the law relating to international treaties). Also, the distinction between mere breach of a contract and a taking of property will have relevance for the determination of any compensation.

It seems to me undeniable that international arbitrators, as a species, are disposed to finding that international law is indeed relevant to such matters, even when faced by a domestic governing law clause. The *Egoth*[25] and *Settebello*[26] cases are clear examples of transnational contracts governed by domestic law: but in both cases international law was given its place. In the former the arbitrators found that reference to a national law necessarily includes international law, as that is part of the law of the land. (Of course, this is an argument that counsel who wants international law to be considered, notwithstanding that the contract is governed by domestic law, will always bring into play. But in some countries international law will have the same status as domestic law; in many others it will be applicable only to the extent that statutes do not provide for incompatible provisions.) In the *Settebello Case* the arbitrators were simply unwilling, given the particular facts before them and their position as international arbitrators, to apply the national law alone. International law *had* to have a role. This was in part a result-oriented determination of the proper law issue and in part an illustration of a principle enunciated by Professor Dupuy when sitting as sole arbitrator in the *Texaco–Libya Case*. There he found that the very fact that there was to be international arbitration

---

[23] R. Jennings, 'State Contracts in International Law' (1961) 37 *BYIL* 156.
[24] *German Interests in Polish Upper Silesia Case* (1926) PCIJ Ser. A, no. 17; *Norwegian Shipowners Claims* (1922) 1 UNRIAA 307.
[25] *SPP (Middle East) Ltd.* v. *Arab Republic of Egypt* (1983) 22 *ILM* 752.
[26] Unreported. For ancillary litigation, see *Settebello Ltd* v. *Banco Totta and Acores* [1985] 2 AER 1025.

'internalized' the contract, making it inevitable that international law would have a role to play.[27] His reasoning was that a foreign investor would be nervous to put himself solely at the mercy of a domestic law, which definitionally a government would be able to change; and that *sole* reliance on domestic law was avoided by ensuring that the case went to international arbitration. Of course, the best way to avoid sole reliance on domestic law is, one has to say, by having a governing law clause that introduces international law. If, in the bargaining process, the private party has been unable to accomplish this, it seems doubtful that international arbitrators should remedy that which one of the negotiating parties was unable to achieve. At the same time, the purpose of the reference to international arbitration certainly merits examination. Was it because the local courts are not trusted or because a different system of law was to be applied?

But the study of arbitral practices tells us this: whether there is only a domestic-law-proper law clause; or whether there is a 'mixed' international-law and domestic-law clause (as in the Libyan arbitrations or in Article 42 of the International Convention for the Settlement of Investment Disputes), international arbitrators are very likely to find international law relevant.

If international law is in play, what does it tell us? A few brief points may be made. First, the concept of the permanent sovereignty over natural resources, which emerged as a concept formulated in UN resolutions and invoked in various tribunals and writings, was challenged in significant part by the industrialized countries. Part of the problem was that no two resolutions which form the stream of source materials that make up the concept say the same thing. Some do require compensation, some do not. Some do refer to international legal standards, some do not. Some do make reference to binding obligations, some do not.[28] I think that, with the passage of time, and the refinement of the issues in the great oil arbitrations,[29] the concept has 'settled down'. It now stands for norms that command a significant common consensus, which I would summarize thus: states have a very special position in regard to their own resources. If, in their infancy as independent states, they assumed obligations out of all line with commercial realities, and if such arrangements were made for very

---

[27] 53 ILR 389. I should make it clear that in the *Texaco Case* there was a complex applicable law clause which, unlike those in *Egoth* and *Settebello*, made reference to international law as well as to domestic law.

[28] See the different terms of GA Res. 1803 (XVII); GA Res. 3171 (XXVII); GA Res. 320 (S-VI); GA Res. 3281 (XXIX).

[29] *Petroleum Development Limited* v. *Sheikh of Abu Dhabi*, 18 ILR 37; *Saudi Arabia* v. *Aramco*, 47 ILR 117; *Sapphire International Petroleum Ltd.* v. *NIOC*, 35 ILR 136; *BP* v. *Libyan Arab Republic*, 53 ILR 297; *Texaco* v. *Libyan Arab Republic*, 53 ILR 389; *Liamco* v. *Libyan Arab Republic*, 62 ILR 140; *Kuwait* v. *Aminoil*, 66 ILR 518.

long periods of time, tribunals look sympathetically at ways to liberate the state from the disadvantageous contract. In particular, clauses that seek to 'freeze' the situation at the moment of contracting are being accorded less and less efficacy by tribunals. Either they will not be regarded as stabilization clauses at all (as in the *Khemco Case*)[30] or it may be said that they must in terms prohibit nationalization for them to be interpreted to have that effect (as held in the *Aminoil Case*).[31] Attempts to secure negotiated change will today be tolerantly regarded.

At the same time, nationalizations do require compensation, and will only be lawful if they are not discriminatory and serve a public purpose. The concept of permanent sovereignty over natural resources does not leave a state free to ignore contracts it has voluntarily entered into.

I want to conclude with some comments on a current debate on one aspect of compensation.

What Elements are to be Included in Compensation for a Lawful Nationalization?

In the *BP–Libya Case* sole arbitrator Lagergren simply found that the Libyan Nationalization Law did 'constitute a fundamental breach of the BP concession' and 'further, the taking by the Respondent, of the property, rights and interests of the claimant clearly violates public international law as it was made for purely extraneous political reasons and was arbitrary and discriminatory in character'. He turned immediately to the question of remedies and there follows in the Award a very interesting analysis in which he argues against the availability of *restituto in integrum*. He concluded that 'the claimant is entitled to damages arising from the wrongful act of the Respondent'.[32] The nature and extent of the damage was left to be dealt with on another occasion, and ultimately a negotiated settlement was reached.

In *Texaco–Libya*, sole arbitrator Dupuy, dealing with essentially identical facts, found that the Government of Libya, 'by adopting the nationalization measures promulgated in 1973 and 1974, has failed to perform its obligations under the Deed of Concession entered into with the plaintiffs'. Unlike Judge Lagergren, Professor Dupuy believed *restituto* a remedy in principle available in international law, and called for performance of the contract.[33] Nothing more is in the public domain about damages in lieu of performance.

In the *Liamco Case*, sole arbitrator Mahmassani introduced a new

---

[30] *Amoco International Finance Corp.* v. *Islamic Republic of Iran* (1988) 27 *ILM* 1314.
[31] 66 ILR 518.   [32] 53 ILR 297 at 355.   [33] 53 ILR 389 at 507–8.

refinement into these matters. He made clear the concessions were both contractual obligations and incorporeal property. On the one hand, sanctity of contract is an integral part both of international law and Islamic law. On the other hand, the dominant trend of international opinion allowed states substantial rights over their natural resources. Unlike the other arbitrators, he then took separately the remedies for premature termination of contract and for the taking of property by nationalization. In fully accepting that the nationalization required compensation, he readily found that the damages should include, as a minimum, the *damnum emergens*, which he described as 'the value of the nationalised corporeal property, including all assets, installations, and various expenses incurred'.[34] But he thought much more controversial the question of whether the compensation should also include *lucrum cessans*, the loss of profits. He felt that the answer might depend upon whether the taking was lawful or not, and that *lucrum cessans* might be payable if the nationalization was unlawful. But the evolution of international law meant that states had the sovereign right to nationalize their natural resources; and Arbitrator Mahmassani concluded that 'it is lawful to nationalise concession rights before the expiry of the concession term, provided that the measure be not discriminatory nor in breach of treaty, and provided that compensation be duly paid'.[35] Turning to the question of *lucrum cessans* for a lawful nationalization, Arbitrator Mahmassani found primary applicable law (international law and Libyan law) unclear on the point, and resorted to the formula of 'equitable compensation'—by reference to which claims based on *lucrum cessans* were in effect excluded.

Professor Virally, in his important Award in the Anglo-Iranian Tribunal in the *Khemco Case (Amoco Finance)* took the analysis several stages further. Whereas Mahmassani, like every arbitrator before him, had emphasized the sanctity of contracts and had accepted that a nationalization required compensation for a prematurely ended contract, Professor Virally simply rejected that sovereign states are bound by contracts with private parties as, in his view, this would allow 'private interests to prevail over duly established public interest, making impossible actions required for the public good'.[36] I have to say I do not agree: a state may still engage in what it sees as actions in the public good that violate contracts; but there is no reason why the foreign investor should underwrite this exercise in state sovereignty. But our main point today is the different one of *lucrum cessans* and *lucrum emergens*. Professor Virally had found Iran not responsible for breach of contract; and the nationalization to be a lawful one. So, as with Liamco (but unlike BP and Texaco), the issue addressed

---

[34] 62 ILR 140 at 201.   [35] Ibid. 207.
[36] (1988) 27 *ILM* 1314, para. 178.

was the liability to pay *lucrum cessans*—lost profits—in a lawful national-ization. The *Chorzow Factory Case* provided for *restitutio* or, if impossible, its money equivalent:[37] but that was a case about an unlawful taking. Professor Virally noted that the Permanent Court had said that reparation must wipe out the consequences of the illegal act and re-establish the situation which would, in all probability, have existed if the act had not been committed.[38] And he pointed to a dictum of the Permanent Court in which it said that a limitation of compensation to value at the moment of dispossession would only have been possible 'if the Polish Government has had the right to expropriate, and if its wrongful act consisted merely in not having paid . . . the just price of what was expropriated'. He concluded that in a lawful expropriation only 'the just price of what was expropri-ated', representing 'value at the moment of dispossession', should be paid. Thus there would be *damnum emergens* (actual loss) but no *lucrum cessans* (loss of profits).

I have difficulties with this—and, I must frankly say, with the way things were put by the Permanent Court. I begin by saying that I do not believe a central element in the law of compensation should be resolved by making deductions from an *obiter dictum* of the Permanent Court forty-five years previously, when it was addressing only (and was only *thinking* about) a different situation—an unlawful taking. That being said, I am puzzled by the assumption that 'the just price of what was expropriated', by reference to 'value at the moment of dispossession', *does* exclude future profits. The value of property is what the market will pay for it. And if, at the moment of dispossession, an arms-length willing buyer could be found for that property, the price he would offer would (at least if the business was a going concern) reflect his estimate of certain profits. There is no 'real' value of property, to which the estimate of profits is then added. In a ten-year contract, if nationalization takes place in year 5, the value of the enterprise *as at year 5* will include the purchaser's estimate of unspeculative profits in years 6–10.

The issue of the contemporary place of *damnum emergens* and *lucrum cessans* presents us with an ideal case for resolution by policy analysis of alternatives, rather than by poring over a 1928 dictum of debatable economic reality. Inevitably, the arguments were finely balanced. If Professor Virally's view is right, then again foreign investors bear the burden of a state's economic freedom. It does not really suffice to say that, even if they do not secure compensation for future profits, they have been 'put back where they were' and thus sustain no real loss. In the economic sense they *do* sustain real loss, because their investment, which represents lost economic opportunities elsewhere, has been made on a calculation of

---

[37] (1928) PCIJ Ser. A, no. 17.   [38] (1988) 27 *ILM* 1361, para. 196.

these future profits. On the other hand, if there is not a softer valuation standard for lawful takings, and if the compensation will be the same, then there is no incentive for capital importing states to act lawfully: they might as well expropriate in a discriminatory fashion, for political objectives.

The answer might seem to lie not in excluding *lucrum cessans* from the valuation of lawful expropriations, but in including a penal element in the valuation of unlawful takings. But this assumes that the role of arbitral tribunals is to 'punish' states, to deal in penal damages rather than civil compensation. And this is not the case. My conclusion, for the moment, is that the value of the property does not change by virtue of the lawful or unlawful nature of its taking; and it is loss of confidence, rather than 'penal' valuation, that will provide the incentive to states none the less to expropriate lawfully, in accordance with international law.

9

ACCOUNTABILITY AND LIABILITY: THE LAW
OF STATE RESPONSIBILITY

JUST as it is important to understand how international law allocates competences among states, so it is important to understand how it determines the international responsibility of states. The law of jurisdiction is about *entitlements to act*, the law of state responsibility is about *obligations incurred when a state does act*. In the law of jurisdiction there are some areas of certainty and some more problematic aspects. In the law of state responsibility one might be forgiven for thinking that there is almost nothing that is certain. But it is traditionally regarded as an area of major importance, and a central element in the whole theoretical structure of international law. This chapter examines whether this traditional view is justified.

The study of state responsibility is inextricably bound up with the treatment of the subject by the the International Law Commission. The ILC, a body of experts in international law elected in their individual capacity, fulfils for the General Assembly of the United Nations the task given to it in Article 13 of the Charter: to 'initiate studies and make recommendations for the purpose of . . . encouraging the progressive development of international law and its codification'. It has long been accepted that these two tasks cannot be separated out, that codification necessarily entails some development, and that progressive development can encourage the prospects for codification. The question of state responsibility has been on the agenda of the ILC since 1953—and the conclusion of work on this topic is nowhere in sight. The difficulties that the ILC has had with the topic reflect the main different possible approaches and the fact that the topic has been handled by a series of different special rapporteurs, each with his own perspective. The first Special Rapporteur on the topic was Garcia Amador, appointed in 1955. He submitted six reports between 1956 and 1961. In 1962, seeking to take stock of the matter, the ILC appointed a subcommittee under the Chairmanship of Professor Ago (now Judge Ago of the International Court of Justice, and President of the Curatorium of the Academy). This subcommittee reported in 1963, following which the ILC entrusted Ago with the task of carrying the work forward. He was appointed as Special Rapporteur and produced eight reports between 1969 and 1979. Some thirty-two articles on State Responsibility were adopted by the Commission, on the basis of Ago's proposals, during the period 1973–9. But this was only part of a very much larger work project, and upon the resignation of Ago in 1979 that was carried forward by Professor Riphagen, who took over as Special Rapporteur. Between 1980 and 1986 he presented seven reports.[1] But since 1980 the Commission has in fact adopted only a further five articles. In 1987 Professor Arangio-Ruiz was appointed as Special Rapporteur. From 1988 to 1992 he produced four reports, but the topic has not received any special priority on the agenda of the ILC—indeed, at the forty-third session the Commission could not make time for any discussion of the third Arangio-Ruiz report. The third and fourth reports were taken together at the forty-fourth session of the ILC in 1992.[2] At its 2176th to 2180th meetings the Commission considered draft articles and a detailed and scholarly commentary on 'reparation by equivalent', interest, and satisfaction.

The work of each one of these rapporteurs represented not so much a continuation of what had gone before, but rather a great shift of direction. And these intermittent changes of direction reflected the deeply different views as to what the topic of state responsibility is all about, and how to proceed with its codification. It will be necessary to come back to this from time to time.

What, then, is the law of state responsibility all about? The most basic starting-point, and one that would command general agreement, is that it is about accountability for a violation of international law. If a state violates an international obligation, it bears responsibility for that violation. How could such an obvious matter lead to forty years' unresolved work? It seems unbelievable. Clearly some explanation is called for.

We must begin by asking what purpose even this basic formulation— accountability for internationally wrongful acts—serves. What does it *mean* to say that a state is 'accountable'? To say that a violation of an obligation is 'accountable' seems self-evident. But it can also mean two things. We say that a person is 'accountable' when we mean that he had the intention to perform the acts and/or the mental capacity to understand what he was doing. But the word 'accountable' also carries another overtone—that there is a liability for internationally wrongful behaviour and that that liability must be discharged.

Once we have put it this way, it can be seen that this simple, self-evident statement—'a state is accountable for a violation of an international obligation'—opens up a plethora of subsidiary questions. First of all, what

---

[1] For a useful resumé of the work of the ILC on state responsibility during this period, see M. Spinedi and B. Simma (eds.), *United Nations Codification of State Responsibility* (1987), 326–93.

[2] A/CN.4/440 and Add. 1; A/CN.4/444 and Corr. 1 and Add. 1, 2 and 3; see also A/CN.4/421 and Corr. 1 and A/CN.4/432.

do we mean by 'the state'? Is it *individuals* who are accountable? Or the state *in abstracto*? For whose acts exactly is the state responsible—for formal governmental decisions, or for acts of its employees? Can it ever be responsible for the acts of private persons? Then there is a completely different set of questions opened up by our initial proposition: What constitutes a violation of an international obligation? First of all, of course, one has to know what the obligation *is* before one can examine whether it has been violated. And then it is necessary to ask whether intention, or malice, is needed for a violation to have occurred. Are there circumstances in which acts that would normally be regarded as violations of an international obligation are *not* so to be regarded? And when we talk about violations of international obligations, are we speaking of *acts* or of *omissions* also? There is yet another avenue laid open by the commonplace observation 'a state is accountable for violations of an international obligation': namely, the equation of 'accountability' with redress. The law of state responsibility, it is said, entails the proposition that a state must provide redress for its breach of obligation.[3] But *what* redress? And to whom? Does harm have to be shown before compensation is due? And how is compensation to be determined and assessed?

One can now begin to see why a topic that should on the face of it take one summer's work has taken forty years. It has been interpreted to cover not only issues of attributability to the state, but also the entire substantive law of obligations, and the entirety of international law relating to compensation. As if all these difficulties were not enough, a further one has been added. Is there such conduct, for which states are responsible, that we should term not only violative of international obligation, but *criminal*? What does it mean to speak of 'an international crime', and what are the consequences, in terms of responsibility, for doing so?

In the literature, cases, and ILC discussions, these matters are often rolled up together. But it is useful to try to look at each of them in turn.

State Responsibility as Attributability of Prohibited Conduct

The Draft Articles adopted so far by the ILC have undoubtedly taken on a certain importance. They are widely invoked and are often spoken of as if they are authoritative—that is to say, reflecting (because they were so carefully prepared and submitted to governments before adoption) a widespread consensus, even though they are not a source of international

---

[3] 'It is a principle of international law that the breach of an engagement involves an obligation to make reparation in an adequate form' (*Chorzow Factory Case* (Jurisdiction) (1927) PCIJ Ser. A, no. 9, p. 21; see also *Chorzow Factory* (Indemnity) (1928) PCIJ Ser. A, no. 17, p. 29).

law in the formal sense of the term. Article 1 provides: 'Every internationally wrongful act by a State gives rise to international responsibility.' Article 3 continues:

An internationally wrongful act exists where:
   (a) Conduct consisting of an action or omission is imputed to a State under international law; and
   (b) Such conduct in itself or as a direct or indirect cause of an external event, constitutes a failure to carry out an international obligation of the State.

It is noteworthy that responsibility can lie for *omissions* that constitute a breach of international obligation, as well as for *commissions*. Ago characterized the attribution of acts and omissions as the 'subjective' element and the breach of the obligation as the 'objective' element, a classification that has certainly taken root,[4] though one could wonder why attributability is categorized as 'subjective'. But, in any event, I am here addressing the former concept, that of *attributability*. We think of the state as an abstract notion, but, as the Permanent Court of International Justice pointed out long ago in the *German Settlers in Poland Case*: 'States can only act by and through their agents and representatives.'[5] It has been a central element in the law of state responsibility that, where organs of state (such as government departments, or its courts), or individuals or groups in the employment of the state (the police, the army, customs officers) act in a way that violates international law, their conduct is attributed to the state, and the state is internationally responsible for such conduct. Many of the older cases that—in English law schools at least—form part of the syllabus of state responsibility are directed to this point. Thus in the *Youmans Case*,[6] before the Mexican–US General Claims Commission of 1926, it was held that the Mexican Government was responsible for the opening of fire by Mexican troops upon American citizens. The Tribunal cited in its award the formulation that had been advanced by the United States:

It seems almost needless to remark that such conduct on the part of soldiers . . . on the plainest principles of international law and independent of [the] treaty stipulations between the two nations . . . renders the Government in whose service they are employed, justly liable to the government of the men [whose lives were lost].

---

[4] R. Ago, Second Report on State Responsibility, *Yearbook of ILC* (1970), ii. 177 at 187. See also E. Jimenez de Arechaga, 'International Responsibility', in M. Sørensen (ed.), *Manual of Public International Law* (1968), 534; C. F. Amerasinghe, *State Responsibility for Injury to Aliens* (1967), 37.
[5] (1923) PCIJ Ser. B, no. 6, at p. 22.
[6] *Thomas H. Youmans (USA) v. United Mexican States* (1926) 4 RIAA 110.

Again, the *Caire Case*,[7] between France and Mexico, affirms the fact that the very fact that forces of a state engaged in an unlawful execution engaged the responsibility of the state. The forces *are* an emanation of the state. That very fact, it was made clear in the *Caire Case*, makes it unnecessary to show any *fault* or *malice* on the part of 'the state'.

Certain other things logically follow. The state will be responsible even if it did not specifically order the conduct concerned of its servants—if there was not any separate 'fault' of this type. Further, the state will be responsible even if its servants acted in ways clearly beyond what they were ordered to do. The case law and all the writers agree that a state will be responsible even for the *ultra vires* acts of its servants, that is to say, even when they acted beyond their powers.[8] Indeed, one can go further and say that, if an organ of state, or public servants of states, acted in a way expressly forbidden by the state and which violated international law, the state would still be responsible for that wrongful conduct.

Sometimes it has been suggested that this principle needs to be qualified, to exclude from state responsibility unlawful conduct by very low-ranking public officials. But this cannot be right, and indeed it has been rejected by the ILC in the way that it has formulated its draft articles[9] on this point. Referring to conduct by *organs* of states, Article 6 provides that it matters not what *type* of organ of state is concerned, or what internal function it performs, nor 'whether it holds a superior or subordinate position in the organisation of the state'. Article 8 deals with attribution to the state of the conduct of persons acting on behalf of the state. Although it does not say in terms that, here too, it matters not whether the persons held superior or subordinate positions, the fact that attribution of their conduct to the state is cast in general terms leads one to the same conclusion.

A graphic example is to be found in the acknowledgement by France of its responsibility for the acts of its security agents who in 1985 blew up the *Rainbow Warrior* in Auckland Harbour, New Zealand. These agents were acknowledged by the French Prime Minister to have acted on orders; but President Mitterrand fully accepted that the act was unlawful and engaged the international responsibility of France.[10] As to acts that are *ultra vires* or contrary to instructions, Article 10 provides:

The conduct of an organ of a State, of a territorial governmental entity or of an entity empowered to exercise elements of the governmental authority, such organ

---

[7] *Estate of Jean-Baptiste Caire (France)* v. *United Mexican States* (1929) 5 RIAA 516.

[8] Arechaga, 'International Responsibility', 548; T. Meron, 'International Responsibility of States for Unauthorized Acts of their Officials' (1957) 23 *BYIL* p. 85.

[9] Draft Articles 1–35 of Part I are published in *Yearbook of ILC* (1980), ii. pt. 2, pp. 30–4. Draft Articles 1–5 of Part II are published in the Report of the ILC on the work of its thirty-seventh session (1985), A/CN.4/L.478, pp. 2–3. These articles have been adopted on first reading.   [10] See *The Rainbow Warrior*, 74 ILR 241, esp. at 256–7, 261, 263.

having acted in that capacity, shall be considered as an act of the State under international law even if, in the particular case, the organ exceeded its competence according to internal law or contravened instructions concerning its activity.[11]

As for illegality, it is also clear that the fact that conduct is unlawful, indeed even exactly contrary to state instructions, does not avoid the responsibility of the state. That is because, from the perspective of outside, *all* organs and servants of the state *are* 'the state', and it is meaningless to be told that they acted contrary to the instructions of the state. This possibility was firmly rejected long ago by the Tribunal in the *Youmans Case* and then by the ILC.[12]

Some have contended that violation of commercial obligations cannot entail state responsibility. Thus Professor Reuter contended in the ILC discussion on State Responsibility:

legal acts of a commercial nature, such as acts of exchange or sale were never attributable to the State even if carried out by a State body. By contrast, in the case of issuing banks, for example, regardless of their internal status—whether they were private companies or State bodies—the issuing of currency was a regalian privilege, so that in international law the acts of issuing banks in monetary matters could be attributed to the State.[13]

What is of interest is that Reuter is using the classification familiar to the law of immunity for purposes of international responsibility. But these are two separate issues. In most domestic legal systems it is axiomatic that states are indeed responsible (liable) for the acts they engage in, whatever their nature. But the international law of state immunity, being interpreted and legislated upon at the local level, will determine whether there is an immunity from legal process in respect of such liability. Today it is widely accepted that there is immunity for *acta jure imperii* (the acts of 'regalian privilege', to use Professor Reuter's terminology); and no immunity for *acta jure gestionis* (commercial acts). But, unless there is a potential *liability* in domestic law, the exempting principle of *acta jure gestionis* has nothing to bite on.

Is there some principle that makes states not responsible for their commercial acts at the level of international law, even if they are liable in most municipal legal systems? It is hard to see what such a principle might be. If the Department of Agriculture of Ruritania acts fraudulently in its commercial relations with Company X, incorporated in Lilliput; and if the contract is said to be governed by international law and in due course

---

[11] *Yearbook of ILC* (1975), ii. 60. On *ultra vires* and state responsibility, see I. Brownlie, *System of the Law of Nations: State Responsibility*, pt. I (1983), 145–50; Amerasinghe, *State Responsibility for Injury to Aliens*, 104–14; and B. D. Smith, *State Responsibility and the Marine Environment* (1988), 31–4.

[12] (1926) 4 UNRIAA 110 at 115–16; and Art. 7, ILC Draft Articles, respectively.

[13] *Yearbook of the ILC* (1974), i. 1253rd meeting, p. 16.

Lilliput takes up the claim of Company X, is it really the case that there is no state responsibility of Ruritania for the unlawful commercial acts?

Other authors have suggested, in this context, that the key is a distinction to be made between torts and other acts. Thus Lady Fox has written:

> the conduct with which state responsibility is concerned is distinct and different from that involved in the private law of tort. State responsibility does not concern itself with private law commercial acts of the State, even where they have a tortious form: 'the fact that it is an alien who is the victim of the offence of theft or an act of pillage does not make it a matter of international law' (*British Claims in the Spanish Zone of Morocco* (1925) Report of Judge Max Huber on State Responsibility, 2 RIAA 615 at 641).[14]

But why should that be so? There seem to be two possible elements that might lead to this conclusion (though I do not believe it to be the right conclusion). First, the classic international law of state responsibility has been largely concerned with physical maltreatment of foreigners rather than with wrong done through commercial means. Secondly, there are those who think that no international wrong occurs until local remedies have been exhausted. Let us look at each in turn.

It is true that the old cases on state responsibility have in part been concerned with physical maltreatment of foreigners. They have been even more concerned with harm occasioned through the taking of the property of foreigners. Bernhard Graefrath, offering a Marxist perspective of this undeniable historical truth, has written: 'Since there was no prohibition of intervention, of war, of racism or colonialism . . . the whole system was confined to "civilized nations" and based on justification of colonialism and successful use of force.'[15] Be that as it may, there is no inherent reason why responsibility should attach at the international level only for certain types of harm done, and not for others—no reason why physical harm and the taking of property should be said to engage a state's responsibility, but fraudulent trading not to do so. The prime question of whether there is any international obligation not to breach an international contract, or cause injury by a tortious act,[16] appears capable in principle of an affirmative response.

---

[14] H. Fox, 'State Responsibility and Tort Proceedings against a Foreign State in Municipal Courts' (1989) 20 *Netherlands Yearbook of International Law* 3 at 12.

[15] B. Graefrath, 'Responsibility and Damages Caused: Relationship between Responsibility and Damages', *Recueil des cours* (1984, II) 9 at 24.

[16] I leave aside here the further complicating factor of a contract governed by local law, which is then altered to allow what would otherwise have seemed a breach of the contract by the state. The diverse views on the place of state responsibility in this scenario are well presented in F. A. Mann, 'State Contracts and State Responsibility' (1960) 54 *AJIL* 581; R. Jennings, 'State Contracts in International Law' (1961) 27 *BYIL* 156; C. F. Amerasinghe, 'State Breaches of Contracts with Aliens and International Law' (1964) 58 *AJIL* 881.

What then of the local-remedies rule? Is not the traditional stipulation correct—namely, that no international wrong (and thus no responsibility therefore) arises until local remedies have been exhausted? This received wisdom follows only if one accepts the starting-point—that the assault, or the breach of contract, or the fraudulent trading are not *themselves* international wrongs, being of interest only at the level of municipal law. From that starting-point (for which, as I have said, I certainly see a certain historical tendency, but no reason of principle or policy), it necessarily follows that the international wrong is only the failure to provide a remedy for a violation or breach of an obligation on the domestic plane.

As I believe that the obligations are substantive obligations of international law, I take the view that the obligation to go to the local courts operates to meet the requirements of the local-remedies rule—not to attach responsibility to the state for the first time. The field of human-rights law provides a graphic illustration of this principle. The obligations of states parties to the International Covenant on Civil and Political Rights is to guarantee the human rights of those within its jurisdiction. There is a quite discrete obligation to provide a remedy for any violation. Thus a state's obligation is 'not to maltreat Mr X'. It is not 'not to maltreat Mr X without paying compensation'. Nor does anything turn upon the fact that these obligations happen to be articulated in a treaty: the principle is applicable as a matter of obligation under general international law. It is true that human-rights violations are more analogous to public-law torts than to private-law torts of a commercial character. But it is hard to see that, if states act in the private-law area, they have no responsibility under international law for such acts, or only after local remedies have been exhausted.

If the basis for attributability of acts of organs or state servants is, quite properly, broad, what is the position concerning the acts of private individuals? Private conduct is not in principle attributable to the state. However, private conduct may still come to involve the responsibility of the state through a variety of possibilities. Let us look at them in turn. First, although private conduct is not the conduct of the state, the state has a general obligation to seek to protect the welfare of aliens by acting against lawlessness and promoting an orderly and safe society. We may call this a general duty to prevent attacks and harm on foreigners. That does not mean, of course, that, if an individual attacks a foreigner in a bar— even because he is motivated by xenophobia or racial hatred—that individual's government is responsible. The state's responsibility is to endeavour, through due diligence, to prevent harm to others. It thus follows that a state is not responsible for harm that is done to a foreigner as a consequence of civil disorder or of revolution. The Iran–USA Claims Tribunal has had occasion to affirm this on many occasions. Only if the revolutionaries are in fact those who become the new government, and only if their acts are specifically directed against foreigners, will the new government be responsible under international law.[17]

A state can become responsible for the acts of private individuals—if it encouraged them, and if the individuals effectively act as agents in the performance of these acts, and if it endorses as its own the acts of the individuals. These elements have been much discussed in a number of cases. The Iran–US Claims Tribunal had not been prepared to find that the strongly expressed anti-Americanism of the leaders of the revolution was the cause of violence against US personnel. But in some cases Chamber One has found that, although the Revolutionary Guards were not at the time an official organ of the Iranian state, 'their actions were attributable for the acts of private persons if it is established that those persons were in fact acting on behalf of the state'. The Tribunal determined that the Revolutionary Guards were exercising governmental authority, with the knowledge and acquiescence of the revolutionary government, which made Iran responsible for their acts.[18] But Chamber Two found, on very similar facts in another case,[19] that the acts of the Revolutionary Guards were not to be attributed to the State of Iran. The principles of law to be applied were clear to both Chambers; they read their application to the facts differently.

In the *US Hostages Case* the International Court of Justice noted that those attacking the US Embassy had no status as recognized agents of the state, and their conduct was not to be imputed to the state on that basis. Like the Iran–US Claims Tribunal, the Court would also not interpret the general declarations of the Ayatollah Khomeini as authorizing such operations. Nor even were the subsequent congratulations enough to alter the character of the militants' attack on the Embassy as non-governmental.[20] The Court in this case limited its finding of responsibility on the part of Iran to Iran's violations of duties owed under the 1961 Convention on Diplomatic Relations, with all its requirements to protect the Embassy and the diplomats, coupled with its omission to act and failure to establish control.

Revolutionary movements provide their own problems from the perspective of state responsibility. Article 14 of the ILC Draft Articles affirms that the conduct of an insurrectional movement is not to be considered the act of the state. Article 15 of the ILC Articles states that the act of an insurrectional movement which becomes the new government of a

---

[17] See e.g. *Short* v. *Islamic Republic of Iran* (1987) 16 Iran–USCTR 76.
[18] *Yeager* v. *Iran* (1987) 17 Iran–USCTR 92 at 104.
[19] *Rankin* v. *Iran* (1987) 17 Iran–USCTR 135.
[20] *Case Concerning United States Diplomatic and Consular Staff in Tehran* (*United States of America* v. *Iran*), ICJ Reports (1980) 3 at 30.

state *shall* be considered as an act of that state. This was not found applicable in the *US Hostages Case*, as the Revolutionary Guards never became the new government, but remained distinct from the government of the Ayatollah Khomeini. The Iran–US Tribunal has also made it clear that there is no responsibility under international law for loss occasioned by revolution. Revolution is not an internationally unlawful act, and, although the incoming government is responsible for any unlawful acts committed while it still had the status of a revolutionary movement, the revolution itself incurs no responsibility. In other words, there is no international responsibility, both because the acts are not attributable to the state, and because they would not entail a breach of an international obligation.

The same principles apply to national liberation movements, as the ILC makes clear in its commentary to Article 14.[21]

In its judgment on the merits of the *Nicaragua–US Case*, the Court again had to look at issues of state responsibility for acts of persons not their servants and not organs of state. Here the relationship in question was that between the United States and the Contras. The Court stated that, on the basis of the evidence before it, it was not satisfied that all the operations by the Contras reflected the strategy and tactics of the United States. At the same time, some operations were planned in collaboration with US advisers, and the legislative and executive bodies expressly took responsibility for military and financial aid in the region. When analysing whether the acts committed by the Contras in Nicaragua could be attributed to the United States, the Court observed: 'For the conduct to give rise to legal responsibility of the United States, it would in part have to be proved that that state had effective control of the military or para-military operations in the course of which the alleged violations were committed.'[22] And this was not the case. This is notably *not* a due diligence test.

The Standard of Care for Responsibility to be Engaged

We have noted that, where the conduct of individual servants of the state is concerned, rather than of state organs as such, the state's responsibility

---

[21] But there are those who criticize the ILC for treating national liberation movements and insurrectional movements on the same basis, contending that the former have a recognized international status and, seeking self-determination, act lawfully; e.g. H. Atlam, 'National Liberation Movements and International Responsibility', in M. Spinedi and B. Simma (eds.), *United Nations Codification of State Responsibility* (1987), 35–57. But Arts. 14 and 15 deal only with the attribution of conduct, not its lawfulness, and attributability has never depended upon distinctions between lawful and unlawful conduct.

[22] *Military and Paramilitary Activities* (*Nicaragua* v. *USA*) (Merits), ICJ Reports (1986), 14.

comes into play if it has failed to exercise the due diligence which could reasonably have prevented such conduct.[23]

There has been debate as to whether the due diligence standard is objective, or whether it has to be looked at in the light of all the resources available to the state. On that second view, a poor state with limited resources would have a low due diligence standard to meet, in seeking to control private behaviour that harms others. In the literature and in the case law there are different views advanced on this question. Thus in the *Montijo Case*,[24] before the US–Colombia Claims Tribunal, the Tribunal found a failure of due diligence to prevent injury to aliens, notwithstanding the problems the state had in exercising this standard of care. But a more Latin American perspective was offered by the contrasting treatment of the topic in Garcia Amador.[25] The matter is not addressed at all satisfactorily in the adopted ILC articles, and the only guidance is the obscurely worded Article 23.[26]

The International Court of Justice, in its judgment on the *Tehran Hostages Case*,[27] appeared to be embracing the 'relativist' approach, though the point is not addressed in terms, and perhaps too much should not be read into the Court's choice of words. Finding that the Iranian authorities had failed in their duty of care to US diplomats, even though the actual harm to them had been caused by individuals, the Court said that the Iranian authorities 'were fully aware of their obligations . . . had the means at their disposal to perform their obligations; [and] completely failed to comply with these obligations'.

It may be the case that, with regard to particular obligations, a standard *higher* than due diligence may be required. For example, Article 22 of the Vienna Convention on Diplomatic Relations of 1961 places a special duty of care upon a state to protect a diplomatic mission from attack, harassment, or impairment to its dignity. Some rather positive, specific measures of protection may be expected from the state—a policeman at the door of a foreign embassy, the monitoring and controlling of demonstrations in the immediate vicinity, and further. Thus in the *Tehran*

[23] The due diligence standard is affirmed in, e.g., *Short* v. *Islamic Republic*, Iran–United States Claims Tribunal (1987).

[24] *The Montijo Case* (1874) (*US* v. *Colombia*), Moore, ii., *Arbitrations* 1421 at 1444.

[25] F. Garcia Amador, *Draft Articles on the Responsibility of the State for Injuries Caused in its Territory to the Person or Property of Aliens*, repr. in F. Garcia Amador, L. Sohn, and R. Baxter (eds.), *Recent Codification of the Law of State Responsibility for Injury to Aliens*, i. (1974), 130. For an interesting view of this topic, see Smith, *State Responsibility and the Marine Environment*, 36–43.

[26] Art. 23 provides: 'When the result required of a state by an international obligation is the prevention, by means of its choice, of the occurrence of a given event, there is a breach of that obligation only if, by the conduct adopted, the state does not achieve that result.'

[27] *Case Concerning United States Diplomatic and Consular Staff in Tehran* (*United States of America* v. *Iran*), ICJ Reports (1980) 3 at 30.

Hostages Case the Court noted that the overrunning of the US Embassy and the seizure of the hostages occurred over three hours 'without any body of police, any military unit or any Iranian official intervening to try to stop it or to impede it from being carried through to completion'.

There is keen debate on the care that states must exercise over activities—sometimes its own but sometimes also the activities of private persons or firms—in the environmental sphere. The *Trail Smelter Case*[28] (notwithstanding that it was technically an agreed application of US law), other leading cases (notwithstanding that they were based on interpretations of treaty obligations),[29] and evolving standards in relevant treaties and declarations, all make clear a duty of care to prevent injury.[30] The *standard* of care is still unclear. But, with regard to *some* activities of an inherently hazardous nature, it is increasingly suggested that there is an absolute duty of care, reflected in resultant strict liability.[31]

But we must realize this: once we enter into discussion of varying standards of care, we pass from the essence of state responsibility—the concept of accountability for international wrong—and enter the *substantive law of obligations*. The standard by which the duty of care in regard to an obligation is to be tested is determined *by reference to the particular requirements of that obligation*. The law of state responsibility does not tell us the answer to this: we can say only that a state is responsible for failing to take, either generally or with respect to the conduct of individuals, duly diligent care or care to such other standard as the particular obligation requires. We will shortly return to the point in a slightly different context.

An interesting question, relating to the state's duty of due diligence to prevent harm, is whether there is also a comparable due diligence due to punish the individuals who have caused the harm. Again, this is not directly dealt with by the ILC Draft Articles, but the idea of a duty to punish nationals who harm foreigners finds much support. Ago put it this way in his Fourth Report to the ILC[32] when writing of attacks upon aliens:

Prevention and punishment are simply two aspects of the same obligation to provide protection and both have a common aim, namely to discourage potential

---

[28] *Trail Smelter Case (USA v. Canada),* 3 UNRIAA 1905; *Corfu Channel Case (UK v. Albania),* ICJ Reports (1949) 4.

[29] *Diversion of Water from the Meuse* (1937) PCIJ Ser. A/B, no. 70; *Lake Lanoux Case (France v. Spain)* (1958) 62 RGDIP 79.

[30] Arts. 194 and 198, UN Law of the Sea Convention, 1982; Brussels IMCO (IMO) Liability Convention on Pollution, 1969, Arts. 3 and 7. And see, *inter alia,* A. Boyle, 'Marine Pollution under the Law of the Sea Convention' (1985) 79 *AJIL* 347 ff.; J. Schneider, *World Public Order of the Environment* (1976), ch. 6; L. Goldie, 'Concepts of Strict and Absolute Liability and the Ranking of Liability in Terms of Relative Exposure to Risk' (1985) 16 *Netherlands Yearbook of International Law* 175.

[31] Art. II, Convention on International Liability for Damage Caused by Space Objects.

[32] Ago, Fourth Report on State Responsibility, C/CN.4/264 and Add. 1, *Yearbook of ILC* (1972) ii. 71.

attackers of protected persons from carrying out such attacks. The system of protection that the State must provide therefore includes not only the adoption of measures to avoid certain acts being committed but also provision for, and application of, sanctions against the authors of acts which the implementation of preventive measures has failed to avert.

His comment, of course, is equally applicable to other examples of international obligation. Brian Smith has put it thus: 'The obligation to apprehend and punish wrongdoers, then, is but an expression of the general obligation to prevent private individuals from engaging in conduct in which the state is prohibited to engage.'[33]

This is not quite the same thing as saying that a state owes an obligation to an injured alien to ensure that on every occasion an offender is diligently pursued: the obligation probably is rather to ensure that non-prosecution and punishment of certain prohibited activity does not occur with regularity, thereby contributing to a general non-prevention of the activity concerned.[34] Interestingly, this question has arisen in the specific context of human-rights obligations under the International Covenant on Civil and Political Rights. The Committee on Human Rights, which monitors compliance by state parties with their obligations under the Covenant, has held that claimants have no legal right under the Covenant to obtain the punishment of a particular human-rights violator. There is thus no issue of state responsibility.[35] The European Court of Human Rights has also, in *Ireland v. United Kingdom*,[36] rejected the idea of a breach of obligation because of a failure to punish violators. (In *Ireland v. United Kingdom* the violators were servants of the state; in Latin American countries their status is often keenly contested. But the points of principle would seem the same.) In its other function of examining the reports of states on their human-rights performance, however, it has been concerned with what Ago called 'the two aspects of the same obligation'. States which have issued amnesties for massive human-rights violations (and this has been true of several South American countries) have been pressed as to whether it is in reality an encouragement to further violation in the future—even if no duty lies to specific alleged victims to bring particular offenders to justice.[37]

---

[33] In his stimulating book, *State Responsibility and the Marine Environment* 37.
[34] To the same effect, see the *James Case* (*US* v. *Mexico*) (1925) 4 UNRIAA 82 at 118.
[35] See e.g. *HCMA* v. *Netherlands*, Communication 213/1986, Report of the Human Rights Committee, GAOR 44th sess., suppl. 40. On the general topic of the obligation to prosecute, see the interesting article by D. Orentlicher, 'Settling Accounts: The Duty to Prosecute Human Rights Violations of a Prior Regime' (1991) 100 *Yale Law Journal* 2539.
[36] *Ireland* v. *United Kingdom*, 25 *European Court of Human Rights*, Judgments, European Court of Human Rights Ser. A (1987), para. 10.
[37] See e.g. the examination by the Committee on Human Rights of the Second Periodic Report of Uruguay (CCPR/C/28/Add. 10), at its 876th–879th meetings, held 27–8 Mar. 1989 (CCPR/C/SR/876–9).

Much of the early discussion in the International Law Commission focused on the substantive international law on the treatment of aliens— including the question that now happily can be relegated to another age, that of whether aliens only have not to be discriminated against, so that the only obligation is to treat them no worse than nationals were treated; or whether there was a minimum standard of treatment that is required. International law has firmly come down on the side of required minimum standards of treatment. The way forward for nationals who sadly may be treated less well is through the development of the law of human rights, which applies to national and foreigner alike. The national's standards must be moved up to those required for the foreigner under international law; they must not be tied down in misery together. This is one of the ways in which human-rights law touches upon the obligations of states. But in my view this has almost nothing to do with the law of state responsibility. It is part of the substantive law of obligations. And those obligations could be *anything*—not just obligations relating to the physical treatment of aliens and their property. This is evident from the examples already given concerning diplomatic protection, or the use of force abroad through irregulars. This point will become more apparent as we proceed.

But before I elaborate this theme further, there are more philosophical questions about *the nature of a state's responsibility* which require our attention. We turn away from the question 'for whose acts may a state be responsible?' to the question 'What are the required elements of responsibility?'

The Required Elements of Responsibility

The key question here is whether there has to be either negligence or intent for responsibility to be engaged. Over the years there has been keen debate on this topic. Some writers have taken the position that *culpa* (fault) is a requirement of responsibility for any breach of an international obligation.[38] Others have limited the requirement of *culpa* to the duty of states to protect foreigners from harm by private individuals.[39] Garcia Amador in his ILC drafts required *culpa* as an element for responsibility for omission.[40] The text of the *Corfu Channel Case*[41] has been pored over

[38] e.g. J. Brierly, *The Law of Nations* (6th edn., 1963), 289; H. Rolin, 'Les Principes de droit international public', *Recueil des cours* (1950), ii. 302 at 445.

[39] e.g. P. M. Dupuy, 'Responsabilité internationale des états', *Recueil des cours* (1984, V), 13 at 23 ff.; C. de Visscher, 'La Responsabilité des états', *Bibliotheca Visseriana* (1924), ii. 86 at 88. For a helpful succinct summary of the issues and literature thereon, see Smith, *State Responsibility and the Marine Environment*, 12–15.

[40] Garcia Amador, *Draft Articles*, 27.

[41] *Corfu Channel Case (UK v. Albania)*, ICJ Reports, (1949) 4.

in another exercise to 'find the law' in unclear pronouncements by the International Court of Justice. In that case the issue was whether Albania was to be treated as internationally responsible for the mines that appeared in the Corfu Channel, although it denied any knowledge of how they came to be there. The United Kingdom had based the foundations for Albanian responsibility on the claim that the minefields were laid 'by or with the connivance or knowledge of the Albanian government'. The Court stated that the mere fact that minefields had been laid within its territorial waters did not of itself indicate knowledge on the part of Albania. But, taking all the evidence together, and the presumptions that operated in respect of them, the Court drew the conclusion that the laying of the minefields could not have been accomplished without the knowledge of the Albanian government. And knowledge that minefields exist in the path of shipping and failure to give a warning violated international law. Some writers[42] have viewed this as supporting the need for *culpa*—if *culpa* was not necessary, it would not have been necessary to decide if Albania *had* pre-knowledge (Lauterpacht). Others insisted—correctly in my view—that the judgment is neutral on *culpa*. It simply says that a failure to warn about what one knew violated an international obligation.[43]

The alternative view has been that it is the violation of international law that engages responsibility, without any fault other than the violation itself being necessary.[44] It was sometimes put this way: there had to be *fault* for there to be international responsibility, but the fault lay in the violation, not in any requirement of negligence or malice. But, once again, we have stepped into discussing the substantive law of obligations, while purporting to talk about the requirement of state responsibility. Amerasinghe implicitly acknowledges this when he writes: 'The basis [of state respons-ibility] will vary with the content of the international obligation. This may be a strict basis or the basis of risk in some circumstances, while in others it may involve malice or culpable negligence, or, conceivably, malice.'[45]

This seems clearly right when the question is: 'Is the state responsible for its own unlawful actions, even when it had no malice and was not negligent?' But the question of *culpa* still comes into play when the issue is a state's responsibility for acts performed by others. It does not carry things

---

[42] See Oppenheim, *International Law*, ed. H. Lauterpacht (8th edn., 1955), i. 343.

[43] But certainly two of the dissenting judges, Judges Krylov and Ecer, spoke in clear terms of the need for *culpa*, or for malice or culpable negligence; see ICJ Reports (1949) 72 and 128 respectively. See the good summary in Smith, *State Responsibility and the Marine Environment*, 12–15.

[44] e.g. D. Anzilotti, *Cours de droit international* (6th edn., 1929), 496–51; I. Brownlie, *System of the Law of Nations: State Responsibility*, pt. 1 (1983), 38–46; Jiminez de Arechaga 'International Responsibility', in Sørensen (ed.), *Manual of Public International Law*, 531 at 535.   [45] *State Responsibility for Injury to Aliens* (1967), 45.

forward to say that the issue of whether the state is responsible without *culpa* is established by reference to the obligation. The tests for *culpa* may well have been met by those actually performing the unlawful act; but that cannot tell us whether the state is to be liable if it has no *culpa* itself. The answer here appears still to be that the law of state responsibility most usually requires due diligence rather than its own *culpa* as the test for attributed responsibility.

Turning to the substantive law of obligations, we have already noted a growing contemporary tendency for certain categories of obligations to entail 'strict liability'—that is to say, responsibility by reference to events, with *culpa* as much an irrelevance as the due-diligence test. This is clearly a growing phenomenon in the international environmental field, and we may mention the Vienna Convention on Civil Liability for Nuclear Damage, 1963, the Brussels Convention on the Liability of Operators of Nuclear Ships, 1962, and the Convention on International Liability for Damages Caused by Space Objects, 1972.

The ILC has adopted responsibility for results requiring no *culpa*, for actions and omissions alike. The only requirement is causality. But now we have a puzzle: Articles 29–34 list circumstances that 'preclude wrongfulness'. Some of the provisions *do* preclude wrongfulness—for example, a lawful measure of self-defence will not be a wrongful act. But some of the provisions listed seem to me clearly to go to *fault* and not to *wrongfulness*. Thus Article 31 says that 'wrongfulness is precluded if the act was due to *force majeure*'. But how does this fit with result-based responsibility? All *force majeure* has done is to remove the existence of *fault*; it has *excused* a breach of an obligation, but it has *not* 'precluded' it. A breach of an international contract by reason of *force majeure* remains a breach; it merely means the breaching party has acted without fault. Therefore, in a responsibility system based on result, not fault, it should be irrelevant to international responsibility. The sections on *distress* and *necessity* seem to me misconceived for the same reasons, confusing 'preclusion' of an obligation with 'defences to breach' it.

State responsibility arises for a breach of an international obligation.

Although with Ago the ILC has turned away from discussion of particular obligations, the world outside the ILC continues to pour out material on specific obligations under the guise of writings on state responsibility. All around us journals contain writings on 'state responsibility and violations of human rights', 'state responsibility and marine pollution', 'state responsibility and the permanent sovereignty over natural resources'—the list is endless. Certain university courses seem to fall into the same lamentable practice, entitling a rag-bag of topics 'State Responsibility'. State responsibility is *not* about the entirety of the obligations relating to every single norm in international law. This is to use the term 'state responsibility' when it is simply sufficient to say 'state obligations in relation to topic X'.

But, although the ILC has avoided immersing itself in what it terms 'the secondary role of state responsibility'—an unfortunate name for what is nothing more than the entire law of international obligations—it has set off on an equally curious path. It has begun detailed work on what it terms 'the "instrumental" consequences of an internationally wrongful act'.[46] In other words, it is embarking on a study of 'the measures that an injured state may take against a state having committed an internationally wrongful act'. Thus the study of state responsibility is now to include the entire corpus of international law on what are termed 'countermeasures'—self-defence, reprisals, intervention, etc. One can admire the work presented by the Special Rapporteur on 'Countermeasures',[47] while believing that it is fundamentally misconceived that these vast themes of international law should be brought within the scope of the ILC's work on state responsibility.

The *consequence* of state responsibility is the liability to make reparation. That principle is clearly stated in the famous *Chorzow Case*[48] and in the *SS Wimbledon*.[49] In *Chorzow* the Permanent Court said that it regarded 'reparation as the corollary of the violation of the obligations resulting from an engagement between states'. But it seems to me misconceived for the ILC currently to be directing its energies to a vast treatise on compensation. The substantive law of compensation is a quite separate topic. In my view, the codification of the law of state responsibility entails neither the detailing of the entire substantive law of obligations, nor a treatise on countermeasures, nor the detailing of the entire body of law on reparation and compensation.

There seems to be no topic that is not embraced by 'state responsibility'. It covers, in the view of some, the law of every substantive obligation; the law of 'instrumental consequences' to breach of obligations; and the detail of the law of reparation. It is my opinion that it is exactly this tendency to make state responsibility 'the law of everything' that has led to such problems in achieving a concluded programme of work on the topic in the ILC. If the law of state responsibility is to have a distinct meaning, then none of these elements is needed. The essence of responsibility is not the substance of obligations; nor in permitted responses thereto; nor in the detailing of reparation. It lies in the concept of liability for an international wrong, coupled with a duty to make reparation; and the detail required

---

[46] See A/CN.4/L/478, 15 July 1992, para. 12.
[47] See especially the third and fourth reports of Professor G. Arangio-Ruiz, A/CN.4/440 and Add. 1; and A/CN.4/444 and Corr. 1, and Add. 1, 2, and 3; and Chapter III of the Report of the ILC 15 July 1992, A/CN.4/L.478.   [48] (1928) PCIJ Ser. A, no. 17, p. 29.
[49] (1923) PCIJ Ser. A, no. 1, p. 3.

should be limited to questions of attributability and to what, so far as the element of liability is concerned, is specific to the law of responsibility itself. Although state responsibility assumes a violated obligation and requires reparation, if it exists at all as a separate topic its sole focus must lie elsewhere: *whose* unlawful acts engage the responsibility of the state, and, if responsibility lies for the acts of others, is the responsibility dependent upon some fault or negligence by the state itself?[50]

There is yet a further problem that we must mention: that is the relationship of wrongfulness to harm and the implications for responsibility. We have seen that the Permanent Court in *Chorzow* stated that reparation is the corollary of the violation of an obligation. And, in the *Wimbledon Case*, the Court held that, once it was determined that an obligation had been violated, the state responsible for the loss occasioned by the violation must compensate for it. Two questions arise. The first, what if there is no loss? Does responsibility arise if the unlawful act generates no loss or harm? The answer seems to be that it does—responsibility is for the unlawful act, not for the loss. Compensation for the loss is the *consequence* of responsibility. Ago, indeed, and his draft regarded this as a 'non-question', believing that *all* violations incur damage—if there is no physical loss then the damage is 'moral damage'. The required reparation may be modest, but the responsibility exists. There is a second question relating to this nexus between international wrongfulness and harm.[51] We have just suggested that, if there is an international wrong, but no harm, or only 'moral harm', there still will be responsibility. But what if it is the other way around? What if there is harm, but it results from an act that is lawful? The *Trail Smelter Case* is a classic example: there was nothing unlawful in having a smelter plant, but the activities of the plant caused harm to the neighbouring state. The state in which Trail Smelter was located was held responsible for that harm.

Is this still caught by the Draft Articles, which clearly require 'an internationally wrongful act' (Article 1) as the precondition for responsibility? The answer is in the negative, because the ILC has introduced a separate topic for development and codification—namely, 'Liability for

---

[50] These misgivings on current concepts of state responsibility are carried further by Philip Allott in his provocative and stimulating essay, 'State Responsibility and the Unmaking of International Law' (1985) 29 *Harvard International Law Journal* 1. Allott denies any intellectually sustainable role *at all* for state responsibility. He argues that liability flows from the nature of a particular wrong, and the remedy requirement is 'a function of integrating the nature of the liability in the given case with the nature of the particular wrongful act' (p. 12). He contends: 'To determine the legal content of responsibility is to create a category between wrongdoing and liability for its consequences. This category is not only unnecessary but dangerous . . .' (p. 13).

[51] See A. Tanzi, 'Is Damage a Distinct Condition for the Existence of an Internationally Wrongful Act?', in Spinedi and Simma (eds.), *United Nations Codification of State Responsibility*, 1.

Injurious Consequences of Acts not Prohibited by International Law'. The Special Rapporteurs—Professor Quentin Baxter and, on his untimely death, Professor Barboza—are focusing largely on environmental matters. Cases like *Trail Smelter*—which we had all in our youth thought was something to do with international responsibility for harm to your neighbour (and a clear example of the absence of need of malice, or *culpa*)—are *not* now questions of state responsibility but are put into another category. But problems remain. If the contemporary law of state responsibility has resolved the debate on *culpa*, and settled for result-based responsibility, why cannot it cover this type of act as well? The answer given is that the result has to be caused by an illegal act—and most environmental harm is caused by actions that are themselves perfectly legal. But *why* does this have to be so? Why, if result rather than *culpa* is what concerns us, why then can responsibility not attach also for results from lawful acts as well as unlawful acts? Of course, the accepted Draft Articles so far adopted would have to be recast, and that seems to be a course that no one in the ILC is prepared to countenance—they are set in stone, even though the cement around them has yet to dry.

Instead—and, it seems to me, against all logic —harm caused by 'acts not prohibited by international law' is being dealt with quite separately. The approach is entirely different from that of state responsibility, the approach is what we may term the law of co-operation, the sort of approach exemplified by Professor Stephen McCaffrey's handling in the ILC of the law of international watercourses.[52] The direction of the work is towards the sharing of information, notifications, participation in mutual studies, etc. One can see the sense in this—but it is a tendency that emphasizes the lawfulness of the activities, and carries the implication that prevention of harm is not an absolute duty. The standard is thus less than strict liability; even in respect of very high-risk activity. Results such as those in Chernobyl and Bhopal would not (as they would be, if dealt with under the law of state responsibility) attract the strict liability of states on the basis of no-fault result. Some environmental lawyers point out that this pulls in the opposite direction from the developing international law of the environment, which increasingly identifies a strict liability in relation to activities that are manifestly high risk.[53]

[52] See e.g. Sixth Report on the Law of Non-Navigational Uses of International Watercourses, A/CN.4/427/Add. 1.

[53] K. Zemanek, 'Causes and Forms of International Liability', in B. Cheng and E. D. Brown (eds.), *Contemporary Problems of International Law: Essays in Honour of Georg Schwarzenberger* (1988), 319. See also the persuasive criticism of A. E. Boyle, 'State Responsibility and International Liability for Injurious Consequences of Acts not prohibited by International Law: A Necessary Distinction?' (1990) 33 *ICLQ* 1. Generally, see also (1985) 16 *Netherlands Yearbook of International Law: Symposium on State Responsibility and Liability for Injurious Consequences Arising out of Acts not Prohibited by International Law.*

Would it not be preferable to bring all responsibility for harm within the general heading of state responsibility, and to note again that the duty of care relating to the harm (that is, whether there is a due-diligence duty or an absolute-liability duty) depends upon the primary obligation itself? In the case of environmental matters, no doubt some activities would be on the one basis, and some on the other—that would develop and change as the substantive law on the environment develops and changes. Responsibility would attach for harm, coupled with a failure to meet the required standard of care.

If it were *really* thought impossible to alter the State Responsibility Articles so far adopted, to achieve this end, it seems to me it could still be done by appropriate interpretation of what we have. If what is required for something to fall within the law of state responsibility is an internationally wrongful act, then what is internationally wrongful is *allowing* (even without *culpa*) *the harm to occur*. A nuclear plant is a lawful activity; but failure to meet a strict-liability or due-diligence standard of care, with resultant harm—*that* is the internationally wrongful act, for which state responsibility attaches.

The Character of International Responsibility: The Question of Criminal Responsibility

Article 19 (1) of the ILC Draft Articles affirms that responsibility can lie for a breach of an obligation, regardless of the subject matter of the obligation breached. Paragraphs (2) and (3) of Article 19 go on to speak of the notion of an international crime, to specify some examples. Paragraph (4) stipulates that any internationally wrongful act which is not an international crime in accordance with these provisions constitutes an international delict.

19 (2) An internationally wrongful act which results from the breach by a State of an international obligation so essential for the protection of fundamental interests of the international community that its breach is recognized as a crime by that community as a whole, constitutes an international crime.

(3) Subject to paragraph 2, and on the basis of the rules of international law in force, an international crime may result, *inter alia*, from:
(a) a serious breach of an international obligation of essential importance for the maintenance of international peace and security, such as that prohibiting aggression;
(b) a serious breach of an international obligation of essential importance for safeguarding the right of self-determination of peoples, such as that prohibiting the establishment or maintenance by force of colonial domination;
(c) a serious breach on a widespread scale of an international obligation of

essential importance for safeguarding the human being, such as those prohibiting slavery, genocide and apartheid;

(d) a serious breach of an international obligation of essential importance for the safeguarding and preservation of the human environment, such as those prohibiting massive pollution of the atmosphere or of the seas.[54]

There has been great controversy about Article 19, and about the ideas that underlie it. Why, it has been asked, was it thought necessary at all to distinguish between crimes and delicts? Why was it not simply sufficient to speak of international wrongs, of whatever character? Various answers have been given. Graefrath offers a commonsense answer when he says: 'Obviously, there are different categories of violations of international law which entail different legal consequences.'[55] In his Reports to the ILC, Ago offered as reasons for distinguishing delicts from crimes the UN institutional system under Chapter VII, and the emerging interest in the concept of obligations *erga omnes* that had been articulated by the International Court of Justice in the *Barcelona Traction Case*.[56]

The institutional system under Chapter VII of the Charter is also much relied on by Graefrath—'the security system of the United Nations is based on such a differentiation'.[57] I find quite unpersuasive the suggestion that the Chapter VII system of the United Nations requires a new category of international crime for purposes of state responsibility. Whereas it is true, as Graefrath suggests, that Articles 40–2 of the UN Charter have the closest link with the classical categories of international crime (the waging of aggressive war), neither the history nor the text of these provisions suggests that they are a penal sanction against a crime.[58] As Pierre-Marie Dupuy has observed, Articles 41 and 42 of Chapter VII of the Charter have 'the aim not of individually punishing the culprit of a wrongful act, but of terminating a *situation* that attacks peace or is a threat to it'. In his view— and it is a view I share—these Articles, along with Article 51, 'are measure of constraint and not of responsibility'.[59] Certainly it is hard to read into them any requirement that delicts be differentiated from crimes.

I find equally puzzling the suggestion that the *erga omnes* concept requires the formulation of the category of international crimes of state.

[54] *Yearbook of ILC* (1976), ii. pt. 2, p. 73 at pp. 95–122.

[55] B. Graefrath, 'International Crimes: A Specific Regime of International Responsibility of States and its Legal Consequence', in J. Weiler, A. Cassese, and M. Spinedi (eds.), *International Crimes of State* (1989), 160, 161.

[56] R. Ago, Fifth Report, *Yearbook of ILC* (1976), ii. pt. 1, p. 3 at pp. 26–57; and his comments at ibid. i. p. 7 at pp. 8, 56–61.

[57] Graefrath, 'International Crimes', 162.

[58] See R. Russell and J. Muther, *A History of the United Nations Charter* (1958), 234.

[59] See P. M. Dupuy, 'The Institutionalization of International Crimes of State', in Weiler, Cassese, and Spinedi (eds.), *International Crimes of State*, 170 at 176. See also, generally on state responsibility, the same author at *Recueil des cours* (1984, V), 55; *Annuaire Français de Droit International* (1979), 539; *RGDIP* (1980), 449; *RGDIP* (1983), 537.

Apart from the fact that the dictum in the *Barcelona Traction Case* is endlessly cited very much more than, properly analysed, it can bear,[60] the linkage is again unpersuasive. It requires sliding from the concept of *erga omnes* to the category of *jus cogens*, and then making the further assumption that the breach of either is necessarily an international crime. The notion of *erga omnes* is concerned with standing; that of *jus cogens* with the non-derogable quality of the norm. There may be a measure of overlap, but the two things are not the same. Not all human rights, for example, are non-derogable rights, or even rights that may not be legitimately qualified if certain conditions are met. Further, as Henkin, Schachter, and Smit have correctly observed: 'it does not follow that a breach of an obligation *erga omnes* is necessarily an international crime. The [ILC] noted that some rules of the Law of the Sea imposed obligations *erga omnes*, but that their breach was not an international crime.'[61]

What, functionally speaking, is served by classifying certain offences as crimes? One could envisage two important possibilities. The first is that the classification serves to place beyond doubt an offence clearly within the category of offences in respect of which there is universal jurisdiction. But Article 10 is concerned with *state* responsibility, and the examples mentioned in Article 19 (3) are examples of acts that are engaged in for the most part by *states*, rather than by individuals. The clause speaks of aggression, self-determination, slavery, genocide, and apartheid, and massive pollution of the environment. The authorizing of universal jurisdiction over offending *states* is not what Article 19 is directed to. The second possible purpose of classifying an offence as a crime is to identify the appropriate reparation as *punishment*, or punishment coupled with monetary compensation. We have already observed that Chapter VII of the Charter is not properly to be regarded as a new form of 'punishment' for 'crimes'. And it is hard to disagree with those who say that no tribunal has ever yet imposed anything we might recognize as 'criminal punishment' against states. The normal panoply of remedies—declaratory judgments, reparations—are all that is really available for offences, whether they be termed 'delicts' or 'crimes'. As Gilbert has written: 'The concept of punishment for criminal behaviour manifestly cannot be applied in a straightforward manner to the treatment of offending states, for, in part, it implies a vertical society. Yet it is an essential element of crime.'[62]

If the idea of the international criminal responsibility of states is fraught

---

[60] See, Ch. 4, p. 57.

[61] *International Law, Cases and Materials* (1980), 567. See also M. Mohr, 'The ILC's Distinction between "International Crimes" and "International Delicts" and its Implications', in M. Spinedi and B. Simma (eds.), *United Nations Codification of State Responsibility* (1987), 134–5.

[62] G. Gilbert, 'The Criminal Responsibility of States' (1990) 39 *ICLQ* 345 at 356.

with difficulty, the development of the concept of the international criminal responsibility of individuals seems more worthwhile. Some interesting developments in this direction are now taking place. Thus the recent ILC Draft Code of Crimes against the Peace and Security of Mankind[63] envisages the responsibility not only of agents of the state, but also of private individuals who engage in genocide or trade in narcotics. (One can still wonder why neither here nor in Article 19 of the ILC Articles on State Responsibility is torture regarded as an international crime.) But agreement is still awaited on the provisions relating to punishment.

Meanwhile, a working group of the ILC has done vigorous work on the possibilities of an international criminal court, addressing institutional and jurisdictional issues.[64] Here again the suggestion is to provide a court for individuals charged with international crimes. The proposals stand separate from the ILC's Draft Article 19 on state criminal responsibility.

We can conclude our survey of state responsibility by saying that it should mean something rather precise, but has over recent years come increasingly to mean everything. State responsibility is surely a topic of which it can be said that less is more.

[63] Draft Code of Crimes Against the Peace and Security of Mankind, A/CN.4/L.471, 6 July 1992.
[64] Ibid., Report of the Working Group on the Question of an International Criminal Jurisdiction. This Report was at the end of 1992 approved by the General Assembly, which has instructed the ILC to proceed with the drafting of a statute.

10

THE UNITED NATIONS

THE stated purposes of the United Nations, listed in Article 1 of the Charter and to be read against the background of the preambular provisions, are centred on the maintenance of peace, the settlement of disputes, and the promotion of social, economic, and humanitarian welfare. In the Charter these are a seamless web. There is full recognition in the Charter that, if disputes are not settled, the peace may not be maintained; and that injustice and economic and social deprivation provide the breeding ground for instability and international terrorism.

I cannot attempt—and nor would it be appropriate—to survey all that the United Nations has endeavoured to do, and its successes and failures, across the broad front of its interconnected objectives. My focus is rather on the containment of disputes in a somewhat narrower sense, emphasizing legal matters, though always remembering the broader context in which they arise.

The United Nations is a key institution in the endeavour to avoid, contain, and resolve disputes. Leaving aside its work on economic and social and humanitarian matters, and indeed even on arms control and disarmament negotiations, it has had to act on the basis of certain prescriptions in the Charter: it is charged with the promotion and development of international law; it has a role in the settlement of disputes; and it is intended to play a central role in the provision of collective security. Some brief comments will be made on each of these in turn.

The Formal Consideration of International Law within the United Nations

The study of legal issues in part proceeds within the United Nations in contexts that are relatively removed from immediate disputes before the General Assembly or Security Council. Thus the Sixth Committee of the General Assembly is entrusted with the consideration of legal issues that are engaging the attention of the Assembly: current and recent matters include work on strengthening the role of the organization; status of national liberation movements; the status of the Protocols additional to the Geneva Conventions of 1949 relating to the protection of victims of armed conflict; the consideration of how the security of diplomatic and consular missions and representatives could be better protected; the general problem of peaceful settlement of disputes; and the question of an additional Protocol to the Vienna Convention on Consular Relations. On all of these topics the Sixth Committee makes its own report. In addition, it has the task of examining reports on legal matters that other bodies present to the United Nations—for example, when the International Law Commission reports on its work to the General Assembly, it is the Sixth Committee that examines the specific proposals on the particular topics on which the ILC has been working.

Article 13 of the Charter provides that the General Assembly shall initiate studies and make recommendations for '(*a*) promoting international co-operation in the political field and encouraging the progressive development of international law and its codification'. In fulfilment of this task the ILC was set up, and for over forty years has been engaged in legal work centred on codification, but necessarily entailing, as part of that process, progressive development. Reference has already been made to its work on different topics in earlier chapters. It has for a long time been dealing with the codification of state responsibility; and has made good progress in its work on state immunity and on the law of non-navigational uses of international watercourses. It has adopted on first reading a draft code of crimes against the peace and security of mankind,[1] on which there is bound to be further controversy and highly divergent views from the states which now have a further opportunity to comment upon it.[2] After grappling with the second part of the topic of Relations between States and International Organizations, the ILC decided in 1992 not to pursue it further. I think it fair to say that the record of the ILC is a mixed one. The topics ripe for codification (albeit with a necessary element of development) need to be selected with care. There is a recent welcome tendency to go for topics of manageable dimensions, with the intention of being able to conclude them within a reasonable time-scale. And, although there was some anxiety, from the point of view of work methods, about the consequences of having significantly enlarged the Commission, the Commisson now seems to have settled into a new routine and to be engaged in very productive work.

Peaceful Settlement of Disputes

Chapter VI of the Charter contains specific provisions on the Pacific Settlement of Disputes. First, it provides the mechanisms for the bringing of disputes before the Security Council and General Assembly. The

[1] A/CN.4/L.459/Add. 1, 5 July 1991.
[2] In Oct. 1992 the General Assembly invited the ILC to proceed with certain aspects of this work.

Secretary-General may himself, under Article 99 of the Charter, bring to the attention of the Security Council any matter which in his opinion may threaten the maintenance of international peace and security. This power, very sparingly used in the early days, is now used rather more. Within Chapter VI, Article 35 provides that members may bring any dispute to the attention of the Security Council or General Assembly—whether they are parties to that dispute or not. And Article 35 (2) further provides that a state which is not a member of the United Nations, but is a party to the dispute, can also bring the matter to the United Nations. Other provisions in the Charter (Articles 31 and 32) ensure that non-members of the Security Council shall be allowed, under various conditions, to participate in the debates of the Security Council.

The Security Council can investigate any dispute, and over the years some use has been made of fact-finding missions. The neutral verification of the facts is not only often necessary where the facts are in dispute, but is itself a means of containing and defusing a situation. Such missions will not be able to go into the territory without the consent of the party concerned, but it will often suit a party to show that it has nothing to hide by allowing in such a fact-finding team. The early constitutional controversy as to whether the Secretary-General may himself establish a fact-finding mission, or whether this can be done only upon authorization by the Security Council, seems to be resolved in favour of the Secretary-General so to act.[3] The success of the fact-finding missions has been variable, depending upon the co-operation of the state concerned and the quality of the team.

A wide range of dispute-settlement possibilities is envisaged in Article 33 beyond enquiry as to the facts: negotiation, mediation, conciliation, arbitration, judicial settlement, and resort to regional agencies. Sometimes assistance in the pursuit of these measures will be suggested by the Security Council itself; sometimes assistance in respect of these functions is offered by the Secretary-General, as part of his mandate. Occasionally the Secretary-General himself will put proposed solutions to the Security Council. More usually, the Security Council devises the proposals (and the tendency for initiatives to flow from the Security Council rather than, even informally, the Secretariat has become more pronounced since the improvement of East–West relations). But either way, it is often the

---

[3] e.g. the Secretary-General has sent, on his initiative, fact-finding missions to: enquire into the conditions of prisoners of war in Iran and Iraq (see *Report of the Mission*, UN Doc. S/16962, 1985); investigate allegations of chemical-weapons use in the Iran–Iraq war (see *Report of the Mission*, UN Doc. S/20134, 1988); and gather information on the measures taken to end the apartheid system in South Africa (see United Nations Press Release 19 June 1990, UN Doc. DH/665). See further, M.-C. Bourloyannis, 'Fact-Finding by the Secretary General of the United Nations' (1990) 22 *New York University Journal of International Law and Politics* 641.

Secretary-General who is required to make the proposals for peaceful settlement operative. This interplay is well evidenced in resolutions that have asked, in broad terms that leave maximum flexibility, the Secretary-General to use his good offices—for example, in the Netherlands–Indonesia dispute;[4] in the enforcement of the Arab–Israeli armistice agreements;[5] in supervising a cease-fire in Kashmir;[6] in sending a representative to East Timor; in the Falklands dispute;[7] the list is almost endless.[8] The Secretary-General routinely assists in the holding of negotiations—sometimes in private, sometimes in public. He has facilitated and played an active role in direct negotiations, in a situation generally under the scrutiny of the Security Council: his role in the talks between the Turkish Cypriot and Greek Cypriot authorities is a case in point. He can equally assist in indirect negotiations, where one or more of the parties is unwilling to sit down with the other. The Arab–Israeli armistice negotiations in 1949 afford an example. The Security Council has also asked the Secretary-General to provide conciliators and mediators. In the Dutch–Indonesian disputes of 1949–54, and in the early years of the Cyprus situation, a conciliator and mediator were respectively much relied on. While Article 33 identifies the required third-party methods, it does not insist that only the United Nations provides the personnel. There has often been an interplay between consideration of a matter by the Security Council, and a role as conciliator played by statesmen from various well-placed countries, acting on the instructions of their government but in support of the peaceful solution sought by the UN community as a whole.

As for resort to regional agencies, Article 33 is of course referring to pacific settlement. (The interplay between regional agencies and the Security Council in enforcement measures is dealt with elsewhere in the Charter.) The Council of Europe system, the Inter-American system, and the OAU Unity all have their own procedures for pacific settlement, and these have been of the greatest importance. This has been confirmed by the Secretary-General in his report 'An Agenda for Peace' which emphasizes the important role such regional organizations play in the maintenance of international peace and security.[9] Some commentators view the creation of dispute-settlement mechanisms by regional organizations as expression of a regional desire for local resolution of the dispute and the exclusion, so far as is possible, of any interference by the Security Council.[10] Practice is often more complex. Sometimes it is the United

---

[4] SC Res. 35 (1947).   [5] SC Res. 113 and 114 (1956).
[6] SC Res. 210 and 211 (1965).   [7] SC Res. 505 (1982).
[8] For useful information and discussion, see S. Morphet, 'Resolutions and Vetoes in the Security Council: Their Relevance and Significance' (1990) 16 *Review of International Studies* 341 at 356.
[9] Report of the United Nations Secretary-General, *An Agenda for Peace* (1992).
[10] See e.g. D. Bowett, *Law of International Institutions* (1982), 313–16.

Nations that wishes to avoid dealing itself with an issue.[11] In the context of the Organization of African States, the difficult problems of the Western Sahara and the dispute between Chad and Libya evidence the point. In the case of Western Sahara the OAU has fully co-operated with the United Nations at all stages in an attempt peacefully to settle the dispute between the two parties to the conflict, Morocco and Frente POLISARIO. The OAU has welcomed the United Nations' expertise in helping organize and supervise a referendum on self-determination for the people of Western Sahara within the framework of the settlement plan adopted by the Security Council in Resolutions 658 (1990) and 690 (1991).[12] Similarly in the case of the border dispute between Chad and Libya, the OAU and the United Nations have co-operated in a joint effort peacefully to resolve the situation.[13] In both cases the United Nations has been reluctant to grapple alone with the problems.

The relationship of regional agencies to the United Nations in matters of peaceful settlement is complex and somewhat unsatisfactory. There seems to be no clear indicia to guide decision-makers as to when it is more appropriate to go for the regional, rather than the global, agency. While the United States and the Soviet Union were in confrontation, reference to a regional body could avoid politicization of a problem. But since the end of the cold war the reference to a regional body often reflects a lack of general interest in a problem—a feeling that it is 'somebody else's problem'. Moreover, certain protagonist states have a great power and influence within a region, and can command greater support there than they would be able to in the United Nations. The desire for regional stability will often cause regional bodies to seek to accommodate the more powerful of the two protagonists, at the expense of the other.

Peace and Collective Security: Intention and Innovation

But it is in relation to its powers under Chapter VII of the Charter, in the direct handling of peace and security issues, that the United Nations has

---

[11] See e.g. 'Cooperation between the United Nations and the Organisation of African Unity', *Provisional Verbatim Record of the 60th Meeting of the General Assembly*, A/47/PV.60 at pp. 16–34.

[12] For further examples of OAU and UN co-operation in respect of this issue see SC Res. 725 (31 Dec. 1991); and reports by the Secretary-General on the situation concerning Western Sahara: S/21360, 18 June 1990, and S/22464, 19 Apr. 1991.

[13] See OAU resolutions AHG/Res. 184 (XXV) and AHG/Res. 200 (XXVI); the 'Framework Agreement on the Peaceful Settlement of the Territorial Dispute between the Republic of Chad and the Great Socialist People's Libyan Arab Jamahiriya', in *Memorandum on the Chad–Libya Border Dispute*, S.21114, 26 Jan. 1990, at p. 11; and SC Draft Res. S/15013.

assumed such an important role in the containment of disputes. The keystone of international peace was the provision of collective security by the Big Powers, the Second World War allies. It was that collective security that was to make it unnecessary for states to act in self-help; their unilateral use of force was now restricted to self-defence—and *that* was to be monitored by the Security Council. The Big Powers would, through the Security Council, arrange for standing UN forces to be contributed by each of the member states (Article 43). A Military Staff Committee of the Big Powers was to assist in the realization of these plans (Article 47).

As is well known, these intentions, so clearly specified in the Charter, came to nothing. The unity of the Big Powers, on which all the rest was predicated, rapidly dissolved; and no agreement was possible on UN forces to keep the peace. Instead of collective security, there was instead the Cold War. Every aspect of the UN's work—economic, humanitarian, and military—was, during its first decade, coloured and limited by the reality of East–West conflict. Not only did the Charter envisage collective military action; it also intended that it should *not* be used against any of the Big Five. The Soviet Union, the United States, China, France, and the United Kingdom were given a veto—that is, the power to defeat a decision of the Security Council by a single negative vote. At the time of drafting the Charter there were understandings between the Big Five that the veto was to be used only if the passage of a resolution could otherwise culminate in military action against one of them.[14] It became the practice, however (first by the Soviet Union, and in later years by the other Powers too), to use the veto more broadly, both to stop the possibility of any sanction directed against an ally, and indeed even to stop a mere critical resolution directed against an ally. The Security Council became increasingly impotent to act, either militarily or politically.[15]

The West looked for alternatives to allow the United Nations some role in keeping the peace. It was argued that the failure of the Security Council to agree on the establishment of a UN Force meant only that the peace could therefore not be enforced; nor could UN members be *compelled* to offer troops. But if, the argument went, the peace could be kept not by enforcing it, but by policing a territory at the *request* of a state; and if other UN members *volunteered* for such a police force, then such action could be taken. While it was not what the Charter had envisaged, it was not prohibited by it, and it was directed towards a Charter objective—peace. This was the view of the United States and the West generally, and was

[14] L. Goodrich and E. Hambro, *Charter of the United Nations: Documents and Commentary* (1946), 129.
[15] See the examples in S. Bailey, *The Procedure of the United Nations Security Council* (1988), 216–21.

supported by those relatively few Third World countries who were already UN members.

It was not, however, the view of the Soviet Union and its allies. They took the view that the Charter had very specific provisions for the use of force by the United Nations, exemplified by the agreements on UN forces to be agreed under Article 43, and it followed that, if those procedures could not be acted upon, alternatives *not* provided for in the Charter were necessarily unlawful. There were two further points of contention. The Charter envisaged, through the control given to the intended Military Staff Committee (i.e. the Chiefs of Staff of the Big Five) that an effective veto would obtain over the operations of a UN force. But a police force operating outside the envisaged Charter plans would avoid control by veto, and indeed would be under the day-to-day control of the Secretary-General. Was this not to move beyond what the founding instrument had intended?

Further, it was contended by supporters of the idea of UN peace-keeping that a UN police force could be ordered not only by the Security Council, but even by the General Assembly, should the operation of the veto in the Security Council make it impossible for that body to act. These ideas were acceptable to the West, which could at that time with ease command a majority in voting in UN bodies, and which had confidence in the Secretary-General. They were totally unacceptable to the Soviet Union, which, finding itself in a constant minority, needed to rely on the veto whenever possible.[16]

It was against this background that the first UN peace-keeping force was established in 1956. After the UK–French–Israeli intervention in Suez, and the use by the United Kingdom and France of the veto to prevent a condemnatory resolution in the Security Council, Secretary-General Dag Hammarskjold proposed the establishment of a UN peace-keeping force by the General Assembly. This force would oversee a cease-fire and would monitor the withdrawal of the British, French, and Israeli forces from Egyptian territory. The invading forces and Egypt all welcomed the idea of such a force. The Soviet Union, while obviously wishing the United Kingdom and France out of Suez, was opposed to the idea of the UN Emergency Force (UNEF) for the reasons of principle that I have outlined. When the costs of UNEF were distributed among UN members, in the same proportions and way as other UN expenses, the Soviet Union and its allies refused to pay, as did France. From the outset, the financing of UN peace-keeping was insecure and problematic.

The peace-keeping activity itself was successful, however. UNEF did

[16] For the detail of the arguments, see R. Higgins, *United Nations Peacekeeping: Documents and Commentary* (4 vols.); in respect of the Middle East, see i. (1969), 260–72; in respect of the Congo, iii. (1980), 58–61, 274–304.

indeed oversee the withdrawal of all foreign troops, and kept the peace in
that area from 1956 to 1967. It was followed by the successful UN Observer
Group in the Lebanon in 1958 (UNOGIL), and many other UN peace-
keeping operations around the world—in the Congo, Indian subcontinent,
Cyprus, and elsewhere. The idea of peace-keeping has taken deep roots.

The Soviet Union refused to pay its assessed share. Other states
inevitably took advantage of the situation, and failed also to pay that part
of their budget assessment attributable to UN peace-keeping. The
operations all had a precarious financial basis.

None the less, UN forces were successfully established and deployed,
and within the Secretariat there grew up a very considerable body of
expertise in this area. Even if, because of the veto, the United Nations
could not control the use of force by the Big Powers, it seemed that it had a
constructive role to play in controlling force by smaller states. The
Lebanon, the Congo, Cyprus, India, Pakistan, Indonesia, Israel, the Arab
countries—all found themselves beneficiaries of UN peace-keeping.

In the 1950s and 1960s the United Nations was at the centre of US
foreign policy. It supported a liberal reading of what could be done under
the Charter. It supported the expansion of the role of the Secretary-
General to carry out these organizational programmes. It supported, too,
the other major activities of the United Nations—the formulation of early
declarations and treaties on human-rights standards, and the Development
Programme. By contrast, the Soviet Union during this period withheld all
support from these activities, insisted on a strict literal reading of the
Charter, sought to curtail the activities of the Secretary-General, and
directed its foreign policy to minimizing the role of the United Nations on
the international stage.

In the 1960s there was some modest confluence of interest that allowed
peace-keeping to flourish. The Soviet Union allowed forces to be
established in Cyprus in 1964, in Kashmir in 1972, and in the Congo in
1960, withholding its veto. But it still did not pay for them. The West,
for its part, began to believe it unwise for the General Assembly to have
too great power over peace-keeping, and set up all subsequent peace-
keeping (with the exception of that in West Irian) through the Security
Council.

It is only by means of this brief history of the evolution of peace-keeping,
and the traditional attitudes of the United States and the Soviet Union to
this and other important UN activities, that we can today have some sense
of the enormous changes that have taken place in the attitudes of the major
Powers to the United Nations. If the 1950s–1970s reflected the attitudes of
the Cold War, the 1980s showed something of a role reversal by the United
States and the Soviet Union.

In the late 1980s the Soviet Union, embarking upon its historic new path, began to see the advantages of a greater use of the United Nations, supporting UN activities about which it had been ambivalent (such as UN peace-keeping). It not only indicated an intention to pay in the future for UN peace-keeping but coupled that with a commitment to pay for accrued expenses relating to UN peace-keeping;[17] this was a clear indication that it now believed there *was* a legal obligation to pay, and that its change of heart was not simply a change in policy but also a reassessment of the duties of UN members under the Charter and international law. The Russian Federation (the continuation of the Soviet Union) pays all that is required of it under the regular budget and has made some inroads into its accrued debts for past peace-keeping.

But, ironically, just as the Soviet Union was becoming more sympathetic to the United Nations as an instrument for avoiding, containing, and resolving disputes, the United States seemed to start moving in the other direction. It felt, in the 1980s, that it was surrounded by a largely hostile UN membership, and was inevitably outvoted in the General Assembly. It disapproved of much of what that numerical majority was seeking to do, which did not accord with its political philosophy. Further, the United States noted that there was massive financial and administrative inefficiency within the United Nations. As the largest contributor to the UN budget, it was having to pay the lion's share for a budget that could be set at any figure, policies of which it often did not approve, in an organization plagued with bureaucracy and inefficiency.

It has to be said that the United Nations' shortcomings are real, and not merely the invention of those who have political reservations about its programme. While the Secretariat has had many outstanding servants of exceptional dedication and ability, the requirements of proportionate geographic distribution has meant that many posts are not filled by the most capable people. Planning, management, and budgetary control have left much to be desired. There is inefficiency, time-wasting, and waste of resources. Every month tens of thousands of pages are published, containing resolutions and the speeches of delegates. The paper that is operationally relevant is but a tiny fraction of this. And the ever-widening range of topics that the United Nations brings within its remit has led to con-siderable duplication of effort, and often, indeed, to incoherence of result.

The United Nations has not been unaware of these deficiencies, and periodic attempts at reform have taken place.[18] In 1985 the Bertrand

---

[17] See Gorbachev's statement of 7 Dec. 1988, as reported in *Pravda*, 8 Dec. 1988.

[18] See e.g. 'Jackson Report': R. Jackson, *A Study of the Capacity of the United Nations Development System*, UN Doc. DP/5 1969; Joint Inspection Unit, *Some Reflections on Reform of the United Nations*, prepared by Maurice Bertrand (1985), JIU/REP/85/9; and Report of the UN Secretary-General, *Report on the Work of the Organisation* (Sept. 1992), 9–16.

Report[19] on institutional arrangement was produced. Maurice Bertrand, an official of the United Nations' Joint Inspection Unit, was emboldened by the prospect of imminent retirement to produce a report of devastating frankness. He was deeply critical of UN organization and procedures and made far-reaching proposals.

The US reservations about the United Nations were translated into a policy of withholding funds. In August 1985 the Congress approved an amendment to the Foreign Relations Act—the Kassebaum amendment[20]—which provided that the United States should pay no more than 20 per cent of the assessed contributions to the budgets of the United Nations and its specialized agencies until those organizations adopted weighted voting based on the amount of a member's contribution, on budgetary questions. Any adoption of weighted voting in the plenary of the General Assembly would require amendment of Article 18 of the Charter. As Charter amendments under Chapter XVIII require a two-thirds vote in the Assembly to have legal effect, such an amendment is unlikely ever to occur. Moreover, the introduction of weighted voting in the General Assembly would represent an affront to an underlying principle on which the United Nations is based—namely, the sovereign equality of all its member states. Later on, another piece of legislation, the Gramm–Rudman Act of December 1985,[21] further reduced Congressional appropriations for international organizations. The withholdings applied not only to the United Nations, but to the specialized agencies. The United States rapidly accrued huge arrears of sums owed under the financing provisions of the Charter and the various constituent instruments of the other agencies. The effect on the United Nations was devastating. While it had in the past been able to absorb the adverse effects of the financial shortcomings of contributors who paid a smaller share, the witholdings of a large percentage of US funds (which represented a high proportion of the total) put the United Nations into crisis. The European Community countries felt obliged to express their deep concern:

The Twelve wish to express their concern that recently enacted US legislation, in particular the Gramm–Rudman–Hollings act and the Kassebaum amendment, is significantly affecting the Administration's ability to comply with its international treaty obligations. The implementation of such legislation will result in the United States not fully meeting its financial obligation to the United Nations as contained in Article 17, paragraph 2, of the Charter . . . Selective adherence to the principle 'pacta sunt servanda' erodes the very foundation of the international order. In this

[19] M. Bertrand, *Some Reflections on Reform of the United Nations* (1985).
[20] 22 USC 278e (99 Stat. 405, 424, 1985).
[21] The cuts that resulted from execution of the Gramm–Rudman Act were implemented through the Balanced Budget and Emergency Deficit Control Act of 1985 (99 Stat. 1037, approved 12 Dec. 1985, codified principally at 2 USC 901).

respect financial obligations are not different from any other international obligations.[22]

It was in this context that another stage of reform was instigated from within the United Nations. In February 1986 a group of intergovernmental experts was set up by the General Assembly, to be appointed by the President of the General Assembly.[23] This group, which became known as the 'Committee of Eighteen', produced a report in 1986 which focused on a new agenda item of UN reform: that of achieving greater efficiency in the use of resources.[24] As a consequence of this report a compromise was reached between the United Nations and the United States which involved giving a primary role to the intergovernmental Committee on Programme and Co-ordination (CPC) and a lesser role to the Advisory Committee on Administrative and Budgetary Questions (ACABQ) when the Secretary-General is seeking advice as to the outline budget of the UN. Both bodies have traditionally advised the Secretary-General as to the outline budget, with the opinion of the ACABQ, composed of individual experts, carrying somewhat more weight. As the CPC is small and composed of inter-governmental representatives, this new arrangement gives the states that contribute a greater share to the United Nations' coffers greater influence in the determination of the budget.

Things have now somewhat improved. The setting of the budget has been brought under better control and there have been certain serious attempts at cutting down on waste and improving efficiency. The US administration in turn advised the Congress that proper payment of its assessed dues should be resumed and has had talks with the Secretary-General about the payment of its back dues. The Congress has not been willing fully to respond to the desires of the administration, but a higher percentage of payments owed is now coming through and the situation is less immediately critical. In 1990–2, after the collapse of the old order in the Soviet Union, the United States again harnessed its foreign policy to the United Nations and became heavily committed in UN peace-keeping and in UN-authorized military action.

The financial and legal implications of the unilateral withholding of contributions by the United States are wide-ranging in scope and pervasive in nature. The clear violation by the United States of its legal obligation under Article 17 of the Charter to pay its assessed contributions has encouraged other states to follow this lead. As of September 1992 only fifty-two member states had paid in full their dues to the regular budget of

---

[22] Memorandum to Secretary of State Shultz, 14 Mar. 1986, repr. in (1986) 25 *ILM* 482.
[23] GA Res. 40/237, 1985.
[24] *Report of the Group of High Level Intergovernmental Experts to Review the Efficiency of the Administrative and Financial Functioning of the United Nations*, GA Official Records, suppl. no. 49, A/41/49, 1986.

the United Nations.[25] With the persistence of the violation of this legal obligation, a paralysing contradiction has developed in UN affairs. On the one hand, states proclaim their desire for expansion in the role of the United Nations in such areas as maintenance of international peace and UN peace-keeping. On the other, lack of provision of finances to achieve the greater possibilities that now exist is accepted as a reality of international politics.

The problem is chronic, and has spread far beyond the changing positions taken over the years by the Soviet Union and the United States. Failure to pay budgetary dues, whether general or related to peace-keeping, is endemic within the United Nations. It is regrettable that, when there are such improved prospects for the United Nations to aid significantly in containing disputes, because of the improved East–West climate, it is still so constrained by financial problems. As of September 1992 the United Nations was still owed more than £1 billion by its member states. The UN Iraq–Kuwait Observation Mission, which has had such a critical role to play in the aftermath of the Gulf War, is owed, as at 31 October 1992, more than $25 million in assessed member states' contributions.[26] The UN Interim Force in the Lebanon (UNIFIL) had a deficit of more than $227 million. In the meanwhile, UN members want the long-standing conflict over Western Sahara brought to a conclusion through a UN-organized referendum, the technical side of which would be supported by a military component. Although the referendum has temporarily been postponed, outstanding assessed contributions from member states as at 30 September 1992 totalled over $21 million.[27] Countless other examples could be given.

It is an oversimplification to suppose that, with the end of the Cold War, only financial constraints prevent the full realization of the United Nations' potential in the field of collective security. The euphoria that followed the enforcement measures authorized by the United Nations against Iraq in 1990–1 has given way to a new and disturbing reality. Wars and inhumane behaviour rage everywhere. No real machinery for collective security through enforcement measures is in place. The United States is financially unable and politically unwilling to bear all the burden of enforcement action. The choices it does make are necessarily seen as selective and not directed in an even-handed fashion.

The end of the Cold War, and the Gulf War precedent, has raised expectations without addressing the preconditions for their fulfilment. The tragic events in the former Yugoslavia illustrate the deeply unsatisfactory

---

[25] *Status of Contributions as at 30 September 1992* (1993), ST/ADM/SER.B/387 4–9.
[26] *Status of Contributions as at 31 October 1992*, ST/ADM/SER.B/391, 39.
[27] See *Status of Contributions as at 30 September 1992*, ST/ADM/SER.B/387, 48.

nature of fragmented institutional approaches. There has been involvement by the European Community, the Western European Union, the Conference on Security and Co-operation in Europe (CSCE), and the United Nations, sometimes simultaneously, sometimes sequentially. The UN peace-keeping force—UNPROFOR—has been placed in certain locations, with an ever-changing mandate. Unlike any previous peace-keeping force, it is operating against the background of a UN arms embargo and economic sanctions. All the lessons of the necessary conditions for UN peace-keeping seem to have been forgotten; and all the alternative possibilities under the Charter ignored. UN peace-keeping, together with collective measures under Chapter VII of the Charter, appears to be entering a period of deep incoherence.

Political Bodies and Quasi-Judicial Activities

Article 1 enjoins the United Nations 'to bring about by peaceful means and in conformity with the principles of justice and international law, adjustment or settlement of international disputes'. Thus all the routine political activities of the United Nations must comply not only with the specific requirements of the Charter, but with general international law. From time to time the political organs of the United Nations have, in the context of dispute resolution, made decisions that, often in an incidental fashion, make determinations of international law. An early resolution on whether belligerent rights could be claimed after an armistice came into existence affords a rather clear example.[28] The Security Council has on several occasions passed resolutions determining entities claiming to be independent governments as 'having no validity', or as being 'illegal regimes'. Resolutions on Southern Rhodesia ('an illegal racist regime') and the situation in South-West Africa are cases in point.[29] It is, of course, desirable that the Security Council should be keen to play a role in upholding international law, and invoking international law is an important element in application. But certain points would seem to fall for consideration. The first is when determinations that purport to pronounce authoritatively on international law are made. It is important that they are made with care, upon proper legal advice, with an understanding of the issues—and not merely as an almost casual description for political purposes. It has been observed that to call a government 'illegal' in just the same way as it is termed 'racist' is to use the term adjectivally, but not

[28] See SC Res. 95 (1951), 1 Sept. 1951, in which the Security Council called upon Egypt to terminate its restrictions on the passage of international commercial shipping and goods through the Suez Canal.
[29] SC Res. 217 (1965); SC Res. 276 (1970).

seriously.[30] But serious legal consequences are said to follow. It should not be thought from these remarks that my views on the status of any of the above claimants to independence is different from that arrived at by the Security Council: it is simply that there was little evidence in the debates that the Security Council reached its determinations by careful legal analysis.

The second point we must consider is the extent to which quasi-judicial determination by the Security Council is in fact appropriate. This is a very difficult question, but one that has been made particularly pertinent by recent events. But let us retrace our steps.

Occasionally the Security Council will not merely point the parties towards the various options open to them for the political settlement of disputes, but will make its own proposals for the substance of the solution. Without in terms saying so, it is necessarily implied that the specified elements in the solution are those required by international law. The celebrated Resolution 242 (1967), on a solution to the Arab–Israeli dispute, affords an excellent illustration. This resolution affirms the following elements as necessary for a solution, all of them resonant of international law obligations: the inadmissibility of the acquisition of territory by war; the withdrawal of armed forces from occupied territory; the termination of claims of belligerency; the acknowledgment of the sovereignty, territorial integrity, and political independence of every state; the right to live in secure boundaries free from threats or acts of force; freedom of navigation through international waterways; a just settlement of refugee problems. So here we have an example of the rights and wrongs of claims made being implicitly passed on in the context of decisions as to how peaceful settlement should be achieved.

In the resolutions referred to above on non-recognition of certain claimant governments, there has been explicit assertion of international legal requirements, and reference to legal consequences that flow from these determinations. Determinations of international law are now part and parcel of decision-making on collective measures (non-recognition, the withholding of diplomatic relations) in response to human-rights violations or to international aggression. If the availability of collective measures (Article 41) for the containing of human-rights violations is uncertain (and I shall come back to this in my penultimate chapter), the entitlement so to act in respect of aggression is beyond doubt. And it is into this last category that Security Council Resolution 662 (1990) falls, when it 'Decides that the annexation of Kuwait by Iraq under any form and whatever pretext has no legal validity and is considered null and void'.

---

[30] See E. Lauterpacht, *Aspects of the Administration of International Justice* (1991), 39; also R. Higgins, 'The Place of International Law in the Settlement of Disputes by the Security Council' (1970) 64 *AJIL* 1.

Other determinations of international law can also be considered as a necessary element in the Security Council's role of maintaining peace and security. It could, for example, certainly not have failed in the Gulf conflict to have taken a position on the applicability of the Geneva Conventions and on humanitarian law generally. But, interestingly, not only were the parties reminded that they had to comply with those international law obligations, but the Resolution twice referred to 'Iraq's responsibility in this regard'.[31] Again, it was understandable and appropriate, in responding to events, that the Security Council should determine that there had been violations by way of the law relating to the protection of diplomatic personnel and premises—and once again the phrase was used that 'Iraq is fully responsible for any use of violence against foreign nationals or against any diplomatic or consular mission'. Security Council Resolution 667, of 16 September 1990, in terms spoke of violations of international law, as did subsequent Security Council Resolution 670, which declared the mistreatment of Kuwaitis and their property as violating international law. But subsequent resolutions on the Gulf seem to go very much further, and contain determinations that it is extremely unusual to see coming from a political body. Let me give some examples. In Resolution 674 of 29 October 1990 the Security Council stated that 'under international law it [Iraq] is liable for any loss, damage or injury arising in regard to Kuwait and third states'. That is an assertion of international law that a tribunal might want to make in somewhat more qualified terms. Further, the Resolution invited states to collect relevant information concerning claims. In Resolution 687 of 3 April 1991, passed after hostilities had ceased, the Security Council drew attention to the legal position of Iraq in relation to chemical and biological weapons. The Resolution also determined that the international boundary should be delimited on the basis of what had been agreed between them in 1964. It is one thing for the Security Council to insist that one state cannot use force to settle its frontier with another. It is another thing for it to purport to determine, in a sentence or two, where the frontier should run. Although I believe that legal analysis would show that the 1964 agreement was still in effect between the states concerned, the Security Council's determination of these matters simply ignores the recent Iraqi claims that for various reasons the 1964 treaty no longer applied. Had the matter of where the boundary lay fallen for determination by a legal tribunal, it would have been expected that an opportunity would have been given for these arguments to be deployed, and legal reasons for rejecting them (if that was the tribunal's conclusion) would have been given. It was further affirmed (without any legal hearing, and notwithstanding that a tribunal might well have reached comparable

[31] SC Res. 666 (1990).

decisions) that Iraq was liable for direct[32] loss and damage for environmental harm, depletion of natural resources, injuries to foreign governments, nationals, and corporations, as a result of the invasion. The
repudiation by Iraq of its foreign debt was declared 'null and void', as
though the Security Council was a tribunal of competent jurisdiction. And,
as we know, a fund was set up to pay for compensation for claims and a
Commission established to administer the fund.[33]

This makes an interesting contrast with the Iran–US controversy over
the taking of the hostages and the subsequent events. There are, of course,
obvious differences—in that case Iran has claims against the United States
as well as the United States against Iran. And, although Iran was
determined by the International Court to have violated the Vienna
Convention on Diplomatic Relations, it had not committed international
aggression. The determination of issues of responsibility and questions of
compensation was left to a tribunal established for the purpose (the Iran–
US Claims Tribunal). In the Iraq affair, the Security Council made the
legal determinations of liability.[34] It will also handle the compensation to
be paid out, through a staff that will include, but will not be limited to,
lawyers. We have to see how all of this works out, but we should
understand that it is very, very different from anything we have expected of
the Security Council before. Whether it would be wise or prudent for the
Security Council to move, in other cases too, into the heart of what we
normally see as judicial activity—that is to say, functions that tribunals are
by their training and experience and familiarity with the relevant norms
very well placed to carry out—must be doubtful.

Conclusion

In speaking about the role of the United Nations in containing disputes, I
have talked about the past, and about the present. This has been done to
show that the Charter is an extraordinary instrument, and that a huge
variety of possibilities are possible under it. This chapter has emphasized
peace-keeping, not at all envisaged under the Charter, but now an
important reality. In the improved international climate it has been
possible, in 1990 and 1991, to envisage that the Security Council might
behave rather more as was originally intended under the Charter. But
there are indications that it is now setting out on other new paths, which
significantly risk legal incoherence. In so far as these entail enforcement
action and intervention, they will be the subject of my final chapter. But

[32] SC Res. 674 (1990) had omitted to limit liability to *direct* loss and damage. This
qualification was then introduced in SC Res. 687 (1991).
[33] See SC Res. 687 (1991).   [34] Ibid.

peace-keeping will not now go away. It will exist side by side with a return to other forms of more orthodox international co-operation, or with yet further variations on the intentions of Chapter VII of the Charter.

The UN Charter is full of possibilities. The changing history of attitudes that I have outlined shows that, while the possibilities are there, they can only be realized if the states want to do so.

DISPUTE SETTLEMENT AND THE INTERNATIONAL COURT OF JUSTICE

WE have seen that, in a decentralized system, a variety of participants invoke international law in advancing claims against each other. They do so with varying degrees of seriousness over the extent to which they really believe that their conduct or claims comply with the requirements of international law. But, at the moment at which the parties to a legal controversy believe that the preferred solution is to have the issue resolved authoritatively by a third party, there arises the possibility for an international tribunal to act. There are really three kinds of data that are particularly interesting to look at: the first is the potential for the International Court of Justice taking jurisdiction over various states; the second is the actual use of the Court by various states; and the third is the subject-matter upon which cases have been brought before the Court. Let us take them one by one.

The Potential for Jurisdiction

The competence of international tribunals is essentially founded on consent, though, as we shall see, it has become increasingly tolerated for that consent to be given in a rather general way, so that it is a consent of principle rather than a consent in relation to a particular dispute with a particular opponent. Standing international courts are themselves established by international treaty. Thus the Inter-American Court on Human Rights, the European Court on Human Rights, the Court of the European Community, and the International Court of Justice each owes its existence to international agreements between states. But to exist is one thing; to have competence in respect of particular states in regard to particular claims is another. It is the founding treaty itself which elaborates how it is that a court may have jurisdiction in a particular dispute. The Inter-American Convention on Human Rights, the European Convention on Human Rights, the Treaty of Rome, and the UN Charter all provide their own different answers.

The Inter-American and European Courts on Human Rights, and the Court of the European Community, are constrained by their founding treaties as to the subject-matter they can determine; and by the restricted parties to those treaties as to the states who may bring claims before them. Two Asian states may not go before the Inter-American Court on Human Rights to resolve a fishing dispute. But the International Court of Justice is properly viewed as the senior of all the International Courts, not only because of its long and distinguished history, but because of the breadth of the possibilities before it. Any state that is a party to the Statute (which means any member of the United Nations and any other state that has made special application to be a party to the Statute) can potentially come before it. And the Court can deal with any question at all of international law.

Article 38 of the Statute of the International Court of Justice stipulates that its function is 'to decide in accordance with international law such disputes as are submitted to it', and of course the Article goes on to say exactly what the Court will apply in fulfilling this task: the well-known sources of international law—namely, custom, treaties, general principles, judicial decisions, and the writings of the leading publicists. There is thus an enormous potential for the use of the Court, both as to parties and as to subject-matter. Some forty-eight years after the establishment of the United Nations, and the International Court in continuation of the Permanent Court, a picture begins to emerge.

Actual Use of the Court

Article 36 (1) provides that the jurisdiction of the International Court of Justice comprises cases which the parties refer to it and all matters specially provided for in the UN Charter or in treaties or conventions in force. Every party to the Statute can of course bring, *ad hoc* and on the basis of agreement, a case with another Statute party before the Court. The joint reference in 1987 by Italy and the United States of the *ELSI Case*[1] to the Court is just such an example. It was simply agreed between the two states that they would avail themselves of the advantage of being parties to the Court, and submit the case to the Court. Although the potential is enormous, relatively few cases have been brought before the Court on this basis. But since the very early 1980s there has been a much greater use of *ad hoc* agreed reference to the Court. Since 1983 it has been used by the United States and Canada in the *Gulf of Maine Case*;[2] by Libya and Malta in their continental shelf dispute;[3] by Burkina Faso and Mali in their frontier dispute;[4] by Libya and Tunisia in the latter's application for

[1] *Elettronica Sicula Case*, ICJ Reports (1989) 15.
[2] *Delimitation of the Maritime Boundary in the Gulf of Maine Area*, ICJ Reports (1984) 246. [3] *Libya–Malta Case*, ICJ Reports (1985) 13.
[4] *Burkina Faso–Mali Frontier Dispute*, ICJ Reports (1986) 554.

revision and interpretation of a judgment;[5] by Italy and the United States in the *ELSI Case*;[6] by Denmark and Norway in the problem regarding maritime delimitation;[7] and by Finland and Denmark in the passage through the Great Belt.[8] It is noticeable that there is an accelerated trend to use the Court on this basis (it is now a high percentage of all references) and that a wide spread of states, from various regions of the world, is taking advantage of the possibility. It is no coincidence that by 1992 the Court had over twelve cases waiting for disposal. This is exactly because states from all over the world are coming to the Court, not reluctantly dragged there by reference to instruments they now wished they had never signed, but voluntarily. This undoubtedly reflects an increasing confidence in the Court, not only as an institution of great competence and impartiality but one perceived as capable of ensuring that its interpretation of international law is at once predictable and responsive to diverse legitimate needs.

Article 36 (1) speaks not only of cases that are simply referred to the Court, but of treaties as a basis of its jurisdiction. Any treaty, whether bilateral or multilateral, can include a clause which stipulates that disputes that arise about the interpretation and application of the treaty are to be referred for judicial resolution. (Whether such a clause allows of reservations depends, as the Court explained in the famous *Reservations Case*[9] about just such a clause, upon whether that would be compatible with the objects and purposes of the treaty concerned.) There are over 260 treaties, multilateral and bilateral, which envisage such a possibility. Again, the range of parties thereto in multilateral treaties is enormous. Such multilateral treaties include the 1989 International Convention against the Recruitment, Use, Financing and Training of Mercenaries and the 1980 Convention on the Conservation of Antarctic Marine Living Resources. There is such a clause also, for example, in the 1961 Vienna Convention on Diplomatic Relations, which is a very widely ratified treaty. As for the bilateral treaties, again they reveal a rather wide spread of states potentially prepared to go to the International Court over any dispute that might arise regarding the treaty. They include Canada and the United States, several European countries (France, Italy, the United Kingdom, Norway, Switzerland); Brazil and Venezuela; Sudan and Saudi Arabia; and Togo, Guinea, and Liberia. It is noticeable that the African countries

---

[5] *Tunisia–Libya Continental Shelf Case. Application for Revision and Interpretation of the Judgment of 24 February 1982*, ICJ Reports (1985) 192.
[6] *Elettronica Sicula Case*, ICJ Reports (1986).
[7] *Jan Mayen Continental Shelf Delimitation Case*, ICJ Reports (1993).
[8] *Passage through the Great Belt (Finland v. Denmark)*, Provisional Measures, ICJ Reports (1991) 12. This case was later settled and withdrawn from the lists.
[9] *Reservations to the Genocide Convention Case*, ICJ Reports (1951) 23.

have been prepared to accept this reference to the Court in bilateral treaties with developed countries—but there is no evidence of any such potential reference to the Court in their bilateral treaties with each other. It seems that, in inter-African bilateral relations, judicial settlement procedures are not the norm, and reference *ad hoc*, should the parties agree, is preferred. Other things are noticeable too. There is a total absence of any interest by Asian states in referring bilateral treaty matters (no matter who the other party is) to the Court. Further, the tendency to include jurisdiction clauses in either multilateral or bilateral treaties is markedly declining. In the early years the Soviet Union and Eastern European states used to refuse any such reference to the Court, insisting on entering reservations to multilateral treaties that contained such clauses. Now all such objections have been withdrawn, but, ironically, the general interest in including such clauses has greatly diminished. In 1951 there were thirteen such treaties; since 1980 there have been two, more usually one, a year. This trend may partly reflect a growing variety of alternative dispute-settlement procedures on offer. Parties to multilateral treaties often envisage entirely different ways of working out their disputes and ensuring compliance with treaty obligations.

Article 36 (2) of the Statute provides for what is known as 'Optional Clause' jurisdiction, stipulating that a state party to the Statute may at any time declare that it recognizes as compulsory *ipso facto* and without special agreement, in relation to any other state accepting the same obligation, the jurisdiction of the Court in legal dispute. In this acceptance, a state effectively signs a blank cheque, as it does not know what will be the subject-matter of a future dispute that will be submitted under it to the Court, nor does it know the other party to the dispute—only that it will have accepted the same obligations as to jurisdiction. Acceptance of the Optional Clause may be indefinite, or upon notification of termination, or for a fixed period of years. It used to be the case that Western members of the United Nations were disproportionately represented among those who had accepted the Optional Clause, and that relatively few Third World countries had accepted it. Socialist countries, who until very recently have not accepted the idea of third-party judicial settlement, have never accepted the Optional Clause. The position now is significantly changed. The United Kingdom is alone among the Permanent Members of the Security Council in accepting the Optional Clause. The acceptances of France and the United States have both been withdrawn upon notice. France had found itself subject to Orders for Interim Measures in the *Nuclear Tests Case*[10] and was also concerned at the possibility of jurisdiction being established over it in the future in respect of comparable issues. The United States deeply resented the way in which jurisdictional

[10] *Nuclear Tests Case*, ICJ Reports (1974) 253.

issues were handled by the Court in the *Nicaragua* v. *United States Case*.[11] China and the USSR never had accepted the jurisdiction of the Court, under the Optional Clause or otherwise.

Although in 1991 there were fifty states parties to the Optional Clause, only eleven out of the fifty were from European countries. Australia and Japan, however, add to the number of industrialized countries party to the Optional Clause. But virtually all of the rest are Third World countries, including fourteen African states and seven central and southern American states. Asia is still under-represented in this form of jurisdiction-giving, as in others, with only Japan, India, Pakistan, and the Philippines (and Cyprus).

The evidence seems clear that, although the commitment to the Optional Clause has declined, the Third World commitment relative to that of the West has advanced. After a difficult period in the mid-1960s to mid-1970s—in part the legacy of the *South West Africa Cases*[12]—the Court today clearly commands the confidence of a very wide spread of countries. Of course, while this is an expression of confidence in the impartiality of the Court, and its ability to assist in resolving today's problems, it is also a vote of confidence in international law. For it is international law that the Court has to apply, and there seems no remnant of the view often expressed in the 1960s that, no matter how impartial the Court may be, it would have to apply a corpus of law that was biased in favour of those who had formed it and had little to offer the newer states. There is now a wide appreciation that international law, with its in-built procedures for evolution and development, can assist all nations in resolving their disputes.

Clearly, in the last decade such countries as Libya, Tunisia, Malta, Nicaragua, El Salvador, Honduras, Guinea Bissau, Senegal, Chad—as well as Canada, the United States, Denmark, Norway, Australia, and Finland—have all felt the advantage of litigating before the Court. About half of the last twenty cases have been on the basis of agreed referrals, and the other half have been cases brought against reluctant defendants. Of course, the more reluctant the defendants—as the cases brought on the basis of the Optional Clause will often be—the more will such defendants seek to avail themselves of opportunities to argue that the Court in fact has no jurisdiction to proceed. The Optional Clause, as we will shortly see,

---

[11] *Military and Paramilitary Activities in and against Nicaragua*, Jurisdiction and Admissibility, ICJ Reports (1984) 392. For US debate, see Editorial Comments (1985) 79 *AJIL*: H. Briggs, ibid. 373; T. Franck, ibid. 379; A. d'Amato, ibid. 385; E. Highet, ibid. 992; M. Reisman (1986) 80 *AJIL* 128.

[12] *South West Africa Cases* (Second Phase), ICJ Reports (1966) 3. See R. Higgins, 'The International Court and South West Africa: The Implications of the Judgment' (1966) *International Affairs* 573.

offers many such opportunities, and in the past a substantial proportion of the Court's hearings and judgments were directed not towards the substantive issues of international law at the heart of a case, but at issues concerning its own jurisdiction. With the declining emphasis on the Optional Clause and an increased use of *ad hoc* referrals to the Court, this necessary preoccupation with jurisdictional issues is receding somewhat—another healthy trend. (At the same time, to any international lawyer, some of the jurisdictional issues are of the very keenest interest and make absorbing study: we may cite the jurisdictional phase of the *South West Africa Cases*,[13] the *Nicaragua–United States Case*,[14] and *Nauru* v. *Australia*,[15] as examples.

The Subject-Matter of Litigation before the Court

In contentious litigation, the Court has been called upon to deal with a wide subject-matter. Delimitation disputes (whether of zones or inter-national frontiers, both maritime and territorial, take up a large amount of the Court's workload. Thus there have been important cases concerning the width of territorial seas and the method for drawing baselines for this purpose.[16] Vital issues relating either to the allocation of land, or to the more precise problems of drawing a boundary, have arisen in such cases as the *Frontier Lands* dispute between Belgium and the Netherlands;[17] the Minquiers and Ecrehos Islands (between Britain and France)[18] and the frontier dispute between Mali and Burkina Faso.[19] In June 1993 the Court commenced hearings of the case that deals with a frontier dispute between Chad and Libya.[20]

The Court has also had to deal with other issues falling within the broad area of law of the sea—passage through straits in the particular factual circumstances of the *Corfu Channel Case*[21] and the *Great Belt Case*[22]

---

[13] *South West Africa Cases* (Preliminary Objections), ICJ Reports (1962) 319.
[14] *Military and Paramilitary Activities Case* (Jurisdiction), ICJ Reports (1984) 392.
[15] *Certain Phosphate Lands in Nauru*, ICJ Reports (1992) 240 at para. 55.
[16] *Anglo-Norwegian Fisheries Case*, ICJ Reports (1951) 139; *North Sea Continental Shelf Cases*, ICJ Reports (1969) 1; *Tunisia–Libya Continental Shelf Case*, ICJ Reports (1982) 1; *Continental Shelf (Libyan Arab Jamahiriya/Malta Case)*, ICJ Reports (1985) 13; *Delimitation of the Maritime Boundary in the Gulf of Maine Area*, ICJ Reports (1984) 246; *Fisheries Jurisdiction Case*, ICJ Reports (1974) 1; and *Land, Island and Maritime Frontier Dispute*, ICJ Reports (1992) 351.
[17] *Sovereignty over Certain Frontier Lands Case*, ICJ Reports (1959) 225.
[18] *Minquiers and Ecrehos Islands Case*, ICJ Reports (1953) 47.
[19] *Burkina Faso* v. *Mali*, ICJ Reports (1986) 554.
[20] *Territorial Dispute (Libyan Arab Jamahiriya* v. *Chad)*.
[21] *Corfu Channel Case*, ICJ Reports (1949) 5.
[22] For an Order by the Court in this case, see *Case Concerning Passage through the Great Belt*, Order of 10 September 1992, ICJ Reports (1992) 348.

providing fascinating and contrasting examples. And from time to time the Court has cases involving peace and security issues, conflicts relating to the use of force between states whose relations are generally hostile. The dispute over the shooting down by the United States of an Iran Airways plane,[23] which concerns interesting questions about responsibility for mistake in the absence of *culpa*, and the *Nicaragua–US* litigation[24] are cases in point, along with the cases concerning transboundary armed actions in South America (*Nicaragua* v. *Honduras*; *Nicaragua* v. *Costa Rica*).[25]

In principle, as we have seen, the Court can in its contentious litigation deal with any legal dispute: the subject-matter is potentially enormous. An interesting question arises from this. There is nothing in the Statute that requires the Court *not* to accept jurisdiction if the parties have in fact agreed to use alternative dispute-resolution procedures. The Soviet Union and its allies, until recently opposed to any form of third-party settlement, recently indicated, in a series of virtually identical statements, that they would like to see the International Court of Justice resolve a variety of legal issues, including those in the area of human rights. Reservations to treaties referring disputes to the United Nations would be withdrawn.[26] While the general sentiment in these statements—formally issued as documents of state—is welcome, the precise meaning to be attached to them is a puzzle. This is because these countries are all parties to the International Covenant on Human Rights, which treaty has its own quasi-judicial procedures for the settlement of legal disputes concerning human rights. It seems that the intention is not to ignore these, as Estonia, Mongolia, Hungary, Lithuania, Poland, Russia, and the Ukraine have accepted further optional possibilities for human-rights litigation in the framework of the Covenant procedures.[27] A suggestion has also been explored, in private meetings, that the Permanent Members of the Security Council should agree *inter se* to resolve a range of pre-identified categories of disputes by reference to the Court. It is not clear whether this would be done by acceptance of the Optional Clause, making use of the permitted reservations as to subject-matter and parties, or otherwise. If a separate mechanism is envisaged, it would be a form of consent-based advance jurisdiction, existing in parallel to the Optional Clause. If it were done under the Optional Clause, presumably it would be done by the Soviet

---

[23] The Case Aerial Incident of 3 July 1988 is pending. For an Order by the Court in this case, see *Aerial Incident of 3 July 1988*, Order of 13 December 1989, ICJ Reports (1989) 132.

[24] *Military and Paramilitary Activities* (Merits), ICJ Reports (1986) 3.

[25] *Border and Transborder Armed Actions* (Admissibility), ICJ Reports (1988) 69.

[26] See Letter of 28 Feb. 1989 from Soviet Minister for Foreign Affairs Schevardnadze to the Secretary-General, reproduced in (1989) 83 *AJIL* 457.

[27] Annual Report of the Human Rights Committee 1992, A/47/40, GAOR 47th sess.

Union, France, the United Kingdom, China, and the United States each agreeing that, in relation *to each other* and in respect of *defined categories of dispute*, there will be reference to the Court. But further progress on this issue seems to be at a standstill.

The Question of Reservations

It is well known that the reservations permitted under the Optional Clause have meant that jurisdiction nominally given under Article 36 (2) of the Statute can in fact be a very limited grant of jurisdiction indeed. Article 36 (3) simply states that declarations of acceptance under the Optional Clause—by which a state recognizes the jurisdiction of the Court in relation to any other party making the same obligation—may be made unconditionally or on condition of reciprocity, on the part of several or certain states, or for a certain time. This seemingly simple clause, when coupled with the conditions in Article 36 (2) itself—that acceptance is in respect of the state accepting the same obligation—has caused endless complications. The *condition* mentioned in Article 36 (3) is that of reciprocity on the part of certain or several states ('I accept, on condition States A and B accept also to settle disputes with me'). In addition, an acceptance may be made for a certain time ('I accept, for the next five years'). But the Optional Clause has also been treated as a treaty engagement, and that in turn has led to the possibility of *reservations* as a matter of general treaty law, over and above what is specifically permitted as *conditions* of acceptance under Article 36 (3). The contractual, treaty element (between the various parties to the Optional Protocol) was emphasized by the Court in the *Rights of Passage Case*.[28] In the *Nicaragua* v. *United States Case* the Court stated that, if the declarations of acceptance under the Optional Clause were to be treated as treaties, a declaration of acceptance could not be withdrawn without reasonable notice of termination. It found that the purported modification by the United States of its declaration of acceptance was in effect a termination *vis-à-vis* certain named states, and was done without reasonable notice. It did not therefore succeed in withdrawing jurisdiction from the Court.[29]

But *reservations* are permitted too and sometimes these are ingeniously directed—thus the Portuguese reservation in the *Rights of Passage Case* exactly reserved the possibility of terminating acceptance immediately on notification. (The US acceptance of the Optional Clause had no such

---

[28] *Rights of Passage Case* (Preliminary Objections), ICJ Reports (1957) 125 at 145–7.
[29] *Military and Paramilitary Activities Case* (Jurisdiction), ICJ Reports (1984) 392 at para. 14.

reservation, so the 'due-notice' treaty rule[30] was held to apply.) Normally a reservation to a treaty can only be made upon ratification of or accession to a treaty. Thus, if the Optional Clause is accepted for an indefinite period, it is at the moment of acceptance that any reservations must be made. Or, if the Optional Clause is accepted for a five-year period, then no new reservations can be made until the beginning of the next period for which an acceptance is made. But some states, such as Malta, have made a reservation which purports exactly to allow them to make *further* reservations. The legality of such a reservation has yet to be tested before the Court.

Three types of reservations have been usual, and broadly acceptable: (1) reservations relating to other parties ('I accept the jurisdiction of the Court, save that I will not agree to litigation of disputes with States Y and Z': reservations *ratione personae*); (2) reservations relating to time ('I accept in 1990 the jurisdiction of the Court in respect to all disputes save those concerning events that occurred in 1985': reservations *ratione temporis*); and (3) reservations as to subject-matter ('I accept the jurisdiction of the Court, but not for the settlement of aviation disputes': reservations *ratione materiae*). Under this last category there have been attempts at reservations which preclude subject-matter within a state's domestic jurisdiction—sometimes 'as determined by itself'. This type of reservation, adopted initially by the United States but embraced by other states also, is of doubtful legal status, because it is the Court that must determine its own jurisdiction. Judge Lauterpacht took the view that an Optional Clause with this type of reservation was no real acceptance of the Court's jurisdiction *at all*.[31] The result of that view, ironically, is not that that state has not accepted the Court's jurisdiction, albeit with a regrettably wide reservation, but has not accepted the jurisdiction at all. This matter has received some attention from the Court in the *International Norwegian Loans*[32] and *Rights of Passage Case*,[33] without ever being determinatively resolved.

Because under the Optional Clause a state accepts the Court's jurisdiction only in respect of another state who accepts the same obligation, the jurisdiction of the Court exists only in respect of what is common between them. Put differently, State A accepts the jurisdiction of the Court over itself, only in respect of what State B has accepted *after* its reservations and any conditions have been taken into account. Thus every

[30] Rosenne rejects the full treaty analysis: *Documents on the International Court of Justice* (2nd edn., 1979), 358–61. See also the discussion by L. Gross, 'Compulsory Jurisdiction under the Optional Clause: History and Practice', in L. Damrosch (ed.), *The International Court of Justice at a Crossroad* (1987) 19 at 30.
[31] See *Norwegian Loans Case*, ICJ Reports (1957) 9; sep. op. at 34–66.
[32] The Court felt no need to consider the validity of the French reservation as it was not an issue between the parties (ibid. 27). [33] ICJ Reports (1957) 125.

party to the Optional Clause can rely to escape jurisdiction when the prospect of litigation actually looms on the horizon, on every limitation by the other party as if it were its own. It is not surprising that controversy as to the actual scope of the Court's jurisdiction in a given case has taken up much of its time, often requiring lengthy preliminary hearings. The increased tendency to *ad hoc* reference to the Court, often by agreed compromise, will hopefully reduce the proportion of the Court's time determining litigation about its own jurisdiction.

Legal Disputes

Article 36 (2) contains one further requirement—that the matter brought before it is a 'legal dispute'. The Court, before it accepts jurisdiction, has thus to be satisfied both that the matter before it is 'legal' and that it constitutes a 'dispute'. Generally speaking, the Court has taken a robust attitude as to what is a 'legal' matter. It has said (in the context of its advisory jurisdiction in the *Admissions Case*[34]) that it matters not that the *motive* in coming to the Court is political. All that is required is that there are issues that involve any of the matters listed in Article 36 (2), which speaks of legal disputes that concern: (*a*) the interpretation of a treaty; (*b*) any question of international law; (*c*) the existence of any fact which, if established, would constitute a breach of an international obligation. It is irrelevant if any of these matters arise in a politically charged context (as often they do). The Court still has a legal task to perform. Again, as early as 1932 in the *Free Zones Case*,[35] the Permanent Court of International Justice (the predecessor of the International Court) had made clear that it was prepared also to address matters of great economic importance, provided always that they arose in the context of legal questions to be answered. The views expressed by the Court in 1966, in the *South West Africa* affair, that the issues brought to it were 'really' political, and better left for determination by the Security Council,[36] were out of line with the otherwise consistent attitude of the Court that neither motive nor context matters: all that matters is that it is required to interpret a treaty, or determine a question of international law, or pronounce upon a breach of obligation, or deal with the nature and extent of reparation. So, even such highly charged cases as *Nicaragua* v. *United States*,[37] and the cases brought

---

[34] *Conditions of Admission of a State to Membership in the United Nations*, ICJ Reports (1948) 57.
[35] (1932) PCIJ Ser. A/B, no. 46, p. 167.
[36] ICJ Reports, (1966) 6 at paras. 49, 64, 89–98.
[37] *Military and Paramilitary Activities Case* (Jurisdiction), ICJ Reports (1984) 392.

by Iran against the United States,[38] will not be struck out as being 'political' rather than 'legal'.

The Court has jurisdiction over legal *disputes* and from time to time it has had to deal with the situation where one party endeavours to start litigation under the Optional Clause, and the other party insists that there is no 'dispute' between them. This is usually put in the form that, while for the moment the two sides have expressed different points of view, the relationship has not deteriorated to a 'dispute', that there is still a good possibility that the matter could be resolved by negotiation, and that it is therefore premature to speak of a 'dispute'; or that the prospective defendant does not believe that there *is* a 'dispute'. The International Court of Justice has adhered to the definition first provided by the Permanent Court in the *Mavrommatis Case*[39] that 'A dispute is a disagreement on a point of law or fact, a conflict of legal views or interests between two persons.' Neither the fact that one party insists there *is* a dispute, nor the fact that the other party insists there is *not*, will be determinative of the issue. The Court has made it clear that it is an objective question for the Court to determine on the facts of a given case. The question of a 'dispute' has in fact had some importance in a variety of situations, going beyond the strict confines of jurisdiction under Articles 36 (2) and 38 (1). Sometimes, when an organ of the United Nations or a specialized agency has asked the International Court of Justice for an advisory opinion on a point of law, a state will urge the Court *not* to give the advice, saying that the request marks the *existence* of a 'dispute' on the matter, to which it itself is a party. I will return to this aspect shortly. So the matter arises as an objection to the assertion of competence by the Court, whether in contentious litigation or in its advisory functions. In contentious litigation a potential defendant insists there is *no* 'dispute'. And in advisory jurisdiction a state may claim that the advice should not be given because there actually *exists* a 'dispute', and that it is not appropriate to give advice to a UN body that would entail the determination of a dispute between states. And sometimes a particular clause, whether founding the Court's jurisdiction or whether a substantive matter before the Court, may make it necessary to decide if there exists a dispute. Let me give an example. The claimed jurisdictional basis of the action brought against South Africa in 1960 by Ethiopia and Liberia was the old League of Nations Mandate. This authorized reference to the Permanent Court by the parties to the Mandate Treaty when there was a dispute. South Africa, in a preliminary objection,

---

[38] For an Order by the Court in the *Aerial Incident of 3 July 1988 Case*, see *Aerial Incident of 3 July 1988*, Order of 13 December 1989, ICJ Reports (1989) 132. The *Oil Platforms Case* is pending. For an Order by the Court in this case, see ICJ Reports (1992) 763.

[39] (1924) PCIJ Ser. A, no. 2, p. 11.

insisted that it had no dispute with Ethiopia or Liberia. But the Court, applying the test in the *Mavrommatis Case*, found a dispute did exist. That is an example of the requirement of a 'dispute' to found the Court's jurisdiction under a treaty providing for reference to the Court. The recent *UN Headquarters Case*[40] provides an interesting example of the existence of a 'dispute' forming part of the substantive issue upon which the Court was called to decide. The United States of America was party to an agreement with the United Nations—the Headquarters Agreement of 1947—which provided in s. 21 that 'any dispute between the United States and the United Nations concerning the interpretation or application of this Agreement . . . shall be referred for final decision to a tribunal of arbitrators'. In 1974 the Palestine Liberation Organization (PLO) had been given observer status by the General Assembly.[41] It had consequently established an observer mission in New York City. In May 1987 a bill was introduced into the US Senate, the purpose of which was 'to make unlawful the establishment and maintenance within the United States of an office of the PLO'. In due course this bill (which had not been the wish of the Administration) became law, and the Attorney-General of the United States indicated that he would feel obliged to act to support the law and ordered the mission to be closed. The State Department, for its part, acknowledged to the United Nations that the closing of the mission would violate the obligations of the United States as the host state to the United Nations. Given the dispute between the various branches of the US government, the Secretary-General was unable to get an assurance that the mission would in fact not be closed. He concluded that a dispute had arisen between the United Nations and the United States concerning the interpretation and application of the Headquarters Agreement and proceeded to the dispute-settlement procedure envisaged under the treaty. The United States took the view that, while there was undoubtedly a problem, no 'dispute' existed. The mission had not yet been ordered closed. The General Assembly requested an advisory opinion from the International Court of Justice—not on the merits of the issue, but on exactly whether a dispute existed, requiring the arbitration procedures of the Headquarters Agreement to be put into effect. The Court found that neither the fact that different views existed within the US administration, nor the fact that the PLO office had not actually been closed down, meant that a dispute did not exist. A dispute was objectively held to exist, with the consequence that the settlement procedures of the Headquarters Agreement came into play.

---

[40] *Applicability of the Obligation to Arbitrate under Section 21 of the United Nations Headquarters Agreement of 26 June 1947*, Advisory Opinion, ICJ Reports (1988) 12.
[41] GA Res. 3237 (XXIX).

Some Issues Relating to Advisory Opinions

I have spoken so far about the contentious jurisdiction of the International Court of Justice, though I have explained that some issues—the requirement that the matter be a legal one, and the issue of whether a dispute exists—can arise also in advisory opinions. Some further comments may be made about the Court's advisory jurisdiction. Article 65 of the Statute provides that the Court may give an advisory opinion on any legal question at the request of whatever body may be authorized by or in accordance with the UN Charter to make such a request. In fact, quite a substantial number of UN organs and specialized agencies have been authorized to make such a request, though a relatively small number of such authorized bodies have availed themselves of the opportunity.

But such requests for advisory opinions have from time to time been made. The Court regards its role as the provision of advice so that the requesting organ may proceed with its work in the knowledge that it is acting in accordance with international law. At one level, the advisory jurisdiction of the Court is very different from its contentious jurisdiction—there are no adversarial proceedings and there will be no judgment binding on the parties, but only advice as to the state of the law. But Article 68 of the Statute provides that in the exercise of its advisory functions the Court shall apply the same procedures as in contentious cases 'to the extent to which it recognises them to be applicable'.

Broadly speaking, similar procedures are in fact followed. Further, states parties to the Statute get notified under Article 66 of the request for an advisory opinion and have the opportunity of presenting their views on the legal issues—even though they are not parties to the case and even though no action is being brought against them. Indeed, there are no parties in advisory proceedings, and, at the end of the day, the Opinion is rendered to the requesting organ.

What application to advisory opinions can the principle have that the Court will not determine in their absence upon the rights of third parties? That principle—*audiatur et altera pars*—underlies consent as the basis for the Court's jurisdiction and has been reaffirmed in respect of contentious litigation by the Court in the *Monetary Gold Case*.[42] Its scope and application has recently been elaborated in the judgment of the Court in the preliminary phase of the *Phosphates Case*.

In the *Phosphates Case* Nauru brought a legal action against Australia, claiming, *inter alia*, violation by Australia of obligations owed under the Trusteeship Agreement for Nauru of 1947. New Zealand and the United

---

[42] *Monetary Gold Case*, ICJ Reports (1954) 19.

Kingdom—who were not defendants in this action—were co-trustees under that Agreement. Australia contended that to proceed with the case would entail the Court pronouncing on the legal obligations of states not before the Court, and would offend against the *Monetary Gold* principle.

The Court, noting that it had had to address this problem in other recent cases,[43] took as its test whether the legal interests of the third party that was not before the Court was 'the very subject matter of the decision'. It found that the interests of New Zealand and the United Kingdom did not constitute 'the very subject matter' of the judgment to be rendered.[44] The situation was therefore not the same as that in the *Monetary Gold* situation. The Court will have an opportunity to refine this further in the *East Timor Case*.

As early as 1923 the Permanent Court had stated, in the *Eastern Carelia Case*,[45] that it will not in its advisory jurisdiction depart from essential rules guiding its activity as a Court. Consent to jurisdiction for the determination of disputes would be an essential practice guiding its activity. In that case the Permanent Court declined to give an advisory opinion when it found that the question put to it related to the main point of a dispute actually pending between two states, so that answering the question put to it for an Advisory Opinion would be the equivalent to deciding the dispute between the parties. Of course, at the formal level it can be said that, just as a judgment is only determinative for the parties before it, so an advisory opinion cannot be determinative in respect of a dispute between two states which would definitionally not be bound by an advisory opinion. In fact, the trend has been for the Court to take a somewhat robust attitude to the rights of third parties. So far as contentious litigation is concerned, Article 62 of the Statute allows a state not party to the litigation in the Court to intervene should it consider that 'it has an interest of a legal nature which may be affected by the decision in the case'. Article 63 refers to a case which entails the construction of a Convention to which other states are parties. These states are to be notified about the case, and 'every state so notified has the right to intervene in the proceedings'. There has been a tendency by the Court (at least until the late 1980s) to make it very hard for a state to intervene[46]—even under Article 63, the wording of which

---

[43] *Paramilitary Activities in and Against Nicaragua*, ICJ Reports (1984) 392 at 431; *Land, Island and Maritime Frontier Dispute*, ICJ Reports (1990) 92 at 116.

[44] *Certain Phosphate Lands in Nauru*, ICJ Reports (1992) 240 at para. 55.

[45] *Eastern Carelia Case* (1923) PCIJ Ser. B, no. 5, p. 2.

[46] See especially *Nuclear Tests Case, Application by Fiji for Permission to Intervene*, ICJ Reports (1973) 334; *Continental Shelf Case (Libyan Arab Jamahiriya v. Malta), Application by Italy for Permission to Intervene*, ICJ Reports (1984) 3; *Military and Paramilitary Activities in and against Nicaragua, Declaration of Intervention by El Salvador*, ICJ Reports (1984) 215. Cf. *Law, Island and Maritime Frontier Dispute (Nicaragua Intervening)*, ICJ Reports (1990) 92.

appears to give a clear right to states falling within its scope to do so. The Court has been apt to point to Article 59 whereby a judgment only binds the parties to a case, to deny that an applicant state can have an interest of a legal nature which *could* be affected by the case. That attitude is hard to reconcile with the reasoning in *Eastern Carelia*, even if we might think the Permanent Court in that opinion perhaps went too far in the other direction. Undoubtedly, the possibility of intervention under Articles 62 and 63 of the Statute presents new problems—it introduces elements outside what the parties who have brought the case want considered. It upsets their timetable. It raises difficult issues about whether a state can intervene under these articles if it itself has no jurisdictional nexus to the subject-matter of the case and to the other parties thereto. There are many other problems also: is the appropriate stage for an intervention at the jurisdictional stage (to stop a judgment or opinion from occurring on the grounds that it would essentially entail a determination upon *its* legal position, which it has not consented to put before the Court)? Or at the stage of the merits (so that its views on the substance may be heard)? Logic would seem to direct one to the jurisdictional phase as the moment for an Article 62 intervention—but the Court has found such an application 'premature'. The question of intervention by legally interested third parties remains very much a live issue before the Court. The increasing interdependency of the international community is likely to make this a growing problem. And the endless factual variables that are possible mean that the Court will surely have to refine its practice in this area. The rationale for its decision-making in this area seems to me at the moment uncertain and there is a resultant substantial unpredictability.

The position of third parties has arisen not just in relation to intervention in a case, but in relation to advisory opinions that—on the *Eastern Carelia* formula—states have perceived as being potentially tantamount to pronouncing upon their legal rights in a dispute. The Soviet Union claimed that the Court should have declined the request of the Assembly to give an advisory opinion in the case of *Certain Expenses of the UN*,[47] because it was in dispute with other states, and with the UN, in respect of this. The Court gave the opinion none the less. South Africa claimed that for the Court to give the requested advisory opinion in the *Namibia Case*[48] would mean that the Court was pronouncing upon South Africa's legal rights in respect of that territory, when it had not submitted to the jurisdiction of the Court. The Court gave the opinion none the less. And the matter was graphically illustrated by the *Western Sahara Case*.[49] In that case the Court

[47] ICJ Reports (1962) 151.
[48] *Legal Consequences for States of the Continued Presence of South Africa in Namibia*, ICJ Reports (1971) 16.
[49] ICJ Reports (1975) 12.

was asked by the General Assembly to advise on whether Western Sahara was, at the time of colonization by Spain, a *terra nullius*? And, if not, what was the nature of the legal ties between it and Morocco and Mauritania? Morocco insisted that it was a party to a legal dispute with Spain actually pending on this issue;[50] and the same claim was made by Mauritania. Spain too insisted that an Advisory Opinion would have implications for an existing dispute. The Court found that there *did* exist between Morocco and Spain, at the time of the request for an advisory opinion, a legal dispute. But, instead of concluding that, on the basis of the old *Eastern Carelia* principle, it would not proceed with an advisory opinion, it instead proceeded with the opinion—but allowed Morocco an *ad hoc* judge on the Bench, as there was already a Spanish judge. But in principle *ad hoc* judges are available only to the 'parties in a case' (Article 31 of the Statute) and there should be no 'parties' in an advisory opinion. One may wonder whether, given this very basic and important difference, the matter of provision of *ad hoc* judges in advisory opinions is really satisfactorily dealt with as an application of the principle, purportedly under Article 68 of the Statute, that advisory procedures should also follow those of contentious procedure.

In any event, the Court in the *Western Sahara Case* distinguished the *Eastern Carelia Case*, noting that in that case one of the key states was neither a party to the Statute, nor indeed a member of the League. Spain and Morocco, by contrast, were members of the United Nations and had accepted the Charter provision whereby the Assembly has responsibilities for decolonizing. They could not prevent the Assembly seeking legal advice on that function.

What is critical, in this very complicated question of third-party rights, and underlying disputes, in relation to advisory opinions, is that the issue has arisen not bilaterally but in the context of the work of the requesting organ. The United States would not have been able to request an advisory opinion on Soviet arguments on expenses for peace-keeping; Ethiopia and Liberia could not have requested an advisory opinion on Southern Africa's duties under the mandate for Namibia; and neither Spain nor Morocco could have requested an advisory opinion on the issues in the *Western Sahara Case*. But in each of these cases an organ had important tasks to perform, in relation to assigning the budget, seeking compliance with the mandate, and decolonization. The International Court of Justice has shown that it will rather robustly preserve its right to provide advice to authorized requesting organs in these circumstances.

---

[50] A claim which led in turn to a demand for an *ad hoc* judge should the case proceed—a request also made by Mauritania. Mauritania did not succeed in its application.

Dispute Settlement and Law Development

The Court's function is to settle disputes between states and to provide advice to authorized organs. It is not to develop international law in the abstract. But, of course, the very determination of specific disputes, and the provision of specific advice, *does* develop international law. This is because the judicial function is not simply the application of existing rules to facts. The circumstances to which it will be said to apply, the elaboration of the content of a norm, the expansion upon uncertain matters, all contribute enormously to the development of international law. It is, in fact, hard to point to a case in which all the Court has done is to apply clear, existing law to the facts. Through a series of maritime cases the Court has developed a corpus of law about maritime delimitation. It has clarified contentious topics in the use of force, including self-help (*Corfu Channel*)[51] and use of force in response to low level unlawful military activity (*Nicaragua* v. *United States*). It has, in various cases on territorial title, built on the classic law to clarify further the legal role of *effectivités* in establishing title. It has developed the law on the stability and finality of boundaries and explained the place of *uti possidetis* in current international law. In the field of international organization, its advisory function has entailed the development of the concept of implied powers, and of *vires*. It has confirmed the existence of self-determination as a legal norm and very much else besides.

Of course, at the formalistic level this is of limited consequence, because the decisions of the Court are said to be a subsidiary source of international law (Article 38 (1) (*c*) of the Statute) and because any judicial determination is subject to Article 59, whereby it is only binding upon the parties before it. But it is a commonplace that the reality is otherwise. Far from being treated as a subsidiary source of international law, the judgments and opinions of the Court are treated as authoritative pronouncements upon the current state of international law. And the Court itself knows that intellectual coherence and consistency is the cornerstone of continuing respect for its jurisprudence. Thus, even though a particular determination of law will be binding only upon the parties before it, it will invariably, in the course of making such a determination, invoke previous jurisprudence and *dicta* pertinent to the present facts. States which have no dispute before the Court follow the judgments of the Court with the greatest interest, because they know that every judgment is at once an authoritative pronouncement on the law, and also that, should they become involved in a dispute in which the same legal issues arise, the Court, which will always

[51] ICJ Reports (1949) 4.

seek to act consistently and build on its own jurisprudence, will reach the same conclusions. Although at the formal level the judgment of the Court in the case of State A v. State B will not bind State Z, State Z *is* bound by the relevant rule of international law, which has been articulated by the Court, and which would no doubt be directly applicable to it also, if the occasion arose.

Even advisory opinions have a role of great importance. Of course, there *are* no parties to a request for an advisory opinion, and an opinion is not technically binding on any state. But Judge Lauterpacht early said that there *is* a duty upon each state seriously to consider in good faith whether it should not accept what the Court has pronounced in an advisory opinion. The stakes have to be rather high for a state visibly to reject the arguments upon which an advisory opinion was based (although the United Kingdom did so in respect of part of the Court's reasoning in the Namibia advisory opinion of 1972).[52] Very often, the organ requesting an advisory opinion will then pass a resolution 'appreciating' or 'accepting' that opinion. This was done, for example, in the *Reservations Case*[53] and in the case concerning *Legal Expenses of the United Nations*. Of course, that will not convert an opinion into a legal obligation, either for the organisation or for members. But it is a public affirmation of the authoritative quality of the advice that has been rendered. As we have seen, behind many advisory opinions are disputes between states in relation to the activities of the United Nations. In some cases, though it must be said not many, the advice of the Court has assisted in a resolution of the underlying conflict. One could point to that connection, for example, in the case concerning the regional office of the WHO in Egypt,[54] or in the *Admissions Cases*,[55] or in the *Mazilu Case*[56] on the applicability of Article VI, s. 22, of the Convention on the Privileges and Immunities of the United Nations. The outcomes to the underlying problem were undoubtedly facilitated by the advice given.

In other cases the causal link has been more tenuous. It is only now that the advice given by the Court in the *Western Sahara Case* is beginning to be followed. States have in large numbers ignored the finding of the Court in the *Expenses Case* that they are under a legal obligation to pay for certain peace-keeping operations (and thus, by implication, for other comparable ones). In yet other cases the importance has been in legal seeds that were sown. It is hard to exaggerate the operational importance, from the point of

---

[52] See R. Higgins, 'The Advisory Opinion on Namibia: Which UN Resolutions are Binding under Article 25 of the Charter?' (1992) 21 *ICLQ* 270.
[53] *Reservations to the Genocide Convention Case*, ICJ Reports (1951) 15.
[54] *Interpretation of the Agreement between the WHO and Egypt*, ICJ Reports (1980) 73.
[55] *Conditions of Admission of a State to Membership in the United Nations*, ICJ Reports (1948) 57.   [56] ICJ Reports (1989) 314.

view of practice of various international organizations, of the Court's findings on implied powers in the *Reparation for Injuries Case*. And, while an amalgam of factors has contributed to the ultimately successful outcome to the *Namibian* situation, who would doubt the importance of the constant stream of legal reasoning that underpinned the political and diplomatic efforts to secure independence?

Of course, the fact that the Court does have such a role in the development of international law leads one to wonder how overt the Court should be about this function. In particular, should it merely say as much as it has to say to decide the issue before it, or should it consciously contribute to the development of norms by offering views on a wider and less restrictive basis? My own opinion is that the judicial function is more than an allegedly mere application of rules to facts—the Court is necessarily choosing, explaining, and refining. But it should still do so in respect of the particular issue it is required to decide or upon which it is asked to advise. This discipline—the discipline of relevance and pertinence—is part of the authoritativeness which commands international respect.

12

THE ROLE OF NATIONAL COURTS IN THE
INTERNATIONAL LEGAL PROCESS

IN the textbooks it is customary to find a chapter entitled 'international law and national law'. In university courses on general international law, the lecture on international law and national law is invariably the very first of the year. I always give this lecture as the very *last* of the year, believing that it is quite unintelligible to students on their first day, and will remain so until they have covered the substantive ground that will give them their bearings in the debates on international and national law.

At the heart of any chapter on international and national law is always an explanation of the two theories of monism and dualism. Monists contend that there is but a single system of law, with international law being an element within it alongside all the various branches of domestic law. For the monist, international law is part of the law of the land alongside labour law, employment law, contract law, and so forth. Dualists contend that there are two essentially different legal systems, existing side by side within different spheres of action—the international plane and the domestic plane.[1] Of course, which ever view you take, there is still the problem of which system prevails when there is a clash between the two. One can give answers to that question at the level of legal philosophy; but in the real world the answer often depends upon the tribunal answering it (whether it is a tribunal of international or domestic law) and upon the question asked. The International Court of Justice has indicated that for it domestic law is a fact.[2] On some matters even an international court will need to apply this law—for example, as the applicable law governing the redemption of bonds. But when the issue is whether an international obligation can be avoided or excused because of a deficiency or contradiction in domestic law, then for an international tribunal the answer is clear—it cannot, and the obligation in international law remains.[3] The domestic court may be faced with a difficult question, when the domestic law which it is its day-to-day task to apply entails a violation of an international obligation. Different courts *do* address that problem differently. Leaving the theoretical aspects aside for a moment, it is as a practical

---

[1] D. Anzilotti, *Corso di Diritto Internationale* (3rd edn., 1928), i. 43 ff.; and L. Henkin, General Course, *Recueil des cours* (1990, IV) 19.

[2] *Serbian and Brazilian Loans Case* (1929) PCIJ Ser. A, nos. 20–1, pp. 18–20; *Nottebohm Case*, ICJ Reports (1959) 4 at 20–1.

[3] *The SS Wimbledon* (1923) PCIJ Ser. A, no. 1.

matter difficult to persuade a national court to apply international law, rather than the domestic, if there appears to be a clash between the two. But it is more possible in some courts than in others. And, although I have sympathy with the views of those[4] who think the monist–dualist debate is passé, I also think it right[5] that the difference in response to a clash of international law and domestic law in various domestic courts is substantially conditioned by whether the country concerned is monist or dualist in its approach.

I say 'substantially' conditioned, because in reality there is usually little explanation or discussion of these large jurisprudential matters in the domestic court hearing. The response of the court to the problem is often instinctive rather than explicitly predicated. And, if the truth be told, the response is often somewhat confused and lacking in an intellectual coherence. The fact that not everything is dependent upon whether a country accepts the monist or dualist view is evidenced by the fact that, even within a given country, different courts may approach differently the problem of the relationship between international law and national law.

Related to this great jurisprudential debate is a further reality not to be found in the textbooks, but which must be mentioned. This is the reality of legal culture. In some jurisdictions international law will be treated as a familiar topic, one that both the judge and the counsel before him will expect to deal with on a routine basis, the introduction of which occasions no special comment or interest. Of course, this attitude is more to be expected in systems accepting the monist view. But I speak of very practical matters: the judge and lawyers in his court will have studied international law and will be familiar with it, just as they are familiar with other everyday branches of the law. But there is another culture that exists, in which it is possible to become a practising lawyer without having studied international law, and indeed to become a judge knowing no international law. Psychologically that disposes both counsel and judge to treat international law as some exotic branch of the law, to be avoided if at all possible, and to be looked upon as if it is unreal, of no practical application in the real world. Of course, this attitude is mostly to be found in those countries that embrace (in so far as they think about it at all) the dualist system. It is a not unfair description of some courts in the United Kingdom. But the lack of background in international law (which is why I speak of it as a legal culture, as much as a question of legal philosophy) manifests itself in various ways, for there are individual cultures as well as national cultures. Some judges are simply rather contemptuous of

---

[4] J. Frowein, 'Treaty-Making Power in the Federal Republic of Germany', in F. Jacobs and S. Roberts (eds.), *The Effect of Treaties in Domestic Law* (1987), 63.

[5] P. Pescatore, 'Treaty-Making by the European Communities', in Jacobs and Roberts (eds.), *The Effect of Treaties in Domestic Law*, 171 at 191.

everything to do with international law, which they doggedly regard as 'unreal'. Others are greatly impressed by international law, but feeling insufficiency familiar with it seek at all costs to avoid making determinations upon it: strenuous efforts are made *not* to decide points of international law, but to locate the *ratio decidendi* of the judgment on more familiar ground. And yet others find international law potentially relevant and important and immerse themselves in it and are fully prepared to pronounce upon it.

Any student of the international tin litigation in the English courts will recognize all these elements. In the Court of Appeal, Kerr LJ was moved in his judgment to comment on the unfortunate emphasis by all the lawyers (and by the judges below, who had given their judgments on the basis of the submissions made to them) on the minutiae of an English statutory provision. For Kerr LJ this was a case about the status and powers of an international organization, and therefore 'the logical starting point must be international law'.[6] His judgment entails a detailed analysis of many important points of international law. But for the House of Lords, where the cases went on appeal, the matter was simply 'a short question of construction of the plain words of a statutory instrument'.[7] A different culture prevailed, and there was clearly an impatience with much of the international law argument that had been deployed.

It was in my view this particular culture, as much as the logic of the argument, that led the House of Lords to find that a statutory instrument which gives certain status and powers to an international organization in English law 'creates' this organization in English law. To an international lawyer, that simply departs from reality. As an objective fact, an international organization, set up by treaty, *exists*. It is fanciful to speak of domestic instruments which entitle an existing organization to act on the local plane as 'creating' it. The legal consequences of this attitude to the objective reality of international law, and the insistence that this factual reality is not to be acknowledged without domestic law itself *creating* (not even *recognizing*) the existence of the organization concerned, are disturbing. In the UK case of *Arab Monetary Fund* v. *Hashim*[8] the House of Lords held that, in the absence of a statutory instrument 'creating' the Arab Monetary Fund as an entity with legal status in English law, the Fund did not exist as an international organization—in spite of the fact that it was established by treaty, had thousands of employees, and engaged in a variety of transactions in London. In what seems to an international lawyer as a further departure from reality, the House of Lords then determined that this international organization was actually a foreign bank incorporated

---

[6] [1988] 3 AER 257 at 275F.   [7] [1989] 3 WLR 969 at 980D.
[8] (No. 3) [1991] 2 WLR 729.

under the law of Abu Dhabi, where it was headquartered. Domestic lawyers are wont to speak pejoratively of international law as 'unreal', but to an international lawyer there is no doubt as to which system is more in touch with objective reality.

These comments form a necessary background to a further theme—not the textbook subject of international law and national law, but rather something *within* that, namely, the contribution that national courts make to the operation of the international legal system.

Article 38 of the Statute of the International Court of Justice refers to judicial decisions as a source of international law. Of course, we think of the judgments of the International Court of Justice and its advisory opinions, as being the judicial decisions there referred to. But there is nothing in the wording of Article 38 that limits the reference to the International Court of Justice at The Hague. And it is not specified that the judicial decision be an international one at all. Although it is natural that the judicial decisions of the International Court of Justice will have a great authority, it is also natural in a decentralized, horizontal legal order that the courts of nation states should also have a role to play in contributing to the norms of international law.

States will not normally litigate with each other in their domestic courts; the principle of sovereignty makes them prefer to litigate in an international court, or before an international arbitral tribunal. So some types of questions that are frequently the subject-matter of inter-state litigation— questions relating to treaties, or the use of force, for example, would simply not normally arise in a national court. Whether there is any *question of principle* which makes these matters unsuitable for determination by a national court is something to be explored shortly. For the moment, let us simply say that some international law issues rarely arise in a national court; but others arise there with a certain frequency. Some issues can arise in either an international or a domestic court. Questions relating to maritime delimitations—perhaps of the continental shelf, perhaps of the territorial sea—are, of course, typical issues before the International Court of Justice. But sometimes a national court will also have to pass on such issues—for example, in deciding whether its national legislation extends to vessels within such maritime zones[9] or what is the breadth of the territorial waters.[10] In the *Tehran Hostages Case*[11] the International Court of Justice had made determinations about the Vienna Convention on Diplomatic Relations; but matters relating to diplomatic immunities often also arise in national courts. Yet other international law matters arise almost solely in domestic courts. We have seen that the whole law of state immunities is

[9] *Post Office* v. *Estuary Radio Ltd.* [1968] 2 QB 740.
[10] *R.* v. *Kent Justices, ex parte Lye* [1967] 2 QB 153 at 188–90.
[11] *US Diplomatic and Consular Staff in Teheran*, ICJ Reports (1980) 3.

about immunity from the local territorial jurisdiction. It is not surprising that the judicial determinations on this issue, that form a great part of the corpus of the sources of the international law on the matter, are those of diverse national courts. One has only to open the special volumes of the International Law Reports that were given over to the topic of state immunity to see how many important cases have come from so many different national courts.[12] And national courts have to pronounce on the legal significance of recognition, on international human-rights standards, on nationalization compensation standards for foreigners, on international environmental standards, on extraterritorial jurisdiction—and on a myriad of other issues that we think of as being 'international law' issues.

Can we give some shape to all of this? Can we try to categorize what it is that domestic courts are faced with when confronted with international law issues? Can we try to make some order out of what at first sight appears to be a random intersecting of international law with the domestic legal order? Some conceptual grouping of the apparently random issues may be useful. Domestic courts are sometimes called upon to interpret or apply international treaties; they are sometimes required to decide whether to apply customary international law; they are sometimes faced with human-rights considerations; and they are sometimes told *not* to apply a governing law, because that law offends international law.

International law will require the treaty to be honoured as between the parties, regardless of what rank it is accorded in domestic law, or whether it is received into domestic law at all. And international law will not allow any of these diverse practices of domestic law to be offered as a reason for failure to comply with an obligation under the treaty. But in many systems, as we will see, domestic courts feel exactly compelled to the opposite position—to insist that domestic law is upheld, even if it entails a violation of an international obligation. Put differently, an international obligation could not be offered as a reason for non-compliance with domestic law.

The 'Receipt' of International Law in the National Legal System

Treaties

It is a commonplace that different countries treat differently the 'receipt' of international legal obligations. The more *monist* a country, the more will international legal obligations, whether arising under treaty or under customary international law, be treated as simply part of the law to be given effect and directly applied. The more *dualist* a country, the more

---

[12] Vols. 63–5 of the International Law Reports. Subsequent cases on immunity appear as integral parts of the later volumes.

difficulty there is in giving direct legal effect to international obligations without an intervening domestic legal act to accomplish that.[13]

From the perspective of international law, an international obligation is an international obligation, whether it stems from treaty or from custom. And some monist domestic systems acknowledge this by giving all treaties the status of domestic law (sometimes indeed a superior status, equivalent to the law of the constitution), and simply treating customary international law as a law that can be directly invoked and applied, along with any other. Logic might have indicated that strongly dualist systems require *all* international law obligations (whether emanating from treaty or otherwise) to have been 'incorporated' by local affirming legislation before they can be given domestic legal effect. But in fact this approach is extremely rare— remarkably few dualist domestic systems refuse to apply general international law in the absence of domestic implementing legislation.[14] They reserve the requirement of 'translation' into domestic law for treaty obligations. Of course, *how* that is done, and, indeed, the decision as to whether it is required for all treaty obligations or only for some,[15] is a matter for national determination. The extent to which treaty obligations may be examined or analysed in domestic courts, or give rise to claims in domestic courts, is a matter for domestic law. The existence of the treaty obligations as a commitment between the state parties thereto is a matter for international law.

Customary international law

Customary international law is binding on all nations. It is widely accepted that it may be invoked before domestic tribunals, and in principle it is thus to the sources of international law that a court will turn to discover the content of the law that it is asked to apply. In state immunity cases the domestic courts regularly look at the few relevant international treaties, international law writings, and the decisions of other leading jurisdictions, to discover what international law requires.[16] An answer is not invariably found. Sometimes a national court will, having undergone that exercise, declare that the international law on the topic that it has to decide upon is 'uncertain': this was the reaction of the Supreme Court of the United

---

[13] See Pescatore's description of UK as 'radically dualist' ('Treaty-Making', 191).

[14] See the flirtation of Lord Denning with this idea, before firmly rejecting it: *Trendtex Corp.* v. *Central Bank of Nigeria* [1977] 2 WLR 356 at 365.

[15] In the United States 'self-executing' treaties are applied directly by the courts, who also decide whether an international treaty falls into that category; see e.g. *Islamic Republic of Iran* v. *Boeing Co.* (1986) 80 *AJIL* 347. Cf. *Diggs* v. *Dent* (1975) 14 *ILM* 797. See also L. Henkin, 'International Law as Law in the United States' (1984) 82 *Michigan Law Review* 1555.

[16] e.g. *1° Congreso del Partido* [1981] 2 AER 1064.

States when, in the *Sabbatino Case*,[17] it was asked to determine that the taking of property of foreigners without compensation violated international law. Sometimes it will indeed decide not that the state of the law is currently uncertain, but that there is no existing international rule on a particular matter—as the United Kingdom Court of Appeal found, after the most thorough survey, when asked to decide if international law required states to be liable for the debts of defaulting international organizations of which they are members.[18]

There seems no difficulty in the courts identifying and applying the relevant norm of international law—though, as has been noted earlier, there is sometimes a nervousness or disinclination about getting into this area. But the normal jurisdictional rules apply, so a court will be reluctant to take jurisdiction over international law violations that have occurred elsewhere. If State A unlawfully seizes the property of a foreigner, Mr B., the courts of State C will see no reason to address the issue at all unless it can be brought within its normal jurisdictional rules. This has nothing to do with the subject-matter being international law but the application of the normal rules of jurisdictional competence.

An interesting exception has occurred through the existence, in the United States, of the Alien Tort Statute.[19] This provides that federal district courts shall have 'original jurisdiction of any civil action by an alien for a tort only, committed in violation of the law of nations or a treaty of the United States'. On the basis of this Statute, the US Court of Appeals, 2nd Circuit, in the celebrated *Filartiga Case*,[20] assumed jurisdiction over a case in which it was alleged that a Paraguayan, temporarily in the United States as a visitor, had under the authority of his government, and while in Paraguay, tortured and killed the son of the plaintiff. To have jurisdiction the Court had to be sure that it was dealing with 'a violation of the law of nations'. It thus had the occasion to test torture systematically against the recognized sources of international law. It was prepared to meet the high test that a prohibition on torture had to be generally assented to, so that it could not be said that 'the courts of one nation might feel free to impose idiosyncratic legal rules upon others, in the name of applying international law'.[21] It described its findings as diametrically opposed to the uncertain state of the law that the Supreme Court had believed itself faced with in *Sabbatino*: 'there are few, if any, issues in international law today on which opinion seems to be so united as the limitations on a state's power to torture persons held in its custody.'[22] The judgment is an impressive survey

---

[17] *Banco Nacional de Cuba* v. *Sabbatino*, 376 US 398, 84 S. Ct. 923, 11 L. Ed. 2d 804 (1964).
[18] *Maclaine Watson and Co. Ltd.* v. *International Tin Council* [1988] 3 WLR 1169.
[19] 18 USC s. 1350 (1982).   [20] *Filartiga* v. *Pena-Irala*, 630 F. 2d 876 (1980).
[21] Ibid. at 881.   [22] Ibid.

of the sources of international law that support this conclusion. Other cases
brought under the Alien Tort Statute have reached their own conclusions
on different matters. In the *Forti Case* the Court found that prolonged
arbitrary detention also violated the law of nations, but rather surprisingly
was unable to find that causing the disappearance of an individual
constituted a violation of international law.[23] But, upon appeal, the
District Court of California overturned this decision, as it found that there
did exist a universal and obligatory international proscription of the tort of
'causing disappearance'. The Court found that the abduction which state
officials had carried out, when coupled with a refusal to acknowledge the
abduction or disclose the detainee's fate, constituted a violation of
international law.[24] In yet other cases there have been arguments about the
scope of the jurisdiction of the Alien Tort Statute: that is beyond our
concern, which is to show that international law can come before a national
court in a variety of ways.

Now, when a court is dealing with a claim under the Alien Tort Statute,
or when it is deciding if a foreign state has immunity, the parties before it
are either two individuals or a private party and the state. It would be
virtually unheard of for two states to agree to litigation in a domestic court,
so a local court would not be faced with seeking to apply international law
to such parties. But, if local courts can apply international law to an
obligation or relationship between a state and a private party, whether as a
jurisdictional matter (state immunity) or a combination of jurisdiction and
cause of action (as in the Alien Tort Statute), is there any reason why it
should not pronounce upon an international law obligation between two
states if it is relevant for purposes of litigation between private persons?

The House of Lords has decided that this involvement in international
law goes too far. In the *Buttes Gas Case*,[25] Lord Wilberforce determined
that 'there was a general principle . . . of judicial abstention from
adjudicating directly on the transactions of foreign sovereign states. The
principle was not one of discretion but was inherent in the very nature of
the judicial process.' He declined to pronounce at all on certain
controversial acts of maritime delimitation by two sovereign states in the
Persian Gulf, although the validity of the acts under international law had
direct relevance to the claims of the individuals being heard in that court.
This doctrine of complete judicial abstention over transactions of sovereign
states has become known as the English act of state doctrine. I believe its
formulation is unique to the United Kingdom, and I must admit that I
cannot understand why, if it is appropriate to pronounce upon international law as it operates between one state and a private person (not to

---

[23] *Forti* v. *Suarez-Mason*, 672 F. Supp. 1531 (ND Cal. 1987) at 1543.
[24] *Forti* v. *Suarez-Mason*, 694 F. Supp. 707 (ND Cal. 1988) at 711.
[25] *Buttes Gas* v. *Hammer (Nos. 2 & 3)* [1981] 3 AER 616 at 628.

torture, not to be exempted from jurisdiction for *acta jure gestionis*), it is not appropriate to pronounce upon international law as it operates between two states.

This principle has been affirmed by the House of Lords in the tin litigation,[26] where it was said that the reason was because 'the transactions of independent states between each other are governed by other laws than those which municipal courts administer; such courts have neither the means of deciding what is right, nor the power of enforcing any decision which they may make'.[27] Several comments may be made. First, international law surely *is* the law which municipal courts administer. It is not a foreign, unknown law. Secondly, it is depressing that the supreme court of a leading jurisdiction in 1990 thinks it has not the means of deciding 'what is right'. Why not? All it has to do, with the assistance of counsel before it, is to examine the sources of international law on the topic to hand. Finally, the fact that it has not the means of enforcing its judgment is neither here nor there. As we have seen, it has limited means of enforcing a judgment against a state given a breach of contract, but that does not stop it pronouncing upon the merits of the case. Further, in a case such as *Buttes Gas* 'enforcement' was never in issue. All that was required was for the court to draw legal consequences for private parties from its analysis of the international law.

A more frequent problem that has arisen in the context of the application of customary international law by national courts is this: what is a national court to do if, while quite willing in principle to do its best to find and apply international law, it is also faced with contrary domestic law? For a domestic court, this immediately confronts it with the problem of hierarchy of norms. If general international law is simply part of the law of the land, then like any other branch of the law it gives way in the face of a specific, contrary, subsequent law. It could only be otherwise if international law was regarded as a separate system of law which is hierarchically superior to domestic law in the face of a clash. In most countries it will be extremely hard to set aside a domestic law on the grounds that it violates general international law—quite apart from the issue of hierarchy, in many jurisdictions the domestic courts have no authority to set aside or strike down legislation. Their powers are limited to applying and interpreting the law. In some jurisdictions, however, a constitutional court may be authorized to strike down legislation incompatible with the Constitution; and the Constitution itself may be closely based on, or include, international human-rights law provisions. Beyond this, however, the general situation would seem to be that a statute of local

---

[26] *J. H. Rayner Ltd.* v. *Department of Trade* (HL) [1989] 3 WLR 969 at 1001–2.
[27] Citing *Secretary of State in Council of India* v. *Kamachee Boye Sahaba* (1859) 13 Moo. PCC 22 at 75.

law will prevail over a contrary rule of general international law, from the perspective of the local court. If local legislation authorizes territorial limits of twenty-five miles, a plea by a foreign vessel that it should have been allowed innocent passage fifteen miles from shore, and that the statutory claim of twenty-five miles violates contemporary general international law, is unlikely to find favour. The court may well accept that the statute is contrary to general international law, but feel obliged to give effect to it.

But the situation is not necessarily the same when the international law obligation arises from a treaty rather than from general international law. Again, it will depend upon the jurisdiction we are speaking about, and generalizations are difficult. In some countries treaties not only have effect on the domestic level without further incorporation or legislation of the state being necessary, but they are also accorded an important hierarchical status. Thus under French law all treaties, once signed, ratified, and published, take precedence under domestic statutes, posterior or anterior.[28] In the United Kingdom, not only are the circumstances in which an unincorporated treaty is to be interpreted very limited, but it will not, in any event, take precedence over subsequent contrary legislation, even if fully incorporated. Once incorporated it becomes English legislation like any other. Subsequent legislation, where there is a conflict, always takes priority over earlier legislation. No special 'exempted status' from this general rule is afforded, because earlier legislation happens to contain, or paraphrase, the terms of an international treaty. As it was put by Diplock LJ in *Saloman* v. *Commissioner of Customs and Excise*: 'If the terms of the legislation are clear and unambiguous they must be given effect to whether or not they carry out Her Majesty's treaty obligations.'[29] This was approved very recently by the House of Lords in the *Brind Case*.[30]

Sometimes an attempt by a local court to interpret a statute in a way compatible with international law will go to surprising and indeed heroic lengths. A recent example occurred in the context of the *UN Headquarters Case*.[31] In this case the United States was bound by the substantive provisions of the Headquarters Agreement it had entered into with the United Nations, under which it was to provide free access for those attending UN sessions. It had come, as a matter of practice, to be accepted that this included the obligation to allow entities granted observer status to set up permanent missions. Since 1974 the PLO had maintained an office in New York. In 1987, Act 436 made 'unlawful the establishment and

---

[28] Art. 55 of the Constitution. See *Ministry of Finance* v. *Chauvineau* 48 ILR 213.

[29] [1967] 2 QB 143 at 166.

[30] *R.* v. *Secretary of State for the Home Department ex parte Brind* [1991] 1 AC 696.

[31] *Applicability of the Obligation to Arbitrate under s. 21 of the UN Headquarters Agreement*, ICJ Reports (1988) 12.

maintenance within the United States of an office of the PLO'. The PLO's mission to the United Nations was its only office in the United States. The issue went to the International Court of Justice for an advisory opinion— not on the merits, but to resolve whether the United States was now obliged to follow certain dispute-resolution procedures. At the same time, the substantive matter came before the courts of the United States. The State Department had readily admitted that the new legislation (which it regretted) was contrary to the United States' obligations under the Headquarters Agreement. But it was generally supposed that a US court would none the less have to give effect to the statutory law of the country— just as the Justice Department had felt obliged to do in ordering the closure of the mission. But on 29 June 1988 the New York district judge, in a judgment full of reference to international law, found that, because the terms of the new Act had been cast in terms of rendering PLO offices *generally* unlawful, and because it had not specified in terms that the office in New York was to be closed, it was not to be presumed that the Congress sought to legislate in a manner inconsistent with the treaty obligations of the United States. He found that 'the Headquarters Agreement remains a valid and outstanding treaty obligation of the United States. It has not been superseded by the antiterrorism act which is a valid enactment of general application.'[32] The Justice Department decided not to appeal against this judgment, and, by a remarkable piece of judicial reasoning, at once admirably purpose-orientated but unpersuasive, the crisis was defused.

Now there are of course important legal consequences that flow from these diverse legal positions (and from the almost endless variations of them that exist in all the different national jurisdictions of the world). In France, as a treaty takes precedence over even subsequent statutes,[33] the terms of the treaty can continue to be invoked as a reason for not applying the statute. Further, old cases where, for example, persons subject to deportation orders could not challenge them by relying on the European Convention on Human Rights[34] have now been overruled. It will no longer be held that invocation of the treaty was *moyen inopérant*. In three important new cases, the Conseil d'État has held that henceforth an examination of France's obligations under Article 8 of the European Convention on Human Rights (family life) will form part of every judicial review of deportation orders.[35]

[32] *United States* v. *Palestine Liberation Organisation* (1988) 27 *ILM* 1055.

[33] See the *Vabré Case* in the Cour de Cassation, 1975, and the *Nicolo Case* in the Conseil d'État, 1985.

[34] *Touami Abdessahn* (25/7/80), rec. p. 820; *Chrouki* (6/12/85); see Errera, *Business Law Brief* (May 1991), 16.

[35] Errera Report on cases of *Beldjoudi* before the Conseil d'État (18/1/91), and *Belgacom*, and *Babas* (19/4/91) (*Business Law Brief* (May 1991), 16).

The contrast with the United Kingdom is striking. In several cases courts have held that, in the matter of judicial review, no regard need be had to the provisions of international treaties.[36] In fact, the judgments turned largely upon the fact that the treaties concerned had not been incorporated into English law and were thus 'extramunicipal' factors. But, even if they had been made part of English law, a subsequent statute that conflicted with them would have prevailed. Of course, where there is an ambiguity, it is a principle of construction that, where possible, a domestic statute be interpreted to be in accordance with international law obligations. But first of all the court has to decide that there *is* an ambiguity on the face of it which allows it to apply this principle at all. But the House of Lords has recently made it clear that, when Parliament by statute authorizes a Minister to exercise a discretion, there is no presumption that he is directed to exercise it within the limitations imposed by an unincorporated treaty (the European Convention on Human Rights) to which the state is party. That would be, said the House of Lords, to introduce the Convention into English law 'by the back door', so that, although Parliament had chosen not to incorporate it (when it *could* have made it part of English law), the courts would effectively apply it in every judicial review case. This, concluded the House of Lords, would be a judicial usurpation of the legislative function.[37]

I think it is a very real dilemma, and the hesitation of the House of Lords is understandable. But the outcome is that, in jurisdictions where treaties are not made part of domestic law, the domestic courts can play no part in monitoring compliance with them, even when 'transactions between states' are not in issue, but only individual rights under human-rights conventions designed actually to guarantee them rights, and which the state has freely entered into. The dualist doctrine which refuses internal effect to a treaty without domestic incorporation allows the courts little scope as guarantors of international law. In consequence, they can contribute relatively little to the development of international law—and, in turn, that law continues to be regarded as 'coming from the outside' and unfamiliar, alien, and thus little to do with the local courts. None the less, there is evidence from recent case law that that indefinable element referred to earlier as 'legal culture' is coming into play. A changing legal culture, in which international human-rights law particularly is felt increasingly to be part of English public life, is encouraging the courts to find ever more imaginative ways of allowing reference to these principles, notwithstanding the absence of incorporation of the international treaties which contain them.[38]

[36] Taylor J. in *R. v. Secretary of State for Transport, ex p. Iberia Lineas Aereas de Espana*, unreported, 5 July 1985; *R. v. Secretary of State for the Home Department, ex p. Fernandez*, unreported, 21 Nov. 1980.

[37] *R. v. Secretary of State for the Home Department, ex parte Brind* [1991] 1 AER 720.

[38] See *Derbyshire County Council v. Times Newspapers* [1992] 3 WLR 49.

National Courts and Foreign Acts Illegal under International Law

It seems to be a general practice that courts will seek, where possible, to give effect to the public acts of foreign recognized governments within their own jurisdiction. This doctrine is most fully articulated as 'the act of state doctrine' and is sometimes said to be an Anglo-American doctrine; but in its general sense, and shorn of the constitutional underpinnings that have developed the doctrine in the United States, it is a general practice. Its origins are often said to be found in the much quoted dictum of Fuller CJ in *Underhill* v. *Hernandez*: 'Every sovereign state is bound to respect the independence of every other sovereign state, and the courts of one country will not sit in judgment on the acts of the government of another within its own territory.'[39] And in *Oetjen* v. *Central Leather Co.* the Supreme Court said: 'To permit the validity of the acts of one sovereign state to be re-examined and perhaps condemned by the courts of another would very certainly imperil the amical relations between governments and thus the peace of nations.'[40]

But should we expect this understandable principle to apply when the acts of the foreign state are manifestly in violation of international law? Should one domestic court give effect to the acts of another state when those acts are not merely politically or economically controversial (a debate into which our court should certainly not enter) but clearly contrary to international law? What if the foreign acts at issue entailed confiscation of property on a discriminatory basis, or without compensation? What if they involved violations of human rights? This has been a very controversial question. In a series of 'hot-oil' cases in continental Europe, and in Japan, the question has to a large extent been avoided through findings that the acts in question were not necessarily to be regarded as violative of international law. Courts in Italy and Japan were being asked to return to BP petroleum that was said to have been wrongfully taken by Libya. The judgments do not attempt any systematic analysis of the then current state of international law and place much emphasis on the sovereign entitlement of a state to legislate within its own territory. Again, in the *Sabbatino Case* in the United States the Supreme Court declared itself unconvinced that the nationalizations did violate international law, and thus applied the act of state doctrine (giving effect to the Cuban legislation) in the classic manner.[41]

In the United Kingdom the matter is somewhat uncertain. An early case

---

[39] (1897) 168 US 250 at 252.   [40] (1918) 246 US 297 at 304.
[41] The US Congress in the Hickenlooper Amendment then directed the courts not to give effect to foreign acts of state that violated international law by taking without compensation the property of US nationals.

law[42] clearly rejects the application of the act of state doctrine when the act in question violates international law—which it found it did in that case. And, in a series of cases in which the courts were faced with the issue of whether they should give effect to Nazi legislation which confiscated the property of Jews, it was made clear that, as a matter of public policy, that would not be done.[43] The emphasis has been on *human rights* and on *public policy*. In other words, it has been made clear that the English courts, as a matter of public policy, will not give effect here to foreign law that offends human rights.[44] But it is still uncertain whether foreign acts violating international law *other* than in human-rights matters would still be given effect under the act-of-state doctrine. It seems that the breaches of international law that most offend national courts—or perhaps are easiest for them to feel confident *do* represent breaches of international law—are human-rights violations. The familiar hesitation reappears in the face of other aspects of international law.

Conclusion

Through Article 38 of the Statute and the reference to judicial decisions as a source of international law, national courts are provided with the opportunity of contributing to the formulation of international law. They are often surprised at this, and feel ill equipped for the task.

The opportunity for them to examine international law matters is significantly reduced in dualist systems whereby interpretation and application of treaties is broadly permissible only when the treaty has been directly incorporated. And when the very issue before the court is not the determination of the substance of an applicable norm of international law, but rather the primacy to be given to a domestic statute or an international obligation, the answer will necessarily depend upon the internal doctrine of the state on this matter.

But important opportunities do remain for national courts to contribute to international law. In a decentralized legal order it is important that they do so, and efforts must be made to overcome a cultural resistance to international law.

---

[42] *The Rose Mary* [1944] 1 WLR 246.
[43] *Oppenheimer* v. *Cattermole* 1976 AC 249; *Frankfurter* v. *Exner* [1947] CH.629.
[44] *Williams and Humbert* v. *W.& H. Trademarks (Jersey) Ltd.* [1986] 1 AER 129. For criticism, see F. A. Mann, 'The Effect in England of the Compulsory Acquisition by a Foreign State of the Shares in a Foreign Company' (1986) 102 *LQR* 191.

13

OILING THE WHEELS OF INTERNATIONAL LAW: EQUITY AND PROPORTIONALITY

EQUITY and proportionality are not substantive norms of international law in the same sense as, for example, jurisdiction, or recognition, or the use of force. But they are concepts that are much invoked, by judges, advocates, and scholars alike. They do not so much comprise the norms of international law as ease their appropriate application in particular cases. The purpose of this chapter is to study the content of these concepts and to examine their role in oiling the wheels of international law.

Equity

Legal doctrine identifies three possible applications of equity: *infra legem*, *praetor legem*, and *contra legem*.[1] The first category is said to refer to the possibility of choosing between several different interpretations of the law. The making of such choices is inherent in the function of the judge and, as such, needs no special consent of the parties in a dispute.[2] What is gained by terming the need to make choices as 'equity', is less certain—especially if no pretence is made that equity assists in *how* one makes choices (save by some general reference to 'justice').

In any event, that is the sense in which the notion was identified by the Institut de Droit International in its Resolution of 1937: 'l'Equité est normalement inherente à une saine application du droit.'[3] For some others—de Visscher, Huber, and Sørensen among them—every rule has various interpretations, all acceptable from the legal point of view, and equity allows the judge to choose in accordance with justice, having regard to the circumstances and balancing the rights and obligations of the parties.[4] How that is done is not made clear. Whether this is done by the

---

[1] See V. D. Degan, *L'Équité et le droit international* (1970), 26; C. de Visscher, *Théories et réalités en droit international public* (3rd edn., 1966), 450–1.

[2] Indeed, K. Strupp says that it would need positively to be excluded: 'Le Droit du juge international de statuer selon l'équité', *Recueil des cours* (1930, III), 486.

[3] Resolution of the Institut de Droit International (1937) 38 *Annuaire de l'Institut de Droit International* 271.

[4] Degan, *L'Équité et le droit international*, 28; de Visscher, *Théories et réalités*, 450; M. Huber (1934) 38 *Annuaire de l'Institut de Droit International* 233; M. Sørensen, *The Sources of International Law* (1946), 197.

use of compromise, or by giving different weight to alternative interpretations of law, or by focusing on the desired result, is never specified.

The second application of equity is said to be that of equity *praetor
legem*—here equity takes on the role of the filling of lacunae, or the
elaborating of rules whose content is too general. The importance attached
to this role depends upon an interior debate—namely, whether indeed
there are lacunae in international law. This is a question on which different
views are held.[5] In so far as there may be said to be lacunae or lack of
specific content, a further debate occurs: does the application of this type
of equity require the consent of the parties? Bin Cheng takes the view that
such authorization is indeed required;[6] but there is disagreement among
the others.[7] For some authors equity *praetor legem* is not acceptable,
because, while they believe that lacunae do exist, they hold that the role of
the judge is simply to pronounce a *non liquet*.[8]

The specifying by the Court of criteria for shelf delimitation closely
resembles equity *praetor legem*; but it is never characterized by the Court
as such.

The third category is that of equity *contra legem*—that is to say, a
softening of the application of an applicable norm, for extra-legal reasons.

There is an almost infinite number of purposes which courts and writers
see equity as fulfilling. For some, it allows the decision rather to embrace a
'just' solution. Thus the International Court of Justice, in the *Tunisia–
Libya Continental Shelf Case*, said that: 'When applying positive international law, a court may choose among several possible interpretations of
the law to one that appears, in the light of the circumstances of the case, to
be closest to the requirements of justice.' This would be the application of
equity *infra legem*.[9] The requirements of justice are, in my view, a
subjective concept, of essentially the same kind as 'equitable result'. To
label something as the result 'justice requires', or the 'equitable result', is
merely to avoid justifying and making specific certain policy objectives. In
1969 the Court, when elaborating a general basis of equity, said: 'Whatever
the legal reasoning of a court of justice, its decisions must by definition be
just and therefore in that sense equitable.'[10] Justice is thus said to be the
end served by equity; but also to be synonymous with equity. It is at once
unclear and an appeal to subjectivity.

In the *Tunisia–Libya Case* the Court insisted that this search for justice,
for the equitable result, was not an operation of *distributive* justice.[11] The

    [5] See Strupp, 'Le Droit du juge international', 469.
    [6] B. Cheng, 'Justice and Equity in International Law' (1955) 8 *Current Legal Problems* 185
at 209–10.
    [7] See the discussion in Degan, *L'Équité et de droit international*, 30–2.
    [8] Strupp, 'Le Droit du juge international', 469.
    [9] ICJ Reports (1982) 18 at para. 71.   [10] ICJ Reports (1969) 48.
    [11] ICJ Reports (1982) 11 at para. 71.

Court returned to this theme in the *Libya–Malta* Case in 1985, where it listed *an example of an equitable principle*, the principle that there can be no question of distributive justice (para. 46). In so far as distributive justice is understood to mean a move to the overall equality of the parties, that must be right. But where it is decided that 'undue weight' will not be given to actual geographic realities, in order to reach an unspecified 'equitable result', the line between 'equity to soften the result' and 'equity as distributive justice' is a fine one.

Certainly there is a widely held perception that the main function of equity is corrective. Some speak of it as 'l'adoucissement de la rigeur du droit' warning that that amelioration can only take place consistent with the rules of law—i.e. not *contra legem*.[12] Sometimes it is said that this 'corrective' role of equity serves to move it away from the harshness of the law to a position that is more 'reasonable'[13]—another subjective term, we may note. Sometimes 'reasonableness' is tied into the idea of a balancing of the interests of the parties, of reaching an equilibrium. This is the language of compromise, with 'reasonableness' being given a meaning internal to the claims of the parties.[14] For some there is a certain common-sense quality to equity, a security that it represents 'un certain bon sens et . . . une ethique commune'.[15] It is a perception I do not share.

There is a different role also advanced for equity. It is suggested that it is a concept lacking specific content, that it is rather a process of taking account of all the relevant circumstances. This was the view of Huber.[16] The Court in the *Tunisia–Libya Case* put it the other way around: it was 'virtually impossible to achieve an equitable solution to any delimitation without taking into account the particular relevant circumstances of the area'.[17] All rational judicial decision-making should take into account all of the relevant factors. It is only the most mechanistic approach to the judicial function that would purport to 'apply rules' without examining the entire context in which they are to be applied. Examination of the entire context, and all factors, is necessary to ensure that norms are being applied in circumstances comparable to those in which they were enunciated; and that the policy objectives are fully in view. None of this is dependent on notions of equity.

[12] See Strupp, 'Le Droit du juge international', 462.

[13] See the Report of the ILC for its 31st Session, 1979: 'L'Équité . . . est davantage un facteur d'équilibre, un élément correctif destiner à preserver le caractère "raisonnable" . . .' (p. 45, para. 16).

[14] D. Bardonnet, 'Équités et frontières terrestes', in *Melanges offerts à Paul Reuter* (1981) 35 at 41.   [15] Ibid.

[16] See Huber (1934) 46 *Annuaire de l'Institut de Droit International* 233. On this aspect, see A. Munkman 'Judicial Decision and the Settlement of Territorial and Boundary Disputes' (1972–3) 146 *BYIL* 1 at 14.

[17] ICJ Reports (1982) 1 at para. 72.

One further theme runs through the writings: the notion of equity as the means for rendering specific laws of general application. Thus Reuter, in his *L'Équité en droit international*, writes:

La marge qui sépare la règle juridique d'une situation concrète est . . . parfois très large. Le passage des faits concrets à la régle écrite doit traverser un champ plus où moins large où regne le pouvoir d'appréciation du juge, où triomphe l'équité.[18]

For de Visscher, in a striking phrase, 'l'équité est la norme du cas individuel'.[19] Bardonnet ties together, rightly, the concretization of the particular case with study of all the circumstances: having spoken of 'l'appréciation individualisée d'un cas concret', he refers to 'des faits, des situations, et notamment des situations géographiques (milieu physique spécial, environnement particulier), des interêts ou des pretensions des Parties'.[20] These are indeed essential elements. But it is only if one takes a positivistic approach to law that one believes that these matters cannot enter save through the door marked 'equity'. Further, the invocation of the concept of equity provides no guidance in selecting among those various factors, and at the end of the day the 'appréciation individualisée d'un cas concret' remains subjective if the invocation of equity is the only guide to the task.

Article 38 (2) in the Statute of the International Court of Justice allows a decision to be rendered *ex aequo et bono*, upon the request of the parties. Thus parties to a dispute are free to agree that the dispute should be resolved by reference not to the law, but to notions of fairness. However, this has proved an unattractive method of dispute resolution and there has been no practice under Article 38 (2), before either the Permanent Court or the International Court of Justice.

It is clear that no decision *ex aequo et bono* may be rendered without the consent of the parties. But it is said that equity is part of international law, and has a separate life within Article 38 (1) of the Statute. What is this 'separate' equity, that is something other than a decision *ex aequo et bono*?

We can begin by saying that equity is a general principle of law—that is to say, it is an ever-present factor, in much the same way as is the notion of good faith. While general principles of law may have a place in the overall picture, they are unlikely to provide, by themselves, a satisfactory basis for decision. Standing alone they are too imprecise. They go to notions of fairness, of appropriate conduct—notions that may be an element in the determination of a legal issue but are of themselves too unsubstantive to determine the outcome. Some examples illustrate the point. In arbitration awards on nationalizations and expropriations, consideration of good faith

[18] Reuter, *L'Équité en droit international* (1900), 166.
[19] De Visscher, *De L'Equité dans le Reglement Arbitral ou Judiciare des Litiges de Droit International Public* (1972), 6.
[20] Bardonnet, 'Équités et frontières terrestres', 42–3.

in adhering to contracts is often invoked. But such claims will be but an element in a decision-making process that will be centred on the substantive law on interference with property. Again, in a dispute over the application of a treaty, the conduct of the parties may raise equitable considerations; but these will not of themselves determine the matter, but rather will be an aspect of a dispute centred on the substantive law of treaties.

In the *North Sea Continental Shelf Cases* 1969, the Court rejected equidistance as an emerging rule of general international law. It also rejected the notion of a 'just and equitable share', as contended for by the Federal Republic of Germany. The Court did, however, find that there existed a customary rule of international law to the effect that shelf delimitation must be determined by reference to equitable principles.

Actual rules of law are here involved which govern the delimitation of adjacent continental shelves . . . it is not a question of applying equity simply as a matter of abstract justice, but of applying a rule of law which itself requires the application of equitable principles . . .[21]

We may usefully pause here. In most disputes, it is not suggested that the decision be reached by reference to equitable principles. We do not see this suggested in respect of, for example, the treatment of aliens; or treaty interpretation; or diplomatic immunities. We would have been surprised to have seen the Court say in the *Elsi Case* (about shareholdings) or in *Nicaragua* v. *United States* (about the use of force) that there was a customary rule of international law that required it to reach its solution by reference to equitable principles.

Where did such a customary rule as the Court held it had to apply in the *Continental Shelf Cases* come from? Even more importantly, when did it feel it had to apply over a rule? Put differently, was the evidence for such a rule so overwhelming that it was to be applied, even though it had no place in most of the Court's judicial decision-making? And, if not, what were the unspoken factors that impelled the Court to take the first steps down this path?

The Court did not make out a very weighty case for the existence of a rule that required it to deal with shelf delimitation by reference to equitable principles. It referred to a single sentence in a report of a committee of cartographers assisting the ILC in 1953, in which they said that the strict application of the concept of equidistance might in certain circumstances give rise to an inequitable solution. The evidence relied on by the Court for the existence of a customary rule can be contrasted with that it applied to the task of showing whether the equidistance principle had become part of general international law.

[21] *North Sea Continental Shelf Cases*, ICJ Reports (1969) 3 at 46–7.

What, we may ask, were the real, the hidden reasons for insisting that such a rule existed in the matter of shelf delimitation? The answer is not hard to find. In many substantive areas of international law the application of well-accepted norms to the particular facts makes it clear whose claim is well founded. But in the area of maritime delimitation the task before the Court of determining whose claim is well founded is only the preliminary to the *real* task of allocating resources between claimants. Further, the reality is that there were no precise rules to apply to this task. It is in the nature of shelf delimitation that each side has to have *something*—it is not the type of subject-matter in which one state can be found to be 'right' (and therefore entitled to everything), while the other state is 'wrong' (and entitled to nothing). The seeds for compromise are already there, and the absence of specific rules perhaps encouraged the assertion that there exists a 'rule of law which itself requires the application of equitable principles'.

It is not coincidental that it is in the area of resource allocation—law of the sea, the law of international water courses—that such frequent reference is made to equitable considerations.[22]

If, as I believe, the reality is that specific rules do not exist for the delimitation of adjacent shelves, then it might have been thought that any role for equitable principles was in *equity praetor legem*—in the filling of lacunae. But, with its insistence that it was applying an 'actual rule of law' (i.e. one which itself requires the application of equitable principles), the Court achieved two results: it avoided taking a stand on the controversy about whether lacunae can properly be filled by reliance on equitable principles; and it maintained the fiction that the judge always decides on the basis of pre-existing norms.[23] The reality is that there are few substantive norms to guide decision-making on shelf delimitation.[24] Decisions will in reality, and necessarily, reflect policy preferences. These policy preferences should be articulated and tested against stated desired outcomes. In this way the objectives would be transparent and the methods objectively verifiable. Instead, the path embarked on in the *North Sea Continental Shelf Cases* has allowed the Court to insist it is applying 'an actual rule of law'—but one that is opaque and not capable of scrutiny or review.

In the *Fisheries Jurisdiction Case* the Court affirmed its celebrated dictum in the *North Sea Continental Shelf Cases*, and added: 'It is not a matter of finding simply an equitable solution, but an equitable solution

[22] See the articles adopted in 1989–91 by the ILC on international watercourses: Report of the ILC on the work of its 43rd session, GAOR 46th sess., A/46/10, pp. 161–97.

[23] A point well made by T. Rothpfeffer 'Equity in the North Sea Continental Shelf Cases' (1972) 42 *Nordisk Tidsskrift for International Ret* 81 at 115.

[24] A point made in both the *Gulf of Maine Case*, ICJ Reports (1984) and the *Guinea* v. *Guinea-Bissau* arbitration, 77 ILR 635.

derived from the applicable law.'[25] Again, this is to be taken not only as a rejection of an equitable solution that is *contra legem* or *ex aequo et bono*, but also *praetor legem*.

Matters were further developed in the *Tunisia–Libya Continental Shelf Case*.[26] While the Special Agreement providing the Court with jurisdiction specifically required equitable principles to be taken into account, it was in any event made clear that as a matter of general international law equitable principles were of cardinal importance in shelf delimitation. The Court said that, since it was 'bound to decide the case on the basis of equitable principles, it must first examine what such principles entail'.[27] It might have been thought that the Court was for the first time to explain what it understood by 'equitable'. But not so. Its examination of what 'equitable principles entail' led to the startling conclusion that

The result of the application of general principles must be equitable . . . It is not every such principle which is in itself equitable; it may acquire this quality by reference to the equitableness of the solution . . . 'equitable principles' . . . refers back to the principles and rules which may be appropriate in order to achieve an equitable result.[28]

So, equitable principles are simply those principles—and, it seems, rules too—which lead to an equitable result. We are never told, in any of the Court's shelf jurisprudence, what constitutes an equitable result. The Court presumably believes it to be self-evident. Putting *North Sea Continental Shelf* and *Tunisia–Libya* together, we are left with the proposition that there is an actual rule of law that requires one to apply those principles that lead to an equitable result—which is itself not defined. The Court decides upon an outcome, that, through the process of later terming it 'equitable', it avoids having to articulate. It then achieves that outcome by selecting principles designed to achieve it (which thereupon become equitable principles). The Court itself acknowledges that it 'is not entirely satisfactory because it employs the term equitable to characterize both the result to be achieved and the means to be applied to obtain this result'.[29] But, with respect, this seems only one aspect of what is not satisfactory.

In the *Libya–Malta Continental Shelf Case*[30] the Court again emphasized that the equitable result, rather than the equitable principles used to achieve it, is 'the primary element in this duality of characterization'. Again, we are not told what constitutes an equitable result.

The Chamber in the *Gulf of Maine* case again emphasizes the requirement of an equitable solution; but in many other regards it adopts a

---

[25] *Fisheries Jurisdiction Case*, ICJ Reports (1974) 3 at para. 78.
[26] ICJ Reports (1982) 18 at 58–62.   [27] Ibid., para. 69.   [28] Ibid., para. 70.
[29] Ibid., para. 70.   [30] ICJ Reports (1985) 29.

notably different tone on equitable criteria. Although the Court in 1969 had spoken of an 'actual rule' of international law which required it to decide shelf delimitation by reference to equitable considerations, the Chamber says that these criteria are not in themselves principles and rules of international law. The implication is that equity may be a principle of international law; but that equitable considerations applicable in a particular case are not. Neither the content nor the significance of this finding is easy to understand.

We have spoken of the Court's reluctance to define an equitable result. Let us return for a moment to the point of departure in 1969—the Court's insistence that equidistance was inequitable. In that case the Court spoke of:

three states whose North Sea coastlines are in fact comparable in length and which, therefore, have been given broadly equal treatment by nature except that the configuration of one of the coastlines would, if the equidistance method is used, deny to one of these States treatment equal or comparable to that given the other two.[31]

It is hard to disagree with the critic who has written that the 'Court's criterion for qualifying the three states as equal, namely the length of the coastlines, have no other apparent theoretical basis of validity than the fact the Court classified this criterion as being determinative of equalness.'[32] And I share the difficulty of another learned author when he writes that by this philosophy the Court 'regards the inequalities caused by the differences between coastal and landlocked states, or between states with long and short coastlines, as facts of nature which have to be accepted while the fact that one state's coastline is straight or convex, and another's is concave is "unnatural".'[33]

My purpose here is not to debate the merits of the equidistance principle, but rather to emphasize the subjective nature of equitability. Judge Sir Robert Jennings has written that 'the doctrine of the "equitable result" . . . if allowed its head, leads straight into pure judicial discretion and a decision based upon nothing more than the court's subjective appreciation of what appears to be a "fair" compromise of the claims of either side'.[34] He then acknowledges that the doctrine of the equitable result provokes the questions 'of where do the mental processes of the judges begin? Do they begin with a boundary line they assume to be

---

[31] ICJ Reports (1969) 50.

[32] Rothpfeffer, 'Equity in the North Sea Continental Shelf Cases', 115.

[33] W. Friedmann, 'Selden Redivivus—Towards a Partition of the Seas?' (1971) 65 *AJIL* 757.

[34] R. Jennings, 'Equity and Equidistance Principles', *Annuaire suisse de droit international* (1986) 27 at 31.

"equitable" and then select supporting principles to lead to this result? Is equity then just the lawyers' name for subjective judicial decision . . .'[35] Building on Judge Gros's contention, in his dissenting opinion in the *Gulf of Maine* case, that equity must be controlled if it is to be predictable, Jennings finds that equitability was handled by the Chamber in that case in a more rigorous manner, with less emphasis on result and more emphasis on the application of specific equitable criteria.

Reliance on equitable principles may be deplored by those who believe that the proper task of a Court is simply to apply positive rules of international law. That is not my position. But one does not have to be a positivist to be uneasy with the way the notion of equitable principles has developed in the shelf delimitation jurisprudence of the Court. As Jennings has rightly said, 'There must be in the final stage an area of judicial discretion; in any case which justifies litigation there is no way in which a court can ultimately avoid the making of choices.'[36] But choices cannot be made without reference to result. This is necessarily so when the 'equitable principles' consist of a list of relevant factors, with no guidance as to the weight to be given to any one of them. What is disturbing about the 'equitable principles to produce equitable results' formula is not that there are choices being made to achieve a result—but that the result is nowhere articulated other than the self-serving description of 'equitable'. Further, the factors that are termed 'equitable principles' for purposes of shelf delimitation are really no more than a compendium of somewhat disparate principles. Let us look at the equitable principles listed by the Court in the *Libya–Malta Case*.[37] The principle that equity does not imply equality is said, with a certain circularity, itself to be an equitable principle. The principle that there is no question of refashioning geography, or seeking to make equal what is unequal, is clear as a rejection of the notion of 'proportionate share'; but thereafter it is clearly *not* allowed its full application. The principle of non-encroachment by one party on the natural prolongation of another may be thought not to carry one very far. And the principle of respect due to relevant circumstances hardly needs justification through designating it as an 'equitable principle'.

Because judicial decision-making inevitably entails choices, and because thinness of applicable norms allows a certain freedom in that choice, it is important to make the choices to achieve justifiable and desired ends. But those ends must be articulated, and cannot be hidden behind the term 'equitable result'; and the means to achieve those ends are the normal tools of judicial decision-making, requiring no classification as 'equitable principles'.

The invocation by tribunals of the principle of equity often has the result

---

[35] Ibid.   [36] Ibid. 35.   [37] ICJ Reports (1985) 13 at para. 46.

of a conclusion being arrived at upon which the parties have not had the opportunity to present argument. Thus, in the Anglo-French (Western Approaches) arbitration, the Tribunal considered a list of factors which had to be taken into account 'to balance the equities'. It then concluded that the Channel Islands were to be given an enclave of continental shelf to a width of twelve miles. There is no explanation as to why consideration of the equities led to twelve miles, rather than to six or nine.[38] Nor was argument addressed to the Tribunal on this point. Reliance on equitable principles too often serves to allow a tribunal to reach conclusions on which the full argument of the parties has not been heard.

Once equity is viewed not only as a general principle of international law, but also as the outcome required, can it really be said to be different from a decision *ex aequo et bono*, which, as we have seen, requires the consent of the parties for its application? Is this the application by the back door of Article 38 (1) of the discretion envisaged under Article 38 (2)? The Court has shown itself sensitive to this charge and in the *Tunisia–Libya Continental Shelf Case* said this:

Application of equitable principles is to be distinguished from a decision *ex aequo et bono*. The Court can take such a decision only on condition that the parties agree (Art. 38, para. 2 of the Statute), and the Court is then freed from the strict application of legal rules in order to bring about an appropriate settlement. The task of the Court in the present case is quite different: it is bound to apply equitable principles as part of international law, and *to balance up the various considerations which it regards as relevant in order to produce an equitable result.*[39] (Italics added.)

Proportionality

Maritime delimitation

In the law of maritime delimitation proportionality has appeared as an *element of* equity. The interrelationship of the concepts is illustrated in a series of cases (*North Sea Continental Shelf Cases*;[40] *Anglo-French Continental Shelf Arbitration*;[41] *Tunisia* v. *Libya*;[42] *Gulf of Maine*;[43] *Libya* v. *Malta*.[44] Proportionality here is not a synonym for 'equitable', but a rather specific notion that addresses whether there should be a relationship between the amount of shelf awarded (when equidistance is not to be used) and the relative length of coastlines. The idea of such a linkage had in fact

---

[38] This point is elaborated, with respect to both the *Western Approaches* arbitration and the *North Sea Continental Shelf Case*, in H. Lauterpacht, 'Equity, Evasion, Equivocation and Evolution in International Law', *Proceedings and Committee Reports of the American Branch of the ILA* (1977–8), 33–47.   [39] ICJ Reports (1982) 18 at para. 71.

[40] ICJ Reports (1969) 3 at 52–4.   [41] (1979) 18 *ILM* 397.
[42] ICJ Reports (1982) 75 at para. 103.   [43] Ibid. (1984) 246 at 335–9.
[44] Ibid. (1985) 43 at para. 55.

been advanced by Sir Francis Vallat as long ago as 1946, when he suggested that 'where a bay or gulf is bounded by several states . . . the most equitable solution would be to divide the submarine area outside the territorial waters among the contiguous states in proportion to the length of their coastline'.[45]

This suggestion was effectively embraced by the Federal Republic of Germany in the *North Sea Continental Shelf Case*, initially in the rather broad formulation of Sir Francis Vallat, and then in a rather more modest formulation. This latter formulation stepped back from suggesting a rule of general applicability, whereby any state in any given situation could claim a share of continental shelf proportionate to the length of its coast.[46] Instead, it was proposed that proportionality would be appropriate in the geographic circumstances of the particular case. The Court dealt with proportionality not as a distinct principle of delimitation, but as one of the factors to be considered in ensuring that equitable procedures were applied. The final paragraphs of the judgment said in somewhat general terms that one of the factors to be taken into account was 'the element of a reasonable degree of proportionality, which a delimitation carried out in accordance with equitable principles ought to bring about between the extent of the continental shelf areas appertaining to the coastal State and the length of its coast . . .'.[47] But the passage of the Court's judgment of which this was effectively the summary made it clear that the 'reasonable degree of proportionality' as an aid to delimitation in accordance with equitable principles came into play when a balance had to be struck between states with straight, and those with markedly concave or convex, coastlines.

In the *Anglo-French Continental Shelf Arbitration* on the delimitation of the continental-shelf boundary in the Channel and south-western approaches, the Tribunal affirmed that proportionality had a role to play not as a general principle of delimitation but as a means to express 'the criterion or factor by which it may be determined whether [such] a distinction results in an inequitable delimitation of the continental shelf'.[48] What the Court in the *Continental Shelf Cases* had expressed in positive terms, the Tribunal in the *Anglo-French* arbitration expressed in negative terms: 'It is disproportion rather than any general principle of proportionality which is the relevant criterion or factor.'[49] The Tribunal said in specific terms that proportionality was thus a means of determining whether 'distorting' geographic features (a concave coast in the *Continental*

---

[45] (1946) 23 *BYIL* 333 at 355–6.
[46] See D. McCrae, 'Proportionality and the Gulf of Maine Boundary Dispute' (1981) 19 *Canadian YBIL* 287 at 292.
[47] ICJ Reports (1969) 3 at 54. [48] (1979) 18 *ILM* 397 at 427.
[49] Ibid.

Shelf Case, off-shore islands in this case) produced inequity. But it was 'not a general principle providing an independent source of rights to areas of the continental shelf'.

In 1982 the Court returned to the matter in the *Tunisia–Libya Continental Shelf Case*. It spoke of proportionality as a function of equity, and seemed to think it had relevance in a situation where both states were making claims around coasts of generally similar configuration. The Court stated that 'the element of proportionality is related to the lengths of the coasts concerned'.[50] In this case the Court is essentially using proportionality as a substantive principle of delimitation.

But by 1985, in the *Libya–Malta Case*, the Court was once again insisting that there was certainly no general principle of *strict* proportionality of coastal lengths—and, indeed, no substantive delimitation rule of proportionality at all. Once again, the emphasis was on proportionality as an element of equity, whose function was to provide 'correctives'. The Court tied this into a further principle—that nature must be respected.[51] Coasts which are broadly comparable ought not to be treated differently because of 'quirks of configuration'. It is not entirely clear to me why 'quirks of configuration' are not part of the nature that should be respected, and why only 'general direction' is said to reflect nature. In any event, the Court was explicit that proportionality was not a method of delimitation in its own right.[52]

The *Gulf of Maine Case*—a Chambers Judgment in 1984—affirmed that proportionality was not an autonomous method of delimitation—but then went on to say that that did not preclude 'the justified use of an auxiliary criterion serving only to meet the need to correct appropriately' by reference to the 'inequalities noted'.[53] But the inequalities here were hardly 'quirks of configuration' but were those that followed from what nature had provided in the region.

The concept of proportionality in maritime delimitation remains, for me, full of uncertainties and problems.

The use of force

The concept of proportionality is used in an entirely different sense in the law on the use of force. It is here not one technique among many to achieve an equitable outcome in the face of special geographic circumstances. It is used in a way that we will see reflected in other areas of the law—namely, to limit permitted harm done to others. The use of force against the territorial integrity and political independence of others is unlawful. But force in self-defence is lawful. That permitted action, which will necessarily

---

[50] ICJ Reports (1982) 18 at para. 104.
[52] Ibid. 13 at paras. 55–8.

[51] ICJ Reports (1985) 13 at para. 56.
[53] ICJ Reports (1984) 246 at para. 218.

cause harm to others, is however limited by the requirement of proportionality. This limitation on self-defence is one known to all systems of domestic law[54] as well as to international law. But the requirement of proportionality as a constraining factor inevitably prompts the question 'proportionate in respect of *what*'? The *Caroline* incident, which is frequently cited as the authority for the requirement of proportionality in the exercise of self-defence, does not really carry matters much further forward. In the relevant passage, Arbitrator Webster says that self-defence must be 'nothing unreasonable or excessive; since the act, justified by the necessity of self defence, must be limited by that necessity and kept clearly within it'.[55] Brownlie perceptively comments that 'the emphasis on proportionality as a "special requirement" in the law of nations may represent an attempt to create the necessary distinction between defence and self help'.[56] If one goes beyond the necessity of defending oneself, the use of force will entail self-help.

In the law relating to the use of force (*jus ad bellum*) it may be said that the answer to the question 'proportionate in respect of what?' is to be answered 'proportionate in relation to the injury being inflicted'.[57] In the *Nicaragua–US* case the International Court introduced a requirement of proportionality into non-forceful countermeasures which were held by the Court to be the appropriate response to low-level uses of force that did not amount to an armed attack.[58] This follows the pattern of proportionality being used to control permitted harm to others.

In a single incident of use of force, which occasions the right of self-defence, it is easy to see that the response must be proportionate to the harm inflicted. It would be disproportionate to respond to a raid across a border by exploding a nuclear device. But, when the armed attack is a sustained one, requiring prolonged and multiple responses, the relationship becomes difficult. A state defending itself from invasion does not, realistically, put itself in a defensive position in respect of each successive blow being rained on it, ensuring that its response to each separate hostile act is proportionate to *that specific injury received*. Rather, proportionality then becomes a proportionality in *respect of the object legitimately to be achieved*. It is exactly this shift in answer to our question 'proportionality in respect of what?' that marks the transition from *jus ad bellum* to *jus in bello*. The difficulty of knowing which is the requirement—proportionality to the injury just received or to the object to be achieved—is emphasized

---

[54] I. Brownlie, *International Law and the Use of Force by States* (1963), 261–4.
[55] Parliamentary Papers (1843) lxi; British and Foreign State Papers, xxx. 193.
[56] Brownlie, *International Law*, 261–4.
[57] J. Hargrove, 'The Nicaragua Judgment and the Future of the Law of Force and Self-Defence' (1987) 81 *AJIL* 135 at 136.
[58] *Nicaragua Case*, ICJ Reports (1986) 14 at paras. 210, 249.

by the fact that in today's world major extended military actions are carefully designated actions in self-defence—but the scale of hostilities is such that the laws of war apply. The Falklands/Malvinas conflict was just such an example. Again, when an unlawful use of force occurs, and force is used to repel it, there can for a variety of reasons (geography, or because attempts are being made at a peaceful resolution) be a prolonged period of time before the military response to the initial act occurs. Both the Falklands hostilities and the 1991 Gulf conflict would be examples of that. Proportionality here cannot be in relation to any specific prior injury—it has to be in relation to the overall legitimate objective, of ending the aggression or reversing the invasion. And *that*, of course, may mean that a use of force is proportionate, even though it is a more severe use of force than any single prior incident might have seemed to have warranted. Judgments still have to be made. In the Falklands rather substantial firepower was regarded as necessary to dislodge the Argentinians and to secure a withdrawal; but any bombing of the Argentinian air force or navy while in Argentina or in port would have been regarded as disproportionate. In the Gulf conflict the coalition forces, with the approval of the United Nations, regarded the massive action against military and strategic targets in Iraq as proportionate to securing Iraqi withdrawal from a different location, Kuwait.

The substantive law of *jus in bello* is largely based on the concept of proportionality. Indeed, one leading team of scholars sees it as a codification of the requirement of proportionality. Examining the matter in the context of the two Protocols additional to the Geneva Conventions of 1949, Bothe, Partsch, and Solf[59] view proportionality as one of two elements comprising necessity, the other being relevance.

Once again we have the idea of proportionality as a limiting element upon otherwise permitted harm. This is illustrated by a brief examination of certain provisions. Article 35 of Protocol I repeats the already well-established rule that 'In any armed conflict, the right of the parties to the conflict to choose methods or means of warfare is not unlimited.' The second paragraph elaborates another well-established rule. 'It is prohibited to employ weapons, projectiles and material and methods of warfare of a nature to cause superfluous injury or unnecessary suffering.' Although there is no mention of proportionality, Bothe *et al.* interpret the clause as justifying military violence if measures are employed which are relevant and proportionate to securing the prompt submission of the enemy with the least possible expenditure of economic or human resources.[60] The principle of necessity is what justifies military violence; the principle of

---

[59] M. Bothe, K. Partsch, and W. Solf, *New Rules for Victims of Armed Conflict* (1982), esp. pp. 192–8, 297–320, 348–69.   [60] Ibid. 195.

EQUITY AND PROPORTIONALITY

humanity forbids *measures* that are not necessary—that is, relevant and proportionate. Relevance means that the violence is appropriate for the purposes of the specific military advantage sought. Casualties and damage must not be disproportionate to the military advantage anticipated.

Article 51 of Protocol I raises the question of the protection of the civilian population and 'collateral damage'. The civilian population 'as such' may not be the object of attack. Indiscriminate attacks are also prohibited, and these are defined and examples given. Again, we have the codification of a customary principle of international law, which for Bothe *et al.* sets 'in fairly concrete terms . . . the principle of proportionality as it applies to the protection of civilians against the collateral effects of attacks directed against military targets'. What some would simply describe as a prohibition upon attacks which are indiscriminate is to Bothe *et al.* a realization of the principle of proportionality, by which it is accepted that not *all* harm to civilians can be avoided, but limitations on result are none the less imposed. Indeed, he terms para. 5 (*b*) of Article 51 (which lists indiscriminate attack) 'the first concrete codification of the principle of proportionality as it applies to collateral civilian casualties', and returns again to his theme of the duality of necessity and humanity, the one permitting destruction if it is relevant and proportionate and the latter prohibiting destruction if it is not relevant and proportionate. Proportionality is thus introduced not only as a silent condition of necessity, but as an element in an alleged separate negative prohibition. I have difficulty in seeing that 'humanity' exists separately from an element that has gone into identifying the legal norm of necessity itself. We also cannot ignore the fact that attempts to introduce the terms 'proportionate' and 'disproportionate' into the text of Article 51 failed.[61] But for Bothe the fact that there has to be a balancing between the foreseeable extent of incidental or collateral civilian casualties or damage, on the one hand, and the relative importance of the military objective as a target, on the other, *is* the operation of a rule of proportionality.

Again, Article 57 on precautionary measures to be taken for the protection of civilians in the face of attack is regarded by Bothe as evidence of the obligation of proportionality. He terms the requirement to refrain from attacks which would cause civilian injury 'excessive in relation to the concrete and direct military advantage anticipated' as one of proportionality. Articles 35 (1) and (2), Article 49 (4), Articles 51–6 and 57 taken together are, on this view, the law of proportionality as an integral element of the law of armed conflict, notwithstanding that the concept finds no specific mention.

[61] Karlshoven, Conference II (1978) 9 *NYIL* 116; CDDF/215/Rev. 1, paras. 47, 57; CDDH/III/264/Rev. 1, XV Official Records 347.

The critical point in this: the rules on armed conflict *fully subsume* the doctrine of proportionality. No conduct that fails to meet the specific requirements of the substantive *jus in bello* can be justified on grounds that it is still 'proportionate'.

By contrast, as we shall see, the substantive obligations of human-rights law do *not* subsume proportionality: it is said to exist over and above the provisions specified. And it is to that that I now turn.

The law of human rights

Proportionality also appears as an element in the international law of human rights. As in humanitarian law, it finds no mention in the relevant instruments. But it is widely invoked by the leading tribunals. If it operates in humanitarian law where a harm is permitted, to limit that harm, in human-rights law it operates where a restriction upon a right is permitted, to control that restriction.

Some human rights are, of course, non-derogable. They may never be restricted. But a large number of rights do allow limitation. It is a standard formulation under the European Convention on Human Rights that a permitted limitation must be prescribed by law and is necessary in a democratic society. 'Necessity' here carries various overtones. As the Court has held in a line of cases, necessity *means* necessity, and not convenience or desirability.[62] So the need to limit *at all* will be tested against necessity. But the Court will also want to satisfy itself that the *measures* are necessary in a democratic society. In this different task the Court will look to see whether alternative, less harsh measures of limitation might have been available: thus, in the *Lawless Case*,[63] the Court looked at the options to non-jury trial. But the test of 'necessity in a democratic society', by reference to possible alternative methods, of course supposes *also* a legitimate objective and demonstrated need. The starting-point is for the state to show that events have occurred which, as the guardian of the public good, it feels it must redress. It must show a legitimate objective in introducing limitations to human rights—and show further that those limitations are necessary to secure the achievement of the legitimate purpose, and that no other less severe measures (perhaps also limitations) would have served the same end.

All of this is fairly straightforward, and flows from the text of the clauses themselves (see Articles 8, 10). But the Court has introduced a further element in judging a limitation, namely, the element of proportionality. In the *Sunday Times Case*[64] the Court, addressing a contempt of court order in the United Kingdom, claimed by the UK to be necessary to protect the

---

[62] See e.g. *Sunday Times* v. *United Kingdom* (1979), Ser. A, no. 30, para. 59.
[63] Judgment of 1 July 1961, Ser. A, no. 3, paras. 31–8.
[64] Judgment of 26 April 1979, Ser. A, no. 30, paras. 42–68.

authority of the judiciary, said that the limitation on the right of freedom of speech

did not correspond to a social need sufficiently pressing to outweigh the public interest in freedom of expression within the meaning of the Convention . . . That restraint proves not to be proportionate to the legitimate aim pursued; it was not necessary in a democratic society for maintaining the authority of the judiciary.[65]

Now here the Court was addressing the *need at all* for the limitation (not whether one measure rather than another was acceptable). It is hard to see what the invocation of proportionality achieves that is not already fully achieved by applying the test specified in the Convention—that the limitation be necessary in a democratic society. 'Proportionality' seems to serve no separate function. Sometimes proportionality is directed to the particular measures—the Inter-American Court, in its 1987 Advisory Opinion on Habeas Corpus in Emergency Situations, noted that permitted derogations had to be tailored to the exigencies of the situation and read into the words of the Article permitting derogations (Article 27) that the specific measures would have to be judged by reference to the character, intensity, pervasiveness, and particular context of the emergency and 'upon the corresponding proportionality and reasonableness of the measures'. In the *Handyside Case* the European Court on Human Rights stated that what 'necessary in a democratic society' means is that 'every formality, condition, restriction or penalty imposed in this sphere must be proportionate to the legitimate aim pursued'.[66] Proportionality is here used to determine whether particular measures of control are necessary—if the measure selected is more severe than is needed to achieve the legitimate objective, it will not be 'necessary'. Here proportionality does seem to have an operational role to play. At the same time, it is a somewhat subjective term: frequently the Court will simply pronounce a measure 'proportionate' or 'disproportionate' (just as a measure might be deemed in other spheres of law to be 'equitable' or 'inequitable'), as if it is self-evident and no explanation for this conclusion need be given.

The most remarkable use of proportionality is surely in the *Sporrong and Lonnroth Case.*[67] The text of Article 1, Protocol I, appears clearly to restrict compensation to certain specified circumstances. The IP confirm the difficulty of agreement that when these specified grounds exist compensation should be paid. But *proportionality* was said to lead to the obligation for compensation in relation to interferences with property that do *not* necessarily fall within the specified categories of the Article.

[65] Advisory Opinion OC-8/87 of 30 Jan. 1987, Ser. A, no. 8.
[66] Judgment of 7 Dec. 1976, Ser. A, no. 24.
[67] *Sporrong and Lonnroth Case*, Judgment of the European Court of Human Rights, 23 Sept. 1982, Ser. A, no. 52.

Conclusion

Whether proportionality is yet a general principle of law is doubtful. It is a familiar provision of German constitutional law[68] and has also had an important role to play in the administrative law of many civil-law jurisdictions. It has also had a certain impact upon European Community law, which has used it to find that a public authority may not impose obligations on a citizen except to the extent to which they are strictly necessary in the public interest to attain the purpose of the measure. But again one is left with a sense of subjectivity in the decision-making of the Court as to whether burdens imposed are or are not out of proportion to the object sought.[69]

The House of Lords in the United Kingdom has noted[70] that there might be a time when the concept of proportionality could have a useful role to play in English law. But in the *Brind Case*[71] it made clear that that time had not yet come. Proportionality would not be looked at by an English court in judicial review of a ministerial discretion, even when that discretion was in a subject area covered by our treaty obligations under the European Convention on Human Rights. The test would remain the traditional test of *reasonableness*. But there are already indications in recent judgments that the rather special formulation of reasonableness exemplified in the *Wednesbury Case*[72] will not long remain untempered by proportionality.

In international law the principle in maritime law is entirely different from the principle in other areas. In the other areas, there are common elements to the invocation of the principle, but many doubts surround it still—whether, as in the laws of war, it exists as a separate principle at all; and whether, in human-rights law, it has a meaningful separate existence from the notion of necessity.

Conclusion

The great principles of equity and proportionality are meant to oil the wheels of decision-making: but we should be sceptical. The concept of equity, designed to be an aid to decision-making, carries with it serious problems. The concept of proportionality in the law of the sea is entirely

---

[68] T. Hartley, *The Foundations of European Community Law* (2nd edn., 1988), 145.

[69] See Advocate General Dutheillet de Lamonthe in *Internationale Handelsgesellschaft*, Case 11/70 [1970] ECR 1125 at 1146; *Balkan Import-Export*, Case 5/73 [1973] ECR 1091 at 1112; and Hartley, *Foundations*, 146–7.

[70] *CCSU v. Minister for the Civil Service* [1985] AC 375 at 410.

[71] *R. v. Secretary of State for the Home Department, ex parte Brind* [1991] 1 AER 720 per Lord Ackner at 735.　　　　　　　　　　　　　　　　　　　　　　[72] [1948] 1 KB 223.

different from proportionality as it is used in other areas of international law. In the law of armed conflict the specific rules *themselves* reflect the concept; in human-rights law it is largely redundant to what is achieved by the specific obligations. Only in the law of *jus ad bellum* is its contribution to 'oiling the wheels of international law' *really* evidenced.

14

THE INDIVIDUAL USE OF FORCE IN
INTERNATIONAL LAW

SINCE earliest times states have employed military force to pursue their political and economic objectives. As early as the fifteenth century, Grotius insisted that the law of nations limited the use of force to three justifiable causes: 'defence, recovery of property, and punishment.'[1] In that particular sense, it was necessary to restrict the use of force to a just war.[2] The Covenant of the League of Nations sought further to control and contain the use of force, without prohibiting it.[3] The Kellogg–Briand Pact of 1928 outlawed war as an instrument of national policy. This instrument,[4] to which some sixty-three states became party, 'decoupled' the justness of the cause from the entitlement to use force. After the cataclysmic events of the Second World War, it was thought necessary to make it even more specific in the UN Charter that force could be used only in self-defence and not to pursue legal rights or genuinely held notions of justice.

The UN Charter thus limited permitted uses of force to self-defence or to collective enforcement action. But it also envisaged that the United Nations would itself provide the mechanisms for asserting legal rights and pursuing political and social justice. There would thus be no need for the individual resort to force. The United Nations was given powers which were intended to allow states to avoid unilateral reliance on the military instrument to guarantee their own security. One cannot understand the post-war debates about the legal limits to the use of force without appreciating that the contemporary norms were predicated upon a Charter system that until now has been impossible to operate. The assertion of legal rights and the pursuit of economic and social justice has been extraordinarily hard to achieve. Indeed, in a decentralized legal order, the notion of justice has often been in the eye of the beholder. And the immediate replacement of wartime co-operation with the Cold War made the collective security system envisaged by the Charter impossible to achieve. It was not possible to set up standing UN forces as envisaged

---

[1] Book II, *De jure belli ac pacis*, ch. 1, ss. 1.4 and 2; ch. 2, s. 13.

[2] 'For Grotius, his formulated doctrine of the "just war" was a method of controlling the unbridled power of states to act as they chose' (R. Higgins, 'Grotius and the Development of International Law in the United Nations Period', in H. Bull, B. Kingsbury and A. Roberts (eds.), *Hugo Grotius and International Relations* (1990), 267.

[3] See Arts. 15 and 16.

[4] 1928 General Treaty for the Renunciation of War, 94 LNTS 57.

under Article 43 of the Charter; and there was a total absence of political consensus in the Security Council.

Against these realities, states have continued to feel the need to resort to force. There has been a further underlying problem. Not only is the wording of the relevant UN Charter articles full of ambiguity, but the articles were formulated to address the problem of military hostilities between states. In the event, much of post Second World War military history has been about different uses of force—the employment or encouragement of irregulars by one state against another, guerrilla movements, national liberation movements, terrorism. The Charter was also formulated before the development of the atomic bomb. Its provisions were not only predicated upon a collective security system that was never a reality, they did not envisage the new types of violence, and the social conditions that were their origin and their consequence.

Since the collapse of communism in Eastern Europe there have begun to emerge other new realities. The total failure of the collective security system (rooted in confrontation between the West and the Soviet Union) has begun to be replaced by the possibility of co-operation within the UN system. But many political difficulties lie ahead in making that co-operation effective. And the ambiguities of the language of the UN Charter, set against these past and present political difficulties, have generated a variety of legal problems that have had great practical importance. In this chapter we will discuss the question of anticipatory self-defence; what constitutes 'the state' for purposes of self-defence; the question of humanitarian intervention; and what constitutes an armed attack. Each problem is set within the Charter relationship established between Article 2 (4) and Article 51.

The Relationship between Article 2 (4) and Article 51

Article 2 (4) provides that 'All members shall refrain in their international relations from the threat or use of force against the territorial integrity or political independence of any state, or in any other manner inconsistent with the purposes of the United Nations.' At the same time, Article 51 indicates that there are certain uses of force that will not contravene the prohibitions in Article 2 (4). It provides: 'Nothing in the present Charter shall impair the inherent right of individual or collective self defence if an armed attack occurs against a member of the United Nations, until the Security Council has taken measures necessary to maintain international peace and security.' It is then provided that these measures be reported to the Security Council. The text makes it clear that, on the one hand, a state may act in self-defence without first securing the permission of the Security

Council, whilst, on the other hand, the Security Council retains its responsibility to take such action as it deems fit.

The UN Charter is intended to provide for a watertight scheme for the contemporary reality on the use of force. Article 2 (4) explains what is prohibited, Article 51 what is permitted. But almost every phrase in Article 2 (4) and Article 51 is open to more than one interpretation. Further, what happens if Articles 2 (4) and 51 are not in fact a watertight system, are not entirely opposite sides of the same coin? Can there be, for example, a use of force that is *not* against the territorial integrity or political independence of a state (and thus not, on the face of it, violative of Article 2 (4))—but is also not individual or collective self-defence (and thus manifestly permitted under Article 51)? It is unlikely—most uses of force, no matter how brief, limited, or transitory, do violate a state's territorial integrity. A simple aerial military incursion will do so. So, too, will an attempt to exercise self-help even if in international straits. Self-help is the use of force to obtain legal rights improperly denied. In the *Corfu Channel Case*[5] the United Kingdom engaged in minesweeping in the Corfu Straits (an international strait but also Albanian territorial waters) in order to make effective its legal right to free passage. The Court found such action unlawful—the action violated Albanian territorial sovereignty and legal rights were not to be vindicated through the manifestation of a policy of force.

It has been generally accepted, ever since this clear finding by the Court on the question, that self-help is unlawful under the Charter, notwithstanding the failure of the UN system to ensure that states do get the legal rights to which they are entitled. But, where the physical security of states is concerned, the matter has been more contested. So the inability of the United Nations to provide for the collective security of states has led to a rather more prolonged debate on the legal status of reprisals under the Charter. Reprisals consist of action in response to a prior unlawful military attack, aimed not at defending oneself against an attack as it happens, but rather at delivering a message of deterrence against the initial attack being repeated. Under customary international law, reprisals were lawful if certain criteria were met. These criteria, traditionally attributed to the *Naulilaa Arbitration*,[6] were that there must have been a prior deliberate violation of international law; that an unsuccessful attempt must have been made at redress; and that the action taken in reprisal be proportionate to the injury suffered. Reprisals would necessarily involve a violation of Article 2 (4), however, and, not being self-defence, are not brought within the permissive use of force in Article 51. It is undeniable that post-war

---

[5] ICJ Reports (1949) 3.
[6] *Naulilaa Case (Germany* v. *Portugal)* 2 RIAA 1011.

state practice has seen a substantial amount of military activity that has been frankly characterized as reprisals—that has been particularly true of the Arab–Israeli conflict in the Middle East. At times it has seemed as if there is an expectation of reprisals in the face of attack, and that the major concern has been as to the proportionality of the reprisals. But the Security Council has repeatedly condemned reprisals (albeit while often failing to condemn equally the prior illegal acts that led to them); and they are condemned in terms in the General Assembly's Declaration of Principles of International Law Concerning Friendly Relations[7] (which *does* clearly also condemn the organization or encouragement by one state of irregular forces for hostile activity in another). The texts of Articles 2 (4) and 51 clearly do not allow reprisals; and the study of other instruments and practices and judicial decisions does not allow one to conclude that there has been any *de facto* amendment of the Charter on this point— notwithstanding the fact that, in the absence of effective means of self-protection, reprisals may be expected to continue.

When a state is not able to engage immediately in action to defend itself, subsequent action can (wrongly) take on the appearance of reprisals, though it is still action in self-defence. Let us imagine that a state is not in a position immediately to resist an invasion; provided that it does repel the invasion as soon as it is able, or as soon as all attempts to secure a peaceful withdrawal have failed, the action will still be self-defence. The position of the United Kingdom in respect of the Falklands/Malvinas, and of Kuwait in respect of Iraq, illustrates the point. In the former, a period of several weeks elapsed between the Argentinian invasion and the arrival in the area of the UK task force. In the latter, nearly five months elapsed between the invasion of Kuwait by Iraq, and the military response by a coalition of UN members.

A particularly acute variation of this problem occurs when the United Nations secures a cease-fire, perhaps with a UN force to oversee the cease-fire—but does not succeed in obtaining the withdrawal of the invading forces. Does the UN cease-fire, and the passage of time (during which the position of the intervening forces becomes entrenched) really preclude the invaded country from liberating its territory? The decision of the Croatian troops on 22 January 1993 to march across UN lines into Serb-held territory within Croatia graphically illustrates the dilemma. It is hard to see that the United Nations' inability to secure the objectives of its agreed plan[8] after a year should extinguish a suspended right of self-defence.

---

[7] GA Res. 2625 (XXV) 1970, A/8028 (1970).

[8] Return of certain lands to Croatia; demilitarization of Krajina and its placing under UN supervised autonomy; and return of refugees to their homes. See SC Res. 743 (1992) establishing UNPROFOR, and approval of the associated UN plan in SC Res. 740 (1992).

With these preliminary comments behind us by way of background, let us now turn to address each of the problems indicated.

Anticipatory Self-Defence

Article 51 allows self-defence only when an armed attack has occurred. Does this mean that a state has, quite literally, even when it sees that it is about to be attacked, to wait until the blow has been struck before defending itself? In this context, what is meant by the reference in Article 51 to an 'inherent' right of self-defence? Is it simply embellishment? Or does it rather serve to carry forward into Article 51 the customary international law on the matter? Under customary international law, self-defence fell to be tested against the criteria enunciated by US Secretary of State Webster in his diplomatic note to the British in the context of the *Caroline Case* of 1842.[9] He stated, in a widely accepted dictum, that anticipatory self-defence must be restricted to those cases where the necessity 'is instant, overwhelming, and leaving no choice of means, and no moment for deliberation'. That formulation has significance in several ways for the UN Charter system. It must be remembered that the Charter does indeed have its own procedures for dealing with international threats to peace. If the threat is one that could reasonably be contained or turned aside through calling an emergency meeting of the Security Council, the criteria of the *Caroline* probably will not be met. At the same time, in a nuclear age, common sense cannot require one to interpret an ambiguous provision in a text in a way that requires a state passively to accept its fate before it can defend itself. And, even in the face of conventional warfare, this would also seem the only realistic interpretation of the contemporary right of self-defence.[10] It is the potentially devastating consequences of prohibiting self-defence unless an armed attack has already occurred that leads one to prefer this interpretation—though it has to be said that, as a matter of simple construction of the words alone, another conclusion might be reached.

Of course, abusive claims may always be made by states claiming to act in anticipatory self-defence. But in a decentralized legal order that is always possible; there is no avoiding the judgment that third parties will have to make on the claims in the light of all the available facts. But the

---

[9] British Parliamentary Papers, lxi; British and Foreign State Papers, xxix. 1129. Schachter states that this formulation cannot be said to have reflected state practice ('The Right of States to Use Armed Force' (1984) 82 *Michigan Law Review* 1620 at 1635).

[10] For the contrary view—namely, that an armed attack must have occurred—see L. Henkin, 'Force, Intervention, and Neutrality in Contemporary International Law' (1963) *Proc. ASIL* 147, 166; P. Jessup, *Modern Law of Nations* (1948), 164–7.

Webster formula, although suggested so long ago, seems still very useful in providing the required balance between allowing a state to be obliterated and encouraging abusive claims of self-defence. It still has great operational relevance and is an appropriate guide to conduct.

What Constitutes 'the State' for Purposes of Self-Determination

Article 2 (4) prohibits the threat or use of force against 'any state'—a precondition to the entitlement of any right of self-defence. What does this term 'any state' mean? Certainly the use of force is prohibited against a state's dependent territories overseas, as much as against the metropolitan state itself. The military action in the Falklands was a use of force against a state—albeit actually against a dependency of the United Kingdom—and in turn allowed a right of self-defence to the United Kingdom, even though the 'self' was some eight thousand miles away. Again, as a matter of policy, that must be the right interpretation, otherwise all territories other than independent metropolitan territories could be exposed to hostile military action with impunity.

But there is a rather more difficult issue: can a use of force against one's nationals abroad be termed an attack against a state? The importance of the question is apparent. The only use of force that is lawful is self-defence. States think it very important to be able to protect their nationals abroad—but they can do so only if the consequential use of force is justified as self-defence. And it can be justified as self-defence only if there has been an attack upon 'the state'.

When we spoke about jurisdictional matters, we discussed the taking of jurisdiction over persons on the basis of passive personality—that they had harmed one's nationals abroad. We noted it was a controversial basis of jurisdiction. Here the focus is not on the taking of jurisdiction (or bringing someone to trial) but of the actual use of force, this time not necessarily against the individual wrongdoer, but against the state that is believed to have been responsible for the harmful acts. In an interesting interrelationship, questions of jurisdiction, use of force, and state responsibility all bear on the same facts.

We have over the last few years seen a tendency to claim to be able to act in self-defence in response to attacks upon one's nationals. The existence of international terrorism has undoubtedly been an impetus to this claim. States have seen indiscriminate bombings and killings directed at their diplomats overseas, at their military personnel, and, quite frequently, at civilians too. It is the hallmark of terrorism, that violence is not conducted in the state-to-state encounters of armies and airforces envisaged by the Charter, but by these covert, violent, and frequently indiscriminate means.

A claim to be acting in self-defence has been made by the United States in the 1986 bombing raid on Libya, which it believed to have been responsible for a series of attacks on US nationals in Rome, Vienna, and Berlin.[11] Some of these attacks were on diplomats; some on servicemen at a night club; and others upon civilians at an airport.

Even if the occasion for invoking self-defence in these circumstances has in this era of terrorism become more frequent, the idea of treating an attack on one's nationals as an attack on the state is not entirely new. Professor Bowett has suggested that 'it is perfectly possible to treat an attack on a state's nationals as an attack on the state, since population is an essential ingredient of the state'.[12] Professor Bowett also finds it significant that the General Assembly's 1970 Declaration of Principle on Friendly Relations contains no prohibition on the protection of nationals, though reprisals are expressly denounced. But the Declaration is dealing with what constitutes an unlawful action under Article 2 (4), not what constitutes a lawful defence under Article 51. It is not surprising that reprisals are denounced as an unlawful use of force. The question of whether one's nationals may be *defended* by reliance on Article 51 did not arise in that context.

What there is some evidence of in customary international law is the right to humanitarian intervention on behalf of threatened citizens abroad. Sometimes that was spoken of as a free-standing right, but sometimes it was expressed in terms of an exercise in self-defence. In any event, it is now clear that, particularly in the face of terrorism, the claim to self-defence goes beyond a claim to rescue nationals, but in fact covers acts that really have a different character. The claim was explained by former US Ambassador to the United Nations, Jean Kirkpatrick, in this way: 'The prohibitions against the use of force in the Charter are contextual, not absolute . . . The Charter does not require that people submit supinely to terror, nor that their neighbours be indifferent to their terrorisation.'[13] One can be sympathetic with the sentiment but note also that the language of self-defence is being invoked to cover military responses that really bear the characteristics of reprisals or retaliation. This reality is again emphasized by the example of the US military air-strike against Libya in 1986 in response to perceived terrorism against nationals. Having characterized it as self-defence, the President then spoke of the need to

[11] (1989) 87 Dept. State Bull. 87; and M. Leich, 'Contemporary Practice of the US Relating to International Law' (1986) 80 *AJIL* 612 at 632 for US explanations. See also GA Res. 43/38, 1986.
[12] D. Bowett, 'The Use of Force for the Protection of Nationals Abroad', in A. Cassese (ed.), *The Current Legal Regulation of the Use of Force* (1986), 39.
[13] Quoted in V. Nanda, 'The United States Armed Intervention in Grenada—Impact on World Order' (1984) 14 *California Western International Law Journal* 395 at 418.

respond to abuse of one's nationals; and the US Permanent Representative spoke of the action being designed to 'disrupt Libya's ability to carry out terrorist acts and to deter future terrorist acts by Libya'. The former is the language of retaliation, the latter of reprisals. Neither is really the language of self-defence.[14]

Humanitarian Intervention

Under contemporary international law, may a state militarily intervene in another territory to rescue citizens under threat? Under customary international law, such activity was widely tolerated. But is it still allowed under the Charter? Let us examine the legal and policy issues.

Even minor military incursions are unlawful uses of force. It is quite clear, from the practice under the Charter and otherwise, that the Charter law does not simply prohibit major clashes between entire armies, while allowing smaller scale military interventions. Attacks by single planes, for example, are as much a violation of Article 2 (4) as would be an attack by a squadron. And it is not really feasible to engage in a rescue operation of threatened nationals without engaging in some use of force, which is prohibited by the terms of Article 2 (4).

But does that dispose of the matter? There are several reasons for thinking that it does not. First, what Article 2 (4) prohibits is the use of force against the territorial integrity or political independence of a state, or in any other manner inconsistent with the purposes of the United Nations. It can easily be seen that even a single plane attacking a country is a use of force against its territorial integrity. But is the answer so clear when the military intervention is not an attack on the state as such, but an operation simply designed to be able to rescue and remove one's threatened citizens? Is that really a use of force against the territorial integrity of a state, or is it not rather a violation of sovereignty—in the same way as a civilian aircraft which enters airspace without permission will surely be violating sovereignty—but still not attacking the state or its territorial integrity? It would seem that hostile intent, coupled with military activity against the state (and beyond the minimum needed for the rescue), is what would distinguish a violation of sovereignty from an attack upon a state's territorial integrity.

If we can satisfy ourselves that humanitarian intervention does not violate the prohibition against the use of force against a state's territorial integrity, then we can feel fairly confident that no *other* prohibition in

---

[14] For comment on 'expanded' claims to self-defence, see O. Schachter, 'Self Defence and the Rule of Law' (1989) 83 *AJIL* 259.

Article 2 (4) is being violated. A military action to end a hijacking, for example, would not be force against a state's political independence (unless it was intended to overthrow the government), and nor would it seem to be contrary to the purposes of the Charter, being directed towards the preservation of human life.

There is a different way of looking at the whole question—instead of looking to see whether a humanitarian intervention violates Article 2 (4), looking instead at the permitted use of force under Article 51. That approach focuses rather on self-defence, and brings us back to the question of harm to one's nationals and self-defence. It is very similar to, but not quite the same as, the question we asked ourselves before. Instead of saying 'Is an attack on a foreign citizen an attack on the state, which therefore entitles self-defence?' the question is the simpler one of whether a state can claim that military action to *rescue* one's citizens is an exercise of self-defence. Again, cautious support has sometimes been offered for this view. Professor Sir Humphrey Waldock (later Judge Waldock), giving this General Course in 1952[15] said that a state could use force to rescue nationals 'as an aspect of self defence', if the threat of injury was imminent, if there was a failure or inability on the part of the territorial sovereign to protect them, and if the measures of protection were strictly confined to the object of protecting them against injury.' These criteria would all seem to have been met in the Entebbe situation. There an Israeli civilian airliner was hijacked to Entebbe; the then President, Idi Amin, far from endeavouring to negotiate the safe release of the passengers, provided further arms for the hijackers and ominously separated the Jewish from the non-Jewish passengers. The dangers seemed extremely imminent and the rescue operation was directed only at procuring the safety of the passengers.

The following may be noted: a claim of humanitarian intervention based on self-defence could only be advanced in respect of nationals, because it is predicated on the argument that the state is being harmed through injury to its nationals, and can therefore respond in self-defence. But a claim of humanitarian intervention based on the argument that no violation of Article 2 (4) is entailed, would *not* logically be limited to the protection of one's own nationals. Either Article 2 (4) is or is not violated by such activity—but nothing turns upon whether those being rescued are nationals or not.

The general question has yet to be judicially determined, though it did arise in an incidental way in the *Tehran Hostages Case* before the International Court of Justice in 1980.[16] The Court was seized of an application by the United States to deal with the merits of that issue—

---

[15] *Recueil des cours* (1952, II), 451 at 467.   [16] ICJ Reports (1980) 3.

namely, whether the State of Iran was in violation of the Vienna Convention on Diplomatic Relations 1961 or international law more generally, by any attributability to it of the acts of those who had taken US diplomats in Tehran hostage. The matter had already been, for several months, the subject of attempts at resolution elsewhere—there had been Security Council resolutions, a UN fact-finding commission, and an Order of the Court calling for the release of the hostages. No progress had been made. While the merits of the case were before the Court, the United States engaged upon an ill-fated military attempt at rescuing the hostages. If one takes the Waldock tests, one question immediately presented itself: whether the hostages were in immediate danger of injury or harm (over and above the harm already occasioned by their very detention). The Court carefully did not pronounce upon the lawfulness or not of the US action, but in some carefully chosen phrases indicated that it thought it inappropriate for the action to have been mounted while the matter was before the Court.

Many writers do argue against the lawfulness of humanitarian intervention today.[17] They make much of the fact that in the past the right has been abused. It undoubtedly has. But then so have there been countless abusive claims of the right to self-defence. That does not lead us to say that there should be no right of self-defence today. We must face the reality that we live in a decentralized international legal order, where claims may be made either in good faith or abusively. We delude ourselves if we think that the role of norms is to remove the possibility of abusive claims ever being made. The role of norms is the achievement of values for the common good. Whether a claim invoking any given norm is made in good faith or abusively will *always* require contextual analysis by appropriate decision-makers—by the Security Council, by the International Court of Justice, by various international bodies. We can think of recent invocations of the right of humanitarian intervention—ranging from the Belgian and French interventions in Stanleyville in 1963, to the Israeli intervention in Entebbe in 1976, to the US intervention in Grenada in 1987. We are all capable of deciding, on the facts at our disposal, in which of these foreigners were really at imminent risk, which interventions were *bona fide* for reasons of humanitarian necessity, and which were not. Nor am I persuaded by another, related argument sometimes advanced—that humanitarian intervention should be regarded as impermissible, because, in the international legal system, there is no compulsory reference to impartial decision-makers, and states finish up judges in their own cause.

---

[17] e.g. I. Brownlie, 'Humanitarian Intervention' in J. N. Moore (ed.), *Law and Civil War in the Modern World* (1974), 217 at 217–18; R. Falk, *Legal Order in a Violent World* (1968), 339; E. Jiminez de Arechaga, General Course, *Recueil des cours* (1978, I), 116. L. Henkin, General Course, *Recueil des cours* (1989, IV), 154.

There are a variety of important decision-makers, other than courts, who can pronounce on the validity of claims advanced; and claims which may in very restricted exceptional circumstances be regarded as lawful should not *a priori* be disallowed because on occasion they may be unjustly invoked.

What Constitutes an Armed Attack?

Article 2 (4) requires states to refrain from the threat or use of force against the territorial integrity or political independence of other states. In so far as Article 51 is meant to be the obverse side of this prohibition, it might have been expected that Article 51 would provide a right of self-defence if such prohibitions were violated. But it does not—at least not in matching terms. We have already seen that Article 51 does not provide for any self-defence against a *threat* of force, although the threat is a violation of Article 2 (4). For self-defence to be a legitimate response to a threat of force, the threat would have to meet the Webster tests in the *Caroline*.

The other puzzle has always been that self-defence is not even permitted for the other prohibited act—a 'use of force' against the territorial integrity or political independence of a state. It permits it only for 'an armed attack'. Two questions are apparent. The first is whether any non-military coercion can be deemed to trigger the right to self-defence. The second is whether all uses of force are in fact armed attacks.

The answer to the first question is straightforward. In spite of occasional colloquial reference to 'economic aggression', nothing in Article 2 (4) deals with economic or diplomatic duress. The Charter implicitly accepts that it cannot regulate political influence and economic pressure. It may be undesirable, but it is not unlawful under the Charter. And there is certainly no suggestion that it gives rise to any right of military response.

The second question of whether all prohibited force is in fact an armed attack has been examined in great detail by the International Court of Justice in the *Nicaragua* v. *United States Case*. But as long ago as 1970 the problem had been identified with striking prescience by Professor T. Franck. Pointing out that wars of national liberation were leading to new kinds of assistance being given, he noted that 'those new kinds of assistance do not fit comfortably into conventional international concepts and categorizations'. He continued: 'Insofar as one state merely encourages guerrilla movements within another, an "armed attack", at least in the conventional sense, cannot be said to have taken place. The more subtle and indirect the encouragement, the more tenuous becomes the analogy to an "armed attack".'[18] He then observed: 'Since the Charter speaks only of

[18] T. Franck, 'Who Killed Article 2 (4)?' (1970) 64 *AJIL* 809 at 812.

a right to defend against an armed attack, the international community is left to ponder what principles govern the right to retort in instances of lesser trespass.'[19] Franck observed that a 'line of continuity' runs from invasions by tanks and divisions through training, arming, sheltering and infiltrating neighbouring insurgents, all the way down to hostile radio propaganda calling for revolution in a foreign country'.[20] But he thought one still could not ignore the differences.

A state can clearly engage in the use of force either directly or through the acts of irregulars for whom it has assumed responsibility. Law-making resolutions of the United Nations have consistently opposed such indirect military hostile uses of force. The General Assembly Declaration of 1965 on the Inadmissibility of Intervention stipulated that 'no state shall organise, assist, foment, finance, incite or tolerate subversive, terrorist or armed activities directed towards the violent overthrow of the regime of another state, or interfere in civil strife in another state'.[21] There are similar prohibitions in the so-called Friendly Relations Declaration, which forbade 'the organisation of irregular forces or armed bands within the territory . . . of another state'.[22] Neither of these clauses makes an exception either for wars of national liberation or for the promotion of self-determination.

At the same time, and in parallel, the ideas concerning self-determination—first in its colonial context, and then more generally—took hold. How was self-determination to be accomplished against a recalcitrant colonial power save through wars of national liberation? At the same time as the law-making resolutions prohibited outside support for such activities, General Assembly resolutions began calling for support, moral and material, for such activities. In the 1970s this relatively low level transnationally supported violence was largely directed against certain remaining colonial powers. But in the 1980s it started also to be used by those who had previously opposed its legality. Indirect military assistance was provided by the West to the Mujahadeen fighting the Soviet Union in Afghanistan. This time the description was not 'wars of national liberation' but 'assistance in self-defence against an invader'. By the end of the decade it was being suggested in some quarters that armed force could be used to ensure that peoples had the right to freedom of choice in their own country, when faced with oppressive regimes. Internal self-determination became the continuum of wars of national liberation, in the sense that each strongly depended on outside training, finance, and arming. Different countries engaged in various of these activities, apparently regardless of the general prohibitions, and while also denouncing the legality of the action of the other in lending such assistance.

[19] Ibid. [20] Ibid. 813. [21] GA Res. 2131 (1965).
[22] GA Res. 2625 (XXV) 1970..

The matter has come to a head in the case of *Nicaragua* v. *United States*,[23] though I emphasize that the type of indirect military action and support in which the United States there engaged was just one of a long series of comparable activities by many states, each of which insisted that *their* action was lawful (because it was for a war of national liberation, or to assist others in ridding themselves of invaders, or to allow the peoples to overthrow a dictator).

In the *Nicaragua* v. *US Case* the Court found, as findings of fact, that the United States for a period provided funds for military and paramilitary activities by the Contras—Nicaraguans in opposition to their own government, but whose military activity had been characterized by the United States as defence in aid of Honduras, Costa Rica, and El Salvador against Nicaraguan incursions into their territories. Rejecting the self-defence arguments, the Court found this US assistance unlawful. The Court also found that 'an intermittent flow of arms' *had* gone from Nicaragua to the armed opposition in El Salvador, but that the flow was not on a significant scale and the evidence was insufficient to hold the Sandanista government responsible. The Court then further found that certain transborder military incursions into Honduras and Costa Rica *were* imputable to the Nicaraguan government.

The Court next addressed the question as to what military acts would constitute 'armed attack'. Citing the General Assembly Resolution on the Definition of Aggression, the Court said that an armed attack *could* include not merely action by regular armed forces across an international border, but also 'the sending by or on behalf of a state of armed bands, groups, irregulars or mercenaries, which carry out acts of armed force against another state' such as to amount to an actual armed attack rendered by regular forces. The Court found this to represent customary international law (without elaborating how it reached that view) and continued:

The Court does not believe that the concept of 'armed attack' includes not only acts by armed bands where such acts occur on a significant scale but also assistance to rebels in the form of the provision of weapons or logistical or other support. Such assistance may be regarded as a threat or use of force . . .'[24]

To summarize, an armed attack could take place directly, through the use of one's own forces, or indirectly, through armed bands or irregulars. The key is the scale of the activity. If it is not very substantial, it may still be an unlawful use of force, but it will not be an armed attack—and hence no self-defence may be used against it. That finding has occasioned a torrent of criticism, the critics contending that it is an encouragement for low-grade terrorism because the state at whom it is directed cannot use force in

[23] ICJ Reports (1986) (Merits) 14.   [24] Ibid. 104.

self-defence against it.[25] As Judge Schwebel put it in his dissenting opinion: 'The Court appears to offer—quite gratuitously—a prescription for overthrow of weaker governments by predatory governments while denying potential victims what in some cases may be their only hope of survival'—he is there referring to seeking assistance through collective self-defence.[26]

What I find puzzling about the Court's reasoning is this. It refers to the Assembly Resolution on the Definition of Aggression[27] which states that an armed attack occurs if the use of force by bands or irregulars is *equivalent to an armed attack by the regular forces of a state*. But how much force does one need by the *regular* force of a state before it is 'an armed attack' and allows of self-defence? If a division of troops rolls over the border, is the decision as to whether force can be used to repel them the *level of force* they are using? By adopting the unsatisfactory definition of the General Assembly Aggression Resolution, and proclaiming it customary international law, the Court appears to have selected criteria that are operationally unworkable. When a state has to decide whether it can repel incessant low-level irregular military activity, does it really have to decide whether that activity is the equivalent of an armed attack by a foreign army—and, anyway, is not *any* use of force by a foreign army entitled to be met by sufficient force to require it to withdraw? Or is that now in doubt also? Is the question of *level* of violence by regular forces not really an issue of *proportionality*, rather than a question of determining what is 'an armed attack'?

Two final points: the Court was purporting to deal with customary international law rather than the Charter; the Court *in terms* avoided pronouncing upon the implications of all this for the question of whether there exists a right of anticipatory self-defence.

The Doctrinal Debates

All of the questions we have discussed are difficult. And it is not surprising that such difficult questions have occasioned different views. What has been interesting is that the debate on these issues has been one that has not merely addressed the specifics of the particular problem to hand. It has been conducted at the level of legal philosophy. In a series of vigorous exchanges (in which Professors Schachter, Henkin, Franck, Gordon, and Reisman have been leading protagonists), some general questions have

[25] See e.g. A. Sofaer, 'Terrorism and the Law' (1986) 64 *Foreign Affairs* 901 at 919; M. Reisman, 'Old Wine in New Bottles: The Reagan and Brezhnev Doctrines in Contemporary International Law and Practice' (1988) 13 *Yale Journal of International Law* 171 at 195–6.
[26] ICJ Reports (1986) 14 at 350.   [27] GA Res. 3314 (XXIX) 1974.

been asked that are applicable to every one of the problems we have discussed. Are the shortcomings of the international system (the failures of the United Nations, the violations of the Charter, the massive violations of human rights, the frequent absence of democracy) such that the limits on the use of force contained in Article 2 (4) and Article 51 should be set aside?[28] Or should the limitations in those provisions, and other relevant norms of international law, be respected, even though that self-restraint would appear, in our imperfect world, to consolidate the position of the wrongdoer at any particular moment?[29] It is important to understand that this absorbing recent debate is not simply about whether texts should be interpreted as far as possible to support democracy and the values protected by international law. All the protagonists in the debate would agree on this. None of them takes a strict constructionist or conservative approach to textual interpretation. The argument addresses a more radical argument—namely, whether the failure of the international system, coupled with fundamentally changed circumstances since the time when the relevant texts were agreed, makes preferable unilateral action for the common good even if it is at variance with the norms articulated in the Charter and elsewhere.

This question is answered in the affirmative by Professor Reisman, who emphasizes that 'norms are instruments devised by human beings to precipitate desired social consequences. One should not seek a point-for-point conformity to a rule without constant regard for the policy or principle that animated its prescription, with appropriate regard for the factual constellation in the minds of the drafters.'[30]

My own position is that, if it is felt that the erstwhile articulation of norms no longer serves community interests, then those norms can properly be subjected to processes for change. The normal processes for change will include non-compliance. New, or refined, norms often emerge from a process of widespread non-compliance with old norms. But there *is* a distinction between non-compliance, on the one hand, and interpretation *infra legem* to achieve certain outcomes, on the other. And we should not pretend that they are the same. We should, moreover, be very sure that the

---

[28] This view has been forcefully argued by M. Reisman: 'Criteria for the Lawful Use of Force in International Law' (1985) 10 *Yale Journal of International Law* 279; 'Coercion and Self-Determination: Construing Charter Article 2 (4)' (1984) 78 *AJIL* 642; and 'Article 2 (4): The Use of Force in Contemporary International Law' (1984) *Proc. ASIL* 74–87. See also E. Gordon, 'Article 2 (4) in Historical Context' (1985) 10 *Yale Journal of International Law* 271.

[29] This is the position taken by O. Schachter: 'In Defense of International Rules on the Use of Force' (1986) 53 *University of Chicago Law Review* 113; 'The Legality of Pro-Democratic Invasion' (1984) 78 *AJIL* 645; and 'Self-Judging Self-Defense' (1987) 19 *Case Western Reserve Journal of International Law* 121. Also T. Franck, 'Who Killed Article 2 (4)?' (1970) 64 *AJIL* 809.

[30] Reisman, 'Criteria for the Lawful Use of Force', 283.

norms as presently articulated are so irredeemably inappropriate to the factual realities that we do indeed wish to undermine them. I believe that the application of Article 2 (4) and Article 51 has been very unsatisfactory. But I am not yet convinced that they have no useful purpose to perform or that unilateral outcome-directed action without reference to common norms is not dangerous.

How does this philosophical debate apply to the issues we have been discussing? How, for example, are we to interpret 'state', when deciding the reach of the protection allowed by international law against terrorism? The underlying question is a serious and real one, especially for lawyers who believe that international law is not just the dissecting of words as if they have no social context or political reality. And is humanitarian intervention to be permitted? And should indirect force not be allowed if it is to overthrow tyranny and establish democratic choice? In each case there are two essential choices, well illustrated by the permissibility of indirect force. The first choice is to say that, if one is to retain any control over this downward spiral into violence, the basic prohibition against the use of force, direct or indirect, by regulars or irregulars, must be maintained, with the sole exception being for self-defence. The other view is to say that, in a decentralized legal order, each action will have to be looked at on its merits and in context, and appraisals made as to whether the purpose of the military assistance is to support or to crush the values of human respect and liberty that international law should be promoting.

I generally believe that, in our decentralized legal order, facts must be looked at, and legal views applied, in context. But I also believe such policy choices are appropriate when the legal norms leave open alternative possibilities. I believe that to be the case, for example, on the question of humanitarian intervention. But I do not believe the question of the use of indirect force to be comparable. It seems clear to me that such force is prohibited by the relevant legal instruments, and that the common good is best served by terming the indirect use of force unlawful, regardless of the objectives in a particular case.

15

THE USE OF FORCE BY THE UNITED NATIONS

In this chapter I address a cluster of difficult issues of international law that arise in the context of a possible use of military measures by the United Nations itself.

UN Action for, or Authorization of, Enforcement Measures for Humanitarian Purposes

In Chapter 14 I discussed the legal controversies surrounding the claim by states unilaterally to intervene for humanitarian purposes. Since the collapse of communism in Eastern Europe, and with it the traditional differences in political objectives between the Soviet Union and the United States, certain new possibilities have begun to emerge in the Security Council. Perhaps now the Security Council would be able to enforce the peace against aggressors, and even intervene for humanitarian purposes when needed? But the path forward is rarely smooth, and the new possibilities have brought with them a raft of new legal, political, and military problems.

Notwithstanding the risk that unilateral intervention for humanitarian purposes is open to abuse, it is far from clear that such action can properly be authorized by the United Nations. We refer here to military or paramilitary action for humanitarian purposes, not other initiatives by the United Nations. The starting-point for everything is Article 2 (7) of the UN Charter, which provides that the United Nations may not 'intervene in matters which are essentially within the domestic jurisdiction of any state . . .'. But it has long been accepted that critical resolutions are not an 'intervention'. In any event, whatever 'intervention' may mean, it is now clearly recognized that human rights are *not* matters solely within the domestic jurisdiction of a state. And Article 2 (7) itself says that its provisions do not prejudice the application of enforcement measures under Chapter VII—so we still have to turn to Chapter VII to see what place, if any, humanitarian concerns find there. To say, as we confidently may, that human rights are not matters of domestic concern and that action to support them is not impermissible intervention, gets one out of Article 2 (7). But it still does not address whether, by reference to Chapter VII of the Charter, the United Nations may engage in sanctions for humanitarian purposes. Chapter VII has its own requirements, and these still have to be met.

It is clear that the envisaged sanctions provided for by Articles 41 and 42 are for the maintenance or restoring of international peace and security. It is further clear that measures under Articles 41 and 42 depend upon there having been a finding under Article 39 of the existence of any threat to the peace, breach of the peace, or act of aggression. No matter how much one may wish it otherwise, no matter how policy-directed one might wish choice between alternative meanings to be, there is simply no getting away from the fact that the Charter *could* have allowed for sanctions for gross human-rights violations, but deliberately did not do so. The only way in which economic or military sanctions for human-rights purposes could lawfully be mounted under the Charter is by the legal fiction that human-rights violations are causing a threat to international peace. That was the technique introduced long ago when economic sanctions were introduced against Rhodesia; it is still the technique being used in today's ever more complex problems in Iraq and Somalia. When the Government of Ian Smith declared its Unilateral Declaration of Independence (UDI) in Rhodesia, this was regarded as the act of a racist minority government, designed at perpetuating the inferior position of the black majority. That internal act was deemed by the Security Council to constitute a threat to international peace. Thus the scene was set for the application of Chapter VII of the UN Charter.[1] Advantage was taken of the fact that the immediate neighbours of Rhodesia were so deeply resentful of the Unilateral Declaration of Independence (UDI) that a hostile response could have been envisaged—and so, it was said, objectively there was a threat to the peace, and economic sanctions could be mounted.

In Iraq and Somalia the issue has been pressed a step further, because in each of these cases the question has arisen not of economic sanctions but of military sanctions for humanitarian ends. But the legal principles remain the same.

After the invasion of Kuwait by Iraq on 2 August 1990, the Security Council adopted a series of resolutions, culminating in an important authorization of the use of force against Iraq in Security Council Resolution 678 of 29 November 1990. After the hostilities, Security Council Resolution 687 specified what measures further to withdrawal from Kuwait were needed by Iraq for compliance with the initial twelve resolutions. Various of these resolutions had dealt with humanitarian issues as they had arisen in the context of the invasion of Kuwait— treatment of Kuwaitis, the holding of hostages, and other matters.

But what none of these resolutions, or any subsequent one, deals with is

---

[1] See e.g. SC Res. 232 (1966).

the human-rights situation in Iraq. As the position of the Kurds and the Shi'ites deteriorated, the coalition powers urged the Secretary-General to establish a UN force to enter Iraq to deal with the matter. The Secretary-General correctly took the view that he had no authority to do this and that a UN peace-keeping force could go to Iraq only with the consent of that country. Iraq was not prepared to give it and, even more importantly, the Security Council was not prepared even to try to set up such a force in the normal way, namely by Security Council resolution. This was for fear of veto by certain members of the Security Council, who did not wish for UN Forces to deal with humanitarian matters within a country (even with the reluctant agreement of the receiving state).

All the Security Council could agree on was to condemn, in Resolution 688 of 5 April 1991, 'the repression of the Iraqi civilian population in many parts of Iraq, including most recently in Kurdish populated areas, *the consequences of which threaten international peace and security in the region*' (emphasis added). Once again, internal repression was characterized as threatening international peace. And, indeed, there had been a massive flow of refugees across Iraq's borders, to Turkey and elsewhere. The resolution contained an appeal to all member states to assist the Secretary-General in his humanitarian efforts on behalf of the Iraqi population. Acting on this basis, certain coalition members set up security zones within Iraq. In the north such a zone provided a measure of security for the Kurds. Later, Anglo-French troops withdrew from this special zone, but continued to monitor the safety of the Kurds through declaring it a 'no-fly' zone for the Iraqi authorities, and patrolling it. Later a further 'no-fly zone' was established in the south, in an effort to protect the Shia from aerial bombardment by Saddam Hussein.

This humanitarian military intervention has taken place within the framework of objectives set by Resolution 688, but without specific authorization by the Security Council. It would in theory have been possible to have built on the Rhodesian precedent more directly—not only by declaring the human suffering a threat to international peace, but by then ordering military action to alleviate it. But that it was not possible to do, because of disagreement between Security Council members.

What are the normative implications of this? Is there, as the French have suggested, a new *droit ingérance*,[2] which entitles intervention by the international community to alleviate suffering? It is, in my view, too early to feel confident that such a norm has clearly emerged. What we may more cautiously say is that there may be an increasing tendency for the Security Council to characterize humanitarian concerns as threats to international

---

[2] See Foreign Minister Dumas, cited in L. Freedman and D. Boren, 'Safe Havens for Kurds in Post-War Iraq', in N. Rodley (ed.), *To Loose the Bands of Wickedness* (1992), 82.

peace—and thus bring them within the potential reach of Chapter VII of the Charter. The fact that the pictures of suffering appear on our television screens, rightly outraging public opinion around the world, makes more likely the possibility that such characterizations will occur even where the national interests of the military active Security Council members are not directly involved. Such has been the case in Somalia. In Resolution 794 (1992) the Security Council determined that the 'magnitude of the human tragedy caused by the conflict in Somalia' constituted a threat to international peace and security. The United Nations had already sought to provide peace-keeping support for the humanitarian operations, through the establishment of the United Nations Operation in Somalia (UNOSOM).[3] It now declared the situation a threat to international peace and authorized 'the use of all necessary means' to establish a secure environment for humanitarian relief operations. Acting under Chapter VII of the Charter, the Council authorized the participation of states in such an effort, within a unified command. The task was essentially taken on by the United States. It is clear that opening the door to military intervention for humanitarian purposes around the world will place an unbearable burden on the UN enforcement mechanisms, whether through direct UN action or through UN-authorized action.

The Use of Force to Support UN Resolutions

Does all non-compliance with Security Council resolutions necessarily entail a threat to international peace? This question underlines the problem of whether the Security Council can call for the use of force to compel compliance with its own resolutions.

After the invasion of Kuwait by Iraq in 1990, the Security Council, declaring itself to be acting under Articles 39 and 40, demanded the immediate and unconditional withdrawal of Iraqi forces, and called upon Iraq and Kuwait to begin intensive negotiations to resolve all their disputes.[4] Subsequent resolutions invoked 'Chapter VII of the Charter of the United Nations' and imposed and expanded economic sanctions.[5] Although no specific reference was made to Article 41, this is clearly the applicable article under Chapter VII. The failure of Iraq to heed the UN call for withdrawal led to the necessity to consider the possibility of the use of force. In the first place, could a measure of force be used to support the efficacy of the economic sanctions? In other words, even if the Security Council did not pass to military measures *per se* under Article 42 as the

---

[3] By SC Res. 751 (1992).   [4] SC Res. 660 (1990).
[5] See SC Res. 661 (1990); SC Res. 665 (1990); SC Res. 555 (1990).

chosen means to enforce the peace, could certain limited military measures be employed to ensure the efficacy of the alternative means chosen, namely economic sanctions? This question has never been addressed in these terms, but such limited actions have in fact been authorized without any sense that the Security Council was passing from Article 41 to Article 42. In 1965 the Security Council had introduced economic and diplomatic sanctions against Rhodesia.[6] In 1966, concerned at the possibility that oil was being delivered to the port of Beira Mozambique (then under Portuguese rule) for delivery on to Rhodesia, the Security Council called upon

the Government of the United Kingdom of Great Britain and Northern Ireland to prevent, by the use of force if necessary, the arrival at Beira of vessels reasonably believed to be carrying oil destined for Southern Rhodesia, and empowers the United Kingdom to arrest and detain the tanker known as Joanna V upon her departure from Beira in the event her oil cargo is discharged there.[7]

Thus a single country—a Permanent Member of the Security Council who happened to be the constitutional authority in Southern Rhodesia— was authorized to use force if necessary to uphold the efficacy of economic sanctions.

In the case of Iraq's invasion of Kuwait, a wide coalition of countries made available their forces, most operating in close co-ordination with the United States, and some acting separately but to the same end. It was rapidly felt that powers to stop and search vessels were needed if the economic embargo in the Gulf was to be effective. The Security Council once again authorized such action. It

call[ed] upon those Member States cooperating with the Government of Kuwait which are deploying maritime forces to the area to use such measures commensurate to the specific circumstances as may be necessary under the authority of the Security Council to halt all inward and outward maritime shipping in order to inspect and verify their cargoes and destinations and to ensure strict implementation of the provisions related to such shipping laid down in resolution 661 (1990).[8]

Again, the implication was that force could be authorized to implement economic sanctions without that use of force being viewed as military sanctions under Article 42. Just as a minimal use of force by UN peace-keeping operations may be authorized by reference to Article 40 of the Charter, so limited force may apparently be authorized by reference to Article 41—even though neither article envisages that possibility.

Further variations have arisen in respect of the right of the Security

---

[6] See SC Res. 217 (1965).   [7] SC Res. 221 (1966).
[8] SC Res. 665 (1990).

Council to call for military action to uphold its resolutions. The military action in Iraq was undertaken under Security Council authorization, but by coalition forces acting under unified command. At the end of hostilities, Security Council Resolution 686 specified a list of requirements that had to be met for a cease-fire to come into effect. The right of the coalition forces 'to use all necessary means' remained in effect for the moment. Security Council Resolution 687 addressed matters subsequent to the cease-fire. But it was still expressly stated to be under Chapter VII of the Charter, and referred to such matters as the verified dismantling of Iraq's nuclear and offensive military capability, the provision of reparations, and (again) the repatriation of Kuwaiti and third-party nationals.

May force be used to require compliance with the terms of Resolution 687? And, if so, upon Security Council authorization only, or directly by the coalition forces? In January 1993 the Secretary-General reported violations of the Kuwait frontier by Iraq, and interferences by Iraq with UN flights being undertaken in connection with the weapons-inspection programme. Although the Security Council passed no resolution, it issued a statement read by its President[9] demanding that the flights not be interfered with and warning of 'serious consequences which would ensue from failure to comply with its obligations'. The authorization in Resolution 678 to use 'all necessary means' was, in the context of the statements made in the Security Council, an authorization to use force. But the 'serious consequences' warning of the President of the Council in January 1993 cannot, in my view, be read as an authorization to coalition members to use force without further reference if interference with UN flights did not abate.

In the event, a series of military actions followed by some of the coalition parties—the United States, France, and the United Kingdom—in January 1993. Only one such action, directed against a target fifteen miles from Baghdad, was said by the United States to be linked to non-compliance by Iraq of its obligations under the Security Council resolutions. Other actions, taken in the no-fly zones set up to protect the Kurds and Shias, were explained in the language of self-defence. France and the United Kingdom, perhaps feeling on safer legal ground, emphasized their entitlement to patrol these zones for UN authorized purposes; and the danger to these missions when Iraq continued to fly within the zones, or to lock radar on to coalition aircraft, or to endeavour to shoot them down. Such responses are to be tested by the traditional criteria of self-defence. There is no entitlement in the hands of individual members of the United Nations to enforce prior Security Council resolutions by the use of force.

[9] S/5534 (1993).

The Relationship of Military Sanctions under Article 42 of the
Charter to Self-Defence under Article 51

Under Chapter VII there are two circumstances in which the use of force is
envisaged. The first of these is the use of force through the Security
Council under Article 42. If the Security Council considers that economic
and diplomatic sanctions would be or have proved to be inadequate, 'it
may take such action by air, sea or land forces as may be necessary to
maintain or restore international peace and security. Such action may
include demonstrations, blockades, and other operations by air, sea or
land forces of members of the United Nations.'[10] The second envisaged use
of force is not by the Security Council, but by individual members or
members acting collectively. Article 51 provides, as we have seen, for
individual or collective self-defence, in principle available after an armed
attack has occurred.

When is a legitimate use of force to be regarded as one rather than the
other? Put differently, what is the relationship between Article 42 and
Article 51? This issue arose in sharp relief during the Gulf crisis of 1990.

After a period of time it became apparent that Iraqi withdrawal from
Kuwait was unlikely to be achieved through economic sanctions. It became
probable that military action would be needed to reverse the aggression
that had occurred upon the Iraq invasion—that it would be necessary to
compel Iraq's withdrawal from Kuwait by force of arms.

At first sight this would seem to be action under Article 42 of the
Charter—military action taken because Article 41 measures had 'proved to
be inadequate'. It would require a further resolution of the Security
Council and, as such, would be subject to the veto of any Permanent
Member. Certain members of the Security Council spoke frankly of their
anxiety about the possible operation of the veto making it necessary to
base any such action on Article 51 rather than on Article 42.[11]

Forces—and in particular land and air forces—had gone to the Gulf to
assist Kuwait to regain its territory and assist Saudi Arabia in preventing
any further invasion by Iraq. Their very presence had provided an effective
defence for Saudi Arabia. If UN economic sanctions failed to secure Iraq's
withdrawal from Kuwait, could military force by way of collective self-
defence be used to obtain the same objective? The United States and the
United Kingdom insisted that such action would be justifiable under
Article 51. Action in self-defence could be taken without prior authorization of the Security Council, thus avoiding a possible veto.

[10] It is hard to see that the action by the United Kingdom at Beira and the action of the US
fleet in the Gulf are not 'blockade . . . or other operations' within the meaning of Article 42.
[11] See Statement by UK Foreign Secretary Douglas Hurd, Sept. 1990.

The issue is difficult. Resolution 661 (which imposed the initial economic sanctions) also specifically affirmed 'the inherent right of individual or collective self-defence, in response to the armed attack by Iraq against Kuwait, in accordance with Article 51 of the Charter'. This was not reiterated in later resolutions, though the United States and the United Kingdom regarded it as still operative.

Do members effectively have a choice between characterizing military action as collective self-defence under Article 51 or as enforcement measures under Article 42? Action under Article 42 would bind the UN membership as a whole (though for historic reasons UN members could not be legally compelled to participate in such a military activity)—but it would be subject to the veto. Could the very same action be taken, avoiding the veto, by reliance upon volunteer states claiming to be acting under Article 51?

We already know from the Korean precedent in 1950 that action which, by its nature, could have been characterized as enforcement was in fact authorized as lawful by reference to collective self-defence. Then, as now, there were practical problems about authorizing the action under Article 42 (at that time the problem was the Soviet veto). What was different was that the Korean action was *at all times* designated an action whereby UN members were authorized to assist South Korea defend itself. No question of 'mixing' Article 42 and Article 51 arose. Nor was the Gulf action ever under a UN command, though the Korean action was—albeit a command directed by the United States on behalf of the United Nations.

Article 51 provides that self-defence may be relied on 'until the Security Council has taken measures necessary to maintain international peace and security'. The question necessarily arises as to whether, the Security Council having embarked upon economic sanctions, such measures have been taken already, with Article 51 falling away. The answer to that would seem to be in the negative. The very resolution that imposed sanctions spoke of the co-existence of the right of collective self-defence.

Merely being seized of the matter cannot mean that the Security Council has 'taken . . . measures necessary to maintain international peace and security'. However, certain measures had been taken by the Security Council. From the perspective of literal interpretation, we could say that Article 51 does not speak of 'measures *effective* to restore international peace' but of measures *necessary* to do so. Economic sanctions were clearly necessary. From a more policy-oriented perspective, we could say that such nuances of meaning are not to be read into the word 'necessary'. Rather, the intention was that, in a decentralized legal order, members should be free to act in collective self-defence until the Security Council was in a position to take over the task and secure the common objective.

This argument has some attraction, but it also has its difficulties. It

262 THE USE OF FORCE BY THE UNITED NATIONS

would give to those claiming to act in self-defence an unbridled power of appreciation as to whether the Security Council had taken 'necessary' measures. No matter what action was taken by the Security Council, a member disagreeing with its perception of a dispute could insist that 'necessary' action still had not been taken and that it remained free to continue to act under Article 51.

How then can we make more objective the assessment of whether the Security Council has taken the 'necessary' action? It is certainly arguable that, if economic sanctions have been ordered, but not yet military sanctions, and an armed attack has not yet been repelled, that not all action 'necessary' has yet been taken and Article 51 remains available. On the other hand, the intended Charter scheme of things is undoubtedly for economic sanctions to be tried first[12] and then for collective measures to be tightened further by the application of military sanctions. Insistence that that second step can freely be taken under the umbrella of self-defence is to shift away from collective measures half-way through their possible application.

Of course, the attraction in doing so lies either in the possibility that the Security Council is so divided that it is unable to move to a resolution authorizing military measures; or that such a resolution would be vetoed if introduced. But the veto is an integral part of what was provided for in the Charter: the Permanent Members were certainly intended to have this power to control the use of force by the Security Council.[13]

The problem is further compounded by the fact that states may act both as Security Council members and as members who respond to a request for collective self-defence. The question is not easy to resolve. Its application in the Gulf remained ambiguous, because the Resolution eventually authorized the use of force if Saddam Hussein had not withdrawn from Kuwait by 15 January 1991. Although no mention is made in the Resolution of Article 42, this appears to be an authorization of military sanctions. No prior authorization of an Article 51 action would be necessary—though, of course, there is nothing to stop a group of UN members from getting the blessing of the Security Council for any collective defence action that they might otherwise be authorized to take.

---

[12] Though Art. 42 in fact allows the Security Council to move straight to military sanctions, if it chooses.

[13] The circumstances envisaged for the proper use of the veto is another question, beyond the scope of our discussion. But see Statement by the Delegations of the Four Sponsoring Governments on Voting Procedure in the Security Council, UNCIO Doc. 852, III/1/37(1); L. Goodrich, E. Hambro, and B. Simons, *Charter of the United Nations* (3rd rev. edn., 1969), 221–31; S. Bailey, *Voting in the Security Council* (1969), 26–47; R. Higgins, 'The Place of Law in the Settlement of Disputes by the Security Council' (1970) 64 *AJIL* 1.

The Relationship between Military Sanctions under Article 42
and the Means Envisaged for Providing them under Article 43

It is envisaged under Chapter VII of the UN Charter that the Security
Council, once it has determined the existence of a threat to the peace,
breach of the peace, or act of aggression, will recommend or decide upon
enforcement measures to maintain or restore international peace and
security. As we have seen, Article 41 provides for economic and diplomatic
sanctions; and Article 42 allows for military action by air, sea, or land
forces. Article 43 then provides that all UN members undertake to make
available to the Security Council, 'on its call and in accordance with a
special agreement or agreements', armed forces, assistance, and facilities.
These agreements were to govern the numbers and types of forces, their
location and readiness, and were to be concluded 'as soon as possible'
between the Security Council and individual members of the United
Nations, or groups of members. Some forty-five years later these
agreements have not been concluded. The deep divisions between East and
West that emerged immediately after the war made it impossible to proceed.
There was no agreement upon the circumstances in which military
enforcement measures would be used.

In the face of the failure of the Security Council to be able to proceed as
envisaged under Article 42, the question immediately arose as to the
authority of the Security Council to act under Article 42. Is the ability of
the United Nations to act under Article 42 dependent upon agreements for
the provision of UN forces being reached under Article 43? The Soviet
Union insisted that Articles 42 and 43 have to be read together, and that, in
the absence of the latter, the former was inoperative. No military action by
the Security Council could be envisaged.[14] The West took a somewhat
different view. It argued that while the absence of the agreements under
Article 43 meant that military sanctions under Article 42 could not be
proceeded with, military action of a different kind was not thereby ruled
out. If a state requested a UN military presence to keep or restore the
peace between itself and a neighbour, such a peace-keeping activity was
not prohibited under the Charter. Not being prohibited, and being entirely
consistent with the purposes of the Charter, it was permitted.[15] Later,
when such Security Council peace-keeping operations developed, it was
sometimes suggested (both in their governing resolutions and in academic
commentary) that their legal basis was to be found in Article 40 of the
Charter.[16] The Soviet Union doubted the ability of the Security Council to

---

[14] The Soviet views are gathered together in R. Higgins, *United Nations Peacekeeping*
(1969), i. 261–4.   [15] Ibid. 261–2.
[16] See ibid. iii. 54–66 (ONUC); iv. 144 (UNFICYP).

engage in such alternative military action. It contended that the permitted use of force was so specifically indicated in Chapter VII of the Charter that it was impermissible to suggest that other uses of force by the United Nations could be envisaged, provided only that they were not prohibited and served the objectives of the UN. Later the Soviet Union was to become somewhat more pragmatic in its approach. It voted for certain Security Council peace-keeping actions;[17] but continued to insist that they could not be financed under the regular budget and that they should be voluntarily financed, or preferably attributed to those aggressor states whose actions had made such peace-keeping action necessary.[18]

What the West and the Soviet Union both agreed upon was that military enforcement action under Article 42 was not possible in the absence of the envisaged agreements under Article 43. For the Soviet Union, it was not legally possible. For the West, it was a practical reality that military enforcement was not available in the absence of agreements under Article 43. The Secretary-General, after the establishment by the General Assembly of the UNEF in 1956, emphasized that it went to Egypt with the consent of that country, and could not operate without that consent. He continued:

This does not exclude the possibility that the Security Council could use such a force within the wider margins provided under Chapter VII of the United Nations Charter. I would not for the present consider it necessary to elaborate this point further, since no use of the Force under Chapter VII . . . has been envisaged.[19]

He thus left open the point as to whether enforcement action under Article 42 could, as a matter of Charter law, occur in the absence of agreements under Article 43. The matter was effectively reserved again in his celebrated Summary Study on the UNEF experience.[20] He stated: 'As the arrangements discussed in this report do not cover the type of force envisaged under Chapter VII of the Charter, it follows from international law and the Charter that the United Nations cannot undertake to implement them . . . without the consent of the Government concerned.' Whether Article 42 action was legally possible was thus not in issue, and left open.

Nor was the matter resolved when the International Court of Justice had in an advisory opinion in 1962 to address certain legal problems concerning

---

[17] e.g. for ONUC and UNFICYP.
[18] Higgins, *United Nations Peacekeeping*, iii. 274–5.
[19] A/3302, 2nd and Final Report of the Secretary-General on the plan for an Emergency UN Force, 6 Nov. 1956, para. 9.
[20] A/3943, Summary Study of the experience derived from the establishment and operation of the Force, Report of the Secretary-General, 9 Oct. 1958, para. 155.

the financing of UN peace-keeping.[21] Dealing there with the issue of whether the expenses of the UNEF in Suez and of the UN operation in the Congo were to be considered as expenses of the organization within the meaning of Article 17 (2) of the Charter, the Court felt constrained to address first the question of the lawfulness of those actions (though that was not in terms the question it was asked). It emphasized that each of the actions was lawful because it was *not* an action under Article 42 but rather a peace-keeping action, in which the UN military role was at the request of the host state, and not directed against the host state.[22] The Court examined the effect of the failure to conclude agreements under Article 43 of the Charter. But, as it had found UNEP and ONUC not to be enforcement actions under Article 42, it only asked itself the narrower question of whether *peace-keeping* action was permissible in the absence of Article 43 agreements. Answering that in the affirmative, the Court said:

It cannot be said that the Charter has left the Security Council impotent in the face of an emergency situation when agreements under Article 43 have not been concluded . . . it must lie within the power of the Security Council to police a situation even though it does not resort to enforcement action against a State . . .[23]

Although the position about Article 42 action in the absence of Article 43 agreements has been left open, it has popularly been supposed that such action was not possible. It has been a short step from the practical difficulty of attempting Article 42 actions to a general assumption that such actions were legally impossible. I have never regarded that view as correct. Peace-keeping action was deemed sufficient and appropriate for the world we lived in. While this political reality was undeniable, I never understood why the legal possibilities under Article 42 were deemed unavailable. It has consistently been my view that the consequence of the failure to conclude agreements under Article 43 was that UN members could not be compelled to provide forces and assistance under Article 42. But I could see no reason of legal analysis which proscribed any member or members from volunteering forces and the Security Council being able to use them under Article 42. It would remain a matter of political judgment for the Security Council, on any given occasion, to decide if it was preferable to provide for peace-keeping (now read into Article 40) or for military enforcement (under Article 42).

What was for many years a matter of academic interest has now come back into focus in the context of the Iraqi invasion of Kuwait. Are there legal constraints upon the Security Council ordering enforcement action under Article 42? Those states who preferred to avoid UN military actions offered reasons other than a legal inability to rely on Article 42. This has

---

[21] *Certain Expenses of the United Nations*, Advisory Opinion, ICJ Reports (1962) 151.
[22] Ibid. 171–2, 177.   [23] Ibid. 167.

been true both of those who wished to avoid military action altogether, and those who preferred to use collective self-defence. On 25 September 1990 Soviet Foreign Minister Shedverdnaze spoke in the Security Council of the importance of reviewing the possibilities under Article 43, of seeing whether, in the face of the improved relations between East and West, agreements could not now be reached. But it was not suggested that the absence to date of such agreements ruled out the possibility of action under Article 42. Indeed, such action was specifically envisaged in the strong speech of the Soviet Foreign Minister. The community of interest between the West and the Soviet Union conspired to put aside the common assumption of the previous forty-five years—that military sanctions could not be authorized in the absence of the agreements envisaged under Article 43. The prudence of the Secretary-General and the International Court of Justice in leaving this issue open, while focusing on peace-keeping, was apparent; and in my view the right legal answer has at last been arrived at (albeit without any apparent serious public consideration). In the absence of Article 43 agreements, no UN member can be compelled to provide military forces or assistance; but action under Article 42, by those who are willing to participate, can properly be authorized by the United Nations and carried out under UN command. It would also seem perfectly possible for such action to be authorized by the Security Council as an enforcement action under Article 42, even if it was to be carried out by UN members not under a unified UN command. And this was effectively the position achieved by Security Council Resolution 678 (1990) on the Gulf.

CONCLUSION

IN this book I have suggested that international law is a process, a system of authoritative decision-making. It is not just the neutral application of rules. None of the problems explored in these lectures can be satisfactorily resolved by confident invocation of a 'correct rule'. The problem exactly is that various, quite plausible, alternative prescriptions can be and have been argued for. The role of international law is to assist in choice between these various alternatives.

I hope I have demonstrated that what one suggests as the answer to each of our problems depends in large part upon how one looks at the sources of international law as they bear on the particular subject. And how one looks at the sources in turn depends very much on one's legal philosophy. There is no separating legal philosophy from substantive norms when it comes to problem-solving in particular cases.

I hope that this book has assisted in showing 'how the pieces fit together'. My experience is that these linkages are not always apparent. I would like students to understand better, for example, that immunities are really part of the topic of jurisdiction; that competence over events on vessels is part of the law of jurisdiction and not the law of the seas, notwithstanding its customary placement under the latter heading in textbooks; that recognition is relevant to immunity issues and to the problem of act of state.

It is not enough to be familiar with the current 'buzz-words' of international law. There is a contemporary trend of mindless invocation of the fashionable concepts—self-determination, rights *erga omnes*, *uti possidetis*, etc., etc. But these are not *mantras*, the mere chanting of which is sufficient in itself. We have to see, rigorously, what exactly these legal concepts mean, and when they are appropriately applicable. This book has urged that we must resist treating evolving ideas as if they are all things to all men.

We must expect in the international system an endless kaleidoscope of problems. Major changes in the international system—such as those we have witnessed in the last ten years—will change the pattern of the problems, but not eliminate the phenomenon. International law is a process for resolving problems. And it is a great and exciting adventure.

INDEX

abduction:
  precursor for jurisdiction, as 69–73
  violation of international law, occurrence
    of 70–2
Africa:
  international frontiers within 122
  uti possidetis, principle of 123
aggression:
  rules against 20–1
aliens:
  acts abroad by, jurisdiction over 58
  mistreatment, state responsibility for 152,
    157–9
  treatment of 52
arbitration:
  international, increasing importance of 54

central banks:
  state immunity 85
colonialism:
  remnants, transfer to independence 44
compensation:
  nationalization, for 142–5
  proportionality, element of 235
  state responsibility, as consequence of 163
continental shelf:
  delimitation, rules for: equitable 223–7;
    proportionality 228–30
  equidistance and equitability 223, 226
  outer limits of 137
  petroleum deposits on 137
  resources on, ownership of 138
  taxation of companies operating on 137–8
crimes:
  classification of offences as 167
  classification under international law 62–3
  state responsibility for 165–8
Croatia:
  recognition of 44–5
customary international law:
  application of 18
  binding nature of 210
  domestic law, conflicts with 213–14
  evidence for establishment of 30–1
  evidence of practice, as 18
  formation of 19
  national courts, application by 213
  national legal system, receipt in 210–16
  new norms, embracing 29
  normative quality 19–20

norms representing 22
treaties, overlap with 28–32
unilateral practice, formation by 34

developing countries:
  international law, view of norms 11–12
development:
  right to 103–4
diplomatic immunity:
  abuse of 89–90, 94
  archives of diplomatic mission,
    inviolability of 87–9
  family of diplomatic agent, of 87
  person of diplomatic agent, inviolability
    of 87
  policy issues 89
  purpose of 87
  substantive law of 87
  territorial jurisdiction, exception to 87
diplomatic law:
  development of 86–7
diplomatic missions:
  archives, inviolability of 87–9
  conduct of diplomacy through 86
  establishment of 86
discrimination:
  norm as to 20
dualism:
  theory of 205

education:
  right to 100
equity:
  applications of 219
  contra legem application 220
  corrective function of 221
  decisions rendered *ex aequo et bono* 222
  equitable result, doctrine of 226
  infra legem application 219
  interpretations of law, choosing between
    219
  lacunae, filling 220, 224
  praetor legem application 220, 224
  shelf delimitation, rules for 223–7
  tribunals, invocation by 227–8
estoppel:
  procedural rule, as 36
European Community:
  economic unity, concept of 75
  extraterritorial jurisdiction, exercise of 75